Islam & Christianity

A Revealing Contrast

James F. Gauss, Ph. D.

Bridge-Logos

Alachua, Florida 32615

Bridge-Logos
Alachua, FL 32615USA

Islam & Christianity
by James F. Gauss

Printed in the United States of America.

Library of Congress Catalog Card Number: 2009920651
International Standard Book Number 978-0-88270-611-5

Unless noted otherwise, all Bible scripture quotations are from the *Serendipity Bible for Groups, New International Version,* ©1988. Published by Serendipity House, Littleton, Colorado, with scriptures taken from *The Holy Bible, New International Version,* ©1984, Zondervan Bible Publishers.

Scripture quotations designated *NKJV* are from *The Holy Bible, New King James Version,* ©1982, Thomas Nelson, Inc.

Scripture quotations designated *NLT* are from *Holy Bible, New Living Translation,* ©1996, 2004, by Tyndale Charitable Trust. Used by permission of Tyndale House Publishers.

Quotations from the Qur'an are from *The Qur'an,* translated by M.H. Shakir, ©2004. Published by Tahrike Tarsile Qur'an, Inc., Elmhurst, New York.

For current Information on the persecuted Church,
Please Contact:

The Voice of the Martyrs, Inc.

PO Box 443
Bartlesville, OK. 74005
(918)337-8015

G163.316.N.m901.35230

"... the premier, universal authority on Islam today.

"This is now *the* book on Islam! Unlike other books on the topic, it shines a blazing spotlight on the true nature of Islam by comparing it with Christianity point by point by point. It doesn't just discuss Islam and then leave you to try to piece together the comparisons. Probably every question you ever had about Muslim beliefs, history, attitudes, and actions is answered in *Islam & Christianity*—concisely, without wasting a word. You'll find it difficult to put down this solid, even-handed book. And I doubt that any thinking person could remain a Muslim after reading the real story here."

– James Rutz, President, Megashift Ministries
Chairman, Open Church Ministries, author, *Megashift*

"*Islam & Christianity* is a trumpet blast of warning to the West about the imminent spiritual and geo-political threat of Islam. A classic in-depth study of the contrasts between Christianity and Islam, this monumental work is required reading for anyone wanting to understand the greatest struggle for the souls of men in the 21st Century."

– Rev. Peter Marshall, Peter Marshall Ministries

"In an age when the moral equivalence of Islam and Christianity is a dogma that must not be questioned and forms a non-negotiable prerequisite for the public debate, *Islam and Christianity* comes as a detailed exposition of why they are not equivalent, and why the devout adherents of each may behave in such very different ways. Christians will find this book an enlightening and energizing response to the Islamic jihadists' civilizational challenge."

– Robert Spencer, author of the *New York Times* bestsellers
The Politically Incorrect Guide to Islam (and the Crusades) and
The Truth About Muhammad

"*Islam and Christianity* provides a very thorough theological comparison of Christianity and Islam. Dr. Gauss goes into great detail relating the beginning of Islam, its writings and beliefs, in sharp contrast to the Bible and Christianity. For someone who loves theology, has contact with Muslims and would like to be able to intelligently discuss the difference in beliefs, this would be a great resource."

– Tom White, Director, The Voice of the Martyrs

"In every generation, satan raises forces to combat the truth of God and His eternal Word. These forces of darkness are framed within a religion, a philosophy, an ideology, or a political movement. The most forceful of them all is religion. If a religion does not touch the Gospel, its purpose is only the damnation of its adherents. But when religion contradicts the Gospel and also claims superiority over it, then we have an anti-Christ force. Islam is precisely this, an anti-Christ spiritual force.

"The church does not have a pretty history in its combat against Islam. Turkey, Syria, Spain, and Albania are some of the examples of our defeat. These nations were the center of Christendom. What happened then is currently taking place in Great Britain, Europe, and the United States of America. The church became self-centered, indulging in a worldly life, and losing its love for the truth. Consequently, in such spiritual conditions, there will be only a remnant of voices crying out on the roof tops the truth of one true God. These faint voices are men and women who love their God and love the souls of men. They refuse to remain in the status-quo. They are men and women of great conviction.

"Dr. Jim Gauss is one of these voices, raising up a banner against the lies and deceptions of Islam. For a non Muslim to write accurately about Islam takes a lot of research and much study. I commend Dr. Gauss for his accurate description of Islam and his great love for the Muslim people. May this book become an arrow in the heart of Islam, exposing the darkness of this evil religion, and may it open doors of freedom to one fifth of the world's population."
– Pastor Reza Safa, a former radical Muslim
Author of *Inside Islam*

Contents

ISLAM & ISLAMIC BELIEFS

THE MESSENGER

THE MESSAGE

THE MISSION

ADVANCE of ISLAM in the 21st CENTURY

Preface

Americans are bombarded daily with conflicting commentary on the relativity of Islam to Christianity and the debate between Islam as a peaceful religion to one of terror and bloodshed. If we are to take these issues before us and deal with them responsibly, we must not only be informed of what is being presented to the world, but we must also be well-informed on the truth behind this fast-growing religion. To stick our heads in the sand and just take everything at face value may come at great cost, not only in our earthly future, but when we stand before the throne of Christ. As responsible Christians, we have the privilege and responsibility to stay engaged in what is taking place around us and seeing that God's kingdom continues to move forward.

There is an abundance of information grabbing for our attention in the world on the topic of Islam, as well as numerous different slants and opinions. To be valid in the life of a Christian, God's Word must be held up as the comparison, the element that, if you will, "tips the scale" towards what is true. Without this mirror, one is left defenseless in discerning what they read and hear through the media, and much less effective when trying to pray for and explain the truth of the gospel to a Muslim. With the fast-moving world we live in today, none of us are exempt from the issue at hand. We hear it on the news, read it in the paper, or as we are sharing car pools and PTA meetings with Muslims in our own community. To take the Great Commission seriously, we must know what we believe, what the world believes, and how to share truth with them when the opportunity arises.

Many within the Islamic faith do not totally know what they believe; they take everything at face value, but find their hearts empty and searching. My visits to the Middle East have brought me in contact with Christians who were former Muslims and who have shared how empty they felt, and who knew that their faith was not meeting their needs. It was only after they were introduced to the truth of the gospel message that they were able to see what they were longing for. These living examples give even more strength to the fact that we must be students of not only God's Word, but also understand what the Muslim faith professes, so that we may present the truth of God's Word to them, holding it in contrast to their holy book, the Koran. It is up to God to do the rest. Our part is to be informed and ready to share when the opportunity arises.

Dr. Gauss has presented an effective resource in *Islam & Christianity* for the average reader. Here you will find many of the issues addressed that are in the forefront of the minds of Muslims, which compare clearly the life and ministry of Christ with that of Muhammad. God's Word is contrasted with the Koran and gives you a hands-on resource to use in your witness, as well as in your prayer life, for the Muslim world.

As Christians, we understand that the root we must recognize is not social, political, or economic, but spiritual. May this book assist you in standing with God in bringing many who are locked in darkness into His marvelous light.

Tom White
Director of The Voice of the Martyrs

Introduction

Just as in the days of Muhammad, the fundamentalist followers of Islam today are pursuing world conquest

Mark A. Gabriel, *Islam and Terrorism*, 2002

Since September 11, 2001, the apologists and political and media pundits have tried to put a politically correct and appeasing face on Islam for Western civilization and the non-Islamic world. Some—including a few Christian leaders—have even gone so far as to declare that the god of Islam, Allah, is just another name for the same god that Jews and Christians worship. Are they correct in that assessment? Did the biblical prophets and patriarchs of the Old Testament and Jesus Christ and His followers worship the same god as Muslims? The Qur'an, the Muslim holy book, claims that Jesus and the prophets of old did worship Allah and that Allah is *the* God of the Universe. Is the Allah of the Qur'an compatible with and the same as the God of the Old and New Testament Scriptures of the Jews and Christians?

This work is not an attempt to take a close look at the history of Islam, nor a biography of its prophet, Muhammad. It is rather a decided effort to closely compare the ministry of Jesus and the message of the New Testament to that of Muhammad and the message of the Qur'an. As these comparisons are considered, it is important to note that Jesus did not write any part of the New Testament. It was written by several of Jesus' apostles and those that closely adhered to His tenets of faith. The Qur'an, on the other hand, was authored entirely by Muhammad, largely through revelations from Allah that he claimed came through the angel Gabriel.

Why is such a comparison necessary? Why is it important for the Western or non-Muslim world to understand the fundamental differences between Islam and the tenets of the Judeo-Christian populations of the world? Without a shred of melodrama intended, it can simply be stated that the fate of modern civilization and world freedom is at stake.

The tenets of any faith are created or "revealed" for its followers to take seriously and incorporate such instructions into the everyday life of the believer. The Jews are called to worship Jehovah God and Him only and to follow the Law handed down through Moses and the prophets. Christians are called to accept Jesus as the fulfillment of the Old Testament law and to follow His teaching of repentance, redemption, love, and peace. Such a calling to love and peace should not be a threat to anyone. It is the only call—as opposed to turmoil and hatred—that the true believing Christian can accept and follow. Other world faiths have tenets of faith that adherents are to take seriously and act upon.

As the reader will discover, Islam has some teachings, which, if adhered to by the Muslim faithful, will bring much chaos and instability in the world. While politically correct Westerners, as well as others, can only hope that the vast majority of Muslims worldwide are really not true believers of their own faith, the fact remains: All Muslims are called to follow every word of the Qur'an and accept every teaching from Muhammad as the unchangeable will of Allah.

Why should the non-Muslim world be concerned? The Islamic faith is growing by leaps and bounds. Not so much because new converts are convinced of its redeeming theology, but because Muslim populations have some of the highest birth rates in the world. Muslims also "win" converts through coercion, oppression, and threats to one's well-being.

The popular estimate of the Muslim population worldwide in 2006 was 1.2 to 1.3 billion. However, other reliable sources (notably Muslim) put it at 1.5 to 1.8 billion, or upwards to nearly 30% of the world population. There are between 52-55 countries where Muslims dominate the religion and/or politics of the country. Muslims are moving into Western European countries by the millions and are expected to dominate the religion and politics of many, if not most Western European countries within the next couple of decades.

"In twenty to fifty years," wrote Dr. Samuel L. Blumenfeld (*WorldNetDaily*, February 14, 2006), "Western Europe may be dominated by Muslims who will claim it as a Waqf [a territory for Islamic purposes or Muslim religious endowment]."

"For the first time in history," wrote the *Chicago Tribune's* foreign correspondent, Evan Osnos (December 19, 2004), "Muslims are building large and growing minorities across the secular Western world —nowhere more visibly than in Western Europe, where their numbers have more than doubled in the past two decades."

France, the Netherlands, the United Kingdom, and other European countries are already under heavy political assault from the Islamic invasion and rapidly growing population. Many of the Muslims, both leaders and their followers, do not have peaceful intentions, as the Muslim riots in France and the Islamic terrorist acts in England, Spain, the Netherlands, and elsewhere well document. If Islam becomes the dominating force in Western Europe, will Canada and the United States be far behind?

While the birth rate among many non-Muslims has plummeted over the last few decades, the birth rate among many Muslim countries is two to three times that of the United States and other Western countries. Among the top ten countries with the highest birth rate, seven are Muslim-dominated nations. Of the fifty Muslim countries listed in the *2007 Central Intelligent Agency's The World FactBook* (updated May 31, 2007), *all* fifty have birth rates higher than the United States, Canada, Australia, New Zealand and all twenty-seven Western European Union countries. In most of Western Europe the Muslim birthrate is three to four times as high as that of native Europeans. By the year 2020, it is estimated that Muslims will make up 30% of Western Europe's population—large enough to have a significant impact on European culture, religion, society, politics, and law. Europe will never be the same.

While Muslims are rapidly populating Europe, *all* twenty-seven European Union members, except Ireland, have birth rates too low to replace their dying populations. Germans and Italians are disappearing at an alarming rate with two of the lowest birth rates in the CIA's world of 223 countries.

To further exacerbate the declining populations in the non-Muslim world is the high rate of abortions. From 1920 through the end of 2006, there have been nearly one billion babies aborted, the large majority in the non-Muslim world. Abortions are rare in Muslim countries except in the former Soviet Union Republics (Azerbaijan, Kazakhstan, Kyrgyzstan, Tajikistan, Turkmenistan, and Uzbekistan).

According to *The Washington Times* (November 21, 2006), Russia's birth rate is so low at 1.28 births per woman that the country's population is shrinking by 700,000 people per year. To complicate matters, Russia has the highest abortion rate in the world (19.29 abortions per 1,000 population). Russian women terminate 52.5 % of all known pregnancies. That is scary enough, but what really terrifies ethnic Russians is that they are being invaded by Muslims that are birthing six to ten children per woman. With a 40% increase in the Muslim population since 1989, there are now twenty-five million Muslims in Russia –two and a half million in Moscow alone. In another eight years (by 2015), Muslims will represent over 50% of Russia's military and 20% of the population by 2020. "If nothing changes," states *Islam in Russia* authority Paul Goble, "in thirty years, people of Muslim descent will definitely outnumber ethnic Russians."

Shari'a, the Muslim religious law–which is deemed antithetical to Western civilized jurisprudence–is being allowed in the Netherlands and parts of England and Canada. It is the law deemed to be the only true law that governs the life of the Muslim and supersedes the constitutional law of the land. It is the law that is dictated by the Qur'an, the Muslim holy book that condones (among other things) beheadings, amputations, torture, stoning, wife beating and other abhorrent punishments deemed barbaric by much of Western civilized culture and law.

That the Muslim ideology and religious beliefs stifle freedom is apparent worldwide. When the Washington, D.C. freedom watchdog, Freedom House, founded by Eleanor Roosevelt in 1941, released its Annual Report, *Freedom in the World, 2007*, it revealed the following facts:

• Of the 193 countries surveyed, ninety (or 47%) were deemed to be free countries. They represented 46% of the world population.

• Of the fifty-two countries with a Muslim majority of 51% or more, only three were considered to be free. One of them, Indonesia, may be disputed as free by the thousands of non-Muslims that are persecuted and murdered there every year.

In the United States, public school children are being taught Islamic customs and religion, while the faith of the Founding Fathers is banned and ridiculed. Fundamentalist Muslim leaders have gained influence in the re-writing of American published history books in order to shed a more favorable light on Islam. All criticism of Islam in America—the land of free speech—is met with cries of racism and Islamophobia by Muslim clerics and scholars. While Muslims worldwide freely castigate Americans at every opportunity, Muslim leaders attempt to silence Americans in their own free-speech country whenever anything negative is expressed about Islam.

Perhaps the naiveté of the Western world can be summed up in the assessment of Islam's future dominance by Pavel Kohout of the Center for Economics and Politics in Prague. In an article titled, "Why Al-Qaeda Will Dominate the European Union," published October 7, 2004, Kohout wrote:

The first reason extreme Islam will prevail is the intellectual advantage that al-Qaeda leaders have over western European politicians.

The latter want to believe that there is no clash of civilizations; that terrorism is just a product of misery and lack of education; that the solution lies in a multicultural, tolerant society; and that the stubbornness of the Americans and Israelis is to blame for all the problems.

The second reason is the unification of foreign policy in the EU [European Union]. In the UN [United Nations], all member states of the European Union dutifully voted against Israel as a flock of sheep under the leadership of France. France is home to millions of Muslims, who are a decisive factor in its politics.

The third reason is an advantage of the Islamic society in terms of evolution: a high birth rate.

The same gullibility that Europeans have demonstrated to the Islamic invasion and the contempt that Islamic leaders hold against

European society is also well entrenched in America. Our obsession with cultural diversity and political correctness is the Islamic dream come true. They can lambaste Americans for "slandering" Islam while hiding behind our civic pride of a free-speech society as they malign and attempt to change everything American.

It is hard for the patriotic American Christian alike to comprehend the mindset of the Muslim. Christianity is a religion of free choice. You cannot be "born" a Christian. It must be a personal decision to accept Jesus Christ and His teachings and Lordship. Islam is a religion of coercion. The vast majority of Muslims are Muslims because they were born into a Muslim family and dare not leave the faith or they sacrifice family, livelihood, and even their life. The Islamic faith is spread through fear, coercion, persecution, and bloodshed. One becomes a Muslim by birth, through threats or witness to bodily harm, torture, marrying into a Muslim family, or the threat of a gruesome death if one does not bend the knee to Allah and recite the Shahada (statement of faith).

The Qur'an claims that Allah is the God of Muslims, as well as Jews and Christians. "And do not dispute with the followers of the Book except by what is best, except those of them who act unjustly, and say: We believe in that which has been revealed to us and revealed to you, and our God and your God is One, and to Him do we submit (surah 29:46)." Despite this assertion that the God of the Jews, Christians, and Muslims is one and the same, much of the Qur'an spews out hatred toward Jews and Christians ("people of the Book"), referring continually to them as infidels and unbelievers, ones only worthy of the sword or Allah's wrath.

There is some difficulty for the non-Muslim, and perhaps for Muslims as well, in piecing together the message of the Qur'an:

• The Qur'an is not written with any sequential theme; nor is it written in a chronological manner. The chapters (called surahs) are arranged by the longest (that appear first) to the shortest (which appear last).

• It was originally composed on any organic material handy, including bones, leaves, bark, reed mats, stones, or just recorded in the minds of men.

• Since Muslims claim that the only true Qur'an is in Arabic, any other translations are suspect even if translated by Muslim scholars.

This makes it convenient for Muslims to dispute whatever non-believers find objectionable in non-Arabic translations. Muslims can just deny that the translations hold true in Arabic.

- The Qur'an's reliability as Allah's word rests on the character and trust of one person, Muhammad, the prophet of Islam.
- Much of the Qur'an appears to be verses of revelation that Muhammad received that fit his self-serving ambitions at the moment, rather than holy guidance for lost souls.
- Some of the teachings of the Qur'an violate the Ten Commandments that Jews and Christians hold sacred.
- While the Qur'an acknowledges that Jews and Muslims (and Christians through Christ) are descendants of Abraham, much of the Qur'an denigrates and demeans Jews and Christians specifically and calls for violence against them.

The Bible, by comparison, is somewhat easier to follow due to many chronological and historical sequences that put together a story of God's faithfulness or purpose for His people. It is also written by numerous prophets, sages, and apostles who were firsthand witnesses to God's intervention in the lives of His people. In some cases, different authors write about the same events with harmonizing agreement on most details and participants. In the Qur'an, Muhammad is the only participant with Allah as well as the only reporter. There are no collaborating witnesses or recorders of the events to which Muhammad speaks.

So, what is the true face of Islam? On November 20, 2003—a scant two years after the terrifying events of September 11, 2001—the President of the United States, George W. Bush, in a joint press conference in England with Prime Minister Tony Blair, declared that Christians, Jews, and Muslims worship the same God and that Islam is a religion of peace. Is Islam a peaceful religion, as Islamic leaders desire for Westerners to believe and as the President of the United States and leaders of other countries try to assure their countrymen? Are Jews, Christians, and Muslims all "brothers" who are just trying to follow the same God? Do we all have a joint destiny that will end at the same place?

If the Qur'an is God's last word to mankind and Muhammad was the last and greatest of His prophets, as Muslims claim, then it would appear that God has reversed His plan of salvation and freedom for mankind. Instead, He has decided that enslavement would be better; that man could no longer be justified by shedding of His own blood through Jesus Christ and that it must be man's blood shed through the violence of *Jihad* that would bring unbelieving sinners to their repentant senses.

Is Islam a religion of peace? According to *The Sword of Militant Islam* web site (http://www.masada2000.org/islam.html), in the 1400 years of Islamic history, an estimated 270 million non-Muslims have been murdered by Muslim jihadists. Of the conflicts on Earth today, 90-95% involve Muslims. Will this aggression subside as Muslims are introduced to democracy and the ideals of the free West? Absolutely not! Muslim beliefs are incompatible with Western-style democracy and ideology.

The Role of the Church

In the first Book of Chronicles the twelve sons of Jacob are listed (their father whom God renamed Israel in Genesis 32:28). Among the sons of Israel was Issachar. During the time of King David the clans of Issachar numbered 87,000 fighting men. (See 1 Chronicles 7:5.) However, the most important asset the men of Issachar brought to King David was that they "… understood the times and knew what Israel should do …" (1 Chronicles 12:32). Where are the Issachar-type leaders for today's perilous times? A few courageous souls have stepped forward, only to be quickly labeled "fear mongers" or "anti-immigrants" or worse.

In the Old Testament, after the Jews had settled in the Promised Land of Canaan, God commanded them to post *watchmen* at the gates and towers of the city in order to give the people early warning of an approaching enemy. Often, the people failed to heed the warning of the watchmen as described in Jeremiah 6:17-19, 22-26:

> *I* [God] *appointed watchmen over you and said, "Listen to the sound of the trumpet!" But you said, "We will not listen." Therefore hear, O nations; observe, O witnesses, what will happen to them. Hear, O earth: I am bringing disaster on this people, the fruit of their schemes, because they have not listened to my words and have rejected my law.…*

> *This is what the Lord says: "Look, an army is coming from the land of the north; a great nation is being stirred up from the ends of the earth. They are armed with bow* [something for shooting] *and spear* [something to strike with]; *they are cruel and show no mercy. They sound like the roaring sea as they ride on their horses; they come like men in battle formation to attack you, O daughter of Zion."*
>
> *We have heard reports about them, and our hands hang limp. Anguish has gripped us, pain like that of a woman in labor. Do not go out to the fields or walk on the roads, for the enemy has a sword, and there is terror on every side. O my people, put on sackcloth and roll in ashes; mourn with bitter wailing as for an only son, for suddenly the destroyer will come upon us.*

Could this Scripture possibly be a prophetic warning for God's people today? Let us look at the parallels.

• Many, especially former Muslims, as well as Muslim leaders themselves, have been warning the West about the coming Islamic invasion. But the West, and the Christian Church in particular, proclaim *we will not listen.*

• Islam, since it knows no boundaries, would certainly fit the category of a *great nation* [that] *is being stirred up from the ends of the Earth.*

• Muslims have a long history that demonstrates that *they are cruel and show no mercy.*

• They are coming first for the Jews, O *daughter of Zion.*

• The Western world has *heard reports about them*, but their *hands hang limp* with fear and inaction. The West's obsession with cultural diversity and political correctness has tied our hands against an enemy that seeks to destroy us and all that we hold dear.

• *Anguish has gripped* the hundreds of millions who have been oppressed by Muslims worldwide.

• *The enemy has a sword, and there is terror on every side.* The sword is the symbol of Islam and the *Sword of Islam* is the rallying cry of Muslim jihadists as they seek to destroy the world of non-believers; *and there is terror on every side.*

• And as Muslims prepare all manner of destruction and death—from nuclear to biological to chemical and anything else diabolical that they can devise—*suddenly the destroyer will come upon us.*

There is something fundamentally wrong and evil about a religion—its belief system and its prophet—that teaches, encourages, and commands its followers to persecute and murder in the name of their god all those who disagree or cannot and will not accept its theology. There is no other major religion on the face of the Earth with this type of anti-life, anti-freedom, anti-humane theology. Muslim terrorists or terrorists who are Muslims are not mentally disturbed madmen or "fanatics," as the Western press and broadcast media would have us believe. That maniacal fallback might apply to the occasional serial killer, but not to Muslim terrorists. These are very intelligent and calculating men and women who take their inspiration from their holy book and the words of their prophet very seriously. They are not misinterpreting their scriptures or taking them out of context, but rather applying them to everyday life as they have been commanded to do for fourteen centuries.

Mike Evans is an expert analyst on the Middle East and has written three *New York Times* best sellers on the subject, including, *Showdown With Nuclear Iran*. In an interview published in the June, 2007, *Charisma* magazine, Evans stated that "The Islamic revolution, fueled and fired by the Shiite movement out of Iran, is committed to a holy war against the West."

In the Old Testament, the watchmen were in the watchtowers 24/7 to provide the people with an early warning of an approaching enemy. In the New Testament, the watchmen are the pastors and prophets who are called (among other duties) to identify the enemies of Christ, warn the people, and prepare them to do spiritual warfare—to defeat the enemy (Ephesians 6) and bring them to the saving knowledge of Christ.

"One reason why the developed world has a difficult job grappling with the Islamist threat," wrote author and journalist Mark Steyn in his book, *America Alone*, "is that it doesn't take religion seriously. It condescends to it." His book details the decline of Western culture and the rapid rise of Islam worldwide and its portents for the future of freedom and democracy. "If ever there were a time for a strong voice from the heart of Christianity, this would be it," he later penned.

"I'm trying to blow the trumpet so that the Church wakes up and unites together," Evans added in the *Charisma* interview.

If the Church is going to have an effective impact on winning Muslims to the salvation message of Jesus Christ it needs to have a clear and truthful understanding of the Islamic faith and mindset. The purpose of this book is to provide a brief overview of Islam's history and beliefs and then to compare the Messenger, Message, and Mission of Jesus Christ of the Bible and Muhammad of the Qur'an and to answer the question of who is Allah? Is he the Jewish and Christian God by a different name? Are Islam and Christianity similar and compatible?

It is time for Christians to suit up for the spiritual fight of their lives and for the survival of Christianity in the West. The adherents to Islam mean business and it is only the salvation message of Jesus Christ that will turn the tide and win the war.

Islam & Islamic Beliefs

CHAPTER 1

Birth of Islam

Faith is born of the soul, not the body.
Whoever would lead someone to faith needs
the ability to speak well and to reason properly
without violence and threats....
To convince a reasonable soul, one does not need
a strong arm, or weapons of any kind, or any
other means of threatening a person with death....

Byzantine Emperor Michael Paleologos II, 1261-1280 A.D.

In an attempt to understand the complexities of Islam and its dedicated one-and-a-half-billion followers, we must first turn to an unlikely source—the Bible of the Jews and Christians. Interestingly, the Bible does provide some historical and spiritual insights on the origins and fate of the Middle Eastern peoples that gave birth to the Islamic faith. It turns out that the Middle East has had an ancient history of volatility and violence that is well established in the biblical record. Islam has its root in Arabic culture mixed among the belief and tradition of Abraham and his son Ishmael fathering the tribes of the Middle East. If both the people of Islam and those of Judeo-Christian heritage claim Abraham as their patriarch, why have they been forever at each others throats? The answer can be found in the Scripture of both the Old and New Testaments of the Bible.

What the Bible Says

We can gain some insight into this generations-old conflict by picking up the story in Genesis 16 where Abraham and his wife Sarah were first known as Abram and Sarai. Abram was eighty-six years old and Sarai had never bore him any children, yet God had promised him that he would have a male descendant who would bring forth descendants as numerous as the stars of Heaven.

And Abram said [to God], *"You have given me no children; so a servant in my household will be my heir."*

Then the word of the Lord came to him: "This man will not be your heir, but a son coming from your own body will be your heir." He took him outside and said, "Look up at the heavens and count the stars—if indeed you can count them." Then he said to him, "So shall your offspring be." (Genesis 15:3-5)

Frustrated and impatient with the lack of God's immediate fulfillment of His promise, Abram decided (with Sarai's encouragement) to take matters into his own hands. He took unto himself Hagar, Sarai's maidservant, and she bore him a son.

And the Angel of the Lord said to her [Hagar]: *"Behold, you are with child, and you shall bear a son. You shall call his name Ishmael* [viz., God shall hear], *because the Lord has heard your affliction. He shall be a wild man; his hand shall be against every man, and every man's hand against him. And he shall dwell in the presence of all his brethren."* (Genesis 16:11-12, NKJV)

Several things should be noted at this point. First, Abram (meaning, "high father") chose to disbelieve God's promised covenant with him and establish his own covenant by the flesh. Second, his partner in this fleshly covenant was the pagan Egyptian Hagar (meaning one who takes flight). Third, it was God, not Abram, who chose the name of Ishmael for this son to be born *outside* of God's chosen covenant with His people. Fourth, it was God who said at Ishmael's conception, that he would "be a wild man" and that "his hand shall be against *every* man, and *every* man's hand against him." At the same time, "He shall dwell in the presence of all his brethren."

It is important to note that the Hebrew word used for "wild" in the above verse means for one to be like a "wild ass," with no boundaries. The Hebrew word used for "hand" means the "open hand of power." And who were Ishmael's brethren? He had a Hebrew father, Abram, and a pagan Arabic mother, Hagar. His brethren at the time of his birth were both Jews and Arabs.

When Abram was ninety-nine years old, he was still without a true heir by Sarai's womb. God then spoke to Abram and made this covenant with him:

As for Me, behold, My covenant is with you, and you shall be a father of many nations. No longer shall your name be called Abram, but your name shall be Abraham; for I have made you a father of many nations. I will make you exceedingly fruitful; and I will make nations of you, and kings shall come from you. And I will establish My covenant between Me and you and your descendants after you in their generations, for an everlasting covenant, to be God to you and your descendants after you. Also I give to you and your descendants after you the land in which you are a stranger, all the land of Canaan, as an everlasting possession; and I will be their God. (Genesis 17:4-8, NKJV)

Fourteen years after the birth of Ishmael, God fulfilled His intended covenant with Abram (now Abraham) with the birth of Isaac ("laughter") to Sarah ("princess") who was no longer called Sarai ("dominant").

Abraham asked God if "Ishmael might live before you." But God told Abraham:

No, Sarah your wife shall bear you a son, and you shall call his name Isaac; I will establish my covenant with him for an everlasting covenant, and with his descendants after him.

And as for Ishmael, I have heard you. Behold, I have blessed him, and will make him fruitful, and will multiply him exceedingly. He shall beget twelve princes, and I will make him a great nation. (Genesis 17:18-20, NKJV)

God never intended to establish His covenant with Ishmael, because Ishmael was not the child of the promise but of the flesh. God could not establish His covenant with him; He could only bless him. While God blessed Ishmael with fruitfulness, He never made a covenant with him. God's covenant was with Abraham and him only. And, unlike

Abraham and Isaac, God never promised Ishmael and his seed that He would be their God.

Although Arabic Muslims claim Abraham as their heir, biblically they are descendants of pre-covenant Abram, the one who disobeyed God and disbelieved His promise of an heir through Sarah. God could bless Ishmael, but He could never establish His covenant with a sinful seed of the flesh.

Ishmael became the father of twelve Arabian princes (nations) whom God said that He would "multiply ... exceedingly" (Genesis 17:20). Ishmael and Hagar were driven into the Wilderness of Paran to dwell. (See Genesis 21:20-21.) This wilderness covers the eastern Sinai and the southern and southeastern borders of present-day Israel.

Ishmael's sons initially inhabited an area from Egypt and the Sinai Desert, the Arabian peninsula to Assyria (which includes present-day Saudi Arabia, Iran, Iraq, Jordan, Syria, and the lesser Arab kingdoms).

Remember, God promised that Ishmael and his descendants would be wild men whose hand would be "... against every man."

Some Bible translations of Genesis 25:18 state that the descendants of Ishmael after the death of Abraham, "lived in hostility toward" or "in defiance of" all their brethren (*New International Version, New Living Translation,* and *New American Standard*). Other versions (including the *King James, New King James* and *Amplified Bibles*) state only that Ishmael's descendants lived "close to" or "in the presence of" their relatives.

Muhammad and the Muslims have found a simple solution to this dilemma of a negative biblical image. Muhammad asserted that Allah revealed to him that it was Ishmael, not Isaac, that Allah chose to test Abraham's faith; and, therefore, it was Ishmael and all those who are descendants of him that are the true chosen people to fulfill Allah's covenant.

Instead of God calling Abraham to sacrifice his son Isaac on a makeshift altar on Mount Moriah in Jerusalem (the current site of the Dome of the Rock), it was Allah who called Abraham to sacrifice Ishmael on Mount Mina outside Mecca.

According to the Qur'an, Abraham prayed to Allah:

My Lord! Grant me [a son who shall be] of the doers of good deeds [that is, righteous]. So We gave [Abraham] the good news of a boy, possessing forbearance. And when [Ishmael] attained to working with him, [Abraham] said: "O my son! Surely I have seen in a dream that I should sacrifice you; consider then what you see." He said: "O my father! Do what you are commanded; if Allah please, you will find me of the patient ones." So when they both submitted and [Abraham] threw [Ishmael] down upon his forehead, and he called out to him saying: "O Ibrahim! You have indeed shown the truth of the vision; surely thus do. We reward the doers of good: Most surely this is a manifest trial." (surah 37:100- 106)

This version in the Qur'an of Abraham's call to sacrifice his son strongly contradicts the biblical story. "Then God said, 'Take your son, your only son, Isaac, whom you love, and go to the region of Moriah. Sacrifice him there as a burnt offering on one of the mountains I will tell you about" (Genesis 22:2). Notice that God refers to Isaac as Abraham's *only* son. That is because only Isaac was God's choice to fulfill His covenant with Abraham—not Ishmael, the son of the flesh.

In the Genesis account, Isaac had no prior knowledge of his role in the sacrifice:

Isaac spoke up and said to his father Abraham, "Father?"

"Yes, my son?" Abraham replied.

"The fire and wood are here," Isaac said, "but where is the lamb for the burnt offering?"

Abraham answered, "God himself will provide the lamb for the burnt offering, my son." (Genesis 22:7-8a)

Because of Abraham's willingness to sacrifice his only son and not withhold him from God, God promised Abraham that "... through your offspring all nations on earth will be blessed, because you have obeyed me" (Genesis 22:18).

From the present day and historical perspective of the daily violence against mankind by the followers of Islam, it is hard to see that this was God's plan for blessing the nations of the Earth through the descendants of Ishmael. Among the descendants of Isaac, however, was Jesus, the

5

sacrificial lamb who brought salvation to the world by the shedding of His blood and not that of another human being—truly a blessing to all who will receive Him.

The Apostle Paul affirmed that descendants of Isaac are the true heirs of God:

"It is not as though God's word had failed," he asserted. "For not all who are descended from Israel are [of] *Israel. Nor because they are his descendants are they all Abraham's children. On the contrary, 'It is through Isaac that your offspring will be reckoned'* [Genesis 21:12]. *In other words, it is not the natural children who are God's children, but it is the children of the promise who are regarded as Abraham's offspring.* (Romans 9:6-8)

In his letter to the Galatians, Paul reasserted the striking difference between the seed of the pre-covenant Ishmael and the covenant-fulfilling seed of Isaac. He made both historical and spiritual comparison:

For it is written that Abraham had two sons: the one by a bondwoman [or slave], *the other by a freewoman.*

But he who was of the bondwoman was born according to the flesh, and he of the freewoman through promise, which things are symbolic. For these are the two covenants: the one from Mount Sinai which gives birth to bondage, which is Hagar—for this Hagar is Mount Sinai in Arabia, and corresponds to Jerusalem which now is, and is in bondage with her children—but the Jerusalem above is free, which is the mother of us all....

But, as he who was born according to the flesh then persecuted him who was born according to the Spirit, even so it is now.

Nevertheless what does the Scripture say? "Cast out the bondwoman and her son, for the son of the bondwoman shall not be heir with the son of the freewoman." (Galatians 4:22-26, 29-30, NKJV)

Paul makes it clear that Ishmael was the pre-covenant seed of a slave and therefore could not represent God's covenant with His people. Isaac, on the other hand, was a freeman, born of a freewoman as the fulfillment of God's promise to His people. Those who are heirs to the bondwoman of the flesh (viz., Ishmael), will remain in bondage until set free by the salvation of Christ, who is heir to the covenant of the freeman, Isaac.

Paul also pointed out that the descendants of Ishmael will always be persecuting the descendants of Isaac, the freeman, and that the heirs of the two can never share in the inheritance of the freeman. The only hope of sharing this inheritance that the descendants of Ishmael have is to be grafted in through the salvation of Christ.

Muslims claim that Allah is their god, but Jesus said: "If God were your Father, you would love Me, for I proceeded forth and came from God; nor have I come of Myself, but He sent Me" (John 8:42, NKJV). The Islamic faith, because it is not a covenant faith with Jehovah God, cannot accept Jesus as the Son of God and therefore denies the existence of God the Father.

Followers of Islam are taught through their holy book, the Qur'an, to persecute and kill the infidels or non-believers (principally Christians and Jews). While they accept Jesus as a prophet to the Jews, they are taught to despise and hate all followers of Christ and Jehovah God. The question is: If Muslims accept Christ as a prophet of Allah as they claim, then why is it that Jesus, His teachings and His followers are not welcome in any Muslim circle?

Yet, Jesus said, "I and the Father are one" (John 10:30). "I am the way, the truth, and the life. No one comes to the Father except through Me" (John 14:6, NKJV).

The Apostle John, who was the only one to use the term "antichrist" in the Bible, made it abundantly clear that, "Who is a liar but he who denies that Jesus is the Christ? He is antichrist who denies the Father and the Son. Whoever denies the Son does not have the Father either; he who acknowledges the Son has the Father also" (1 John 2:22-23, NKJV).

In his second letter, John continues this theme by stating:

For many deceivers have gone out into the world who do not confess Jesus Christ as coming in the flesh. This is a deceiver and an antichrist.... Whoever transgresses and does not abide in the doctrine of Christ does not have God. He who abides in the doctrine of Christ has both the Father and the Son. If anyone comes to you and does not bring this doctrine, do not receive him into your house nor greet him; for he who greets him shares in his evil deeds. (2 John 7, 9-11, NKJV)

Muhammad, as many before him and after Jesus, definitely brought forth a new and dramatically divergent doctrine or "gospel" than that which was preached by Jesus and His apostles. It was a doctrine that so conflicted with Judaism and Christianity that early converts could only be won over by the threat of the sword.

Birth of Muhammad and Islam

The Prophet of Islam or The Apostle, as Muhammad is called, was born in AD 571 (some sources use 570). His father, Abdullah, died before Muhammad's birth and his mother, Amina, died in 577 when he was only six. Muhammad then stayed with his grandfather until he died two years later. Muhammad was then raised by his uncle, Abu Talib.[2]

"The evidence that a prophet was active among the Arabs in the early decades of the seventh century," wrote Patricia Crone, professor of Islamic history at Princeton University, "must be said to be exceptionally good."[3]

"Everything else about Muhammad," Crone continued, "is more uncertain … we can be reasonably sure that the Qur'an is a collection of utterances that he made in the belief that they had been revealed to him by God."

In 586, at the age of fifteen or sixteen, Muhammad participated in the war of Fijar between the Arabian tribes of Hawazin and Quraish (or Quraysh). Although not a combatant, he had the responsibility of recovering the enemy's arrows for his Quraish uncle.[4, 5]

When he was in his early twenties, Muhammad had the good fortune of being introduced to the wealthy Hadrat Khadija. Muhammad took on the responsibility of managing her prosperous trade caravan. A year later, in 595, although Khadija was fifteen years his senior, Muhammad took her as his first wife. He would live with her monogamously for twenty-five years until her death in 619.[6]

For someone sent by God, Muhammad seemed uncertain of his status. "Say: I am not the first of the apostles, and I do not know what will be done with me or with you: I do not follow anything but that which is revealed to me, and I am nothing but a plain warner." (surah 46:9)

In 610, when he was around forty years old, Muhammad had his first "revelation" from the angel Gabriel in a cave on Mt. Hira. His experience is recounted in the writings of the eighth century Muslim, Ibn Ishaq, in his *Sirat Rasul Allah*:

> When it was the night on which God honored him with his mission, and showed mercy on His servants thereby, Gabriel brought him the command of God. "He came to me," said the Apostle, "while I was asleep, with a piece of brocade whereon was writing, and said 'Recite!' and I said 'What shall I recite?' He pressed me with it so tightly that I thought it was death; then he let me go and said 'Recite!' I said 'But what shall I read?'—And this I said only to deliver myself from him lest he should do the same to me again, but he said:
>
> 'Recite: In the Name of thy Lord who created,
> Created man from blood clotted,
> Recite! Thy Lord is the most beneficent,
> who taught by the Pen,
> Taught that which they knew not unto men.'
>
> "So I recited it, and he departed from me. And I awoke from my sleep, and it was as though these words were written on my heart.
>
> "Now none of God's creatures was more hateful to me than an (ecstatic) poet or a man possessed; I could not even bear to look at them. I thought, 'Woe is me—poet or possessed. Never shall Quraysh [Muhammad's pagan Arabian tribe in Mecca] say that of me! I will go to the top of the mountain and throw myself down that I may kill myself and gain rest.' I raised my head towards heaven to see, and lo! Gabriel in the form of a man, with feet astride the horizon, saying, 'O Muhammad! Thou art the Apostle of God, and I am Gabriel.' I stood gazing at him, moving neither forward nor backward; then I began to turn my face away from him, but towards whatever region of the sky I looked, I saw him as before.
>
> "I continued standing there, neither advancing nor turning back, until Khadija sent her messengers in search of me...."[7, 8]

If it is to be accepted that the above account of Muhammad's first revelation is true, then there are several problems with it. Ibn Ishaq's recounting of Muhammad's experience was written more than a century and a half after the visitation of Gabriel. According to the Muslim Sacred Texts web site, "[Ibn Ishaq's] original work survived only in quotations from it by other authors ... However, it has been possible for modern scholars to re-establish much of the original text."[9] The question must be asked: How does one *re-establish* the original text if the original text was lost? Can one rely on the quotations of others passed down through the centuries as being accurate and true to the original? Translations of the Bible do not try to recreate text from some Scripture that was lost, but only from known and preserved manuscripts, some of which have authenticated multiple and identical copies.

While there are many accounts in the Bible of God sending angels to bring a message to mankind, God always chose to speak directly with His chosen prophets (as recorded in the Old Testament). The prophets in turn always referred to God as the author of their spoken words. Muhammad is the first (of the class of prophets that he put himself in—Moses, David, Isaiah, et al) that proclaimed his prophetic words came from an angel—and one that he first thought was demonic.

"Muhammad's doubts are troubling," wrote Mark Gabriel, "for what major prophet doubts the source of his prophetic revelation?... Certainly no major prophet in the Bible attributes God's revelation to demons, as Muhammad believed...."[10]

After this visitation, Muhammad thought he had been visited by Satan and that he was possessed by a demon,[11] so much so, that he wanted to commit suicide. He thought he was crazy and wanted to die. Not a very fitting beginning for a prophet who later became convinced that he was chosen as Allah's last and most important prophet. It was only after he returned from Mt. Hira to the waiting arms of his wife, Khadija, that his demeanor changed. When he saw her, he said, "Woe is me—a poet, or a man possessed!" Khadija reassured him with these words: "Rejoice, O son of my uncle, and be of good heart! Verily by Him in whose hand is Khadija's soul, I have hope that thou wilt be the prophet of these people."[12] Muhammad did not receive words of reassurance from Allah but from a woman. He considered Khadija's words to be a reliable confirmation of the visitation and his calling, even though later revelations from Allah disclosed that women were only half as intelligent as men and could not be relied upon because they were often deceivers. (See Chapter 5).

The words of God, according to Jesus, are not presented to man by the angels, by mere mortal men (such as Muhammad), or even by sacred writ, but by the Holy Spirit of God himself. "But the Counselor, the Holy Spirit," Jesus told His disciples, "whom the Father will send in my name, will teach you all things and will remind you of everything I have said to you" (John 14:26).

> *But when he, the Spirit of truth, comes, he will guide you into all truth. He will not speak on his own; he will speak only what he hears, and he will tell you what is yet to come. He will bring glory to me by taking from what is mine and making it known to you. All that belongs to the Father is mine. That is why I said the Spirit will take from what is mine and make it known to you (John 16:13-15).*

Throughout human history and in current times God has sent angels to bring a message to His people or to provide protection. However, God's primary method of communication is through the revelation-knowledge of the Holy Spirit.

> *However, as it is written: "No eye has seen, no ear has heard, no mind has conceived what God has prepared for those who love him [Isaiah 64:4]"—but God has revealed it to us by his Spirit.*

> *The Spirit searches all things, even the deep things of God. For who among men knows the thoughts of a man except the man's spirit within him? In the same way no one knows the thoughts of God except the Spirit of God. We have not received the spirit of the world but the Spirit who is from God, that we may understand what God has freely given us. This is what we speak, not in words taught us by human wisdom but in words taught by the Spirit, expressing spiritual truths in spiritual words. The man without the Spirit does not accept the things that come from the Spirit of God, for they are foolishness to him, and he cannot understand them, because they are spiritually discerned.*

The spiritual man makes judgments about all things, but he himself is not subject to any man's judgment:
    "For who has known the mind of the Lord that he may instruct him [Isaiah 40:13]?" *But we have the mind of Christ.* (1 Corinthians 2:9-16)

This dubious beginning for Muhammad's prophethood was further complicated by what followed or did not follow. Unlike the prophets of old where God revealed His Word to them on a regular basis, Allah did not reveal himself again to Muhammad through Gabriel for three years. Once again Muhammad became depressed and suicidal. As he received revelations in the years following, his wives believed the visions were authentic because Muhammad would frequently go into trances or convulsions[13]—a state of being that Jesus attributed to demon possession. (See Matthew 12:22; 17:14-18.)

Unlike Moses and other prophets before him, Muhammad never had a personal encounter with the god of his affections. "Narrated Aisha: 'Whoever claimed that (the Prophet) Muhammad saw his Lord, is committing a great fault, for he only saw Gabriel in his genuine shape in which he was created covering the whole horizon'" (hadith 4:457).

At one point Muhammad even claimed to have communicated with the dead[14] and on numerous occasions changed Allah's revelations to suit himself.[15] Jesus also spoke to the dead, but He did so because He had power over death as demonstrated in the resurrection of Lazarus. (See John 11.)

In AD 613, Muhammad began to preach the tenets of Islam in Mecca. The word *Islam* means *submission to Allah*. To be a Muslim is to be one who is completely submitted to Islam or Allah; to be a slave of Allah. Almost from the very beginning of this new faith, "The goal of Islam [wa]s to produce a theocracy with Allah as the ruler of society, a society with no separation between religion and the state. This society would have no democracy, no free will and no freedom of expression."[16]

Satanic Verses

In 619, Muhammad received a revelation that became known in Islamic tradition as "the Satanic Verses." "According to Islamic tradition, Satan, not Allah, once actually spoke through Muhammad's mouth."[17]

As the story has been handed down, Muhammad yearned for the conversion of his own tribe, the Quraysh, to his new-found religion of Islam. But the Quraysh leaders wanted to continue to worship their gods, al-Lat and al-'Uzza. They offered Muhammad a deal: Muhammad would worship their gods for a year and then they would worship Muhammad's god for a year. In exchange, they would give Muhammad money, wives, and make him their king. Muhammad was tempted, but then this revelation came to him:

Say: What! Do you then bid me serve others than Allah, O ignorant men?

And certainly, it has been revealed to you and to those before you: Surely if you associate (with Allah), your work would certainly come to naught and you would certainly be of the losers.

Nay! But serve Allah alone and be of the thankful. (surah 39:64-66)

The Quraysh persisted, however, and Muhammad sought for a solution to the stalemate. "And finally he hit on a solution. He received a revelation saying that it was legitimate for Muslims to pray to al-Lat, al-'Uzza, and Manat, the three goddesses favored by the pagan Quraysh, as intercessors before Allah."[18] The Quraysh, of course, accepted this new revelation with great enthusiasm and word rapidly spread that the Quraysh had indeed acknowledged Allah as one of their gods.[19]

But then Muhammad received another revelation strongly rebuking him for placing Allah in this grouping of pagan gods.

And surely they had purposed to turn you away from that which We have revealed to you, that you should forge against Us other than that, and then they would certainly have taken you for a friend.

And had it not been that We had already established you, you would certainly have been near to incline to them a little;

In that case We would certainly have made you to taste a double (punishment) in this life and a double (punishment) after death, then you would not have found any helper against Us. (surah 17:73-75)

"The Satanic verses incident," commented author Robert Spencer, "has naturally caused Muslims acute embarrassment for centuries. Indeed, it casts a shadow over the veracity of Muhammad's entire claim to be a prophet....

"... While events may be explained in other ways, those who would wish away the Satanic verses cannot get around the fact that these elements of Muhammad's life were not the inventions of his enemies, but were passed along by men who believed he was indeed the Prophet of Allah ."[20]

During the same year of the Satanic Verses incident, Muhammad's first wife, Khadija, and uncle, Abu Talib, died. A year later, Muhammad began his polygamous lifestyle with his marriage to the widow, Sauda bint Zam'ah (or Sawda).[21,22] At the same time he was also betrothed to six-year-old Ayishah (or Aishah), the one who would become known as his favorite wife at age nine three years later. After his marriage to Ayishah, from 626 to 629, Muhammad would marry ten more women; sometimes for no other reason than to cement tribal alliances. (See Chapter 5 for more on Muhammad's wives.)

Ayishah, Muhammad's favorite wife, would later narrate that, "Once the Prophet was bewitched so that he began to imagine that he had done a thing which in fact he had not done" (hadith 4:400). Exactly what *things* he supposedly did or did not do is not as troubling as the observation by his wife that Muhammad was under the influence of witchcraft. In a following hadith (4:490), Ayishah again proclaims that, "Magic was worked on the Prophet...." In a dream Allah revealed to Muhammad the source of the spell: "A comb, the hair gathered on it, and the outer skin of the pollen of the male date-palm." Muhammad went to the site of the date-palms and discovered, "Its date-palms … are like the heads of the devils." Ayishah asked him, "Did you take out those things with which the magic was worked?" Muhammad answered, "No, for I have been cured by Allah and I am afraid that this action may spread evil amongst the people."

The Night Journey

In 620, perhaps in an effort to solidify his status as the Prophet of Allah, Muhammad revealed his celebrated "Night Journey" or ascension to Paradise and the seven heavens. The event is recounted in the following hadith (or words of Muhammad), narrated by Abu Huraira:

> The Prophet said, "I met Moses on the night of my Ascension to heaven." The prophet then described him saying, as I think, "He was a tall person with lank [lifeless] hair as if he belonged to the people of the tribe of Shanu's." The prophet further said, "I met Jesus." The Prophet described him saying, "He was one of moderate height and was red-faced as if he had just come out of the bathroom. I saw Abraham whom I resembled more than any of his children did." The Prophet further said, "(That night) I was given two cups; one full of milk and the other full of wine. I was asked to take either of them which I liked, and I took the milk and drank it. On that it was said to me, 'You have taken the right path (religion). If you had taken the wine, your (Muslim) nation would have gone astray.'" (Hadith 4:647)

The visionary trip or miraj (ascension) took Muhammad to Jerusalem and the Temple Mount. From there he ascended to the first heaven where he was met by Adam, who tells Muhammad, "You are welcome, O pious son and pious Prophet." Then the angel Gabriel took him to the second heaven where both John the Baptist and Jesus greeted Muhammad with, "You are welcome, O pious brother and pious Prophet."[23]

Muhammad continued his journey with Gabriel through the third, fourth, fifth, sixth, and seventh heavens where he met many of the prophets before him, including Moses and Abraham. When Moses met Muhammad in the sixth heaven, he wept. When Muhammad asked Moses why he wept, Moses said, "I weep because after me there has been sent (Muhammad as a Prophet) a young man, whose followers will enter Paradise in greater numbers than my followers."[24]

When Muhammad reached the seventh heaven, he met Abraham, who told Muhammad that Muslims must pray *fifty* times a day. But the Prophet of Islam balked at such a burdensome number and appealed to

Moses on his journey backwards through the heavens. "The prophet of Islam kept going between Allah and Moses until the number of daily prayers for the Muslims was only five."[25]

This *journey*, at least in the eyes of Muhammad, elevated his status with Allah. In hadith 4:651-652, narrated by Abu Huraira, Muhammad equates himself with Jesus.

"I heard Allah's Apostle saying, 'I am the nearest of all the people to the son of Mary, and all the prophets are paternal brothers, and there has been no prophet between me and him (i.e. Jesus).

"Allah's Apostle said, 'Both in this world and in the Hereafter, I am nearest of all the people to Jesus, the son of Mary. The prophets are paternal brothers; their mothers are different, but their religion is one.'"

It was during his flight into the seven heavens that Muhammad would later relate to his wives, Khadija and Aisha, that Allah wedded him to Mary, the mother of Jesus, the sister of Moses, and to the wife of Pharaoh. "It was Allah's special divine blessing that Muhammad was husband to three of the Bible's most noted women," wrote the Caner brothers. "Clearly he was not bound to the very Qur'an he said he had received ."[26]

Muhammad's claims about the Night Journey were more than some of the followers of this new religion could tolerate. Members of his own tribe, the Quraysh, whom Muhammad had been trying to sway toward Islam, mocked and ridiculed him. Two years later, amid the growing tensions and threats in Mecca, Muhammad and his band of followers fled to Medina.

The Flight to Medina.

After The Hijra, or flight from Mecca in 622, the tenets of the new faith went through a radical transformation. Allah's revelations to Muhammad became more vengeful and oppressive. From a human standpoint, this would make sense, if one were under the threats and oppression of others. But it also illustrates very concretely that Allah is a changeable and vengeful god that apparently has no clear plan for mankind or mankind's salvation. (See chapter 8).

Former radical Shiite Muslim and now author and Christian evangelist, Reza Safa, claims that, "Many rituals practiced within Islam are similar to those of Baal worship. In my opinion, the spirit that raised Baal worship in Phoenicia and Canaan, and later in Babylon, is the same spirit that raised Islam in Arabia."[27] Baal worship—worship of multiple gods—was first mentioned in the Bible during the time of Moses. (See Numbers 22:41.) Baal, the supreme male deity, was worshipped throughout the Canaanite and Phoenician Middle East and such pagan worship preceded the arrival of the Jewish people in the "promised land" of Canaan. During the time of Moses and the prophets of the Bible, many of the region's kings submitted to the worship of Baal.

Muhammad, after settling in Medina, began to receive revelations from Allah, laying down the "Law" to be followed by Muslim adherents. Despite his distaste for the Jews, much of what he received was heavily influenced by Judaism in Medina and beyond. "From nearly the beginning of his prophetic career," author Robert Spencer stated, "Muhammad was strongly influenced by Judaism—situating himself within the roster of Jewish prophets, forbidding pork for his followers, and adapting for the Muslims the practice of several daily prayers and other aspects of Jewish ritual."[28]

"We must realize," concluded Safa, "that many of the teachings of Islam are a reflection of Arabian culture and society of the seventh century. Many rituals and practices enforced by Islam can be traced back to pre-Islamic Arabia." He noted that Muhammad constructed his religion and the Koran from pre-existing material in Arabian culture.[29]

With Muhammad's death in AD 632, at the age of sixty-three, the faith of Islam was left with no clear successor. Muhammad had no male children and no "second lieutenant" in command. According to the traditions of Islam, Muhammad singled out his rich neighbor and one of his first converts, Abu Bakr, as his successor. A small group of Muslims insisted that it was Hadrat Ali (or Ali), Muhammad's son-in-law and cousin that the Prophet had chosen.[30] With his hatred for the Jews, his death came with a twist of irony. Bukhari's hadith 4:165 says, "Allah's Apostle died while his (iron) armor was mortgaged to a Jew for thirty Sas of barley."

Muslims that chose to follow Abu Bakr became known as Sunni or ones that follow the Sunnah (i.e., the traditions of Muhammad). The smaller group that followed Ali became known as the Shi'a or Shiites (i.e., the Party of Ali). Today, Sunni Muslims comprise about 83% of the world's Muslims.[31] They are the predominant form of Islam in such countries as Afghanistan, Algeria, Egypt, the Gaza Strip, Jordan, Kuwait, Libya, the Maldives, Pakistan, Somalia, Sudan, Syria, Tajikistan, Turkey, the United Arab Emirates, Uzbekistan, and the West Bank. The majority of Muslims in Iran and Iraq are Shi'a Muslims or Shiites.[32]

Conclusion

The Arabic Muslims claim to be descendents of Ishmael, the illegitimate son of Abraham. God spoke to Abraham and told him that Ishmael would be a *wild man* and that his hand would be *against every man*. Although Muhammad may have been genuinely seeking for spiritual truth, the revelations he received strongly contradicted God's covenant that He established with Abraham and which was fulfilled through Jesus Christ and His sacrifice on the cross.

That the Muslim peoples of the Earth have been forever a warring people, especially afflicting the people of the Bible (Christians and Jews), should be no great surprise, for this was prophesied by God himself. Muhammad, in establishing Islam as the faith of the Arabic people, facilitated the fulfillment of this prophecy. Islam was birthed in violence and wickedness and has continued in that vein for fourteen centuries. The sin of hatred runs so deep that even Muslims slaughter other Muslims the world over. Nothing will change until the bondage to this oppressive religion is broken and the captives are set free.

Seeking Heaven's Glory

Our father was a wonderful, sincere, mountain of a man. He was in every way our hero—intelligent, warm, loving, handsome, determined, hard-working, and funny. It gave him no pleasure to disown or disinherit his sons. It broke his heart. Yet it was all he could do, given his beliefs and the teachings of Islam. On the August day in 1999 when our father succumbed to cancer, the stark reality of religious systems and our relationship with Jesus Christ as our Savior came into sharp focus.

As you begin [your] investigation into Islam, its teachings, and its adherents, we want you to see the human side of religion—where faith often means the total rejection of culture, ethnicity, family, and friends. To find heaven's glory in Jesus Christ, we Caner brothers lost our father—our earthly hero—as have millions of others worldwide.

... At this moment, for the sake of the Gospel of Jesus Christ, men and women are being bullwhipped into submission, tortured, imprisoned, beaten, battered, and broken. Homes are being burned, families executed, and other lives lost through hateful revenge. If you believe that torture and murder because of belief in Jesus Christ is a thing of the past, then you are tragically mistaken. Across our globe, the blood of Christians runs down cobblestone streets, dirt paths, paved alleys, and concrete prison floors.

... We did not "switch religions." The blood of Jesus Christ saved us. What happened to us was not an act of a religious person; rather, it was God's gracious act of redemption.

Ergun Mehmet Caner and Emir Fethi Caner
Unveiling Islam, 2002

Endnotes

1. *This was no insult to Islam*. The First Post, September 15, 2006. Http://www.Thefirstpost.co.uk/index.php?menuID=1&subID=751&WT.srch=1. Accessed January 4, 2007.

2. Caner, Ergun Mehmet and Emir Fethi Caner. *Unveiling Islam*, 2002. Kregel Publications, div. of Kregel. Inc., p. 40.

3. Crone, Patricia. *What Do We Actually Know About Mohammed?* Open Democracy, August 31, 2006. Http://www.openDemocracy.net Accessed June 2, 2007.

4. *Islamic History (Chronology)*. Http://www.barkati.net/English/chronology. Htm. Accessed January 30, 2007.

5. *Before and After Conversion to Islam*. Http://www.witness-pioneer.org/vil/Articles/companion/01_abu_bakr.htm. Accessed February 1, 2007.

6. Caner & Caner, p. 40-41.

7. *Muhammad the Messenger*. Http://www.sacred-texts.com/isl/isl/isl11.htm. Accessed February 19, 2007.

8. Wood, David. *A Bewitched Prophet? Examining Muhammad's Psychological and Spiritual Stability*. Http://answering-islam.de/Main//Authors/Wood/ bewitched_ prophet.htm. Accessed February 19, 2007.

9. *Muhammad the Messenger*.

10. Gabriel, Mark A. *Islam and Terrorism*, 2002. Published by FrontLine, a Strang Company, Lake Mary, Florida, p. 42.

11. Ibid.

12. *Muhammad the Messenger*.

13. Caner & Caner, p. 44.

14. Ibid, p. 44.

15. Ibid, p.45.

16. Safa, Reza F. *Inside Islam: Exposing and Reaching the World of Islam*, 1996. Charisma House, Lake Mary, FL., p. 19.

17. Spencer, Robert. *The Truth About Muhammad, Founder of the World's Most Intolerant Religion*, 2006. Regnery Publishing, Inc., Washington, DC., p. 78.

18. Ibid, p. 79.

19. Ibid, p. 80.

20. Spencer, p. 82-83.

21. Caner and Caner, p. 56.

22. Gilchrist, John. *Muhammad and the Religion of Islam. 2C. The Circumstances of His Marriages,* 1984. Online edition at: http://www.answering-islam.org/Gilchrist /Vol1/2c.html.

23. Spencer, p. 83-85.

24. Ibid, p. 85.

25. Ibid, p. 85.

26. Caner & Caner, p. 136.

27. Safa, p. 22.

28. Spencer, p. 90.

29. Safa, p. 18-19.

30. Spencer, p. 167-168.

31. Wehner, Peter. *Why They Fight, and What it means for us,* OpinionJournal, from The Wall Street Journal, January 9, 2007.

32. *The World Fact Book*, Updated December 12, 2006. Http://www.cia.gov/cia/publications/factbook/fields/2122.html. Accessed December 19, 2006.

CHAPTER 2

The Holy Bible or the Glorious Qur'an

Allah sent prophets and messengers to proclaim the truth.
. . . God the Father sent His Son to be the truth . . . .

Ergun Mehmet Caner and Emir Fethi Caner,
Unveiling Islam, 2002, p. 31

Author's Note: The extent of historical and biblical errors, fabrications, and extreme contradictions in the Qur'an are too numerous to address in one or two chapters. Some of the more important errors and contradictions will be explored in this and the next chapter and at various points throughout the book.

The Truth, or Contradictions

In an introduction to the version of the Qur'an used in this comparison of Islam and Christianity, Ali Abdur Rasheed wrote:

I invite those who may be reading this Qur'an for the first time to look deeply and objectively into its meaning. The Muslims were promised by Allah that this book would always remain free from falsehood, alteration and misinterpretation. We are the only people following a Divine religion who can claim to have a book which is pure and unaltered, which had been given to the Prophet directly from God and written down in his lifetime and preserved unchanged thereafter.

In the spirit of Mr. Rasheed's invitation, an attempt will be made to look *deeply and objectively* into the Qur'an, its messenger, message, and stated mission compared to that of Jesus Christ, His message and mission. For Muhammad and all his followers during his lifetime and 1400 years hence, Islam is the only true religion: "And whoever desires a religion other than Islam, it shall not be accepted from him, and in the hereafter he shall be one of the losers" (surah 3:85).

A hadith narrated by Aisha, Muhammad's child bride, proclaims, "Allah's Apostle said, 'If somebody innovates something which is not in harmony with the principles of our religion, that thing is rejected'" (hadith 3:861).

At first glance one only has to read parts of the Qur'an and compare it to the New Testament message of Jesus and the apostles to get a grasp of the *truth*. The Bible presents a clear message of God's love, forgiveness, reconciliation, peace, and assurance of eternal life in Heaven. Compare that to the message of the Qur'an and Allah's messenger, Muhammad, where Allah is unforgiving, vengeful, changeable, deceptive, one to be feared, and a god that takes pleasure in the oppression and slaughter of those who do not believe in him. In spite of that image of Allah, "The worst thing the enemies of Allah [or infidels] can do is to persuade Muslims to 'reject the Truth'[1]" of the Qur'an or teachings of Muhammad.

"If they [the infidels] find you, they will be your enemies, and will stretch forth towards you their hands and their tongues with evil, and they ardently desire that you may disbelieve" (surah 60:2).

To justify the apparent changeability of Allah, Muhammad came up with the concept of *abrogation*—the changeable, repealing word of Allah. This convenient idea is what often constitutes the verses of the Qur'an and ahadith. *Nothing, no one* can change the word of Allah proclaimed Muhammad and all the Islamic clerics since his time. "And the word of your Lord has been accomplished truly and justly; there is none who can change His words …" (surah 6:115; 18:27). Surah 6:34 and 10:64 also say that "There is none to change the words of Allah …" or "My word shall not be changed…." (50:29).

But then Allah reveals, "Whatever communications We abrogate or cause to be forgotten, We bring one better than it or like it. Do you not know that Allah has power over all things?" (surah 2:106).

The argument and assumption here in this verse and the verses in the previous paragraph, is that, while man cannot change Allah's words, Allah is free to do so as he wishes.

> And when We change (one) communication for (another) communication, and Allah knows best what He reveals, they say: You are only a forger. Nay, most of them do not know.

> Say: The Holy Spirit has revealed it from your Lord with the truth, that it may establish those who believe and as a guidance and good news for those who submit. (surah 16:101-102)

The revelation above was received by Muhammad while he was headquartered in Mecca, the town of his birth. Muhammad's ancestral tribe, the Quraysh, was pagan. While pagans dominated the area, there were also Jewish tribes and Christians living in the environs of Mecca.[2] When Muhammad started preaching the message of Islam, many of the pagans, Jews, and Christians of the area refused to accept this new theology and rejected Muhammad as a prophet. The Jews and Christians saw him as a false prophet and not one sent by God. To counteract their objections, Muhammad conveniently received this indisputable revelation from Allah.

Muhammad quite often received revelations of convenience to answer his numerous detractors and "quite often during his prophetic career," author Robert Spencer wrote, "he received revelations that answered critics, or solved a disputed question, or gave his particular perspective on a series of events."[3] His most notorious revelation reversal was "The Satanic Verses" incident highlighted in the previous chapter.

When one is reading or studying the Qur'an, it is important to understand that Muhammad received his revelations during three key periods of his apostolic life.[4] There were two Meccan periods (AD 611-615 and AD 616-622) and his Medina period, AD 623-632. During the two Meccan periods, Muhammad was more conciliatory toward the area residents as he tried to convince them of the validity of his message from Allah. Muhammad's revelations in the Qur'an during these two periods reflect his appeasing demeanor. After the Meccans finally ran Muhammad and his followers out of town, he fled to Medina. He remained in Medina until his death in 632. While in Medina, Muhammad had one epiphany after another revealing to him how Allah wanted him to convince the people of Allah's truth. That is when Allah, through Muhammad, revealed his hatred for non-believers, and Muslims started their violent rampages across the Saudi Arabian peninsula and elsewhere, taking captives to convert to Islam or murdering those who refused to convert.

"Don't be deceived, my dear brothers," wrote the Apostle James. "Every good and perfect gift is from above, coming down from the Father of the heavenly lights, who does not change like shifting shadows" (James 1:16-17).

"The biggest contradiction in the Qur'an," wrote Steve Keohane, "is that it says the Qur'an can be contradicted at any time. God can change his mind, and change verses in the Qur'an, with or without telling Muslims."[5]

As an extreme example of this "Doctrine of Abrogation," there are, according to Keohane, 125 verses in the Qur'an calling for patience and tolerance that are repealed by such injunctions as unbelievers "… should be murdered or crucified or their hands and their feet should be cut off on opposite sides or they should be imprisoned …" (surah 5:33), or "slay the idolaters wherever you find them, and take them captives and besiege them and lie in wait for them in every ambush …" (surah 9:5). Both of these surahs (5 and 9), by the way, were received by Muhammad when he was in Medina.

The Qur'an highlights Allah's truth through the words expressed by the prophet Muhammad. Allah's words are true and Muhammad is the messenger *of* that truth. "Surely this Islam," reveals Allah, "is your religion, one religion (only), and I am your Lord, therefore serve Me" (surah 21:92). The New Testament Scriptures of the Bible present God's truth in the person of Jesus Christ. Jesus, the Son of God, *is* the truth—the *only* truth of God, according to the Bible.

"Jesus said to him [the Apostle Thomas], 'I am the way, the truth, and the life. No one comes to the Father [God] except through me'" (John 14:6, NKJV). The Apostle John expressed it this way: "For the law was given through Moses; grace and truth came through Jesus Christ" (John 1:17).

Jesus, in addressing Jewish believers in John 8:31-32 (NKJV), assured His followers, "If you abide in My word, you are My disciples indeed. And you shall know the truth, and the truth shall make you free." The *truth* that Muhammad proclaimed was far from liberating. Rather than setting people free, it brought them into oppression and bondage—either they renounce their freedom of choice and accept Islam or die. In sharp contrast, at the beginning of Jesus' ministry, He went into the synagogue in the city of Nazareth, the town of his upbringing, and read from the scroll of the Prophet Isaiah: "The Spirit of the Sovereign Lord is on me, because the Lord has anointed me to preach good news to the poor. He has sent me to bind up the brokenhearted, to proclaim freedom for the captives and release from darkness for the prisoners" (Isaiah 61:1). After reading this Scripture, Jesus said, "Today this scripture is fulfilled in your hearing " (Luke 4:21).

"Now the Lord is the Spirit," the Apostle Paul said, "and where the Spirit of the Lord is, there is freedom" (2 Corinthians 3:17). Wherever Jesus went, His words, deeds, and spirit embodied a sense of well-being and freedom. This was not the case with Muhammad. Once he took up residence in Medina, his "ministry" took on an atmosphere of fear, chaos, oppression, and death. Those who were free were enslaved, murdered, or tyrannized into Islamic bondage.

Muhammad claimed that he was the "way" and that Allah had revealed to him the "truth;" he commanded by innuendo, intimidation, fear, and violence that *everyone* must follow him and the revelations from Allah or be consigned to death and hell-fire.

In surah 33:36 we read, "And it behoves [sic] not a believing man and a believing woman that they should have any choice in their matter when Allah and His Apostle have decided a matter; and whoever disobeys Allah and His Apostle, he surely strays off a manifest straying."

Jesus did not coerce or threaten anyone to follow Him. He simply stated the truth that God the Father had given Him and demonstrated the way to freedom by His example.

To the non-Christian, Jesus' retort to Thomas in John 14:6 may seem like an outlandish statement. However, Jesus backed it up with words and deeds, healings and miracles, and the witness and testimony of thousands who saw Him live an exemplary godly, sinless life—none of which Muhammad could ever lay claim.

"But when He, the Spirit of truth, comes," Jesus said, "He will guide you into all truth" (John 16:13a). Islam claims, of course, that this is another biblical Scripture that prophesied of the coming of Muhammad. This cannot be true for a number of reasons. **First,** Jesus identifies the source of God's truth as *the* Spirit–not a human being and not *a* spirit, but *the* Spirit of God. **Second,** Jesus says that the Spirit "… will speak only what he hears …." (John 16:13b). Muhammad claimed to speak only that which the angel Gabriel revealed to him. However, on numerous occasions (some discussed in this chapter and others to follow), Muhammad saw fit to change or modify a previous revelation from Allah when it did not quite meet his need. **Third,** Jesus says that the Spirit of truth "… will tell you what is yet to come " (John 16:13b). While the Holy Spirit of God—the Spirit of truth—knows all things (past, present and future), Muhammad was confused about history and knew nothing of the future, nor did he prophesy about it. **Fourth,** and this is the real clincher, Jesus says that the Spirit of truth will give *glory* to Jesus and testify that Jesus and God the Father Almighty are *one*. (The Muslim claim of the presence of Muhammad in biblical prophecy will be explored in detail in the next chapter.)

"He [the Spirit of truth] *will bring glory to me by taking from what is mine and making it known to you. All that belongs to the Father is mine. That is why I said the Spirit will take from what is mine and make it known to you."* (John 16:14-15)

Jesus' message from God was one of complete and instantaneous freedom in an era of slavery and repression. It was a theological and divinely inspired dispatch that far exceeded the reality and expectations of the people and the times. It presented a message of liberation that was previously unknown and unheard of by mankind. Muhammad's message some 600 years later was one of regression—driving people back into bondage, both physically and spiritually. The *truth of God*, as presented by Jesus, was turned into a lie by the despotic revelations of Muhammad. Yet Allah revealed to Muhammad that he was the one that gave the Torah to the Jews for *guidance and light* so that the prophets of the Jews could guide and judge the Jews in matters of *divine knowledge*. If so, why did Allah later reveal to Muhammad, not messages of guidance and light, but ones of misguidance and darkness?

"Surely We revealed the Taurat [Torah] in which was guidance and light; with it the prophets who submitted themselves (to Allah) judged (matters) for those who were Jews, and the masters of Divine knowledge and the doctors, because they were required to guard (part) of the Book of Allah, and they were witnesses thereof; therefore fear not the people and fear Me, and do not take a small price for My communications; and whoever did not judge by what Allah revealed, those are they that are the unbelievers." (surah 5:44)

In the Qur'an and in ahadith (sayings of Muhammad), the Prophet of Islam frequently contradicts or reverses the words he supposedly received from Allah. Jesus never reversed or modified His teachings because they were from the unchangeable God of Heaven and Earth. One glowing example of such a reversal or contradiction appears in hadith 2:541. The subject is alms giving and is narrated by Abu Said Al-Khudri.

… After finishing the prayer, he [Muhammad] delivered the sermon and ordered the people to give alms. He said, "O people! Give alms." Then he went towards the women and said. "O women! Give alms, for I have seen that the majority of the dwellers of Hell-Fire were you (women)." The women asked, "O Allah's Apostle! What is the reason for it?" He replied, "O women! You curse frequently, and are ungrateful to your husbands. I have not seen anyone more deficient in intelligence and religion than you …. "

However, in the second half of the same hadith, Muhammad backtracks on this command of alms giving when he is questioned by the wife of one of his followers.

And when he [Muhammad] reached his house, Zainab, the wife of Ibn Masud, came and asked permission to enter. It was said, "O Allah's Apostle! It is Zainab." He asked, "Which Zainab?" The reply was that she was the wife of Ibn Masud. He said, "Yes, allow her to enter." And she was admitted. Then she said, "O Prophet of Allah! Today you ordered people to give alms and I had an ornament and intended to give it as alms, but Ibn Masud said that he and his children deserved it more than anybody else." The Prophet replied, "Ibn Masud had spoken the truth. Your husband and your children had more right to it than anybody else."

So, the conflicting message given here seems to be: *Give alms, but not if it is going to be a sacrifice for you.* Or, *Give alms, but not if you deserve it more than those in need.* This is just one small example among hundreds of confusing and blatant contradictions that appear in the Qur'an and ahadith.

The Bible or "The Mighty Book"

"… if the Muslim rejects the Bible," wrote Gnana Pragash Suresh, a priest for the Society of St. Pius X in Southern Africa, "he must also reject the Qur'an because it appeals to the Bible as God's Word. On the other hand, if he accepts the Bible, he still must reject the Qur'an because it contradicts the Bible."[6]

"… the [Qur'an] is difficult to use as a historical source," wrote Islamic scholar Professor Patricia Crone of Princeton University.[7] "The roots of this difficulty include unresolved questions about how it reached its classical form, and the fact that it still is not available in a scholarly edition.

"Modern scholars," Crone continued, "usually assure themselves that since the Qur'an was recited from the start, we can rely on the oral tradition to supply us with the correct reading. But there is often considerable disagreement in the tradition …."

The Bible, by contrast, has been shown to be a reliable historic document. The key figures, places, and events have been verified by other historical documents and archeological discoveries. Virtually no scholar of the Bible doubts the veracity of its claims or contextual message.

The same cannot be said about the Qur'an. "… the Qur'an," penned Crone, "is often highly obscure. Sometimes it uses expressions that were unknown even to the earliest exegetes [one who explains a text], or words that do not seem to fit entirely, though they can be made to fit more or less; sometimes it seems to give us fragments detached from a long-lost context; and the style is highly allusive.

"One explanation," Crone offered, is "that the prophet formulated his message in the liturgical language current in the religious community in which he grew up, adapting and/or imitating ancient texts such as hymns, recitations, and prayers, which had been translated or adapted from another Semitic language in their turn."[8]

Muslims generally believe in the Bible, but believe that it was revealed to the Jews and Christians by Allah. In fact, although most Muslims tend to deny or downplay it, they are called to believe in the Bible, as well as in the prophets and apostles of the Bible, as commanded by the prophet Muhammad.

Say: We believe in Allah and (in) that which had been revealed to us, and (in) that which was revealed to Ibrahim [Abraham] and to Ismail [Ishmael] and Ishaq [Isaac] and Yaqoub [Jacob] and the tribes [their descendants], and (in) that which was given to Musa [Moses] and Isa [Jesus] and (in) that which was given to the prophets from their Lord, we do not make any distinction between any of them, and to Him do we submit. (surah 2:136)

Muslims, however, are taught to take this verse differently. This verse, they say, proves that Abraham, Isaac, Ishmael, Jacob, and even Moses and Jesus were, indeed, Muslims. This conclusion is reached despite the fact that Abraham preceded Muhammad and the birth of Islam by about 2,000 years. "When his [Abraham's] Lord [Allah] said to him," verse 131 of the same surah claims, "Be a Muslim, he said: I submit myself to the Lord of the worlds." In verse 135 that follows, Jews and Christians are told to submit to the religion of Abraham, which is Islam. This was "revealed" during Muhammad's Medina period when he was getting frustrated to the point of violence because the Jews and Christians were not accepting his mandate to convert to Islam. However, in three verses of the Qur'an—6:14, 163 and 39:12—it is revealed that Muhammad was to be the first to submit to Allah and Islam, and thus, become the first Muslim.

According to surah 3:49, Jesus could do nothing without Allah's permission. Of course, Jesus' disciples were also Muslims. "But when Isa perceived unbelief on their [the disciple's] part, he said: Who will be my helpers in Allah's way? The disciples said: We are helpers (in the way) of Allah: We believe in Allah and bear witness that we are submitting ones." Muhammad even revealed that Jesus himself proclaimed His faith in Allah. "And when Isa came with clear arguments, he said: I have come to you indeed with wisdom, and that I may make clear to you part of what you differ in; so be careful of (your duty to) Allah and obey me: Surely Allah is my Lord and your Lord, therefore serve Him; this is the right path" (surah 43:63-64).

This is how easy it was for Muhammad to take what he wanted from the Jewish and Christian Scriptures and adapt it to his theology and declare that Jews and Christians were to do the same. After all, how could they resist him? Were not all the Jewish and Christian forefathers and spiritual leaders Muslims? Even Jesus was a Muslim.

> Surely We have revealed to you as We revealed to Nuh [Noah], and the prophets after him, and We revealed to Ibrahim and Ismail and Ishaq and Yaqoob and the tribes, and Isa and Ayub [Job] and Yunus [Jonah] and Haroun [Aaron] and Sulaiman [Solomon] and We gave to Dawood [David] Psalms.

> And (We sent) apostles We have mentioned to you before and apostles we have not mentioned to you; and to Musa, Allah addressed His Word, speaking (to him): (We sent) apostles as the givers of good news and as warners, so that people should not have to plea against Allah after the (coming of) apostles; and Allah is Mighty, Wise. (surah 4:163-165)

Muhammad was not happy just to convert by his word the faithful of the Bible to Islam, but to be complete he had to convert the Bible to that which was revealed by Allah and not by Jehovah God of the Jews. "The revelation of the Book [Bible] is from Allah," he decreed, "the Mighty, the Wise" (surah 46:2). Throughout the Qur'an there are verses that reveal that Allah and Allah alone ordained and revealed the Torah to Moses and the gospel to Jesus.

> Again, We gave the Book to Musa, Allah revealed to Muhammad, "to complete (Our blessings) on him who would do good (to others), and making plain all things and a guidance and a mercy, so that they should believe in the meeting of their Lord. And this is a Book We have revealed, blessed; therefore follow it and guard (against evil) that mercy may be shown to you. (surah 6:154-155)

Allah further revealed that the Gospels of Jesus Christ were his. "And We sent after them [the Old Testament prophets] in their footsteps Isa, son of Marium, verifying what was before him of the Taurat and We gave him the Injeel [Gospel] in which was guidance and light, and verifying what was before it of Taurat and a guidance and an admonition for those who guard (against evil). And the followers of the Injeel should have judged by what Allah revealed in it; and whoever did not judge by what Allah revealed, those are they that are the transgressors. (surah 5:46-47)

And most certainly We gave Musa the Book [Torah] and We sent apostles after him one after another; and We gave Isa, the son of Marium [Mary], clear arguments and strengthened him with the holy spirit.... (surah 2:87)

Indeed, Muhammad—as it was revealed to him by Allah—presents a great mystery here. If Allah, the revealer of the Qur'an, was also the one who revealed the Torah to Moses and the gospel to Jesus, then how come the Qur'an is in such great and constant conflict with the Word of God in both the Torah and gospel? And if Allah revealed the Torah and the gospel, how come Muhammad and his followers did not honor it and follow its teachings? Allah said that those who do not follow his teachings in the Torah and gospel are transgressors. If so, then Muhammad, Allah's agent of "new" revelation, was chief among the transgressors.

Muhammad neither believed in nor followed much of the teachings in the Torah and practically none of the teachings of Jesus in the gospels. Even today, despite their belief *in* the Bible, the Bible is forbidden to Muslims and banned in Muslim countries. This is quite a strange state of affairs for a people that are commanded by their own holy book to believe in the Bible (the message of the prophets and apostles in surahs 2:136, 285; 4:136, 163 and elsewhere). How can they believe in that which is forbidden to them? Could it be that the imams of Islam know that if the truth of the Bible were revealed to the Muslim faithful, Islam could no longer be spread across the world through deception, lies, and fear? Apparently, fear of the truth is pervasive in the Muslim community.

Yet, the Bible, according to the revealed will of Allah, is not only to be read, but to be studied and followed by his followers. "Those to whom We have given the Book [Bible]," surah 2:121 directs, "read [study and follow] it as it ought to be read [studied and followed]. These [that do] believe in it [the Bible]; and whoever disbelieves in it[s truth] these it is that are the losers."

The fact is that Muhammad "borrowed" from both the Old and New Testament scriptural stories or concepts he liked and incorporated them into Islamic theology as revelations from Allah. However, Muhammad and the Qur'an teach that the Bible was corrupted or Scriptures were removed by Jews or Christians, Scriptures that Allah must now reveal through Muhammad to make his (Allah's) word true again. "Islam teaches that the Qur'an is an exact word-for-word copy of God's final revelation, words inscribed on tablets that have always existed in heaven."[9]

Do you then hope that they [the people of the Book] would believe in you, and a party from among them indeed used to hear the Word of Allah, then altered it after they had understood it, and they know (this).

And when they meet those who believe they say: We believe, and when they are alone one with another they say: Do you talk to them of what Allah has disclosed to you that they may contend with you by this before your Lord? Do you not then understand?

Do they not know that Allah knows what they keep secret and what they make known?

And there are among them illiterates who know not the Book but only lies, and they do but conjecture.

Woe, then, to those who write the book with their hands and then say: This is from Allah, so that they may take for it a small price; therefore woe to them for what their hands have written and woe to them for what they earn. (surah 2:75-79)

"Many Muslims," according to the former radical Shi'a Muslim, Reza Safa, "will argue that Allah is the same God that Christians and Jews worship. But by studying the Koran one will see the vast gap of character, nature and personality that exists between the God of the Bible and the Allah of the Koran."[10]

Sometime during his Medina residency (AD 623 to 632), Muhammad had this revelation about the Qur'an's place in God's realm of truth.

> He has revealed to you the Book [Qur'an] with truth, verifying that which is before it, and He revealed the Taurat and the Injeel aforetime, a guidance for the people, and He sent the Furqan [The Criterion or Standard; the Qur'an]. (surah 3:3)

This verse provides a curious contradiction. In surah 2:75-79, also revealed during the Medina period, Allah made it clear to Muhammad that the Bible (the Torah and the gospels) could not be trusted because they had been corrupted by *the people of the Book*—Jews and Christians. Yet, in surah 3, Allah revealed that the Qur'an was given to verify the truth he had previously made known through the Torah (the Old Testament) and gospels (the New Testament). So, was the Qur'an revealed by Allah to confirm old truth, present new truth, or to be the **only** truth? Apparently, neither the Qur'an itself, nor Allah is clear on that point.

Despite such a confusing message from the Qur'an, Muhammad made it clear that, "Surely they who disbelieve in the communications of Allah—they shall have a severe chastisement; and Allah is Mighty, the Lord of Retribution" (surah 3:4).

According to Muhammad, only he was privileged through revelation knowledge from Allah, to know what parts of the Bible were true and what parts had been corrupted by human hands. "And when Our clear communications are recited to them [people of the Book], those who disbelieve say with regard to the truth when it comes to them [via Muhammad]: This is clear magic. Nay! They say: He has forged it. Say: If I have forged it, you do not control anything for me from Allah; He knows best what you utter concerning it; He is enough as a witness between me and you, and He is the Forgiving, the Merciful (surah 46:7-8)." No matter what Muhammad was confronted with, he always came up with a convenient and often self-serving revelation from the god he called Allah.

Again, in surah 98:1-3, Muhammad has this revelation from Allah against his detractors: "Those who disbelieved from among the followers of the Book and the polytheists [Christians] could not have separated (from the faithful) until there had come to them the clear evidence: An apostle from Allah, reciting pure pages, wherein are all the right ordinances."

Of course, since the Qur'an was revealed to Muhammad in Arabic, the Qur'an, according to Islamic teaching, can only be read and recited in Arabic in order to get the true meaning and full blessing of Allah. Other translations are suspect and viewed as faulty and unreliable. As a result, despite the rapid rise in Islam currently, the vast majority of Muslims—perhaps as many as 90 % —have never read the Qur'an and cannot read it because they do not know the Arabic language.

Furthermore, unlike the detailed account of the life of Jesus in the Bible, "The Qur'an," Crone stated, "does not give us an account of the prophet's life …. We see the world through his eyes, and the allusive style makes it difficult to follow what is going on.

"Events are referred to," Crone acknowledged, "but not narrated; disagreements are debated without being explained; people and places are mentioned, but rarely named. Supporters are simply referred to as believers; opponents are condemned as unbelievers, polytheists, wrongdoers, hypocrites and the like, with only the barest information on who they were or what they said or did …."[11]

In comparison, the Bible is very concise and well narrated by numerous groups of actors and verifiable historical figures. The history of the time is well delineated and the context of the dialogue made clear. The faithful in God and their detractors are plainly identified. Above all, the theological message delivered is clear as to its source and its targeted audience.

To reinforce the fact that only he and believers in Allah had the truth, Muhammad had this further understanding revealed to him.

And those who were given the Book did not become divided except after clear evidence had come to them. And they were not enjoined anything except that they should serve Allah, being sincere to Him in obedience, upright, and keep up prayer and pay the poor-rate [submission to Islam tax], and that is the right religion. Surely those who disbelieve from among the followers of the Book and the polytheists shall be in the fire of hell, abiding therein; they are the worst of men. (As for) those who believe [in Allah] and do good, surely they are the best of men. (surah 98:4-7)

In this revelation from Allah, Muhammad makes the following clear:
- The people of the Book and polytheists have gone astray from the truth (verse 1).
- Muhammad is the new messenger of God's truth (verse 2).
- With a new law to be laid down (verse 3).
- When this new truth was revealed, even the Jews and Christians argued among themselves as to its truthfulness (verse 4).
- If Jews and Christians wanted to be in the right religion, they had to follow the right laws (verse 5).
- If not, they would go to hell (verse 6).
- But only true believers, those that followed Muhammad's teachings, were acceptable to God (verse 7).

The Qur'an is a very difficult book to follow (for the reasons cited in the Introduction). What does the reader of the Qur'an actually encounter in the theology of the Qur'an? According to Professor Crone, "… some kind of combination of Biblical-type monotheism and Arabian paganism …."[12] Despite these difficulties and in spite of the *corrupted Bible* stance of Muslims, some "moderate" Muslims and Christian apologists (on the behalf of Islam) maintain that there is much common ground in the scriptures of the Qur'an and the Bible.

There can be no common ground between the Qur'an and the Bible; and there is no common ground. The scriptures and message of both are fundamentally and spiritually diametrically opposed to each other. The Qur'an's message is one of darkness, oppression, and death. The message of the Bible is one of light, freedom, and life.

"When Islamic apologists say terrorists quote the Qur'an on jihad 'out of context,'" author Robert Spencer noted, "they neglect to mention that the Qur'an itself often offers little context. Frequently it makes reference to people and events without bothering to explain what's going on."[13] The Bible, in contrast, is full of collaborating stories full of detail that thoroughly inform the reader of the context in which the event occurred or the message was given.

To fill in this contextual void, Muslims have relied primarily on two early sources of additional information: the *tafsir* (or Qur'an commentary) and the *hadith* (or traditions of Muhammad). Another written tradition, the *sunnah*, follows the example of the Prophet Muhammad. It mostly consists of the hadith. Both the hadith and sunnah attempt to elaborate on the meaning of Qur'anic verses and/or Muhammad's teachings and commandments. Next to the Qur'an, either the hadith or sunnah are considered the most sacred to the Muslim. It is the sunnah that provides the legal foundation for Islamic *shari'a* law.[14, 15]

"From the vantage point of fourteen hundred years later," Spencer asserted, "it is virtually impossible to tell with any certainty what is authentic in this mass of information and what isn't. Muslims themselves acknowledge that there are a great many forged *ahadith* (the plural form of hadith), which were written to give the Prophet's sanction to the views or practices of a particular party in the early Muslim community. This makes the question of what the historical Muhammad actually said and did well-nigh insoluble."[16]

Surprisingly, the Qur'an itself has a solution for Muslims who really want to know the truth. "But if you are in doubt as to what We [Allah] have revealed to you, ask those [Jews and Christians] who read the Book [Bible] before you; certainly the truth has come to you from your Lord, therefore you should not be of the disputers [doubters]" (surah 10:94).

There Is One God

"You shall have no other gods [besides] me" (Exodus 20:3). Yahweh, Jehovah, Elohiym, the great God of the Jews, spoke through the great Prophet Isaiah thirteen centuries before the birth of Islam:

"You are My witnesses," declares the Lord [Jehovah, the self-Existent or Eternal God], *"and My servant whom I have chosen, that you may know and believe Me and understand that I am He. Before Me there was no God formed, nor shall there be after Me. I, even I, am the Lord. And besides me there is no savior. I have declared* [revealed] *and saved, I have proclaimed, and there was no foreign god among you; therefore you are my witnesses,"* says the Lord, *"that I am God. Indeed before the day was, I am He; and there is no one who can deliver out of*

38

My hand; I work, and who will reverse it?" (Isaiah 43:10-13, NKJV)

This same revelation—"And you shall know no God but Me; for there is no Savior besides Me"—was revealed through the Prophet Hosea a few years earlier. (See Hosea 13:4b, NKJV.) In the eyes and mind of Muhammad, this admonition was compounded by the revelation in all four gospels that Jesus was the *Son of God*. Jesus acknowledged that He was, indeed, the Son of the Most High God. (See John 3:16-18; 10:36; 11:4.) To further complicate the issue for monotheists, Jesus said, "I am the way and the truth and the life. No one comes to the Father [God] except through me" (John 14:6). Such professions were enough to convince Muhammad that Christians worshipped more than one god.

> O followers of the Book! do not exceed the limits in your religion, and do not speak (lies) against Allah, but (speak) the truth; the Messiah, Isa son of Marium is only an apostle of Allah and His Word which He communicated to Marium and a spirit from Him; believe therefore in Allah and His apostles, and say not, Three. Desist, it is better for you; Allah is only one God: far be it from His glory that He should have a son; whatever is in the heavens and whatever is in the earth is His; and Allah is sufficient for a Protector. (surah 4:171)

Muhammad had no concept of the Triune God or the Trinity, and, in fact, included Mary, the mother of Jesus, in the Trinity instead of the Holy Spirit. "And when Allah will say: O Isa son of Marium! Did you say to men, Take me and my mother for two gods besides Allah, he will say: Glory be to Thee, it did not befit me that I should say what I had no right to (say) …" (surah 5:116).

The concept of the *Trinity* or the *Godhead, three in one*, is a difficult perception even for the Christian to grasp, much less the non-believer; and it is especially sensitive to the Muslim that firmly believes there can only be ONE God. However, a Muslim could agree that he or she and all mankind is comprised of a *spirit*, a *body* and a *soul* as the Apostle Paul states in 1 Thessalonians 5:23. Each human being is *one* person but created in three entities: spirit, body, and soul. The Christian God is the same as what He created: spirit, body, and soul. God the Father is the body or source of life; Jesus is the incarnated Word and soul of God and the Holy Spirit.

The Apostle John explains it this way: "In the beginning was the Word, and the Word was with God, and the Word was God. He was with God in the beginning …. The Word became flesh and made his dwelling among us. We have seen his glory, the glory of the One and Only, who came from the Father, full of grace and truth" (John 1:1, 14).

A simplified way to explain the Christian God is to look to His creation, the sun. The sun, the fireball in the sky, is a molten body of fire. It produces both heat and light. The molten body would be nothing without heat and light. Without heat and light there would be no life. The indescribable heat is not the sun—it cannot be seen; it can only be felt. Likewise, the sun's brightness can only be seen, it cannot be felt except through its production of heat. All *three* make up the *one* sun—the molten body, the heat, and the light. By itself, the light is not the sun; nor is the heat. All three must function together to be the sun.

Despite Muhammad's assertions in the Qur'an and what Muslims have always been taught, Christians *are not* polytheists. They do not worship more than one god.

"Hear, O Israel: The Lord our God, the Lord is one (Deuteronomy 6:4)!" and "… besides him there is no other (Deuteronomy 4:35)." Jesus would not disagree, for He quoted this Scripture when asked by one of the teachers of the Law, "Of all the commandments, which is the most important?"

"'The most important one,' answered Jesus, 'is this: Hear, O Israel, the Lord our God, the Lord is one" (Mark 12:28, 29).

The prayer of Hezekiah, the king of Judah, echoes what the Jewish sages believed and taught. "O Lord Almighty, God of Israel, enthroned between the cherubim, you alone are God over all the kingdoms of the earth …" (Isaiah 37:16).

The Old Testament prophets, Jesus Christ, and His apostles never claimed anything else than God Almighty, the God of the Jews and Christians, was indeed one God and one only. But Muslims believe that because Christians believe in the concept of the Trinity (God in three persons, the Father, Son and Holy Spirit—or Mary, according to Muhammad), that Christians are polytheistic. Nothing could be further from the truth. For Christians to worship and serve more than God alone would be heretical and not faithful to the Scriptures they have been given through the ages.

"… We believe in that which has been revealed to us and revealed to you, and our God and your God is One, and to Him do we submit" (surah 29:46). Surah 32:4 reaffirms that there is no God but Allah and that there is no "guardian or any intercessor" besides him.

"Allah, (there is) no god but He, the Everliving, the Self-subsisting by Whom all things subsist" (surah 3:2). Other surahs, such as 3:18, 6:102 and 59:23, also proclaim that Allah is the only god or that he is one god and one only. The Islamic mantra or *Shahada* (to bear witness to) is, "There is no god but Allah, Muhammad is the messenger of Allah (or Muhammad is his Prophet)." They are the first words spoken in the ears of a newborn baby boy," noted the Caner brothers. "The creed is repeated at times of prayer, during rights of passage in life and throughout the life of the faithful Muslim.[17]

"Certainly they disbelieve," Allah disclosed in surah 5:72-73, "who say: Surely Allah, He is the Messiah, son of Marium; and the Messiah said: O children of Israel! Serve Allah, my Lord and your Lord. Surely whoever associates (others) with Allah, then Allah has forbidden to him the garden [of paradise], and his abode is the fire; and there shall be no helpers for the unjust.

"Certainly they disbelieve who say: Surely Allah is the third (person) of the three; and there is no god but the one God, and if they desist not from what they say, a painful chastisement shall befall those among them who disbelieve."

Could Allah possibly be the same God that revealed himself to Moses on Mount Sinai? When Moses went up on Mount Sinai to meet with God, the Lord God Almighty "passed in front of Moses, proclaiming, 'The Lord, the Lord, the compassionate and gracious God, slow to anger, abounding in love and faithfulness, maintaining love to thousands, and forgiving wickedness, rebellion and sin'" (Exodus 34:6-7a). Thus, God revealed His temperament and nature to Moses toward all peoples of the Earth. This character of Yahweh or Jehovah God of the Jews that was exemplified in His Son, Jesus Christ, is the antithesis of the character and nature of Allah as revealed in the Qur'an.

Allah is neither compassionate, nor slow to anger. Nor is he abounding in love and forgiveness. Notwithstanding the frequent proclamations throughout the Qur'an that Allah is compassionate, loving, and forgiving, little of those character traits show through the continuous harsh edicts and condemnations presented in the Qur'an, ahadith, or the life of Allah's chief apostle, Muhammad.

"Is God the God of the Jews only?" the Apostle Paul preached. "Is he not the God of the Gentiles [unbelievers] too? Yes, of Gentiles too, since there is only one God, who will justify the circumcised by faith and the uncircumcised through that same faith" (Romans 3:29, 30). By contrast, Muhammad, in the Qur'an, by the words of Allah, continually and consistently condemns non-believers to hell-fire. There is no recognition or acceptance that Allah is the god of infidels.

When Jesus was confronted and persecuted by the Jewish leaders because He was doing ministry on the Sabbath and "… called God his own Father, making himself equal with God (John 5:18)," Jesus had this response for them. "… I tell you the truth, the Son can do nothing by himself; he can do only what he sees his Father doing, because whatever the Father does the Son also does. For the Father loves the Son and shows him all he does. Yes, to your amazement he will show him even greater things than these. For just as the Father raises the dead and gives them life, even so the Son gives life to whom he is pleased to give it. Moreover, the Father judges no one, but has entrusted all judgment to the Son, that all may honor the Son just as they honor the Father. He who does not honor the Son does not honor the Father, who sent him" (John 5:19-23).

Jesus did *only* that which His Father in Heaven showed him to do. He reached out and loved the poor, the oppressed, the sinners—believers and unbelievers alike—with no partiality, discrimination, or condemnation. "I and the Father are one," he revealed. (See John 10:30.) What He saw God do in the Spirit, that Jesus did also on Earth.

When the Apostle Philip asked Jesus to show them the Father, Jesus retorted. "Don't you believe that I am in the Father, and that the Father is in me? The words I say to you are not just my own. Rather, it is the Father, living in me, who is doing his work. Believe me when

I say that I am in the Father and the Father is in me; or at least believe on the evidence of the miracles themselves" (John 14:10-11).

Muhammad, Allah's *only* apostle and prophet, apparently also did what he saw Allah do and carried out Allah's commands of hatred and oppression against all those who refused to accept Muhammad's message. There was no equal love or justice for the believer and the non-believer in Allah's world. No compassion, no forgiveness for the sinner or for those who refused this new religion of biblical contradictions.

> *When tempted, no one should say, "God is tempting me."*
> *For God cannot be tempted by evil, nor does he tempt anyone;*
> *but each one is tempted when, by his own evil desire, he is*
> *dragged away and enticed. Then, after desire has conceived, it*
> *gives birth to sin; and sin, when it is full-grown, gives birth to*
> *death.* (James 1:13-15)

The Birth of Jesus and the Immaculate Conception

Over three hundred prophesies in the Old Testament foretold of the coming of Jesus, the Messiah, the Anointed One, the Son of God —and the birth of Jesus Christ fulfilled all of them. There was not one prophecy in the Old Testament that foretold of Muhammad's birth, his coming or his mission. His birth was not noted as anything other than normal *until* he declared himself to be the Prophet of Allah.

The Old Testament prophets foretold where Jesus would be born (see Micah 5:2; Matthew 2:4-6); how He would be born (see Isaiah 7:14); from what lineage (see Genesis 12:3; 18:17-18; Isaiah 11:1; Jeremiah 23:5-6); and how He would be recognized (see Isaiah 9:2-3, 6-7; 42:1-4; 52:13-53:12). There was no such disclosure about Muhammad by anyone who lived before him.

"In the beginning," the Apostle John decreed, "was the Word, and the Word was with God, and the Word was God.... The Word became flesh and made his dwelling among us. We [the apostles] have seen his glory, the glory of the One and Only [Jesus] who came from the Father, full of grace and truth" (John 1:1, 14).

The Old Testament prophets NEVER prophesied about Muhammad as God's "last" messenger, or about Muhammad at all; but they did prophesy about the coming of a Messiah, one who would bring salvation to the Jews and the entire world. That person was and is Jesus Christ and Him only. Muhammad and his followers (both then and now) claim that the Old Testament did prophesy of his coming, but that the lying Jews and Christians edited out the scriptures that foretold of him. This myth of the foretelling of Muhammad's coming is adhered to even today by the Muslim faithful, although there is absolutely no proof that such scriptures existed, nor that, if they did exist, that the Jews or the Christians removed them from the Torah or the Bible.

The birth of Jesus and John the Baptist are re-told by Muhammad in surah 3:39-61. In verse 47, Mary (or Marium) speaks: "My Lord! When shall there be a son (born) to me, and man has not touched me? He [presumably the angel Gabriel] said: Even so, Allah creates what He pleases; when He has decreed a matter, He only says to it, Be, and it is." Now, if Muslims believe (as they must, because the Qur'an says so) that Jesus was conceived without the intervention of a man and that only Allah was involved, how could Jesus not be Allah's son? Despite this clear Qur'anic description of the Virgin Birth of Jesus, Muhammad and Muslims have always claimed that Allah cannot have any offspring—it is beneath Allah to "procreate." (This conflict of Godly Sonship is explored in greater detail in Chapter 7.)

Muhammad claimed that it was the angel Gabriel who revealed the perfect, unadulterated word of Allah to him. It was the same angel Gabriel of the Bible that delivered the news to Mary that she would give birth to a son—the Son of God.

In the sixth month, God sent the angel Gabriel to Nazareth, a town in Galilee, to a virgin pledged to be married to a man named Joseph, a descendant of David. The virgin's name was Mary. The angel went to her and said, "Greetings, you who are highly favored! The Lord is with you."

*Mary was greatly troubled at his words and wondered what kind of greeting this might be. But the angel said to her, "Do not be afraid, Mary, you have found favor with God. You will be with child and give birth to a son, and you are to give him the name Jesus. He will be great and will be called the **Son of the Most High**. The Lord God will give him the throne of **his father David**, and he will reign over **the house of Jacob** forever; his kingdom will never end."* (Luke 1:26-33, author's emphasis.)

In Gabriel's visitation with Mary, he makes three things clear: Mary's son to be born by the hand of God should be named *Jesus* (or Jehovah is Salvation); He will be the *Son of the Most High* God; and He will descend from the throne of *David* and be of the *house of Jacob*. Jesus' birth was the complete fulfillment of Old Testament prophecies. The Old Testament Scriptures are full of references and prophecies about the coming of God's promised Messiah, His birth, His character, His physical characteristics, His mission, and His suffering. Even Satan believed and taunted Jesus for being the Son of God. (See Matthew 4:1-11.)

> *Then Isaiah said, "Hear now, you house of David! Is it not enough to try the patience of men? Will you try the patience of my God also? Therefore the Lord himself will give you a sign: The virgin will be with child and will give birth to a son, and will call him Immanuel* [that is, God *with us*]." (Isaiah 7:13-14)

Allah cannot have a son—or can he? The Qur'an provides a confusing picture of the birth of Jesus. On the one hand it states clearly that Allah *cannot* have a son. It is beneath him.

Allah has no sons: "Wonderful Originator of the heavens and the earth! How could He have a son when He has no consort, and He (Himself) created everything ..." (surah 6:101). So vehement is Allah's denial that he could have a son, that he threatens to annihilate the Christians for saying so. "... and the Christians say: The Messiah is the son of Allah; these are the words of their mouths; they imitate the saying of those who disbelieved before; may Allah destroy them; how they are turned away!" (surah 9:30).

Numerous verses in the Qur'an staunchly proclaim that God [Allah] could never and would never have a son (see surah 10:68; 18:4-5; 25:2; 19:35; 21:26; 37:151-152; 72:3; 112:3), because "... it is not worthy of the Beneficent God that He should take (to Himself) a son. There is no one in the heavens and the earth but will come to the Beneficent God as a servant" (surah 19:88-83).

Now, if it was Gabriel that delivered to Muhammad the Qur'an as the infallible word of Allah, how could he be so confused as to the relationship between Jesus and God Almighty? In the Qur'an, Gabriel insists (according to Muhammad) that God cannot and would not have a son. Yet, in the Bible, 600+ years before Gabriel "delivered" the Qur'an, Gabriel proclaimed that Mary's son, Jesus, would indeed be the promised Messiah, the Son of the one and only living God.

Or can Allah have a son? According to surah 39:4, Allah can have a son if he wants to. "If Allah desire[s] to take a son to Himself, He will surely choose those He pleases from what He has created...."

Then there is this surah that states clearly that Allah can have a son if he wants to: "And mention Marium in the Book when she drew aside from her family to an eastern place; so she took a veil (to screen herself) from them; then We [Allah] sent to her Our spirit [angel], and there appeared to her a well-made man .... He said: I am only a messenger of your Lord; That I will give you a pure [immaculately conceived] boy. She said: When shall I have a boy and no mortal has yet touched me, nor have I been unchaste? He said: Even so; your Lord [Allah] says: It is easy to Me: and that We may make him a sign to men and a mercy from Us; and it is a matter which has been decreed" (surah 19:16-17, 19-21).

The Crucifixion of Christ

Jesus died an excruciatingly painful death of His choosing at the hands of His accusers and oppressors just as the prophets of old foretold. (See Psalm 22:15-18; Isaiah 53:1-12; Zechariah 12:10.) Only He had the power and the will to freely choose the time, place, and method of His atoning death. (See Matthew 26:3-5; John 13:1.) Jesus died as a true martyr—one who gave His life so that all could live. He was only 33. Muhammad, on the other hand, despite all his calls for others to die as martyrs in Allah's cause, died a quiet, peaceful death of a non-martyr in the arms of his beloved 18-year old Aisha, the girl he had married when she was only nine and Muhammad was fifty-three. He lived a full life and died at sixty-two.

"I am the good shepherd," Jesus said, "I know my sheep and my sheep know me—just as the Father knows me and I know the Father—and I lay down my life for the sheep. I have other sheep that are not of this sheep pen. I must bring them also. They too will listen to my voice, and there shall be one flock and one shepherd. The reason my Father loves me is that I lay down my life—only to take it up again. No one takes it from me, but I lay it down of my own accord. I have authority to lay it down and authority to take it up again. This command I received from my Father" (John 10:14-18).

Not only did Jesus have power over His own death, but He also had the freedom to relinquish that power to the Father so that in His death it would be a loving sacrifice for all mankind—the death of a true and faithful martyr. To accomplish this all-encompassing, atoning surrender of His life for others, Jesus also knew when and how He must die. As the sacrificial *Lamb of God, who takes away the sin of the world* (see John 1:29), Jesus could die at no other time than the Jewish Passover. "When Jesus had finished saying all these things, he said to his disciples, 'As you know, the Passover is two days away—and the Son of Man will be handed over to be crucified'" (Matthew 26:1-2).

Almost 500 years before the birth of Jesus, the Jewish prophet Zechariah prophesied that the King of the Jews, the promised Messiah, would not be an ordinary king or a king in the class of Solomon. He would not only be a king of humble beginnings, but one of humble endings. "Rejoice greatly, O Daughter of Zion! Shout, Daughter of Jerusalem! See, your king comes to you, righteous and having salvation, gentle and riding on a donkey, on a colt, the foal of a donkey" (Zechariah 9:9). This prophecy too was fulfilled by Jesus as recorded in the Gospel of Matthew. (See Matthew 21:1-11.)

When Jesus went to the cross, He fulfilled yet another of the Old Testament prophecies revealed through David. (See Psalm 69:19-21.)

"Later, knowing that all was now completed, and so that the Scripture would be fulfilled, Jesus said, 'I am thirsty.' A jar of wine vinegar was there, so they soaked a sponge in it, put the sponge on a stalk of the hyssop plant, and lifted it to Jesus' lips" (John 19:28-29).

In surah 19 there arises another Qur'anic conundrum: the Crucifixion of Jesus and His subsequent resurrection. The official Islamic position and belief today, as in its entire history, is that Jesus was not crucified, did not die as the Bible states, and was not raised from the dead.

"And their [the Jews] saying: Surely we have killed the Messiah, Isa [Jesus] son of Marium [Mary], the apostle of Allah; and they did not kill him nor did they crucify him, but it appeared to them so (like Isa) and most surely those who differ therein are only in a doubt about it; they have no knowledge respecting it, but only follow a conjecture, and they killed him not for sure" (surah 4:157). (See also surahs 3:144; 4:158; 19:33.)

This is the only verse in the Qur'an that mentions the Crucifixion of Jesus, even though Muslims protest the reality of it with vigor. However, it is the verse that Muslims point to as proof that Jesus was no more than a mere prophet and was not crucified and raised on the third day as the Bible says. It was all a hoax of the first-century Christians, Muslims claim. In spite of such Islamic claims, a closer examination of the verse is warranted. First, the verse *does not* say that Jesus was not crucified. It only says that the Jews "… did not kill him nor did they crucify him." Second, that analysis would be a correct statement according to the biblical witness. While Jewish leaders conspired to have Jesus killed, they themselves did not kill or crucify Jesus. Jesus, through the false witness of certain Jews, was tried and condemned by a Roman court and consigned to the Roman death by crucifixion.

However, in surah 19, Muhammad provides a different revelation about Jesus:

"And peace on him [Jesus] on the day he was born, and on the day he dies, and on the day he is raised to life" (vs. 15). This view is repeated in verses 33 and 34: "And peace on me [Jesus] the day I was born, and on the day I die, and on the day I am raised to life. Such is Isa [Jesus], son of Marium [Mary]; (that is) the saying of truth about which they dispute."

Muhammad believed and the Islamic faith continues to propagate that Jesus did not die on the cross as the Bible says, but someone that Allah made to look like Jesus took His place and that Jesus continued to spread the gospel beyond the year of His supposed crucifixion. The fact that the Qur'an mentions Jesus' bodily resurrection should not be seen as an admission of His resurrection three days after His crucifixion. Muhammad and Muslim adherents, while believing that Jesus was not crucified, do believe that He will be raised from the dead, as will Muhammad and other prophets in the last days.

This apparent conflict in theology could also be explained by Muhammad's changing revelations over his lifespan as "The Prophet" of Allah. Surah 19 was received during Muhammad's second Mecca period (AD 616-622) when many of the doctrines of the faith were being established—a period during which Muhammad was more conciliatory toward the Jews and Christians. Surah 4, however, was revealed during the last ten years of Muhammad's life when he lived in Medina (AD 623-632), a period when he and his followers became militant and intolerant of Jews and Christians and anyone who refused to accept Islam as the only true religion.

Muhammad foresaw nothing about his eventual death and had no power to stop it. Jesus knew exactly when His death would occur, how it would occur and the events leading up to it. Yet, He freely chose to surrender the power He had over His own death in strict obedience to God the Father for the sake of all.

As Muhammad lay dying, he reportedly said: "I have been sent with the shortest expressions bearing the widest meanings, and I have been made victorious with terror (cast in the hearts of the enemy), and while I was sleeping, the keys of the treasures of the world were brought to me and put in my hand."[18]

Muhammad, according to Muslim history and traditions, had a hatred for the cross or anything that resembled it.[19] Not only did Muhammad hate the cross, but Muslims claim that Christ himself not only hates the cross but will destroy it (that is, Christianity) when He returns. Hadith, volume 3, book 43:656 of Sahih Bukhari, narrated by Abu Huraira, states: "Allah's Apostle said, 'The Hour will not be established until the son of Mary (i.e. Jesus) descends amongst you as a just ruler, he will break the cross, kill the pigs, and abolish the Jizya tax. Money will be in abundance so that nobody will accept it (as charitable gifts).'"

A similar hadith from Sunan Abu Dawud and narrated by Abu Hurayrah, says this: "The Prophet (peace be upon him) said: 'There is no prophet between me and him, that is, Jesus (peace be upon him). He will descend (to the earth). When you see him, recognize him: a man of medium height, reddish [h]air, wearing two light yellow garments, looking as if drops were falling down from his head though it will not be wet. He will fight the people [infidels] for the cause of Islam. He will break the cross, kill swine, and abolish jizyah. Allah will perish all religions except Islam. He will destroy the Antichrist [whom the Jews follow] and will live on the earth for forty years and then he will die. The Muslims will pray over him.'"

If the New Testament message was God's highest and last revelation of His character and hope for mankind, then, according to the Qur'an, He made a mistake, changed His mind and decided there was no hope for mankind and that He made a horrendous mistake in sending His only begotten Son to save all mankind from ultimate destruction and must now purge the world through terror. "Islam," according to the Caners, "in order to resolve the matter of the Resurrection, teaches that Judas, not Jesus, was crucified, allowing Jesus to appear three days later."[20]

Apparently, according to this new revelation to Muhammad, God now has decided that mankind was not worthy of such a loving sacrifice through Christ's crucifixion on the cross, and the only way to reach man would be through unrelenting cruelty and bloodshed, which Muhammad was more than willing to carry out on a regular basis—as have Muslim adherents for the past fourteen centuries.

Muhammad, and every Muslim since, believes that the crucifixion story is a sham. Allah revealed to Muhammad that Jesus did not die on a cross, as the numerous Bible witnesses testified and numerous first and second century writers, such as the Roman historian, Tacitus, the Jewish historian, Josephus, Christian leaders like Justin Martyr and Tertullian, and many others gave witness to in their writings.[21]

It was essential to Muhammad's theology and self-serving revelations as Allah's prophet that he discredit the crucifixion story and Christ's sacrifice for the sins of the world. To acknowledge the crucifixion and the shedding of Christ's blood as atonement for sin would mean there would be no need for Muhammad as God's new and last prophet. No new revelations would be needed. For, as Jesus said on the cross, "It is finished" (John 19:30).

"Islam says that Jesus did not die," wrote Keohane. "So, again—Islam has proven to be false; because Muhammad claimed the Gospel is true, and all four Gospels (Injils) testify that Jesus died and rose from the dead."[22]

"Jews demand miraculous signs and Greeks look for wisdom," Paul wrote, "but we preach Christ crucified: a stumbling block to Jews and foolishness to Gentiles" (1 Corinthians 1:22-23). The Apostle Paul and the apostles that walked with Jesus had no doubt that Jesus was crucified. They were either a witness to it or knew it happened from the testimony of other eye-witnesses and they had no reservations in preaching the Gospel of Jesus Christ crucified. In His death and resurrection Jesus fulfilled yet another Messianic prophecy—this one by David. "Therefore my heart is glad and my tongue rejoices; my body also will rest secure, because you will not abandon me to the grave, nor will you let your Holy One see decay" (Psalm 16:9-10).

"The Messiah, son of Marium, is but an apostle;" Muhammad revealed, "apostles before him have indeed passed away; and his mother was a truthful woman; they both used to eat food. See how We make the communications clear to them, then behold, how they are turned away" (surah 5:75). In spite of the overwhelming proof of the Crucifixion of Jesus, Muhammad could conveniently and easily wipe it from history with a self-serving revelation from Allah.

"Anyone," the Apostle John said, "who runs ahead and does not continue in the teaching of Christ does not have God; whoever continues in the teaching has both the Father and the Son. If anyone comes to you and does not bring this teaching, do not take him into your house or welcome him. Anyone who welcomes him shares in his wicked work" (2 John 9-11). Although He was the Son of God, Jesus followed in the footsteps in the men of God before Him. His message built upon the foundation of those who went before Him. Muhammad did not build on that godly foundation, but rather tried to destroy it as a false gospel. Instead, it was Muhammad's gospel that was false and not in keeping with the foundation of love, peace, and forgiveness laid down so firmly by Christ and His apostles.

"The Spirit," the Apostle Paul wrote to Timothy, "clearly says that in later times some will abandon the faith and follow deceiving spirits and things taught by demons" (1 Timothy 4:1). Six hundred years after the death of Jesus, it is apparent that those who chose to follow the teachings of Muhammad did just that.

"… every ritual and belief in Islam," writes Fr. Suresh, "can be traced back to pre-Islamic pagan Arabian culture. Muhammad did not preach anything new. Everything he taught had been believed and practiced in Arabia long before he was ever born. Even the idea of 'only one God' was borrowed from the Jews and the Christians.

"This irrefutable fact casts to the ground the Muslim claim that Islam was revealed from heaven …. we have to conclude along with the Middle East scholars that Allah is not God, Muhammad was not his prophet, and the Qur'an is not the Word of God."[23]

Conclusion

Christians are not polytheists, as Muhammad falsely claimed throughout the Qur'an and Muslim clerics and scholars throughout the centuries have falsely propagated. Christians worship one God—the one and only God of creation. The fact that Jesus came into the world, sent by God, as His only begotten Son, does not detract from God's Oneness as the sole true deity of the universe. That God chooses to express His nature in the presence of His Son and the Holy Spirit does not nullify His completeness as the one and only God.

Islam proclaims to have a new truth by negating the real truth that endured for centuries and continues to endure through the willingness of thousands of Christians to suffer persecution for the love of Christ. Real martyrs die for the love of God; false martyrs die because of their hate for others.

In Search of Truth

After a month of sleepless nights, of weeping and crying, of waiting upon the true God to descend from Heaven to earth to answer me, I got tired of thinking. I then went back to reading the Qur'an, which left me more bewildered and confused. So, I decided to read the holy Bible, that I may find the truth.

But people said that the original version of the holy Bible did not exist anymore. What could I do? I had no choice but to read this corrupted version of the Bible, that I may find the truth between the lines. So I started to read the holy Bible and I discovered Jesus, the name that I had heard about long ago, and the name I had been attracted to. I saw how He healed the sick, freed the captives, forgave the adulterous woman, loved and blessed His enemies. For the first time in my life, I discovered what I had never experienced—the fatherhood heart or the motherhood care—because my parents were separated long ago and I was the eldest daughter.

And now I feel that Jesus is my father and mother. I have sensed Him hugging me, holding me in His arms like a baby. He took away all my heavy loads that burdened my back. For the first time in my life, I feel that I am a real woman—a real person, really beloved; not just a commodity to please men, but created after the image of God ....

Leila
"Behind the Veil"
Into the Den of Infidels, 2003

References

1 Caner, Ergun Mehmet and Emir Fethi Caner. *Unveiling Islam*, 2002. Kregel Publications, div. of Kregel. Inc., p. 35.

2 Spencer, Robert. *The Truth About Muhammad, Founder of the World's Most Intolerant Religion*, 2006. Regnery Publishing, Inc., Washington, DC., p. 34.

3 Ibid, p. 59.

4 Caner and Caner, p. 85.

5 Keohane, Steve. *Muhammad: Terrorist or Prophet?* BibleProbe.com, 200402007. Http://bibleprobe.com/muhammad.htm. Accessed April 1, 2007.

6 Suresh, Fr. Gnana Pragash, *Understanding Islam, Part II*. Society of St. Pius X—Southern Africa, 2001. http://www.sspxafrica.com/documents/2001_September/Understanding_Islam.htm. Accessed March 11, 2003.

7 Crone, Patricia. *What Do We Actually Know About Mohammed?* Open Democracy, August 31, 2006. Http://www.openDemocracy.net. Accessed June 2, 2007.

8 Ibid.

9 Caner & Caner, p. 83.

10 Safa, Reza F. *Inside Islam: Exposing and Reaching the World of Islam*, 1996. Charisma House, p. 23.

11 Crone.

12 Ibid.

13 Spencer, p. 21.

14 Caner & Caner, p. 95-96.

15 Spencer, p. 24.

16 Spencer, p. 25.

17 Caner & Caner, p. 122.

18 Spencer, p. 165.

19 Keohane, p. 23.

20 Caner & Caner, p. 18.

21 *Crucifixion of Jesus*. In His Step Ministries. Http://www.creatingfutures.net/crucifixion.html. Accessed June 21, 2007.

22 Keohane, p. 5.

23 Suresh.

The Messenger

CHAPTER 3

Biblical Prophets and Muhammad

The words the prophet utters are not offered as souvenirs.
His speech to the people is not a reminiscence, a report,
hearsay. The prophet not only conveys; he reveals.
He almost does unto others what God does unto him.
In speaking, the prophet reveals God.
This is the marvel of a prophet's work: in his words
the invisible God becomes audible.
He does not prove or argue. The thought he has to
convey is more than language can contain.
Divine power bursts in the words.
The authority of the prophet is in the Presence his
words reveal.

Abraham Heschel
The Prophets, 1962

O
f the world's major religions, Islam (meaning "submission") is one of the most recent, even though it was birthed over 1400 years ago. Despite that indisputable fact, the official position of Muslim clerics and scholars is that Islam always existed because Allah has always existed, and that Christians and Jews are really Allah worshippers that have gone astray. It is also maintained by followers of Islam that the Jewish prophets, principally Noah, Abraham, Moses, and the like; John the Baptist and Jesus were really prophets of Allah.

To put this controversial view aside for the moment, it must first be determined what a prophet is and how he or she reveals the mind of God to the people. Was Muhammad a prophet of the class of biblical prophets, such as Elijah, Elisha, Isaiah, Jeremiah, Daniel, Micah, and many others? Was Muhammad the *last* prophet sent by the God of the Jews and Christians, even though, at the end of the New Testament God warned the Apostle John on the Isle of Patmos that no one should add to the revelation he had just received? "I warn everyone who hears the words of the prophecy of this book: If anyone adds anything to them, God will add to him the plagues described in this book. And if anyone takes words away from this book of prophecy, God will take away from him his share in the tree of life and in the holy city, which are described in this book" (Revelation 22:18-19).

So what is and who is a prophet? The Hebrew word used in the Old Testament for *prophet* means one who is *inspired*—inspired by God to speak the Word of God. In the New Testament, the Greek word for *prophet* translates to *inspired speaker*, *foreteller* and/or *poet*. According to a reprinted article from the November, 1949, issue of *The Herald*, the *pro* in prophet refers to "in place of." Therefore, "a prophet is one who speaks in place of another."[1] For example, when Moses protested to God that he could not speak for Him because he was a man of stammering speech (see Exodus 6:30), God told him that "... your brother Aaron will be your prophet" (Exodus 7:1).

The prophets of God in the Old Testament intervened in the lives of the people through personal sacrifice and service; through messages from God, prophecies and the performance of miracles to demonstrate God's presence and power. "Almost every prophet in the Old Testament," wrote Ron McKenzie, a minister, economist, and Christian writer in Christchurch, New Zealand, "... appeared first as a foreteller. Through his fellowship with the eternal God, the prophet has access to the future .... However, whatever he sees for the future is always related to the present. He warns of future judgements [sic] ... He speaks of future blessing ...."[2]

The vast majority of the time God spoke directly to His prophets through the presence of His Holy Spirit. They had no doubt that the source of the wisdom and insight they received was straight from the heart of Almighty God. They never led a war against the oppressors of God's people; they let God and His anointed leaders go forth. They led moral lives of sacrificial obedience to God's calling to serve and warn His people.

According to the Old Testament prophet Amos, "The Sovereign Lord does nothing without revealing his plan to his servants the prophets" (Amos 3:7).

"Prophets," wrote Chip Brogden, founder of the School of Christ in Louisburg, North Carolina, "do not bring new truth. Revelation is simply a revealing of what is already true and bringing it to bear upon our heart and soul. Revelation is based upon insight into the written Word of God, not into visions and dreams and prophecies. These other things are simply tools for expressing the Word, they are not the Word...."[3] It is within the context of existing truth that the biblical prophets from Abraham to Jesus expressed God's divine plan for His people. Muhammad, through angelic revelation, brought new truth—*truth* that changed and replaced God Almighty's infallible, unchangeable and irreplaceable truth. The revelations that Muhammad received reversed God's plan of redemption and salvation—a plan that God had set in place since the Garden of Eden and was fulfilled through His Son, Jesus Christ.

"Prophecy is something done *within a context*," wrote Robert Longman, Jr., "the context of God's covenants with human beings, shown through the Word as revealed in Scripture. If it is not within that context and in full accord with it, it is false and not from God, and furthermore it will quite likely prove evil in its effect."[4] Often, in the Qur'an, there is little or no framework from which the reader can draw upon in order to better understand the verse or revelation. The prophets of the Old Testament and Jesus spoke out of the context of their environment, traditions, and history. Jesus also used parables with familiar themes to drive home a point. The Qur'an, on the other hand, provides little such assistance for the reader's fuller understanding. The verses come one after the other, often on different and unrelated topics, neither connecting nor explaining the previous verse or the verse to come. As a result, some surahs (chapters) and the verses within take on an incoherency all their own, leaving the reader baffled as to the message and wisdom that is to be received from the revelation.

Sometimes, even within the same surah, Allah seemingly contradicts himself. Nowhere is this more strikingly clear than in surah 2. In verse 256 Allah reveals, "There is no compulsion [coercion] in religion …" But earlier in the chapter, Allah reveals to the Prophet, "… fight with them until there is no persecution, and religion should be only for Allah …" (verse 193). Yet, Muslims to this day will cite verse 256 as an example that Muslims are not prejudiced toward other religions and that there is freedom of worship in Muslim countries or societies.

Many revelations, both essential to understanding and trivial, dramatically contradict each other, leaving the reader confused or uninformed as to the intent of the revelation. For example, in surahs 22:47 and 32:5 it states that Allah's days are "as a thousand years." But in surah 70:4, it says Allah's "day the measure of which is fifty thousand years."

In the New Testament, the Apostle Peter said, "But do not forget this one thing, dear friends: With the Lord a day is like a thousand years, and a thousand years are like a day" (2 Peter 3:8). Moses, the man that Muhammad admired as a prophet of God, prayed in Psalm 90:4, "For a thousand years in your sight are like a day that has just gone by…."

The Changeable Allah and the Unchangeable God

Even a cursory examination of the Qur'an it becomes abundantly clear that Allah is an indecisive and changeable god. The concept of abrogation in the Qur'an was reviewed in the previous chapter. It is the notion that Allah can change any previous revelation to a more current revelation to suit his needs. Not surprisingly, this usually occurred when it was necessary to meet Muhammad's need to absolve some wrong he or one of his followers committed or to gain the upper hand over some perceived enemy. By comparison, prophets and sages of the Bible and Jesus and His apostles all warned those who would seek to add to or take away from the word of God in the Bible. "Every word of God is flawless [pure]; he is a shield to those who take refuge in him. Do not add to his words, or he will rebuke you and prove you a liar" (Proverbs 30:5-6).

In the Qur'an, Allah says that all the prophets before Muhammad testified to the existence of Allah. "And We did not send before you any apostle but We revealed to him that there is no god but Me, therefore serve Me" (surah 21:25). If Muhammad was a prophet in the tradition of the Old Testament prophets, he apparently was ignorant or misinformed by Allah about the lives of the prophets who came before him. He neither followed their example, nor promulgated their truths, as revealed to them by Jehovah God.

Even King Saul, the first king of Israel was not above God's rebuke. When Saul rejected God's word to destroy the Amalekites, while Saul did not follow God's instructions to the letter, he thought that God would be pleased with him anyway. But God was not pleased and sent His reprimand to Saul through the Prophet Samuel. "He who is the Glory of Israel does not lie or change his mind; for he is not a man, that he should change his mind" (1 Samuel 15:29). This is just one biblical illustration that when God—the God of the Jews and Christians— reveals a thing, He does not repent and go back on His word.

In the Apostle Paul's second letter to his protégé, Timothy, whom he addresses as "my dear son," Paul emphatically states: "All Scripture is God-breathed and is useful for teaching, rebuking, correcting and training in righteousness, so that the man of God may be thoroughly equipped for every good work" (2 Timothy 3:16-17).

In the Qur'an there are so many contradictions within itself and between it and the revealed truth of the God of the Bible that one gets the distinct impression that there is a lot of falsification and lying about God and His character. However, Moses, in his fourth book of the Pentateuch, wrote: "God is not a man, that He should lie, nor a son of man, that He should repent. Has He said, and will He not do? Or has He spoken, and will He not make it good?" (Numbers 23:19, NKJV)?" If God cannot lie and He cannot go back on His word—that He loves the world and all mankind—then who is lying about Him? Who is giving the world the impression that God not only hates sin, but He hates the sinner as well?

Former radical Shi'a Muslim, Reza Safa, in his book, *Inside Islam*, proclaimed clearly that, "An antichrist spirit is a spirit that opposes the work and person of Christ. An antichrist spirit denies the deity of Jesus. It denies and despises the cross. It denies redemption and forgiveness through the shed blood of Jesus. It denies the death and resurrection of Jesus."[5]

Safa further wrote, "Islam denies the deity, death and resurrection of Jesus; therefore, it is an antichrist religion ... that makes Muhammad a false prophet and Islam a false religion."[6]

During his Sermon on the Mount, Jesus corrected those who assumed His mission was to do away with the Law of Moses or the word of the prophets. "Do not think that I have come to abolish the Law or the Prophets; I have not come to abolish them but to fulfill them. I tell you the truth, until heaven and earth disappear, not the smallest letter, not the least stroke of a pen, will by any means disappear from the Law until everything is accomplished" (Matthew 5:17-18). God's Word does not change. God does not change and God's plan for mankind does not change from generation to generation. "I the Lord do not change" (Malachi 3:6). Muhammad, through his supposed revelation from Allah, changed the Word of God, changed the image of God, and changed God's plan.

Every good and perfect gift is from above, the Apostle James, brother of the Lord, wrote, coming down from the Father of the heavenly lights, who does not change like shifting shadows. (James 1:17)

The Word of God cannot pass away or disappear. "But the word of the Lord endures forever. Now this is the word which by the gospel was preached to you" (1 Peter 1:25, NKJV).

God is not the creator of uncertainty or disorder. "For God," writes the Apostle Paul, "is not *the author* of confusion but of peace, as in all the churches of the saints" (1 Corinthians 14:33, NKJV). Throughout biblical history God acted with preciseness and consistency. He never faltered, never went back on His word, never changed His plan for mankind.

Was Muhammad a Prophet of Biblical Proportions?

Muslims, imams, and Muslim scholars claim that both the Old and New Testaments foretold of Muhammad's coming and point specifically to Deuteronomy 18:15 and 18, John 14:16, and other seemingly nebulous Scriptures as concrete proof. However, if the Bible did originally contain verses that foretold of Muhammad's coming as the last and most important of God's prophets, they would also contain a description of the character and ministry of such a significant messenger of God. The Scriptures would have had to foretell that this special messenger of God would be identified, not by signs and wonders, but by butchery, thievery, and deception; by immorality and adultery; by the omen that he killed his own people and the Jews, God's own chosen people.

Jesus' wisdom, knowledge, and understanding far exceeded that of all the prophets that preceded Him. (See Isaiah 9:6-7.) Muhammad's wisdom and knowledge were often confused, ignorant, and erroneous. He often had his historical facts wrong and frequently contradicted himself and the revelations he claimed to have received from Allah.

Surah 61:6 makes the radical claim that Jesus foretold of Muhammad's coming.

> And when Isa [Jesus] son of Marium said: O children of Israel! Surely I am the apostle of Allah to you, verifying that which is before me of the Taurat [Torah] and giving good news of an Apostle who will come after me, his name being Ahmad [variation of Muhammad]; but when he came to them with clear arguments they said: This is clear magic.

The Bible records no such revelation by Jesus. No wonder the Jews and Christians of Muhammad's era responded to his claims of God's apostle as *clear magic*. It was not only magic but complete fabrication inspired by satanic sources. And Jesus NEVER referred to himself as a prophet of Allah. He did, however, refer to himself as the Bread of Life (see John 6:35, 48), the Good Shepherd (see John 10:11, 14), the Light of the World (see John 8:12; 9:5), the Resurrection and the Life (see John 11:25), the Son of God (see Mark 14:61-61; John 1:49; 5:19-26; 8:35-36; 10:36; 14:13), the True Vine (see John 15:1), the way, the truth and the life (see John 14:6), and the I Am (see John 8:58).

Examining Deuteronomy 18:15 and 18

While Muslims believe in the Bible and the Old Testament prophets, they have been taught since the days of Muhammad that the Bible has been corrupted and therefore cannot be fully relied on as God's Word. This, they believe, despite a thunderous silence of any historical proof from any quarter that the Bible has been corrupted in any form, by any person, at any time in history. This, they choose to believe, despite the thousands of historical biblical manuscripts that have been discovered and preserved that fully collaborate the Scriptures, stories, prophecies, the people of the Bible, and the historical records.

In stark contrast, there are no collaborating works that can verify or support the words supposedly revealed to Muhammad in the Qur'an. The Qur'an contains strictly the words of one man who claimed they came from God. There were no witnesses, no subsequent revelations or prophecies to others to confirm or support these one-man revelations—many of which were conveniently self-serving for the prophet himself.

However, one biblical verse in particular Muslims do rely on as a testimony of Muhammad's coming. They cite Deuteronomy 18:15 as evidence that the coming of Muhammad as God's prophet was foretold about 2,000 years before his birth by Moses. There are a number of problems with this assertion. First, the full context of the Scripture carries through verse 22.

*The Lord your God will raise up for you **a prophet like me** [Moses] **from among your own brothers**. You must listen to him. For this is what you asked of the Lord your God at Horeb on the day of the assembly when you [the Israelites] said, "Let us not hear the voice of the Lord our God nor see this great fire anymore, or we will die."*

*The Lord said to me: "What they say is good. I will raise up for them a **prophet like you from among their brothers**; I will put **my words in his mouth**, and he will tell them everything I command him. If anyone does not listen to my words that the prophet speaks in my name, I myself will call him to account. But a prophet who presumes to speak in my name anything I have not commanded him to say, or a prophet who speaks in the name of other gods, must be put to death."*

You may say to yourselves, "How can we know when a message has not been spoken by the Lord?" If what a prophet proclaims in the name of the Lord does not take place or come true, that is a message the Lord has not spoken. That prophet has spoken presumptuously. Do not be afraid of him. (Deuteronomy 18:15-22, author's emphasis)

The particulars of this prophecy of Moses should shed some light on the claim of Islam that this prophecy refers to the coming of Muhammad. **First,** the prophet is to represent the God of the Jews. The word "Lord" in the first verse refers to the self-existent Jehovah God of the Jews. **Second,** the prophet who is foretold is to be like Moses. Moses was a Jew born to the house of a Levite (a Jewish high priest). Muhammad was neither a Jew nor was he born of the house of Levi. **Third,** the prophet was to be "from among your own brothers," that is, from among the Israelites themselves. This does not fit Muhammad either, since he was an Arab, a descendant of Ishmael. **Fourth,** this prophet is to speak only the words of Jehovah God, not Allah or a god by any other name.

Jesus, on the other hand, made direct reference to this prophecy by Moses. As He was speaking to the Jews, Jesus said, "If you believed Moses, you would believe me, for he wrote about me" (John 5:46).

Unlike the prophets of the Old Testament and Jesus, where God chose to speak directly to them, Allah did not or would not speak directly to Muhammad. Allah's revelation or *wahy* came to Muhammad in various forms—dreams, trances, visions, angelic visitation, foaming fits, etc.—but never face-to-face or by personal revelation direct from Allah.

The reason Allah did not speak to Muhammad personally is explained by Muhammad in surah 42:

> And it is not for any mortal that Allah should speak to him except by revelation or from behind a veil, or by sending a messenger and revealing by His permission what He pleases; surely He is High, Wise.
>
> And thus did we reveal to you an inspired book by Our command. You did not know what the Book was, nor (what) the faith (was), but We made it a light, guiding thereby whom We please of Our servants; and most surely you show the way to the right path:
>
> The path of Allah, Whose is whatsoever is in the heavens and whatsoever is in the earth; now surely to Allah do all affairs eventually come. (Surah 42:51-53)

The surah above clearly eliminates Muhammad as the prophet spoken of in Deuteronomy 18:15, a prophet that would be like Moses. There are three distinct characteristics of Moses' ministry that would have to be met by the foretold prophet to come.

First, he would have to know God *face-to-face* as Moses did. The above surah states clearly that Allah *would not* reveal himself to Muhammad. Jesus, on the other hand, descended from the Father and knew God face-to-face, because He was one with God.

Second, Moses was the mediator of God's covenant with the Jews. The prophet to come would also have to mediate God's covenant. Allah made no covenant with Muhammad or his followers and therefore Muhammad could not be the mediator of any covenant. Jesus, however, was the mediator of the *New Covenant*, a covenant based on *better promises*. "But the ministry Jesus has received is as superior to theirs [the Jewish high priests] as the covenant of which he is mediator is superior to the old one, and it is founded on better promises (Hebrews 8:6)."

Third, the prophet foretold in Deuteronomy 18:15 would have to be a miracle worker just like Moses. Muhammad never performed a miracle throughout his lifetime as a prophet. In fact, in response to a request that he perform a miracle, he confessed that he could do none. Jesus' life (which was far shorter than Muhammad's) was differentiated by signs and wonders everywhere he went.

Only Muhammad and the traditions of Islam lay claim that Deuteronomy 18 was a prophecy that foretold of the coming of Muhammad. None of the Jews or Christians of Muhammad's era believed in the least that he was the fulfillment of this prophecy. However, when Jesus performed the great miracle of the feeding of the five thousand (John 6:1-15), the Jewish witnesses readily proclaimed, "Surely this is *the Prophet* who is to come into the world (John 6:14, author's emphasis)." The Jews had been waiting for centuries for the coming of The Prophet and Messiah prophesied by Moses, David, Isaiah, Daniel, Micah, Zechariah, Malachi and others. They knew what to look for and how they could identify him and they without doubt saw Jesus as the fulfillment of the long-awaited prophet. No such acceptance was ever accorded Muhammad during his lifetime. Although the Jews were expecting *the* Prophet and Messiah—and many of the Jews were beginning to accept Jesus as the fulfillment of that expectation—the

Jewish leaders turned against Him when He proclaimed Himself to be the Son of God—a claim the religious leaders saw as blasphemy.

Stephen, one of the seven deacons of the first Christian church and the first martyr of the Church—right before his martyrdom—gave testimony before the Jewish Sanhedrin, that the prophet of whom Moses foretold was indeed Jesus (Acts 7:37).

Robert Spencer, author of the best selling book, *The Truth About Muhammad* (2006), noted that, "as a matter of history, that there is no record of Christians expecting a prophet in Arabia 540 years after the death of Jesus; nor is there any record of any Christian book with signs marking out an Arabian prophet . . . nor is there any record of any Christian heresy that held such beliefs ...."[8]

After the Apostle Peter healed the lame beggar, all the onlookers were amazed. He then gave the following testimony pointing to Jesus as the fulfillment of biblical prophecy:

> *Now, brothers, I know that you acted in ignorance, as did your leaders. But this is how God fulfilled what he had foretold through all the prophets, saying that his Christ would suffer. Repent, then, and turn to God, so that your sins may be wiped out, that times of refreshing may come from the Lord, and that he may send the Christ, who has been appointed for you—even Jesus. He must remain in heaven until the time comes for God to restore everything, as he promised long ago through his holy prophets. For **Moses said**, "The Lord your God will raise up for you **a prophet like me from among your own people**; you must listen to everything he tells you. Anyone who does not listen to him will be completely cut off from among his people.*

Indeed, all the prophets from Samuel on, as many as have spoken, have foretold these days. And you are heirs of the prophets and of the covenant God made with your fathers. He said to Abraham, "Through your offspring all peoples on earth will be blessed." When God raised up his servant, he sent him first to you to bless you by turning each of you from your wicked ways" (Acts 3:17-26, author's emphasis).

After Jesus spoke in the temple courts in Jerusalem, the Jews, "On hearing his words ...," said, "'Surely this man is the Prophet.' Others said, 'He is the Christ'" (John 7:40-41).

"Still others asked, 'How can the Christ come from Galilee? Does not the Scripture say that the Christ will come from David's family and from Bethlehem, the town where David lived? (John 7:40-42).'" Jesus did indeed come from Galilee and the lineage of David and was born in Bethlehem.

After John the Baptist was imprisoned he heard from his followers about the many miracles Jesus performed. He sought to reassure himself that Jesus was the promised Messiah. "When John heard in prison what Christ was doing, he sent his disciples to ask him, 'Are you the one [the Prophet] who was to come, or should we expect someone else?' Jesus replied, 'Go back and report to John what you hear and see: The blind receive sight, the lame walk, those who have leprosy are cured, the deaf hear, the dead are raised, and the good news is preached to the poor. Blessed is the man who does not fall away on account of me (Matthew 11:2-6)'"

At the beginning of His ministry Jesus recruited the brothers Peter and Andrew. He then called Philip to follow Him. All three were from the town of Bethsaida, near the north shore of the Sea of Galilee. "Philip found Nathanael and told him, 'We have found the one Moses wrote about in the Law, and about whom the prophets also wrote—Jesus of Nazareth, the son of Joseph (John 1:45).'"

Once again, after Jesus miraculously fed the 5,000 near the Sea of Galilee, the crowd was abuzz about what they had witnessed. "After the people saw the miraculous sign that Jesus did, they began to say, 'Surely this is the Prophet who is to come into the world' " (John 6:14).

After Jesus' resurrection, He appeared to two of His followers as they walked along the road to Emmaus. "He said to them, 'How foolish you are, and how slow of heart to believe all that the prophets have spoken! Did not the Christ have to suffer these things and then enter his glory?' And beginning with Moses and all the Prophets, he explained to them what was said in all the Scriptures concerning himself (Luke 24:25-27)." If Muhammad was *the prophet* the Jews were expecting, why did they not recognize him or accept him as such? Why was Muhammad unable to get his biblical history and Old Testament prophecies correct? It is simple! Muhammad *was not* the fulfillment of any biblical prophecy, nor was he the prophet foretold in the Bible—in either the Old or New Testament. Only Jesus could and did fulfill all that was prophesied about the coming Messiah, *the* Prophet.

The Apostle Peter, in his testimony about Jesus as he preached to the Jews at Solomon's Colonnade, confirmed Jesus' fulfillment of Old Testament prophecy. "For Moses said, 'The Lord your God will raise up for you a prophet like me from among your own people; you must listen to everything he tells you. Anyone who does not listen to him will be completely cut off from among his people (Acts 3:22-23).'"

Examining John 14:16.

Historically, Muslims have claimed that Muhammad was the foretold "Comforter" or "Counselor" promised by Jesus in John 14:16. "… I will ask the Father, and he will give you another Counselor [Helper; Comforter] to be with you forever." To fully understand this verse it must be put into the context of the verse preceding and following. "If you **love me**," Jesus said, "you will **obey what I command**. And I will ask the Father, and he will give you another Counselor [Helper; Comforter] to be with you **forever**—the **Spirit of truth**. The world cannot accept him, because it neither sees him nor knows him. But **you know him**, for he lives with you and **will be in you**" (John 14:15-17, author's emphasis).

Despite Muslim assertions and hope upon hope, Muhammad cannot possibly be the promised *comforter* or *counselor*. **First**, the Counselor or Comforter will come only to those who *love* Jesus and *obey* His *command*. Neither Muhammad nor any of his followers love and obey the commands of Jesus. **Second**, the Counselor *is* the *Spirit of Truth* who will be with the believers in Jesus *forever*. Muhammad was not a spirit, he was flesh and bone like every other mortal being and he did not live forever. He died a human death, was buried, never to rise again. **Third**, the followers of Jesus, and Him only, will know the Counselor—the Spirit of Truth whom the world cannot see—because He resides within them. Muhammad, being flesh and bone, could not and does not live within any living soul—never did, never will. Likewise, he was far from personifying a "spirit of truth." Far from it! Instead he embodied lies and fabrications to suit his ungodly purposes.

Jesus' further description of the coming Counselor/Comforter in John 15:26 and John 16:7-15 thoroughly eliminate Muhammad from being even remotely considered as the person Jesus was talking about. "When the Counselor comes," Jesus said, "whom I will send to you from the Father, the Spirit of truth who goes out from the Father, **he will testify about me**" (John 15:26, author's emphasis). Muhammad could not and would not *testify* to the true purpose of Jesus' coming. While he recognized Jesus as a prophet, he refused to accept Him as the Son of God; as the vehicle of God's salvation for mankind; as the source of redemption from sin; or that He was crucified, died, was buried and rose again. Truly, only the Holy Spirit, the Spirit of Truth, the Counselor and Comforter could give testimony to such things and bear witness within the soul of every believer.

> *But I tell you the truth: It is for your good that I am going away. Unless I go away, the Counselor will not come to you; but if I go, I will send him to you. When he comes, **he will convict the world of guilt** in regard to sin and **righteousness and judgment**: in regard to sin, because men do not believe in me; in regard to righteousness, because I am going to the Father, where you can see me no longer; and in regard to judgment, because the prince of this world now stands condemned.*
>
> *I have much more to say to you, more than you can now bear. But when he, the Spirit of truth, comes, he will **guide you into all truth**. He will not speak on his own; he will speak only what he hears, and he will **tell you what is yet to come**. He will **bring glory to me** by taking from what is mine and making it known to you. All that belongs to the Father is mine. That is why I said the Spirit will **take from what is mine and make it known to you**.* (John 16:7-15, author's emphasis)

Once again, Jesus makes it abundantly clear that the Counselor/Comforter is the Holy Spirit of God who will *convict the world of guilt* (sin) with all *righteousness and judgment*. He will *guide* the followers of Jesus *into all truth. He will tell you what is yet to come* and *bring glory* to Jesus and *make known* the birthright of Jesus to His disciples. Muhammad, of course, could do none of this. He had no power to convict the world of sin; no God-given righteousness and judgment; possessed no indisputable truth; could not predict anything of the future; did not bring any glory to Christ and made nothing known about the true ministry and purpose of Jesus' life on earth.

Sometime during the second half of Muhammad's Meccan period, surah 6 was revealed to him. Part of this surah reveals that Allah guided the Jewish prophets of the Old Testament, as well as Jesus and John the Baptist:

And We gave to him [Abraham] Ishaq [Isaac] Yaqoob [Jacob]; each did We guide, and Nuh [Noah] did We guide before, and of his descendents, Dawood [David] and Sulaiman [Solomon] and Ayub [Job] and Yusuf [Joseph and Moses] and Haroon [Aaron]; and thus do We reward those who do good (to others).

And Zakariya [Zechariah] and Yahya [John the Baptist] and Isa [Jesus] and Ilyas [Elijah]; every one was of the good [righteous].

And Ismail and Al-Yasha [Elisha] and Yunus [Jonah] and Lut [Lot]; and every one [of them] We made to excel (in) the worlds [above other people]:

And from among their fathers and their descendants and their brethren, and We chose them [all] and guided them into the right [straight] way. (Surah 6:84-87)

According to the surah above, Allah has revealed to Muhammad that He guided all the prophets of old and their descendents, including Jesus and John the Baptist, the one who prophesied about Jesus, along the right path of truth. The Jews, both during the age of the Jewish patriarchs and during the time of Jesus, relied on the *spoken* word of the prophets and the *written* word of the Law (that is the Torah or Pentateuch) for God's guidance in the path of righteousness. Therefore, if Allah guided them in all truth through the spoken and written word, then the Torah and the Gospel must be Allah's true and faithful word. But wait, surah 2:75 states that the Torah and Gospel of "the people of the Book" was corrupted or altered by Jews and Christians. If it was altered, then how could Allah guide the Jews of both the Old and New Testament era along the right path?

Prophets Know Their History

As stated previously, both Muhammad and Islamic leaders proclaim that every word of the Qur'an was delivered to Muhammad from Allah—either personally or through the angel Gabriel—and therefore is perfect and without error. The same proclamation of perfection is put forth for the *ahadith* (the sayings and examples of Muhammad). When it came to recounting biblical stories, it seems that either Muhammad or Allah erred about biblical history. The Jewish prophets of the Old Testament, as well as John the Baptist, Jesus and His apostles knew the history about which they preached and prophesied.

"Prophets must be students of history," penned McKenzie. "They must also be students of contemporary events. The whole of a nation's history is a record of God's dealings with his people. The prophetic message must be spoken in this context."[9]

In an apparent effort to elevate himself among the prophets of old, Muhammad frequently retold a biblical story in the Qur'an or ahadith with a distorted version of the truth or important diversions from the biblical account.

"If a prophet has no personal history with God," wrote Brogden, "no spiritual depth to draw from, no deep root in firm soil established over many seasons of [religious] experience, how can the prophet presume to speak from a position of revelation into what God is telling the [people] ...? Furthermore, if a prophet cannot accurately interpret and read the signs of the present times; if a prophet cannot correctly judge and precisely discern his own generation; if a prophet cannot relate to what God is saying and doing in terms of present truth, how can the prophet presume to speak of future events?"[10]

Not only did Muhammad ignore the centuries of God's revealed truth to previous prophets but he confused the history of God's people and even went against that which was revealed in the Qur'an that was entrusted to him. Even the Qur'an acknowledges that Allah (God) made a covenant with his chosen people, the Jews. "O children of Israel! Call to mind My favor which I bestowed on you and be faithful to (your) covenant with Me, I will fulfill (My) covenant with you; and of Me, Me alone, should you be afraid .... O children of Israel! Call to mind My favor which I bestowed on you and that I made you [to] excel [above] the nations (surah 2:40, 47)." Yet, Muhammad made it his passion, after fleeing to Medina, to slaughter God's chosen, the Jews, the only ones that God had made a blood covenant with until the institution of the New Covenant established by the blood sacrifice of Jesus Christ on the cross.

Throughout Islamic history, Arabic Muslims, following the teaching and example of Muhammad, have relentlessly persecuted the Jews—not only in Palestine, but throughout the world. The claim of Arabic Muslims is that Palestine—that is, Canaan—was always the inherited land of Muslims and that the Jews have no right to it and are to be driven out. Yet, the Qur'an states that Allah promised Moses and the Jews the land of Canaan or the *Holy Land*.

> And when Musa said to his people: O my people! Remember the favor of Allah upon you when He raised prophets among you and made you kings and gave you what He had not given to any other among the nations.
>
> O my people! Enter the holy land which Allah has prescribed for you and turn not on your backs for then you will turn back losers. (surah 5:20-21)

Three things are noteworthy in this surah. **First,** it is revealed that God (*not* Allah) did, indeed, promise the Jews that they would occupy the Holy Land or Canaan. **Second,** there were no kings ruling over the Jews during Moses' lifetime. Moses died before the Jews entered Canaan and almost 200 years before the prophet Samuel anointed Saul as the first king of the Israelites. **Third,** God (*not* Allah) commands the Jews to never give up the land of Canaan that he has *prescribed* for them. It is important to note that Allah *never* spoke to the Jews. But the Qur'an claims that he did. Despite this revelation of the Jews right to Palestine in perpetuity in their own holy book, Muslims are bent on annihilating or forcing the Jews from their rightful homeland as guaranteed to them by God in the Bible and Allah in the Qur'an. Nevertheless, in surah 7:157, Allah commands his followers to follow that which is written in the Torah and the Gospel.

But when it comes to the Jews, Allah is apparently very changeable. "And certainly you have known those [Jews] among you who exceeded [profaned] the limits of the Sabbath, so We said to them: Be (as) apes, despised and hated (surah 2:65)." This derogatory view of Jews by Allah is repeated in surah 7:166. In surah 5:60, Jews are referred to by

73

Allah not only as apes but as swine as well, thus giving Muslims the perceived right to habitually dehumanize Jews by referring to them as pigs and monkeys to this day.

The Qur'an, as it has been stated before, contradicts much of the Bible—in history, teaching and in the spirit of revelation. Muhammad was either ignorant or ill-informed about biblical history.

The Creation

The first two chapters in the Bible (Genesis 1 and 2) clearly state that it took six days for God to create the heaven and the earth and all it contained; the sixth day God created man and "by the seventh day God had finished the work he had been doing; so on the seventh day he rested from all his work (Genesis 2:2).

The Qur'an presents a very confusing image of the creation story. First the Qur'an says that it took Allah six days to create heaven and earth. "Surely your Lord is Allah," surah 7:54 proclaims, "Who created the heavens and the earth in six periods [days] of time …" Surahs 10:3; 11:7 and 25:59 confirm the six day creation period as in the Bible. But then Allah reveals through the angel Gabriel in surah 41:9-12 that it took him eight days.

> Say: What! Do you indeed disbelieve in Him Who created the earth in two periods … And He made in it mountains above its surface, and He blessed therein and made therein its foods, in four periods … Then He directed Himself to the heaven and its vapor … So He ordained them seven heavens in two periods…. (Author's emphasis)

In this case, the *periods* or days add up to eight. Apparently, even Allah does not know how long it took him to create the heavens and the earth.

In the biblical explanation of creation, *before* God started His six day creation process, the "heavens and the earth" already existed by God's hand. "Now the earth was formless and empty … (Genesis 1:2)." But then it took God six days to create light, water and land, the sun, moon and stars, vegetation, living creatures and man. There is no explicit mention of which was created first—the heavens or the earth.

In the Qur'an it is implied that the earth was made first in surah 2:29 and the heavens were made first in surah 79:27-30.

"The Lord God formed the man from the dust of the ground and breathed into his nostrils the breath of life ... (Genesis 2:7)." God created man first and then woman from the rib of the man (Genesis 2:21-22). There is only *one* story of man and woman's creation in the Bible. In the Qur'an, however, there are several and there is no mention of the creation of a woman. In surah 96:2, it says that "He created man from a [blood] clot" or germ cell. Then in 21:30, it states that everything living was made from water by Allah. But then 16:4 and 75:37 say that "He created man from a small seed." To further confuse man's creation, the Qur'an reveals that man was created from dust (3:59); earth (11:61); of "clay (55:14) ... of black mud fashioned in shape" or "dark-slime transmuted" (15:26); or Allah created him out of nothing (19:67). Apparently, Muhammad did not know how Allah created man.

Fate of Noah's Son

"Noah was a righteous man, blameless among the people of his time, and he walked with God. Noah had three sons: Shem, Ham and Japheth (Genesis 6:9-10)." Everyone knows the story of Noah. Noah was commanded by God to build an ark in which to house representative creatures of the earth, as well as his sons and their wives—all entered the ark at the start of the deluge (Genesis 7:13). "Every living thing on the face of the earth was wiped out; men and animals and the creatures that move along the ground and the birds of the air were wiped from the earth. Only Noah was left, and those with him in the ark (Genesis 7:23)." Surah 21:76 agrees with this conclusion: "And Nuh [Noah], when he cried aforetime, so We answered him, and delivered him and his followers from the great calamity." However, surah 11:42-43 makes it clear that one of Noah's sons drowned during the flood because he refused to take refuge in the ark.

Joseph, the Dream Interpreter

In surah 12:36-41 Muhammad attempts to re-tell the Genesis story of Joseph interpreting the dreams of Pharaoh's chief cupbearer and chief baker as revealed to Muhammad by Allah. The summation of Joseph's interpretation of the dreams is revealed in verse 41: "O my two mates of the prison! As for one of you [the cupbearer], he shall give his lord to drink wine; and as for the other [the baker], he shall be crucified, so that the birds shall eat from his head; the matter is decreed concerning which you inquired."

While Muhammad has the general premise of the tale correct, he errs considerably on the fate of the baker. According to the Book of Genesis, chapter 40, the baker's fate as foretold by Joseph was that he would be brought before Pharaoh (the King of Egypt) and beheaded and his body hung on a tree for the birds to eat his flesh (Genesis 40:16-22). Crucifixion, while a sometime practice of early Egyptians, Assyrians and others, was a method of punishment and death reserved for those who were still living and became popular among the Romans during the time of Jesus. To be beheaded first and then hung on a tree or pole would not generally be considered as a crucifixion.[11]

The Adoption of Moses

The story of Moses and his birth is told in Exodus 2. At the command of Pharaoh all newborn Hebrew boys were to be drowned. To avoid detection by the Egyptians, the mother of Moses put him in a basket and set it into the Nile River. Pharaoh's *daughter* found the infant Moses and adopted him as her own (Exodus 2:10). Surah 28:9, in contrast, says that Pharaoh's *wife* found Moses in the river and took him as her own. "... do not slay him," she said; "maybe he will be useful to us, or we may take him for a son ..."

Pharaoh's Fate

When Pharaoh, King of Egypt, finally decided to let Moses and the Hebrews escape after 430 years of captivity in Egypt, the Jews fled across the north end of the Red Sea (current-day, Gulf of Suez). After Pharaoh let the Hebrews go, he had a change of heart and he and all his army pursued the Hebrews (Exodus 14:5-9). Verse 28 pronounces that Pharaoh and all his army drowned while trying to catch the Hebrews. The Qur'an, in surahs 17:103, 28:40 and 43:55 concur with the Bible's fate for Pharaoh. However, surah 10:92 states that Allah rescued Pharaoh from drowning "that you may be a sign to those after you ...."

The Leadership of Gideon's Army

The angel Gabriel apparently got confused in surah 2:249 about King Saul and Gideon and the armies they led and against whom. For one thing, Saul was not chosen king of Israel by the prophet Samuel until 200 years after Gideon. Judges 6 and 7 tell the story of how God called upon Gideon to go against the strong Midianites who were oppressing the Jews. Gideon, a mighty warrior, assembled thousands of fighting men. However, God told Gideon he had too many (Judges 7:2). So God had Gideon use a series of tests to pare down his forces. The last test was to separate out only 300 fighting men based on how they drank water. Those that "lapped with their hands to their mouths," that is, were vigilant, were the ones Gideon was to use for the battle. But surah 2:249 says that King Saul used this test to lead Gideon's army, and not against the Midianites, but against Goliath. Saul did not lead an army against Goliath (a Philistine), only David was sent to fight and kill him.

As a lead-in to this story, in surah 2:246, the angel Gabriel seems to have forgotten who the Jews appealed to for a king to lead them. The prophet Samuel who is clearly identified and is the one who receives this request of the Jews (1 Samuel 8:4-7) is the one who anoints Saul as the King of Israel (1 Samuel 10:1). Despite Samuel being one of the most celebrated prophets of the Jews, he is referred to in the surah above as "a prophet of theirs …" Prophets of Samuel's stature were always given honor and referred to by name.

The Wisdom of Solomon

In hadith 4:637 Muhammad retells the account of the wisdom of King Solomon with a non-biblical twist.

… He [Muhammad] also said, "There were two women, each of whom had a child with her. A wolf came and took away the child of one of them, whereupon the other said, 'It has taken your child.' The first said, 'But it has taken your child.' So they both carried the case before David who judged that the living child be given to the elder lady. So both of them went to Solomon bin David and informed him (of the case). He said, 'Bring me a knife so as to cut the child into two pieces and distribute it between them.' The younger lady said, 'May Allah be merciful to you! Don't do that, for it is her (i.e. the other lady's) child.' So he gave the child to the younger lady."

There are several problems with Muhammad's retelling of the biblical story in I Kings 3:16-28. Yes, there were two women involved. The Bible says that they were both prostitutes that lived in the same house; and yes, they both had an infant son. But that is where the similarity ends. There was no wolf involved in the biblical account. The dispute over the living child came about when one of the women rolled over onto her baby while sleeping and smothered it. The woman of the dead child took the baby and switched it for the live child while the other woman was asleep. "The next morning," the woman with the live son told King Solomon, "I got up to nurse my son—and he was dead! But when I looked at him closely in the morning light, I saw that it wasn't the son I had borne (I Kings 3:21)." The women in the biblical version were never identified as "younger" or "elder"—only as the woman with the dead child or the one with the live child.

King David was no longer king of Israel and had nothing to do with this historical happening. Solomon was now king and was charged with judging the people, not his father, David. It was Solomon that asked God to give him extraordinary wisdom to judge the people, not David. "The Lord was pleased that Solomon had asked for this. So God said to him, 'Since you have asked for this and not for long life or wealth for yourself, nor have asked for the death of your enemies but for discernment in administering justice, I will do what you have asked. I will give you a wise and discerning heart, so that there will never have been anyone like you, nor will there ever be (I Kings 3:10-12).'" There was no appeal from David to Solomon by the women. They went direct to King Solomon and him only. In Muhammad's adaptation, it depicts David as making the wrong decision by giving the baby to the wrong woman, when David was not even engaged in the event.

In Muhammad's version, it is not stated whose child was taken, so how does one know if the living child really belonged to the younger or elder woman? Nor does the hadith reveal that the woman crying out for Allah's mercy was indeed the mother of the living child. The Bible, on the other hand, makes it very clear. "The woman whose son was alive was filled with compassion for her son and said to the king,

'Please, my lord, give her the living baby! Don't kill him!' But the other said, 'Neither I nor you shall have him. Cut him in two!' Then the king gave his ruling: 'Give the living baby to the first woman. Do not kill him; she is his mother (I Kings 3:26-27).'"

Zechariah's Penalty for Unbelief

The story of Zechariah, the father of John the Baptist, is recounted in the first chapter of the Gospel of Luke. Zechariah was a Jewish priest and both he and his wife, Elizabeth, were descendents of Aaron (the brother of Moses). As the biblical story goes, they were both beyond normal childbearing years and Elizabeth could not have children. Still, both had prayed for a child. When Zechariah was in the temple performing his priestly duties, an "angel of the Lord" stood by him and told him his prayer had been heard and that Elizabeth would conceive and bear him a son. Zechariah doubted the veracity of the angel's revelation. Because of his unbelief, the angel told him that he would be unable to speak from that moment on until his son was born. At this point Elizabeth had not conceived. Luke records that Zechariah did not speak again until the eighth day after the birth of John the Baptist—the day of his son's circumcision (Luke 1:59-63). Zechariah was speechless for over nine months. However, when Allah revealed the story to Muhammad, Zechariah was only without his voice for three days (surah 3:41).

In the Bible, of course, one could also point to contradictions in some stories. However, the Bible is made up by many storytellers who might have had varying points of observation or memory. The claim of Muhammad and Muslims is that the Qur'an is perfect in every way because it came from one source—Allah. If so, then why are there so many conflicting revelations within the Qur'an and between the Qur'an and the Bible that Muslims are to respect as the "word of God?"

Muhammad, the Last Prophet

According to Islam Muhammad is the last prophet. "Muhammad is not the father of any of your men, but he is the Apostle of Allah and the Last of the prophets ... (surah 33:40)."

Muhammad died in 632 A.D. Interestingly, according to Islamic scholar Professor Patricia Crone, "a Greek text written during the Arab invasion of Syria between 632 and 634 mentions that 'a false prophet has appeared among the Saracens [Muslims of the Syro-Arabian desert]' and dismisses him as an imposter on the grounds that prophets do not come 'with sword and chariot.'"[12]

While Muhammad claimed to be God's last and most important prophet and to have important and new revelation knowledge for both Jews and Christians, the people of the *Book* and the *polytheists* did not recognize him as such, nor would they have anything to do with him and his incantations and moralistic disclosures. The only way that Jews and Christians submitted to his revelations of "truth" was under the severe oppression from Islamic followers. If they survived Muhammad's murderous raids and submitted to Islamic domination, then they could live as secondary citizens if they paid Muhammad the *poor-rate* or tax of submission.

At the end of the Apostle John's revelation on the Isle of Patmos, Jesus made it clear, "I am the Alpha and the Omega, the First and the Last, the Beginning and the End" (Revelation 22:13).

> *This is what the Lord says—Israel's King and Redeemer, the Lord Almighty: I am the first and I am the last; apart from me there is no God. Who then is like me? Let him proclaim it. Let him declare and lay out before me what has happened since I established my ancient people, and what is yet to come.* (Isaiah 44:6-7)

"When I saw him [the son of man]," the Apostle John wrote, "I fell at his feet as though dead. Then he placed his right hand on me and said: 'Do not be afraid. I am the First and the Last. I am the Living One; I was dead, and behold I am alive for ever and ever! And I hold the keys of death and Hades (Revelation 1:17-18).'" Jesus was the first and the last to reveal God's final and only plan for mankind. There can be no other plan of salvation and no other prophet to reveal a different plan. Any prophet to come after Jesus is sent by God only to confirm what He has already put into motion through Christ, the anointed Messiah.

"Listen to me, O Jacob, Israel, whom I have called: I am he; I am the first and I am the last. My own hand laid the foundations of the earth, and my right hand spread out the heavens; when I summon them, they all stand up together (Isaiah 48:12-13)."

Only Jesus could and did fulfill the Messianic prophecies of Isaiah and other Old Testament prophets. "I will also make you a light for the Gentiles, that you may bring my salvation to the ends of the earth (Isaiah 49:6b)." Only Jesus brought the light of God's truth to both the Jews and the Gentiles (non-believers or infidels). None of the prophets before Him did so. Muhammad brought only persecution, oppression and death to non-believers.

ALL the prophets of the Old Testament foretold of the coming of Jesus, the Messiah, not of Muhammad. As the Apostle Peter testified, "And [Jesus] commanded us to preach to the people, and to testify that it is He who was ordained by God to be Judge of the living and the dead. To Him all the prophets witness that, through His name, whoever believes in Him will receive remission of sins" (Acts 10:42-43, NKJV).

I have heard what the prophets have said who prophesy lies in My name, saying, "I have dreamed, I have dreamed!"

How long will this be in the heart of the prophets who prophesy lies? Indeed they are prophets of the deceit of their own heart, who try to make My people forget My name by their dreams which everyone tells his neighbor, as their fathers forgot My name for Baal. (Jeremiah 23:25-27)

If Muhammad fulfilled anything, it was this prophecy. He convinced many that he had dreamed of a new revelation from the god he called Allah. The new revelations he spoke of greatly contradicted previous revelations, turning the truth of God into a lie, deceiving many and turning them away from the only true God—the God of the Jews and Christians.

Signs of a False Prophet

"Above all," the Apostle Peter asserted, "you must understand that no prophecy of Scripture came about by the **prophet's own interpretation**. For prophecy never had its origin in the will of man, but men spoke from God as they were carried along by the Holy Spirit (2 Peter 1:20-21, author's emphasis)."

Muhammad did not believe in the Holy Spirit, the One who reveals all truth according to Jesus (John 16:13). To believe in the Holy Spirit

81

would mean that Muhammad would have to confirm the crucifixion and resurrection of Jesus was real, because the Holy Spirit could not come until Jesus' glorification was accomplished according to God's plan. "On the last and greatest day of the Feast [of Tabernacles]," the Apostle John wrote, "Jesus stood and said in a loud voice, 'If anyone is thirsty, let him come to me and drink. Whoever believes in me, as the Scripture has said, streams of living water will flow from within him.' By this he meant the Spirit, whom those who believed in him were later to receive. Up to that time the Spirit had not been given, since Jesus had not yet been glorified [that is crucified and resurrected]" (John 7:37-39).

"This is what the Lord Almighty says: 'Do not listen to what the prophets are prophesying to you;' Jeremiah the prophet warned, 'they fill you with false hopes. They speak visions from their own minds, not from the mouth of the Lord (Jeremiah 23:16).'" Despite the numerous world religions worshipping different gods there can only be one true God. The source of Muhammad's revelations is debatable and highly suspicious because they strongly contradicted the word of God that went before him. His revelations directly opposed the known and accepted truth of the God of the Jews and Christians. His proclamation of new "truth" provided only false hope to a desperate people.

"Therefore behold, I am against the prophets," says the Lord, "who steal My words every one from his neighbor. Behold, I am against the prophets," says the Lord, "who use their tongues and say, He says. Behold, I am against those who prophesy false dreams," says the Lord, "and tell them, and cause My people to err by their lies and by their recklessness. Yet I did not send them or command them; therefore they shall not profit [benefit] this people at all," says the Lord. (Jeremiah 23:30-32, NKJV)

God's prophets did not and do not oppress the poor and needy; deprive people of their rights; make widows their prey or steal from the fatherless. As the Lord God of Israel spoke through the prophet Isaiah: "Woe to those who make **unjust laws**, to those who issue **oppressive decrees**, to **deprive the poor** of their rights and **withhold justice** from the oppressed of my people, making **widows their prey** and **robbing the fatherless**. What will you do on the day of reckoning, when disaster comes from afar? To whom will you run for help? Where will you leave your riches?" (Isaiah 10:1-3, author's emphasis). Muhammad did all that the Almighty God commanded one not to do. He made unjust laws and decrees to oppress the people. He stole from anyone he was against—rich or poor. He was not a man of his word or justice and meted out cruel and savage punishment. He made widows out of his enemies and then took their wives captive, often giving their wives and daughters to his fighting men to rape or enter into a three-day marriage of convenience to satisfy their sexual desires (see chapter 5). By pillaging and destroying the property of his enemies, he left the fatherless abandoned and destitute—unless he took them as his captives and slaves.

Muhammad was very familiar with the story of Jesus' birth and the appearance of Gabriel to Mary. The Qur'an repeats the story several times. Is it possible that because of Muhammad's acquaintance with this story, that it was not Gabriel that chose Muhammad to deliver Allah's message, but rather Muhammad chose Gabriel to reveal Allah's word?

"The spirit that raised Islam has three main objectives," wrote Reza Safa: "1) To challenge Christ, His Word and His church. 2) To hinder the end-time world revival. 3) To oppose the Jewish people and take over their God-given land."[13]

"I believe," Safa continued, "Islam is Satan's weapon to oppose God, His plan and His people."[14]

> *But a prophet who presumes to speak in my name anything I have not commanded him to say, or a prophet who speaks in the name of other gods, must be put to death.*
>
> *You may say to yourselves, How can we know when a message has not been spoken by the LORD? If what a prophet proclaims in the name of the LORD does not take place or come true, that is a message the LORD has not spoken. That prophet has spoken presumptuously. Do not be afraid of him.* (Deuteronomy 18:20-22)

The real test as to whether a self-proclaimed prophet was sent by God is in the truth of his word and actions. No true prophet of Almighty God can bring forth a new revelation that would contradict or make false a previous revelation of God. "Then the LORD said to me, 'The prophets are prophesying lies in my name. I have not sent them or appointed them or spoken to them. They are prophesying to you false visions, divinations, idolatries and the delusions of their own minds'" (Jeremiah 14:14).

"Watch out for false prophets," Jesus advised. *"They come to you in sheep's clothing, but inwardly they are ferocious wolves. **By their fruit you will recognize them.** Do people pick grapes from thornbushes, or figs from thistles? Likewise every good tree bears good fruit, but a bad tree bears bad fruit. A good tree cannot bear **bad fruit**, and a bad tree cannot bear **good fruit**. Every tree that does not bear good fruit is cut down and thrown into the fire. Thus, by their fruit you will recognize them.*

"Not everyone who says to me, 'Lord, Lord,' will enter the kingdom of heaven, but only he who does the will of my Father who is in heaven." (Matthew 7:15-21, author's emphasis)

Clearly, when the ministry of Muhammad is compared to that of Jesus, John the Baptist, and the prophets of the Old Testament it fell way short of bearing *good fruit*. To the contrary, it bore extremely *bad fruit*. It led people to accept false and satanic teaching that led them to oppress and kill their neighbors; rape women and children; pillage and destroy whole communities and cause havoc wherever they went. Christian Crusaders were guilty of similar atrocities. However, they were not following the dictates of Jesus or the Bible when doing so.

The same Moses who supposedly foretold of Muhammad's coming also made it clear that the Jews were not to believe in or follow any prophet *or one who foretells by dreams*, trying to get them to *follow other gods*. The Jews were to adhere to the commandments of the one and only true God, Jehovah.

If a prophet, or one who foretells by dreams, appears among you and announces to you a miraculous sign or wonder, and if the sign or wonder of which he has spoken takes place, and he says, "Let us follow other gods" (gods you have not known) "and let us worship them," you must not listen to the words of that prophet or dreamer. The Lord your God is testing you to find out whether you love him with all your heart and with all your soul. It is the Lord your God you must follow, and him you must revere. Keep his commands and obey him; serve him and hold fast to him. That prophet or dreamer must be put to death, because he preached rebellion against the LORD your God, who brought you out of Egypt and redeemed you from the land of slavery; he has tried to turn you from the way the LORD your God commanded you to follow. You must purge the evil from among you. (Deuteronomy 13:1-5)

Once again, God Almighty, through the prophet Jeremiah, warned about lying false prophets who were not sent by Him. False prophets are ones who reveal only *false hopes. They speak visions from their own minds* and not from the word of God. Muhammad often spoke convenient "truths" that benefited only him but insisted they were from the mind of Allah. Muhammad spoke of peace as long as everyone followed his commands; otherwise there was "hell" to pay.

This is what the LORD Almighty says:

*"Do not listen to what the prophets are prophesying to you; they fill you with **false hopes**. They **speak visions from their own minds**, not from the mouth of the LORD.*

*They keep saying to those who despise me, 'The LORD says: **You will have peace.**' And to all who follow the stubbornness of their hearts they say, '**No harm will come to you.**'*

But which of them has stood in the council of the LORD to see or to hear his word? Who has listened and heard his word? See, the storm of the LORD will burst out in wrath, a whirlwind swirling down on the heads of the wicked.

The anger of the LORD will not turn back until he fully accomplishes the purposes of his heart. In days to come you will understand it clearly.

***I did not send these prophets**, yet they have run with their message; **I did not speak to them**, yet they have prophesied.*

But if they had stood in my council, they would have proclaimed my words to my people and would have turned them from their evil ways and from their evil deeds.

"Am I only a God nearby," declares the LORD, "and not a God far away? Can anyone hide in secret places so that I cannot

*see him?" declares the LORD. "Do not I fill heaven and earth?"
declares the LORD.*

*"I have heard what the prophets say **who prophesy lies in my
name**. They say, '**I had a dream! I had a dream!**' How long will
this continue in the hearts of these lying prophets, **who prophesy
the delusions of their own minds**? They think the dreams they
tell one another will make my people **forget my name**, just as
their fathers forgot my name through Baal worship. Let the
prophet who has a dream tell his dream, but let the one who
has my word speak it faithfully. For what has straw to do with
grain?" declares the LORD. "Is not my word like fire," declares
the LORD, "and like a hammer that breaks a rock in pieces?*

*"Therefore," declares the LORD, "**I am against the prophets
who steal from one another words supposedly from me**. Yes,"
declares the LORD, "I am against the prophets who **wag their
own tongues** and yet declare, 'The LORD declares.' Indeed,
I am against those who prophesy false dreams," declares the
LORD. "**They tell them and lead my people astray with their
reckless lies, yet I did not send or appoint them.** They do not
benefit these people in the least," declares the LORD.* (Jeremiah
23:16-32, author's emphasis)

False prophets, according to the words of God spoken through the
prophet Micah, were ones who proclaimed *'peace'* as long as the people
gave them what they wanted. "This is what the LORD says: 'As for the
prophets who lead my people astray, if one feeds them, they proclaim
'peace;' if he does not, they prepare to wage war against him. Therefore
night will come over you, without visions, and darkness, without
divination. The sun will set for the prophets, and the day will go dark
for them. The seers will be ashamed and the diviners disgraced. They
will all cover their faces because there is no answer from God (Micah
3:5-7).'" This was frequently Muhammad's ploy. If people cooperated
with him, he would proclaim peace; if they opposed him, he would
declare war against them and do his best to destroy them.

Another characteristic of a false prophet is that they have *a different
spirit* within them and profess a different *gospel* or word of God then
previously revealed or preached. There is no question that Muhammad

had a different spirit within him than Jesus or any of God's apostles or prophets before him. His spirit was obsessed with coercion and violence against all people who refused to follow him. He continually preached a different gospel or word of God then that which had been preached for centuries before him. His message came against those who were considered to be God's chosen—Jews by covenant; Christians by the blood of Christ and the New Covenant.

> *But I am afraid that just as Eve was deceived by the serpent's cunning, your minds may somehow be led astray from your sincere and pure devotion to Christ. For if someone comes to you and preaches a Jesus other than the Jesus we preached, or if you receive **a different spirit** from the one you received, **or a different gospel** from the one you accepted, you put up with it easily enough.*
>
> *But do not think I am in the least inferior to those "super-apostles." I may not be a trained speaker, but I do have knowledge. We have made this perfectly clear to you in every way.*
>
> *… And I will keep on doing what I am doing in order to cut the ground from under those who want an opportunity to be considered equal with us in the things they boast about. For such men are false apostles, deceitful workmen, masquerading as apostles of Christ. And no wonder, for **Satan himself masquerades as an angel of light**. It is not surprising, then, if his servants masquerade as servants of righteousness. Their end will be what their actions deserve.* (2 Corinthians 11:3-6, 12-15, author's emphasis)

Finally, "Who is the liar?" the Apostle John affirmed. "It is the man who denies that Jesus is the Christ. Such a man is the antichrist—he denies the Father and the Son. No one who denies the Son has the Father; whoever acknowledges the Son has the Father also (1 John 2:22)." Once more John made it clear: "Many deceivers, who do not acknowledge Jesus Christ as coming in the flesh, have gone out into the world. Any such person is the deceiver and the antichrist. Watch out that you do not lose what you have worked for, but that you may be rewarded fully. Anyone who runs ahead and does not continue in the teaching of Christ does not have God; whoever continues in the teaching has both the Father and the Son. If anyone comes to you and does not bring this teaching, do not take him into your house or welcome him. Anyone who welcomes him shares in his wicked work" (2 John 7-11).

Conclusion

Despite the centuries of assertions by the Muslim clerics and scholars, the coming of Muhammad was not foretold in either the Old or New Testament scriptures. However, the birth and ministry of Jesus fulfilled over 300 prophecies in the Old Testament about the coming Messiah and *the Prophet*. Muhammad fulfilled none of the prophecies of the Old Testament prophets, nor those of Jesus. In fact, Muhammad met very few of the characteristics associated with the prophets of the Bible.

The ministry of the prophets of the Bible was normally associated with signs and wonders. No miracles were associated with Muhammad's life. The prophets of Jehovah God never persecuted, oppressed or killed people that disagreed with their message. Muhammad frequently planned and/or carried out murderous raids against those who refused to accept him or his message. Prophets often foretold of future events; Muhammad foretold nothing of the future. Prophets of the Bible knew their history and understood the context of their ministry. Muhammad was repeatedly confused or wrong about biblical history and frequently offered little current context for his message to be understood.

Most importantly, Muhammad's revelations completely contradicted the consistent message that God had revealed through His prophets throughout the ages—a message of hope and redemption. The message Muhammad brought from Allah offered no hope, no redemption, and no plan of salvation to relieve mankind of its sin. If Muhammad was a prophet, he was not a prophet of the same God that Jews and Christians worshipped during his time or since.

Only Jesus

William Deng was terrified. He knew what might happen if he refused to become a Muslim. Though not yet 10 years old, he'd seen the consequences of not becoming a Muslim. But he also knew something else: There is only one God, and it isn't the god of Mohammed.

William was captured from his village of Rumbek, South Sudan, in 1997. The Islamic militiamen came into the village at 7:00 a.m. ...

Hearing the gunfire, William's father began to run, calling to his family and trying to stay ahead of the advancing attackers ....

Almost before William knew what was happening, the radical Muslims had tied up his father. Moments later William's father and sister were dead, shot by the Islamic radicals.

William's mother screamed out in agony and loss, and the men began to beat her.

William was thrown into the river, but he didn't know how to swim ... Fighting off her attackers, William's mother grabbed his arm and dragged him to shore ....

One of the men took William to his home. "I had to look after the sheep and goats," William said ....

"I didn't want to be a Muslim," William said in recounting his horrible experience. "I know there is a real God, and He is not the god of the Muslims. I had been baptized before I was captured, and I knew Jesus was the only God. I am a full Christian, and I love Jesus with all my heart."

The threats came, and the Muslim men surrounding William made plans to kill him. But God provided an escape from an unexpected source.

"There was an old man there, a grandfather," William remembers. "He was a member of that family (of the man who captured William). He said: 'You   should not pull a person to your religion .... If he says he doesn't want Islam, you leave him. But don't kill him ....'"

The old man's speech saved William's life ....

"I don't want Islam," William says now. "I only want Jesus."

"I Only Want Jesus"
The Voice of the Martyrs
December, 2003, p. 4-5

References

1 *The Role of the Prophet*. Reprinted from The Herald, November, 1949. Http://www.heraldmag.org/literature/quest_9.htm. Accessed March 3, 2007.

2 McKenzie, Ron, *Receiving the Word*. Http://www.kingwatch.co.nz/Prophetic_Ministry/receiving_the_word.htm. Accessed March 3, 2007.

3 Brogden, Chip, *The Ministry of the Watchman*. Http://www.theschoolofchrist.org/articles/minwatch.html. Accessed July 14, 2007.

4 Longman, Jr., Robert. *What is Prophecy?* Http://www.spirithome.com/prophecy.Html. Accessed March 3, 2007.

5 Safa, Reza F. *Inside Islam: Exposing and Reaching the World of Islam*, 1996. Charisma House, p. 17.

6 Ibid.

7 Caner, Ergun Mehmet and Emir Fethi Caner. *Unveiling Islam*, 2002. Kregel Publications, div. of Kregel. Inc., p. 110.

8 Spencer, Robert. *The Truth About Muhammad, Founder of the World's Most Intolerant Religion*, 2006. Regnery Publishing, Inc., p.38.

9 Mckenzie.

10 Brogden, Chip, *Prophetic Dissonance*. Http://www.reconciliation.com/n_brogden01.htm. Accessed July 14, 2007.

11 *History of Crucifixion*. AllAboutJesusChrist.org. Http://www.allaboutjesuschrist.org/common/history-of-crucifixion-faq.htm. Accessed June 11, 2007.

12 Crone, Patricia. *What Do We Actually Know About Mohammed?* Open Democracy, August 31, 2006. Http://www.openDemocracy.net. Accessed June 2, 2007.

13 Safa, p. 18.

14 Ibid.

CHAPTER 4

Prince of Peace
or Warrior Prophet

I have been sent with the sword between my hands
to ensure that no one but Allah is worshipped ....

Muhammad

In the 114 chapters of the Qur'an, only fifty-six verses mention the concept of "peace." The majority of the verses, however, refer to the Qur'anic greeting, "peace be unto you," or similar salutation. Others deal with the "peace" that Allah brings after a military conflict. After the difficult Battle of Hunayn in Arabia in 630 A.D.—in which Muhammad and his army were initially overrun, but subsequently prevailed—Muhammad received this revelation from Allah:[1]

"Then Allah sent down His tranquility [peace] upon His Apostle and upon the believers, and sent down hosts which you did not see, and chastised those who disbelieved, and that is the reward of the unbelievers (surah 9:26)." In surah 48:18 and 26 a similar blessing of peace from Allah after conflict is offered.

There are also some interesting references to peace in other verses of the Qur'an. In surah 2:248, the verse reflects on how God brought peace to the children of Israel and King Saul before an impending battle.

And the prophet said to them: Surely the sign of His kingdom is, that there shall come to you the chest in which there is tranquility [peace] from your Lord and residue of the relics of what the children of Musa [Moses] and the children of Haroun [Aaron] have left, the angels bearing it; most surely there is a sign in this for those who believe.

Allah, according to the Qur'an, also bestowed peace upon Nuh (Noah, in surah 37:79), Ibrahim (Abraham, 37:109), Musa and Haroun (37:120), Ilyas (Elijah, 37:130) and all of Allah's apostles (37:181). In an interesting aside, while Muslims revere Elijah as a prophet of Allah, Elijah's name literally means, "his God is Jehovah," the name that Jews attribute to God Almighty and the name for God that Muslims refuse to use.

The Qur'an even exclaims that God's peace was upon Jesus the day he was born. "And peace on him [Jesus] on the day he was born, and on the day he dies, and on the day he is raised to life . . . And peace on me [Jesus] on the day I was born, and on the day I die, and on the day I am raised to life (surah 19:15, 33)." This peace of God that was bestowed on Jesus was something that Muhammad could never claim or aspire to throughout his entire life—nor did most of his life exhibit peace.

Other verses of the Qur'an state that Allah offers a *word* of peace to believers (surah 36:58); that Muslims are never to beg for peace in the midst of battle (surah 47:35); that Allah dispenses peace to increase faith (surah 48:4) but only to select believers (surah 10:25). Does the follower of Allah have any assurance of peace in this life or the next? Is peace—real inner peace of the soul—offered by or guaranteed by Allah to the faithful? No, not really. Faithful Muslims are only offered the illusion or possibility of peace from Allah if they do what is right in the eyes of Allah (surah 6:127). The problem is, not even the most faithful Muslim can be assured he or she has done what is right. An adherent to the faith might receive inner peace—and, perhaps it is the only way in this life—if he makes the pilgrimage to the Ka'bah (site of Abraham's supposed offering of Ishmael to Allah) in Mecca. This offer is not available to females or children, only to adult male believers. If one misses out on this opportunity to receive peace from Allah, then there is always the possibility that Allah will bestow peace on the believer after they get to Paradise (surah 19:62; 50:34). However, it is only the **possibility** of peace.

Noticeably missing from the teachings of the Qur'an are references that Allah grants peace to all those who accept him, or that he is the source of inner peace, or that he is the God of peace. One thing the annals of history and the Qur'an **cannot** attribute to Muhammad, was that he was a man of peace.

According to Mark Gabriel, when he was a freshman Islamic student at the prestigious Al-Azhar University in Cairo, Egypt in 1980, the blind sheikh, Omar Abdel Rahman, was lecturing 500 students on "Quranic Interpretation." In opposition to teachings on peace, love and forgiveness, the sheikh told the students that, "there is a whole surah [chapter 8] called the 'Spoils of War.' There is no surah called 'Peace.' Jihad and killing are the head of Islam. If you take them out, you cut off the head of Islam."[2]

That radical Muslim leader, you might recall, was caught and convicted of being the architect behind the 1993 World Trade Center bombing in New York City.

Unfortunately, he is right in his assessment of the Qur'an's mostly silence on the subject of peace. While the Bible has much to say about and teach about peace at all levels of human existence, the Qur'an offers little guidance to the wayward, sinful man.

God of Peace and the Prince of Peace

In contrast to the Qur'an, the Bible (King James Version) offers 420 verses on the subject of "peace." Interestingly, the *Arabic Life Application Bible*, published by the International Bible Society, has no verses using the word "peace." Twenty centuries of secular and religious history attest to Jesus Christ as the "Prince of Peace." No other deity or human being has or can claim that title. Around 740 B.C., the Old Testament prophet Isaiah heralded the coming of the Jewish Messiah with this revelation from God:

> *For unto us a Child is born, unto us a Son is given; and the government will be upon His shoulder. And His name will be called Wonderful, Counselor, Mighty God, Everlasting Father, Prince of Peace.* (Isaiah 9:6, NKJV)

"Surely," the prophet Isaiah testified, "he [the promised Messiah] took up our infirmities and carried our sorrows, yet we considered him stricken by God, smitten by him, and afflicted. But he was pierced for our transgressions, he was crushed for our iniquities; the punishment that brought us peace was upon him, and by his wounds we are healed (Isaiah 53:4-5)." Certainly, this type of sacrifice for others is not something that Muhammad could lay claim to as Allah's last and most important prophet. Muhammad never took upon himself anyone's sicknesses or sins. He never suffered torture or extreme punishment and pain for the sake of his follower's inner peace and spiritual freedom.

The God of the Christians and Jews is known in scripture and life as the God of Peace. The Apostle Paul, ended his letter to the Jewish and Gentile Christians in Rome and elsewhere in Asia Minor with, "The God of peace be with you all (Romans 15:33)."

Not only is the Judeo-Christian God known as the God of Peace, but He sent His Son to be the example of His peace on earth. Christ established a new covenant built upon the old promises of God, restoring God's peace to mankind through His shed blood on the cross. The Apostle Paul, in his letter to the church at Ephesus, put it this way:

> *For he himself is our peace, who was made the two one and has destroyed the barrier, the dividing wall of hostility, by abolishing in his flesh the law with its commandments and regulations. His purpose was to create in himself one new man out of the two, thus making peace, and in this one body to reconcile both of them to God through the cross, by which he put to death their hostility.* (Ephesians 2:14-16)

It was Almighty God's intention from the beginning to bring His Son into the world to abolish the old covenant that brought enmity between God and His creation. Through Jesus' sacrifice and shedding of blood on the cross, God installed a new covenant of reconciliation and peace. Allah, on the other hand, according to his revelations to Muhammad, used Muhammad to bring about discord and blood shed—not the sacrificial blood of Muhammad, his chosen prophet—but the shed blood of all those deemed to be the *enemies of Allah.*

Jesus taught his followers to demonstrate peace to the world; even toward ones' enemies. "Blessed are the peacemakers," He preached in the Sermon on the Mount, "for they will be called sons of God (Matthew 5:9)." By comparison, Muhammad taught his followers to carry out a "holy war" or jihad against anyone who refused to accept Islam or have faith in Allah. According to the Qur'an, adherents to Islam are to fight against all who stand in the way of the spread of Islam and to fight against anyone who refused to enter into the Islamic faith.

> And fight with them [the unbelievers] until there is no more persecution and religion should be only for Allah; but if they desist, then surely Allah sees what they do. (surah 8:39)

Muhammad's revealed message from Allah brought about extreme conflict and bloodshed between families and among neighbors, both near and far. Jesus, throughout His ministry, continually shared with His disciples and those who would hear Him, about God's love and reconciliation and the coming of God's Holy Spirit to dwell within those who chose to follow Him. "I have told you these things," Jesus told His disciples shortly before His arrest, "so that in me you may have peace. In this world you will have trouble. But take heart! I have overcome the world (John 16:33)." Note that Jesus did not command His followers to go forth and conquer the world for His sake. But, rather, He had already conquered the world in the spiritual realm through His coming and future sacrifice on the cross for all mankind. Allah, by contrast, revealed to Muhammad, that he and those who chose Islam were to go forth and violently subdue the world through bloody conquest.

In the letter to the Jewish-Christians, written in the first century, A.D., the author re-assures the believers who were struggling with their faith under persecution and doubts with these parting words: "May the God of peace, who through the blood of the eternal covenant brought back from the dead our Lord Jesus, that great Shepherd of the sheep, equip you with everything good for doing his will, and may he work in us what is pleasing to him, through Jesus Christ, to whom be glory for ever and ever. Amen" (Hebrews 13:20-21).

While Allah is said to offer peace at times to his followers, only one verse in the entire Qur'an identifies Allah as a god of peace (As-Salam). But the Qur'an does not refer to Allah as the source of inner or eternal peace. As-Salam designates Allah as the source of peace or one who makes peace.[3] It is by implication in this name associated with Allah, that Allah brings inner peace to a believer, but nowhere in the Qur'an does it say that Allah explicitly or irrevocably offers or secures inner peace for those that follow him.

He is Allah, besides Whom there is no god; the King, the Holy, the Giver of peace [or peacemaker], the Granter of security, Guardian over all, the Mighty, the Supreme, the Possessor of every greatness …. (surah 59:23)

Jesus, however, as the *Prince of Peace* and the incarnation of His Father, Almighty God, on earth, overtly and without reservation offered and guaranteed God's inner peace to His disciples. "Peace I leave with you," He said; "my peace I give you. I do not give to you as the world gives. Do not let your hearts be troubled and do not be afraid (John 14:27)." While Jesus offered this clear message of God's peace—because He was the source of peace—the significance of Allah's peace appears to get lost in the overall message of the Qur'an and Muhammad's murderous exploits.

It is hard to see or interpret Allah as a god of peace when the Qur'an is full of verses that command the followers of Islam to "kill [the unbelievers] wherever you find them …" (surah 2:191, as an example). Muhammad, in the name of Allah, the As-Salam, sought to conquer his foes, near and far, and force them into submission to Allah. Christ, through words and deeds of peace and love, sought to reconcile both Jews and Gentiles—believers and non-believers; those who were near and far from God in spirit and distance—with God's saving grace.

But now in Christ Jesus you who once were far off have been brought near by the blood of Christ. For He Himself is our peace, who has made both [Jews and Gentiles] *one, and has broken down the middle wall* [of the law] *of separation, having abolished in His flesh the enmity, that is, the law of commandments contained in ordinances, so as to create in Himself one new man from the two, thus making peace, and that He might reconcile them both to God in one body through the cross, thereby putting to death the enmity.* (Ephesians 2:13-16, NKJV)

The Apostle Paul made it clear that the mission of Jesus was to bring about peace and reconciliation. "For God was pleased to have all his fullness dwell in him [Jesus], and through him to reconcile to himself all things, whether things on earth or things in heaven, by making peace through his blood, shed on the cross (Colossians 1:19-20)." If we are to assume and accept, as the Qur'an and Islam teaches, that Jesus was a great prophet of God (Allah), but *not* the Son of God, then Allah must be one confused and changeable deity. First, he sends Jesus to clearly bring a message and example of peace and reconciliation. Then, 600 years later, he changes his mind, and sends Muhammad, one whose message was the dead opposite—one of conflict, chaos and inner turmoil.

"Let the peace of Christ rule in your hearts," the Apostle Paul wrote, "since as members of one body you were called to peace. And be thankful (Colossians 3:15)." While followers of Christ are called to peace and are called to be peacemakers by Christ (Matthew 5:9), Muslims are called, not to peace, but to jihad, that is, a *continuous* holy war against the infidels, all those who do not accept Allah as God. The Apostle Paul, taking from Jesus' example, called upon all Christians to, "Pursue peace with all people ..." (Hebrews 12:14, NKJV)." Something the prophet Muhammad did not exemplify or encourage his followers to practice.

Even the psalmist, King David, reminded the Jews to, "Turn from evil and do good; seek peace and pursue it (Psalm 34:14)." And again, to "Consider the blameless, observe the upright; there is a future for the man of peace" (Psalm 37:37).

The biography of Muhammad and the many historical accounts of his persona and exploits do not give way to him being a man of peace. Nor does the history of Islam paint a pretty picture of a people or religion of peace. Yes, there are periods and incidents in the history of the Christian faith that paint a dark picture that is contrary to a religion of peace. But, unlike Islam, the teachings of Christ and the Apostles command and demand that His followers take the road of peace wherever possible.

"You will keep him in perfect peace, whose mind is stayed on You, because he trusts in You (Isaiah 26:3, NKJV)." This was and is the promise of God through His prophet, Isaiah. "The fruit of righteousness will be peace; the effect of righteousness will be quietness and confidence forever. My people will live in peaceful dwelling places, in secure homes, in undisturbed places of rest" (Isaiah 32:17-18).

Peace—a Gift of God

Peace, true inner, personal peace that also manifests itself in expressions of outer peace, can only come from God. It is a gift from God. Man cannot manufacture it. It is impossible to have a real sense of inner peace without the presence of God and the knowledge of His presence in the life of one who believes in Him. The word used in both the Old Testament and New Testament parts of the Bible describes a person who is *happy; has a sense of wellbeing; feels safe; is prosperous, healthy and at rest.* That is, a person who experiences to the depth of his or her soul, a state of peace. For the Muslim believer, this state of existence does not and cannot occur. In every Muslim nation in the world there is extreme unrest, turmoil and bloodshed. While Muslim leader after Muslim leader cry out that "Islam is a religion of peace," the worldwide current events and wealth of Islamic history tell the truth of the matter.

Once again, King David, who was no stranger to inner turmoil or outer conflict with his enemies, wrote, "The Lord gives strength to his people; the Lord blesses his people with peace" (Psalm 29:11). While David defended against and in some cases pursued his enemies, he knew God would have him strive for peace.

The Apostle Paul put it this way: "The mind of a sinful man is death, but the mind controlled by the Spirit is life and peace" (Romans 8:6). Man cannot create his own peace; he can only create in his own mind the illusion of peace. He can build walls of defense, train great armies, earn great wealth or do whatever he may imagine will bring him peace, and it will all deceive him. It will not bring him the inherent desire to know true inner peace.

The Apostle Paul, who prior to his conversion to Christianity was a persecutor of the followers of Christ, understood this inner peace concept well. Prior to his meeting Jesus on the road to Damascus (the current capital of Syria), Paul's life was one of inner and outer chaos. Yes, he was an educated Roman citizen and a Pharisee, a Jew by birth, yet he knew nothing of God's peace. He was obsessed with persecuting the followers of Christ and destroying the fledgling Christian Church.

After his conversion he became committed to following Christ, his newfound Lord and Savior. It was then that Paul found true inner peace that was expressed in outer deeds of personal sacrifice and love. "May god himself, the God of peace," he wrote to the church in Thessalonica (a coastal city along the Aegean Sea of ancient Greece), "sanctify you through and through. May your whole spirit, soul and body be kept blameless at the coming of our Lord Jesus Christ" (1 Thessalonians 5:23). Paul now understood what it meant to experience the God of Peace and the inner presence of peace, a peace that only Jesus Christ could bring to him. In an effort to encourage the believers in this Roman-controlled city, he once again wrote: "Now may the Lord of peace himself give you peace at all times and in every way. The Lord be with you all" (2 Thessalonians 3:16).

This peace of God was a conscious part of Paul daily. So much so, that he desired for all of God's children to experience it. He did not presume to understand it. He just knew it existed, was available and he basked in its presence every day of his life. "Do not be anxious about anything," he wrote to the believers in Philippi (another coastal city in ancient Greece), "but in everything, by prayer and petition, with thanksgiving, present your requests to God. And the peace of God, which transcends all understanding, will guard your hearts and your minds in Christ Jesus" (Philippians 4:6-7). Even for the great Apostle Paul, God's peace rose beyond his personal understanding. All he knew was, that through the grace and sacrifice of Jesus Christ, it became available to him and he wanted everyone else to know about it.

Gospel of Peace

"How beautiful upon the mountains are the feet of him who brings good news," the prophet Isaiah wrote, "who proclaims peace, who brings glad tidings of good things, who proclaims salvation, who says to Zion, 'Your God reigns!'" (Isaiah 52:7, NKJV). The people of the world, both ancient and modern, have sought the message and reality of peace for thousands of years. And, just like in the days of old, it continues to elude them.

A scant 30 years after Jesus' crucifixion and resurrection, the Apostle Luke wrote, "You know the message God sent to the people of Israel, telling the good news of peace through Jesus Christ, who is Lord of all (Acts 10:36)." That was and is "good news." Throughout the history of the world, one thing the peoples of the earth have had in common—they all yearned for peace. A similar gospel of peace cannot be found in the Qur'an or among the teachings of Muhammad.

While Jesus was a "prophet" of peace, Muhammad was a "prophet" of war. "O Prophet! Urge the believers to war" (surah 8:65). Again, "It is not fit for a prophet that he should take captives unless he has fought and triumphed in the land" (surah 8:67). The contrast of prophethood could not be any clearer: Jesus offered the world peace; Muhammad offered the world confrontation and hostility. Jesus and His Apostles preached peace and were examples of peace. Muhammad and his disciples proclaimed and carried out war against the infidels.

Once again, Jesus, in His Sermon on the Mount, declared that "Blessed are the peacemakers, for they will be called sons of God (Matthew 5:9)." There is nothing in the world like proclaiming a message of peace as an illustration of God's love.

"On the evening of that first day of the week [after Jesus' crucifixion], when the disciples were together, with the doors locked for fear of the Jews, Jesus came and stood among them and said, 'Peace be with you!' … Again Jesus said, 'Peace be with you! As the Father has sent me, I am sending you'" (John 20:19, 21). Upon seeing His disciples for the first time since His resurrection, Jesus could not have said anything more reassuring than, "Peace be with you!" The disciples were fearful for their lives. Jesus wanted to reassure them, that despite their fear and circumstances, His peace was with them. So much so, that He was sending them out into their hostile surroundings to continue to preach His redemptive message of God's peace and love.

"But the wisdom that comes from heaven is first of all pure;" wrote James, the brother of Jesus, "then peace-loving, considerate, submissive, full of mercy and good fruit, impartial and sincere. Peacemakers who sow in peace raise a harvest of righteousness" (James 3:17-18). The early followers of Jesus understood His message of peace and were willing to die for it; and many of them did.

By comparison, one of Muhammad's most flamboyant and current day disciples preaches a quite different message. In a religious ruling (fatwa) of February 23, 1998, Usama bin Laden (Shaykh Usamah Bin-Muhammad Bin-Ladin) and the leaders of four other Islamic jihad groups, called for the wanton killing of Americans, both civilian and military.[4] In doing so, they quoted the Prophet Muhammad to support their justification. "I have been sent with the sword between my hands to ensure that no one but Allah is worshipped, Allah who put my livelihood under the shadow of my spear and who inflicts humiliation and scorn on those who disobey my orders."

The Apostle Paul reiterated time and again, that Jesus "came and preached peace to you who were far away and peace to those who were near (Ephesians 2:17)." Isaiah prophesied about such a messenger of peace when he said: "'I create the fruit of the lips: Peace, peace to him who is far off and to him who is near,' says the Lord. 'And I will heal him'" (Isaiah 57:19, NKJV).

Allah instructs Muhammad to do otherwise. "O Prophet! Strive hard against the unbelievers and the hypocrites and be unyielding to them; and their abode is hell, and evil is the destination" (surah 9:73). The Apostle Paul, however, as God's anointed Apostle, reminds the faithful, "If it is possible, as far as it depends on you, live at peace with everyone" (Romans 12:18). Again, how can Allah and the God of the Jews and Christians be one and the same? God cannot tell the followers of Jesus *to live at peace with everyone* and then tell Muhammad and his followers to, *Strive hard against the unbelievers ... and be unyielding to them*. Certainly, this is not a message of peace, nor would it demonstrate a god of consistency.

"Flee the evil desires of youth," Paul admonishes the faithful, "and pursue righteousness, faith, love and peace, along with those who call on the Lord out of a pure heart" (2 Timothy 2:22). Christians—true followers of the Lord Jesus Christ—are not only called to live in peace, but they are to pursue peace at every opportunity.

The Qur'an instructs the followers of Allah to do just the reverse: Not only to not live in peace but to pursue the destruction and murder of those who disbelieve in Allah.

"And kill them [the unbelievers] wherever you find them, and drive them out from whence they drove you out, and persecution is severer than slaughter, and do not fight with them at the Sacred Mosque until they fight with you in it, but if they do fight you, then slay them; such is the recompense of the unbelievers" (surah 2:191). Two verses later, this instruction is repeated. "And fight with them until there is no persecution, and religion should be only for Allah, but if they desist, then there should be no hostility except against the oppressors" (surah 2:193).

"Some of these so called 'peaceful' campaigns documented," wrote Islamic researcher, Steve Keohane, "were the massacre of the Jews of Medina, attack and enslavement of the Jews of Khayber, rape of women and children, sale of these victims after rape, trickery, treachery and bribery employed to their fullest extent to grow the numbers of [Muhammad's] new Islamic religion which ironically was supposed to mean 'Peace'! Muhammad organized no less than eighty-six expeditions of rape, plunder and murder; twenty-seven of which he led himself. In nine of these, he fought himself on the battlefield."[5]

Peter, one of Jesus' twelve Apostles, provides a contrary view of God's word. "'Whoever would love life and see good days must keep his tongue from evil and his lips from deceitful speech. He must turn from evil and do good; he must seek peace and pursue it. For the eyes of the Lord are on the righteous and his ears are attentive to their prayer, but the face of the Lord is against those who do evil'" [Psalm 34:12-16] (1 Peter 3:10-12).

Lest the reader think that the verses of the Qur'an above are isolated quotations, they pretty much mirror a theme throughout much of the Qur'an. "And let not those who disbelieve think that they shall come in first; surely they will not escape. And prepare against them what force you can and horses tied at the frontier, to frighten thereby the enemy of Allah and your enemy and others besides them, whom you do not know (but) Allah knows them ... (surah 8:59,60)." *The Noble Qur'an* (an English translation of the Qur'an published by King Fahd of Saudi Arabia in 1998) has this take on surah 8:60: "And make ready against them all you can of power, including steeds of war (tanks, planes, missiles, artillery) to threaten the enemy of Allah ...."[6]

"So when the sacred months have passed away, then slay the idolaters wherever you find them, and take them captives and besiege them and lie in wait for them in every ambush, then if they repent and keep up prayer and pay the poor-rate, leave their way free to them ..." (surah 9:5). This is what Mark Gabriel, an Islamic scholar and former radical Muslim, calls the Jihad Stage of the Muslim movement—the antithesis of peace. "This stage is when Muslims are a minority with strength, influence and power. At this stage every Muslim's duty is to actively fight the enemy, overturning the system of the non-Muslim country and establishing Islamic authority."[7]

This verse of the Qur'an is clear, according to Gabriel, "Muslims are commanded to kill anyone who chooses not to convert to Islam ... There are no geographic limits."[8]

God cannot be a peacemaker on the one hand and a warmonger on the other. He cannot be divided among Himself. "For God is not the author of confusion but of peace ..." (1 Corinthians 14:33) and the followers of Jesus are to preach the Gospel of Peace to the world. (Romans 10:15)

False Prophets of Peace

Muhammad and the modern day imams of Islam are clear examples of what and who the Old Testament prophets warned the Jews about. They cry out that Islam is a religion of peace and that Muhammad was a messenger of peace. They shout, "Peace, Peace!" where there is no peace.

"Therefore this is what the Sovereign Lord says: Because of your false words and lying visions, I am against you, declares the Sovereign Lord. My hand will be against the prophets who see false visions and utter lying divinations. They will not belong to the council of my people or be listed in the records of the house of Israel, nor will they enter the land of Israel. Then you will know that I am the Sovereign Lord.

"'Because they lead my people astray, saying, 'Peace,' when there is no peace, and because, when a flimsy wall is built, they cover it with whitewash, therefore tell those who cover it with whitewash that it is going to fall. Rain will come in torrents, and I will send hailstones hurtling down, and violent winds will burst forth." (Ezekiel 13:8-11)

"To whom can I speak and give warning? Who will listen to me?

Their ears are closed so they cannot hear. The word of the Lord is offensive to them; they find no pleasure in it. But I am full of the wrath of the Lord, and I cannot hold it in ....

"From the least to the greatest, all are greedy for gain; prophets and priests alike, all practice deceit. They dress the wound of my people as though it were not serious. 'Peace, peace,' they say, when there is no peace." (Jeremiah 6:10-11a, 13-14)

The Apostle Paul warned his protégé, Timothy, about such men. "But evil men and imposters will grow worse and worse, deceiving and being deceived" (2 Timothy 3:13, NKJV). We live in an evil and dangerous time. Men still clamor for peace and are willing to do almost anything to achieve or receive it. And evil men are only too willing to say what the ear of the peace-hungry populace wants to hear.

Denied to the Wicked

Islam throughout the centuries gives the distinct impression that it is a religion that is in constant conflict within itself and with its neighbors near and far. Its most outspoken religious leaders neither preach peace nor encourage peace among their followers. "There is no peace," says the Lord, "for the wicked" (Isaiah 48:22). Those who preach and instigate evil deeds can not know peace.

As God spoke through the prophet Isaiah, He said, "But the wicked are like the tossing sea, which cannot rest, whose waves cast up mire and mud. 'There is no peace,' says my God, 'for the wicked'" (Isaiah 57:20-21).

It has been several years since the horrible day of unprovoked attacks on innocent life on September 11, 2001, and there has yet to be a universal outcry from the leaders of Islam to denounce this wicked deed in the name of Islam and issue a call for peace. Men who know no inner peace—the peace of God—are helpless when a call for peace is required.

The Apostle Paul, in his letter to the church in Rome, recounts the mindset and fate of those who do not know God by citing Old Testament scriptures.

As it is written:

There is no one righteous, not even one; there is no one who understands, no one who seeks God. All have turned away, they have together become worthless; there is no one who does good, not even one [Psalm 14:1-3].

Their throats are open graves; their tongues practice deceit. (Psalm 5:9)

The poison of vipers is on their lips [Psalm 140:3].

Their mouths are full of cursing and bitterness [Psalm 10:7].

Their feet are swift to shed blood; ruin and misery mark their ways, and the way of peace they do not know [Isaiah 59:7-8].

There is no fear of God before their eyes [Psalm 36:1]. (Romans 3:10-18)

Once again, the prophet Isaiah spoke vehemently against those of his day that had nothing but evil intent in their thoughts and actions. His words have rung true throughout the centuries and for today.

Surely the arm of the LORD is not too short to save, nor his ear too dull to hear. But your iniquities have separated you from your God; your sins have hidden his face from you, so that he will not hear. For your hands are stained with blood, your fingers with guilt. Your lips have spoken lies, and your tongue mutters wicked things. No one calls for justice; no one pleads his case with integrity. They rely on empty arguments and speak lies; they conceive trouble and give birth to evil .... Their feet rush into sin; they are swift to shed innocent blood. Their thoughts are evil thoughts; ruin and destruction mark their ways.

The way of peace they do not know; there is no justice in their paths. They have turned them into crooked roads; no one who walks in them will know peace. So justice is far from us, and righteousness does not reach us. We look for light, but all is darkness; for brightness, but we walk in deep shadows. Like the blind we grope along the wall, feeling our way like men without eyes. At midday we stumble as if it were twilight; among the strong, we are like the dead. We all growl like bears; we moan mournfully like doves. We look for justice, but find none; for deliverance, but it is far away. (Isaiah 59:1-4, 7-11)

Parting Words

Muhammad's last words to his followers before his death, according to hadith 5:716, were, "Turn the pagans out of the Arabian Peninsula (9, 10)." Muhammad wanted Arabia to be for none other than Muslims. No matter what it took, non-Allah worshippers were to be wiped off the peninsula of Arabia.

Nearing death, these words were also spoken by Muhammad, according to hadith 4:52:220, narrated by Abu Huraira:

> Allah's Apostle said, "I have been sent with the shortest expressions bearing the widest meanings, and I have been made victorious with terror (cast in the hearts of the enemy), and while I was sleeping, the keys of the treasures of the world were brought to me and put in my hand." Abu Hiraira added: Allah's Apostle has left the world and now you, people, are bringing out those treasures (i.e. the Prophet did not benefit by them). [Author's emphasis.]

In stark contrast, Jesus' last recorded words before he ascended into heaven, as reported in the Gospel of Matthew were: "… All authority in heaven and on earth has been given to me. Therefore go and make disciples of all nations, baptizing them in the name of the Father and of the Son and of the Holy Spirit, and teaching them to obey everything I have commanded you. And surely I am with you always, to the very end of the age" (Matthew 28:18-20).

The Gospel of Mark records these last words of Jesus: "… Go into all the world and preach the gospel to every creature. He who believes and is baptized will be saved; but he who does not believe will be condemned. And these signs will follow those who believe: In My name they will cast out demons; they will speak with new tongues; they will take up serpents; and if they drink anything deadly, it will by no means hurt them; they will lay hands on the sick, and they will recover" (Mark 16:15-18, NKJV).

In addition, when Jesus knew His crucifixion was drawing near, He spoke these reassuring words to His disciples:

> *Peace I leave with you; my **peace** I give you. I do not give to you as the world gives. Do not let your hearts be troubled and do not be afraid.* (John 14:27, author's emphasis)

A wider divergence in messages and messengers is hard to imagine. In the life and words of Jesus we have a human being preaching and conveying acts of peace from the first to the last day of His ministry on earth. In Muhammad, we have a self-serving, power-hungry warrior who sought to destroy his neighbors under the guise of Allah's good will and design for mankind. If man desires peace, would not his god also desire and grant peace? If a man's theology causes him to seek conflict instead of peace, then his god must be a god of war and not the God of Peace portrayed in the Bible and throughout Judeo-Christian history.

"… Islam does in fact have an essential and indispensable tenet of militaristic conquest," wrote the Caner brothers.[11] These two American-born brothers should know. Raised in a strict Muslim home, when they converted to Christianity, their father disowned them. Today, as Christian theologians, they educate people on the true tenets of the Islamic faith. "Military warfare," they added, "is an absolute necessity if Allah is to be honored and worshipped."[12]

Conclusion

Is it possible, as Muhammad and the Qur'an attest, that Jesus Christ, the Prince of Peace, was sent by Allah and gave testimony to Allah? Or, from the opposite viewpoint, that Muhammad was the spokesperson or prophet for the god, known to the Jews and Christians as the God of Peace? Could two lives be more diametrically opposed to each other than the lives of Jesus and Muhammad? If they were both messengers of the same god, how could one preach and live peace and the other preach and live a life of hate?

Clearly, Allah is not the God of Peace that the prophets and sages of the Bible talk about and followed. Muhammad could not be the Prince of Peace prophesied by Isaiah. Only Jesus could and did fulfill the image of the God of Peace. The harsh character of Allah portrayed in the Qur'an and demonstrated in the life of Muhammad and his followers would prevent those who have a personal knowledge of the God of the Bible in declaring that He and Allah are one. It is both a theological and practical impossibility.

Seduced by Radical Islam

Before I was an FBI informant, an apostate and a blasphemer, I was a devout believer in radical Islam ....

I believed that non-Islamic governments were illegitimate, that jihadists were brave holy warriors carrying out the will of Allah, that Jews and other non-Muslims were inferiors who had to be conquered and ruled. Funny thing, I was born Jewish. At twenty-three, with my nose in a wool prayer rug, I found myself praying for the humiliation of my parents because true Islam demanded it, or so I believed.

... One summer morning, I realized just how much I had come to accept a worldview that I once would have rejected out of hand.

... During my first year [of law school] at NYU, it was as though I lived in a different universe than my classmates.

... As I read about the need to subjugate women, about how anyone who leaves the Muslim faith and does not repent and return to it "will be killed as a kafir [infidel] and apostate," I realized that I harbored real moral doubts about radical Islam ....

Depressed and confused ... I stopped asking [in prayer] for victory for the mujahedin [holy warriors], or for my heart to be cured of doubts. Instead, I asked God to show me what I needed to know. I no longer was convinced I knew the truth.

Daveed Gartenstein-Ross
When Faith Goes Too Far
Reader's Digest, February, 2007

References

1 Spencer, Robert. *The Truth About Muhammad, Founder of the World's Most Intolerant Religion*, Regnery Publishing, Inc., Washington, DC., 2006, p. 151.

2 Gabriel, Mark A. *Islam and Terrorism*, published by FrontLine, a Strang Company, Lake Mary, Florida, 2002, p. 24.

3 *The Beautiful Names of Allah*, http://wahiduddin.net/words/99_pages/salam _5.htm.

4 *Jihad Against Jews and Crusaders: World Islamic Front Statement*, February 23, 1998. http://www.fas.org/irp/world/para/docs/980223-fatwa.htm. Accessed December 11, 2006.

5 Keohane, Steve. *Muhammad: Terrorist or Prophet?* BibleProbe.com, 200402007. Http://bibleprobe.com/muhammad.htm. Accessed April 1, 2007.

6 Gabriel, Mark A., p. 87.

7 Ibid.

8 Ibid.

9 Caner, Ergun Mehmet and Emir Fethi Caner. *Unveiling Islam*, Kregel Publications, div. of Kregel. Inc., 2002, p. 189.

10 Spencer, Robert, p. 165.

11 Caner and Caner, p. 184.

12 Ibid, p. 185.

CHAPTER 5

Life of Holiness
or Immorality

*Certainly you have in the Apostle of Allah an excellent exemplar
for him who hopes in Allah and the latter day and remembers
Allah much (Qur'an 33:21)*

The prophets of God in the Old Testament led exemplary lives. What example of godly living did Muhammad leave his followers? Those that the Bible refers to as prophets, such as Aaron, Amos, Daniel, Elijah, Elisha, Ezekiel, Habakkuk, Hosea, Isaiah, Jeremiah, Joel, Jonah, Malachi, Micah, Moses, Nathan, Nehemiah, Obadiah, Samuel, Zechariah and numerous others, did not have multiple wives. Most apparently did not have even one wife. They did not steal, lie, covet, or lead murderous raids. They were all men of integrity and honesty with a sincere desire to communicate God's words of truth and warning. Most endured stark and harsh living conditions as a personal sacrifice to remain true to God's calling upon their lives.

Jesus Christ, as God's Son, led a perfect life of peace and love. He taught and prophesied about God's goodness and love for all who would call upon Him. He taught about loving others as you would love yourself and as God loved you; about compassion and forgiveness and going the extra mile for those in need. While some of Jesus' followers assumed He had come to lead the Jews in a holy war, He rejected the assumption and admonished them for believing so. If any of His followers so much as picked up a sword, He stiffly admonished them and set them straight as to His mission of peace. There is no record or mention that He even had a place to call home during His three year

111

ministry. While He was called the Son of God and King of the Jews and other monikers of high honor, He walked and ministered among the poor, the dispossessed and the flagrant sinners of society.

When the Jews started to persecute Jesus because He was performing miracles on the Sabbath He gave this testimony as to the truth of His coming.

By myself I can do nothing; I judge only as I hear, and my judgment is just, for I seek not to please myself but him who sent me. If I testify about myself, my testimony is not valid. There is another who testifies in my favor, and I know that his testimony about me is valid. You have sent to John and he has testified to the truth. Not that I accept human testimony; but I mention it that you may be saved. John was a lamp that burned and gave light, and you chose for a time to enjoy his light.

I have testimony weightier than that of John. For the very work that the Father has given me to finish, and which I am doing, testifies that the Father has sent me. And the Father who sent me has himself testified concerning me. You have never heard his voice nor seen his form, nor does his word dwell in you, for you do not believe the one he sent. You diligently study the Scriptures because you think that by them you possess eternal life. These are the Scriptures that testify about me, yet you refuse to come to me to have life.

I do not accept praise from men, but I know you. I know that you do not have the love of God in your hearts. I have come in my Father's name, and you do not accept me; but if someone else comes in his own name, you will accept him. How can you believe if you accept praise from one another, yet make no effort to obtain the praise that comes from the only God?

But do not think I will accuse you before the Father. Your accuser is Moses, on whom your hopes are set. If you believed Moses, you would believe me, for he wrote about me. But since you do not believe what he wrote, how are you going to believe what I say? (John 5:30-47, NKJV)

Muhammad, by contrast, did not serve the people but only his personal lusts for power and domination over his fellow man. He led a life of immorality. He never prophesied anything concerning God's will for the human race. No one ever gave testimony as to his veracity or the purpose of his existence. Instead of living a life of peace and personal sacrifice in service to God, he led a life of a warrior who slaughtered thousands who would not submit to his will and pleasure. He also demanded that his followers do the same or they too would be killed. Muhammad's life and example did not demonstrate love or compassion toward anyone. To the contrary, he was ruthless and a barbarian in his teaching and practice. He lusted after women and children and had multiple wives to satisfy his urges. "And no wonder," the Apostle Paul wrote, "for Satan himself masquerades as an angel of light. It is not surprising, then, if his servants masquerade as servants of righteousness. Their end will be what their actions deserve" (2 Corinthians 11:14-15).

The Righteous Man

The followers of Yahweh, the God of the Jews and Christians and the disciples of Jesus Christ are called to a life of righteousness. While called, none can attain it as evidenced by the millions of spiritually and morally fallen Jews and Christians worldwide. The Qur'an also provides evidence that the followers of Allah are called to righteousness. "Surely those who believe and those who are Jews and the Sebeans and the Christians whoever believes in Allah and the last day and does good—they shall have no fear nor shall they grieve" (surah 5:69; also 2:62).

"You are the best of the nations raised up for (the benefit of) men," surah 3:110 states; "you enjoin what is right and forbid the wrong and believe in Allah; and if the followers of the Book had believed it would have been better for them; of them (some) are believers and most of them are transgressors."

The theme of righteousness continues in verses 114 and 115: "They [followers of the Book who] believe in Allah and the last day, and they enjoin what is right and forbid the wrong, and they strive with one another in hastening to [do] good deeds, and those are among the good. And whatever good they do, they shall not be denied it, and Allah knows those who guard (against evil)."

Based on the violent history of Islam it would seem that the call to righteousness in the Qur'an is fallacious rhetoric or has mostly fallen on deaf ears of its followers. The official proclamation of Islam and its teachings over the centuries is that "evil is good." Islam's prophet of "change" was evil and barbaric and far from a righteous leader and example. However, the position of Islam and its adherents over the centuries is that Muhammad's murderous raids, pillages, rapes and enslavements were justified, righteous and good—in fact commanded by the "loving" god, Allah. Beheadings and mutilations are also good and remain so to this day. And the Holocaust? That evil did not occur. It is a fabrication of the Jews and Christians. Therefore, evil is good and whatever evil you can deny, that also is good. Righteousness and truth? Do not expect to find them among the teachings and many followers of true Islam.

God's People Are Called to Righteousness

"Righteousness exalts a nation, but sin is a disgrace to any people," wrote the wise King Solomon (Proverbs 14:34). Sin never advances the cause of God or His people—only righteousness. Likewise it is revealed in Proverbs 29:2 that, "When the righteous thrive, the people rejoice; when the wicked rule, the people groan."

Throughout the Qur'an there are numerous verses that stipulate that *Allah loves those who do good to others*. "And what (reason) have we that we should not believe in Allah and in the truth that has come to us, while we earnestly desire that our Lord should cause us to enter with the good people [viz., count us among the righteous] (surah 5:84)?"

"Blessed are those who are persecuted because of righteousness," Jesus preached in His Sermon on the Mount, "for theirs is the kingdom of heaven" (Matthew 5:10). The Qur'an is conspicuously silent on the concept of one being persecuted for the sake of righteousness while speaking volumes on the call to persecute those who disbelieve in Allah and his Apostle.

> And kill them [the infidels] wherever you find them, and drive them out from whence they drove you out, and persecution is severer than slaughter … And fight with them until there is no persecution, and religion should be only for Allah …. (surah 2:191, 193)

In clear distinction, the Apostle Paul calls the disciples of Jesus to a much higher ground. "But you, man of God, flee from all this [evil], and pursue righteousness, godliness, faith, love, endurance and gentleness" (1 Timothy 6:11). This higher ground of morality was also espoused by Solomon when he wrote: "Better a little with righteousness than much gain with injustice" (Proverbs 16:8).

Both the Bible and the Qur'an call upon its adherents to refrain from hateful speech. However, the Qur'an appears to offer a loophole. Once again, Proverbs presents an unequivocal moral ground for God's followers. "The mouth of the righteous is a fountain of life, but violence overwhelms the mouth of the wicked …. The tongue of the righteous is choice silver, but the heart of the wicked is of little value. The lips of the righteous nourish many, but fools die for lack of judgment" (Proverbs 10:11, 20-21).

The Qur'an implies a similar call to morality. "Allah does not love the public utterance of hurtful speech, unless (it be) by one to whom injustice has been done …" (surah 4:148). There is, however, some ambiguity in this verse. Allah's believers are called to abstain from hateful words, unless, of course, they feel they have been victimized—which the violent and abusive Muslim will claim and use as justification for hateful oratory and acts. "The righteous hate what is false, but the wicked bring shame and disgrace. Righteousness guards the man of integrity, but wickedness overthrows the sinner" (Proverbs 13:5-6).

Jesus Is the Example

The sole and only authoritative and pure example of righteousness that God ever placed on earth was Jesus Christ. It was not Muhammad; it was not any of the prophets of the Bible; it was not the Apostles of Jesus. "Whatever happens," the Apostle Paul wrote to the church in Philippi, "conduct yourselves in a manner worthy of the gospel of Christ" (Philippians 1:27a).

Of course, Muslims *do* believe that it is Muhammad that is the premier model for godly living. "Certainly you have in the Apostle of Allah an excellent exemplar [other versions: "beautiful pattern of conduct" or "good example for everyone"] for him who hopes in Allah and the latter day and remembers Allah much" (surah 33:21).

In response, the Apostle Paul would likely retort as he did in his second letter to the Corinthians who were being swayed by false apostles. "Do not be unequally yoked together with unbelievers.

For what fellowship has righteousness with lawlessness? And what communion has light with darkness? And what accord has Christ with Belial [Satan]? Or what part has a believer with an unbeliever (2 Corinthians?" (6:14-15, NKJV).

"The LORD is righteous in all his ways and loving toward all he has made," David wrote (Psalm 145:17). In the popular *The Lord is my shepherd* Psalm 23, David exclaimed in verse three, "He guides me in paths of righteousness for his name's sake." Note that righteousness is not for man's sake but for God's benefit. While righteous behavior brings blessings to the one living in righteousness, it should not bring glory to the person but to God.

In Jeremiah's prophecy about the Messiah, the coming King of the Jews from the lineage of David, he proclaimed Him *The Lord Our Righteousness.*

> *"Behold, the days are coming," says the Lord, "That I will raise to David a Branch of righteousness; a King shall reign and prosper, and execute judgment and righteousness in the earth. In His days Judah will be saved, and Israel will dwell safely; now this is His name by which He will be called: The Lord Our Rightiousness." (viz. YHWH Tsidkenu) (Jeremiah 23:5-6, NKJV)*

Even the Qur'an professes that Jesus is among the righteous. "And Zakariya [Zachariah] and Yahya [John the Baptist] and Isa [Jesus] and Ilyas [Elijah]; every one was of the good [viz. righteous]; and Ismail and Al-Yasha [Elisha] and Yunus [Jonah] and Lut [Lot]; and every one We made to excel (in) the worlds. And from among their fathers and their descendents and their brethren, and We chose them and guided them into the right way (surah 6:85-870." Please note that Jesus and many of the prophets of the Bible are listed among the righteous but Muhammad is not.

"You see," the Apostle Paul wrote, "at just the right time, when we were still powerless, Christ died for the ungodly. Very rarely will anyone die for a righteous man, though for a good man someone might possibly dare to die. But God demonstrates his own love for us in this: While we were still sinners, Christ died for us" (Romans 5:6-8). Muhammad died for no one. As an unrighteous person his death meant nothing in God's plan to save mankind. Only through the sacrificial death of a purely righteous and sinless man could God accomplish His plan of redemption for ungodly, sin-laden man.

The Apostle John clearly understood this sacrifice for sin. "My dear children, I write this to you so that you will not sin. But if anybody does sin, we have one who speaks to the Father in our defense—Jesus Christ, the Righteous One" (1 John 2:1). Not only is Jesus the example of God's righteousness on earth, He is the only one that can act as an advocate for the sinner before the throne of God Almighty. Muhammad was neither an advocate nor an intercessor on the behalf of mankind. He was just a sinner like everyone else—nothing more, nothing less.

"If you know that he [Jesus] is righteous, you know that everyone who does what is right has been born of him" (1 John 2:29).

But None Are Righteous

During the time of Noah mankind had become so depraved that God could not tolerate the wanton sinfulness. "God saw how corrupt the earth had become, for all the people on earth had corrupted their ways" (Genesis 6:12). God's solution was to destroy all mankind with a worldwide flood and save only Noah's family and Noah, "a righteous man, blameless among the people of his time, and he walked with God" (Genesis 6:9). After the destruction, God made a covenant with Noah: "Never again will all life be cut off by the waters of a flood; never again will there be a flood to destroy the earth" (Genesis 9:11). And God has kept His promise. Is it because man has become righteous before God? Far from it. Man has become even more sinful.

"The fool [morally deficient one] says in his heart, 'There is no God.' They are corrupt, their deeds are vile; there is no one who does good" (Psalm 14:1). Mankind has fallen so far from God that the only way back to God was (and continues to be) through a Redeemer—one who would refine mankind, not by flood or fire, but through a blood sacrifice on the cross, washing away the sin of all who would call upon the name of Jesus Christ and Him only.

"As it is written: 'There is no one righteous, not even one'" (Romans 3:10).

Righteousness By Faith

Since no one can achieve righteousness by his own thoughts or deeds, how then, can one attain such a high standard of virtue? Righteousness, according to God, can only be truly obtained through faith in the One who was truly righteous—Jesus Christ. It can not be achieved through good deeds, right thinking, obeying the Law or righteous living. "Therefore," the Apostle Paul instructed the church in Rome, "no one will be declared righteous in his sight by observing the law; rather, through the law we become conscious of sin. But now a righteousness from God, apart from law, has been made known, to which the Law and the Prophets testify. This righteousness from God comes through faith in Jesus Christ to all who believe. There is no difference" (Romans 3:20-22).

After his salutation to the church in Rome, Paul laid down the foundational relationship between righteousness and faith. "For in the gospel a righteousness from God is revealed, a righteousness that is by faith from first to last, just as it is written: 'The righteous will live by faith'" [Habakkuk 2:4] (Romans 1:17). Because God lives within believers in Jesus Christ through the presence of the Holy Spirit, Christians are considered to be the living temple of God on earth. "Don't you know," Paul wrote to the Corinthians, "that you yourselves are God's temple and that God's Spirit lives in you? If anyone destroys God's temple, God will destroy him; for God's temple is sacred, and you are that temple" (1 Corinthians 3:16-17).

Muslims can only represent Allah on earth through good deeds and obedience to his law. They are not the embodiment of Allah on earth. Christians, on the other hand, are presumed to be living temples of God's presence on earth through the personification of God in Christ Jesus through the indwelling of the Holy Spirit. Christians in and of themselves are not righteous, but the Holy Spirit within them by the appropriation of faith in Christ will lead a Christian into all righteousness—if such a believer will permit that to happen.

"Do not offer the parts of your body to sin, as instruments of wickedness," Paul continued in his letter to Roman Christians, "but rather offer yourselves to God, as those who have been brought from death to life; and offer the parts of your body to him as instruments of righteousness" (Romans 6:13).

In the same letter Paul persisted in his theme of personal righteousness through the power of the indwelling Holy Spirit:

You, however, are controlled not by the sinful nature but by the Spirit, if the Spirit of God lives in you. And if anyone does not have the Spirit of Christ, he does not belong to Christ. But if Christ is in you, your body is dead because of sin, yet your spirit is alive because of righteousness. (Romans 8:9-10)

"What is more," Paul penned to the church in Philippi, a coastal city in northern Greece, "I consider everything a loss compared to the surpassing greatness of knowing Christ Jesus my Lord, for whose sake I have lost all things. I consider them rubbish, that I may gain Christ and be found in him, not having a righteousness of my own that comes from the law, but that which is through faith in Christ—the righteousness that comes from God and is by faith" (Philippians 3:8-9). Nothing one can possess can compare with the righteousness of God—not from keeping the law, but from a free gift of faith that God gives to all those who believe in His Son and His salvation work on the cross.

Islamic Teaching and the Ten Commandments

Jews, Christians and Muslims are to reject sin as defined by their respective holy books. But it is the definition of what is sin that Muslims are separated from Jews and Christians. Allah, according to Muhammad's revelations in the Quran, approves of his followers breaking most of the Ten Commandments that Jehovah God gave to the Jews through Moses (whom Muslims count as one of their apostles and prophets)—the same Ten Commandments that Christians are to uphold as well. Yet, as revealed in surah 5:49, Muslims are also to abide by the Ten Commandments.

Hence, judge between the followers of earlier revelation in accordance with what God has bestowed from on high, and do not follow their errant views; and beware of them, lest they tempt thee away from aught that God has bestowed from on high upon thee. And if they turn away [from His commandments], then know that it is but God's will [thus] to afflict them for some of their sins: for, behold, a great many people are iniquitous indeed.[1]

"For of this you can be sure," Paul wrote to the church in Ephesus from his prison cell in Rome, "No immoral, impure or greedy person—such a man is an idolater—has any inheritance in the kingdom of Christ and of God. Let no one deceive you with empty words, for because of such things God's wrath comes on those who are disobedient (Ephesians 5:5-6)." While it is impossible for earthly man to adhere to the Ten Commandments, Christians, by yielding to the power of the indwelling Holy Spirit can achieve such success.

Commandment #1

You shall have no other gods before [besides] *me.* (Exodus 20:3)

According to the Bible and the tenets of faith of both Jews and Christians, there is only one God and He is YHWH (Yahweh) or Jehovah (Greek). He is not Buddha, Zeus, Allah, one of the many Hindu gods or goddesses or a god by any other name, attributes or deification. He is *God*—the Great *I AM* (Exodus 3:14) or *I WILL BE WHAT I WILL BE*. He is the Alpha and Omega, the Beginning and the End and there are *no other gods before* or after Him.

Commandment #2

You shall not make for yourself an idol in the form of anything in heaven above or on the earth beneath or in the waters below. You shall not bow down to them or worship them; for I, the Lord your God, am a jealous God, punishing the children for the sin of the fathers to the third and fourth generation of those who hate me, but showing love to a thousand {generations} of those who love me and keep my commandments. (verses 4-6)

Muslims claim to worship the one and only true god and are commanded to turn from idol worship. However, every year thousands of Muslim pilgrims trek to Mecca to march around the Ka'bah or Ka'aba, a pre-Islamic shrine that housed 360 pagan gods of ancient Arabic peoples, including one named *Allah*.[2, 3]

Commandment #3

You shall not misuse the name of the Lord your God, for the LORD will not hold anyone guiltless who misuses his name. (verse 7)

Here the Jews and Muslims have it over many Christians. Jews and Muslims revere the name of Yahweh and Allah, respectfully. They would never dream of misusing or disrespecting the name of the god they worship. Too many insincere or "nominal" Christians frequently abuse the name of God and Christ in their everyday conversation, much to their disgrace and defamation of the Holy God and His Son.

Commandment #4

Remember the Sabbath day by keeping it holy. Six days you shall labor and do all your work, but the seventh day is a Sabbath to the LORD your God. On it you shall not do any work, neither you, nor your son or daughter, nor your manservant or maidservant, nor your animals, nor the alien within your gates. For in six days the Lord made the heavens and the earth, the sea, and all that is in them, but he rested on the seventh day. Therefore the Lord blessed the Sabbath day and made it holy. (verses 8-11)

True believers, whether Jews, Christians or Muslims, make every attempt to keep their respective Sabbath days holy and set aside to worship their Holy One. For Muslims, the Sabbath is Friday (hadith 2:1); for the Jews, it is Saturday, and for the majority of Christians it has traditionally been recognized as Sunday. In addition, Christians are called to see every day as a holy day in which to give God the glory and honor in everything they do and say.

Commandment #5

Honor your father and your mother, so that you may live long in the land the Lord your God is giving you. (verse 12)

Most God-fearing adherents among the Jews, Christians and Muslims make every attempt to honor their parents. However, it may vary among the societies and cultures in which the respective faiths are practiced. Muslims, in particular, and some Jewish sects place a very high value on honoring their elders.

Commandment #6

You shall not murder. (verse 13)

The majority of the civilized world recognizes murder—the unlawful and unwarranted killing of an innocent person—as a sinful or heinous act. Among the majority of Christians and Jews the only acceptable time to take another person's life is in self-defense or during combat of national defense or the so-called "just" war. Both Jews and Muslims, through their respective holy books are taught to practice an "eye for an eye" mode of justice. The Qur'an provides no prohibitive teaching on the killing of another, except that of not killing one's children or a fellow believer. It does convincingly teach (as will be presented later in this chapter and elsewhere) that killing of infidels—all those who refuse to worship Allah—is permissible at any time; as is the killing of an apostate or son or daughter who dishonors the family. Jihad, the perpetual state of war against the infidel, is seen as just cause for taking innocent life—men, women, children—at any time and any place for the *cause of Allah*.

Commandment #7

You shall not commit adultery. (verse 14)

Adultery is a sin among Jews and Christians. It is clearly forbidden in their holy scriptures. Yet, among both groups it is a sin too frequently committed—especially among Christians. While Muslims too are to abstain from such an act, their holy prophet practiced it and promoted it among his followers, complete with Allah's acceptance.

Commandment #8

You shall not steal. (verse 15)

All three faiths and the world societies and cultures in general believe that stealing at most any level is a transgression that needs to be dealt with under common or religious law. However, among Muslims, stealing from their infidel enemy is seen as permissible. It was taught and practiced with abandon by Muhammad as he pillaged communities of unbelievers near and far. The teaching and tradition of Muslim looting of its neighbors has continued for over fourteen centuries.

Commandment #9

You shall not give false testimony against your neighbor. (verse 16)

Deceitfulness and lying are abhorrent to the God of the Jews and Christians. Muhammad gave his followers permission—with the apparent blessing of Allah—to lie whenever it was convenient or to their advantage, as long as they did not lie about Allah.

Commandment #10

You shall not covet your neighbor's house. You shall not covet your neighbor's wife, or his manservant or maidservant, his ox or donkey, or anything that belongs to your neighbor. (verse 17)

While God chastised David severely for coveting Bathsheba, the beautiful wife of Uriah the Hittite (2 Samuel 12:7-12), Allah approved of Muhammad's lust for the beautiful Zaynab bint Jarsh, the wife of Zayd, Muhammad's adopted son. Muhammad coveted his neighbor's riches throughout his prophetic life; mounting dozens of raids to procure wealth for himself and his army of believers.

"You are not a God who takes pleasure in evil;" wrote the psalmist David, "with you the wicked cannot dwell. The arrogant cannot stand in your presence; you hate all who do wrong. You destroy those who tell lies; bloodthirsty and deceitful men the LORD abhors" (Psalm 5:4-6). There are no gray areas with God Almighty. Sin is sin; righteousness is righteousness; evil is evil and good is good. The same can not be said of Allah and his principles that have been handed down through the centuries via the Qur'an, ahadiths, sunnahs and many of the imams and clerics of Islam.

The only truly obedient and godly life lived on earth before God was that of Jesus Christ—the only one without sin. He was and is mankind's only example of a righteous life. Believers in His saving work on the cross are called to follow His exemplar life in all arenas.

> *Do nothing out of selfish ambition or vain conceit, but in humility consider others better than yourselves. Each of you should look not only to your own interests, but also to the interests of others.*
>
> *Your attitude should be the same as that of Christ Jesus: Who, being in very nature God, did not consider equality with God something to be grasped, but made himself nothing, taking the very nature of a servant, being made in human likeness. And being found in appearance as a man, he humbled himself and became obedient to death—even death on a cross! Therefore God exalted him to the highest place and gave him the name that is above every name, that at the name of Jesus every knee should bow, in heaven and on earth and under the earth, and every tongue confess that Jesus Christ is Lord, to the glory of God the Father.* (Philippians 2:3-11)

Jesus was and continues to be mankind's only genuine servant-leader and teacher of God's truth. The Apostle John gave a clear illustration of Jesus' mindset of servanthood. "When he had finished washing their feet, he put on his clothes and returned to his place," John wrote. "'Do you understand what I have done for you?' he asked them. 'You call me 'Teacher' and 'Lord,' and rightly so, for that is what I am. Now that I, your Lord and Teacher, have washed your feet, you also should wash one another's feet. I have set you an example that you should do as I have done for you. I tell you the truth, no servant is greater than his master, nor is a messenger greater than the one who sent him'" (John 13:14-16).

The Apostle Peter also understood the concept of sacrificial service. In 64 A.D., when Nero looked to the Christians as a scapegoat for the burning of Rome, Christianity became outlawed and its practitioners persecuted. Peter wrote to the Christians in the Roman provinces which would become modern-day Turkey: "To this you were called, because Christ suffered for you, leaving you an example, that you should follow in his steps. 'He committed no sin, and no deceit was found in his mouth [Isaiah 53:9].' When they hurled their insults at him, he did not retaliate;

when he suffered, he made no threats. Instead, he entrusted himself to him who judges justly" (1 Peter 2:21-23). Not long after this and his second letter, Peter was crucified upside down in 68 A.D.—refusing to be crucified as his Lord and Savior.

Of Women and Wives

Jesus honored and respected women on the same level as men and taught His disciples to do the same. He did not discriminate between male or female; Jew or Gentile; believer or non-believer. All were the same in His sight—children of the Living God in need of *The Savior*. Jesus did not even elevate His own mother above others.

Someone told [Jesus], *"Your mother and brothers are standing outside, wanting to speak to you."*

He replied to him, "Who is my mother, and who are my brothers?" Pointing to his disciples, he said, "Here are my mother and my brothers. For whoever does the will of my Father in heaven is my brother and sister and mother." (Matthew 12:47-50)

Just like men, Jesus forgave the sins of women (Luke 7:36-48); blessed them (Luke 7:50); healed them and cast evil spirits from them (Luke 8:1-3a; 13:10-13) and looked to them for support (Luke 8:3b). Jesus had equal empathy toward all, including women. A woman that touched the hem of His garment was instantly healed of chronic bleeding (Matthew 9:20-22) as an example of His unreserved compassion.

One of the most touching of biblical stories and illustration of the compassion of Jesus was when He was presented with a woman caught in the act of adultery. (John 8:3-11) The religious leaders brought her before Jesus and said, "Teacher, this woman was caught in the act of adultery. In the Law Moses commanded us to stone such women. Now what do you say?"

Jesus did not immediately respond, but instead, bent down and wrote something in the dirt with His finger. Finally, He rose up and calmly said, "If any one of you is without sin, let him be the first to throw a stone at her." That simple challenge pricked the collective consciences of her accusers and one by one they all departed. When all her accusers had disappeared, Jesus looked at the woman and asked her, "Woman, where are they? Has no one condemned you?"

The woman responded, "No one sir." To which Jesus replied, "Then neither do I condemn you … Go now and leave your life of sin."

The Apostle Paul, who never walked with Jesus in the flesh, but knew his Master through a vision and revelation knowledge, propagated Jesus' non-prejudicial teachings. In his letter to the young church in Galatia where new Christians were slipping once again under Jewish law, Paul wrote, "There is neither Jew nor Greek, slave nor free, male nor female, for you are all one in Christ Jesus" (Galatians 3:28).

Female Chattel

Muhammad, in stark contrast, had contempt for women and demeaned them and encouraged his followers to see them the same way. In all Muslim societies women tend to be viewed as nothing more than chattel—a human possession for the man to do with as he sees fit. Betrothal, the practice of a father promising his pubescent daughter to marry a man often unknown to her, is commonplace in many Muslim societies. Whether the girl or young woman is in agreement with her spousal selection is of no measure of importance. Hadith 7:62:67 gives the impression that women did have some say in who they married. "The Prophet said, 'A matron should not be given in marriage except after consulting her; and a virgin should not be given in marriage except after her permission.'" And how is one to know if the woman gives her permission? "The people asked, 'O Allah's Apostle! How can we know her permission?' He said, 'Her silence (indicates her permission).'" So, in a society where women can not freely speak their mind, her silence (which is expected of her) is her consigned approval. If she has the nerve to protest or refuses to marry her betrothed she is seen as dishonoring her father and her family. She then can be banished or shunned, or in some cases murdered by her father, brother or uncle in order to remove the "shame" from the family.

"Your wives are your tilth [cultivated field] for you," Muhammad taught, "so go into your tilth [have intercourse] when you like, and do good beforehand for yourselves; and be careful (of your duty) to Allah, and know that you will meet Him, and give good news to the believers" (surah 2:223). For the Muslim woman to decline or resist her husband's sexual desires is unthinkable and forbidden. "The Prophet said, 'If a man invites his wife to sleep with him and she refuses to come to him, then the angels send their curses on her till morning'" (hadith 7:62:121).

Muhammad also permitted women to be demeaned as sex objects through temporary contractual marriages purely of the man's desire to relieve his sexual urges. These usually one-sided sexual trysts could last for only fifteen minutes or up to three days. They were then broken off by the man without any writ of divorce, no obligation of alimony or bequeath of inheritance. The marriage was one solely for immediate sexual pleasure for the man—a sort of legalized use of prostitution initiated by the male believer.

Such a contractual marriage was permitted by Muhammad when his men were away in battle without their wives. "We were on an expedition with Allah's Messenger (may peace be upon him)," narrated Abdullah, "and we had no women with us. We said: Should we not have ourselves castrated? He (the Holy Prophet) forbade us to do so. He then granted us permission that we should contract temporary marriage for a stipulated period giving her a garment ... (hadith of Sahih Muslim, 2:8:3243 and also of Sahih Bukhari" 7:62:13). To justify this perversion of marriage, surah 5:87 was quoted: "O you who believe! do not forbid (yourselves) the good things which Allah has made lawful for you and do not exceed the limits; surely Allah does not love those who exceed the limits."

"This marriage," wrote Egyptian pastor Dr. Saleem Almahdy, "is not bound to any of the rules set in Islam for a normal marriage. In this 15-minute marriage, the man does not write a contract of marriage or divorce after he enjoys her. The only thing the man has to do is to give the woman something, like money or food."[4]

Female Inferiority

The negative and inferior portrayal of women, as well as the approval of mistreatment, is a recurring theme in many ahadith. To make sure that women knew their place in male-dominated Islamic society, Muhammad taught that, "After me I have not left any affliction more harmful to men than women" (hadith 7:62:33). In the same hadith volume and book, verse 30, "Allah's Apostle said, 'Evil omen is in the women, the house and the horse.'" Wives and children were also to be suspected of evil doing. "... And the Statement of Allah: 'Truly, among your wives and your children, there are enemies for you (i.e. may stop you from obedience to Allah)'" (hadith 7:62:29).

Even Aisha, Muhammad's youngest wife complained, "It is not good that you people have made us (women) equal to dogs and donkeys" (hadith 1:498). This is analogous to the Qur'an proclaiming that Jews are nothing more than pigs and monkeys (surah 5:60).

In some verses of the Qur'an it is implied that women have equality. "Whoever does good whether male or female and he is a believer," Muhammad revealed in surah 16:97, "We will most certainly make him live a happy life, and We will most certainly give them their reward for the best of what they did." Although women, as child bearers, were to be accorded some respect, it's hard to imagine that happening on a daily basis when Muhammad taught that women were evil; the primary reason for men turning from Allah and that women dominated the fires of hell.

"The Prophet said, 'I stood at the gate of Paradise and saw that the majority of the people who entered it were the poor, while the wealthy were stopped at the gate (for the accounts). But the companions of the Fire were ordered to be taken to the Fire. Then I stood at the gate of the Fire and saw that the majority of those who entered it were women'" (hadith 7:62:124).

Again, "The Prophet replied, 'I saw Paradise ... I also saw the Hell-fire and I had never seen such a horrible sight. I saw that most of the inhabitants were women.' The people asked, 'O Allah's Apostle! Why is this so?' The Prophet replied, 'Because of their ungratefulness'" (hadith 2:161).

In other ahadith Muhammad continued to put women in their proper subservient place. "After finishing the prayer, [Muhammad] delivered the sermon and ordered the people to give alms. He said, 'O people! Give alms.' Then he went towards the women and said. 'O women! Give alms, for I have seen that the majority of the dwellers of Hell-Fire were you (women).' The women asked, 'O Allah's Apostle! What is the reason for it?' He replied, 'O women! You curse frequently, and are ungrateful to your husbands. I have not seen anyone more deficient in intelligence and religion than you'" (hadith 2:541). Although Muhammad is admonishing the women to give alms as a command from Allah, he later (in the same hadith) reverses himself. When Zainab, the wife of Ibn Masud, came to the Prophet's house to ask if it was acceptable to give away some of her jewelry for the poor, Muhammad told her that her husband and children disserved it more than the poor.

In hadith 1:301, Muhammad clarifies a woman's deficiencies further. "The women asked, 'O Allah's Apostle! What is deficient in our intelligence and religion?' He said, 'Is not the evidence of two women equal to the witness of one man?' They replied in the affirmative. He said, 'This is the deficiency in her intelligence. Isn't it true that a woman can neither pray nor fast during her menses?' The women replied in the affirmative. He said, 'This is the deficiency in her religion.'" Notice that the deficiencies ascribed to women are those assigned them by Muhammad and the male-dominated society of which he was a part and that a woman's *deficiency* had nothing to do with her intelligence but with a biological function beyond her control. Once again, in hadith 3:826, Muhammad asserts a woman's mental lack. "The Prophet said, 'Isn't the witness of a woman equal to half of that of a man?' The woman said, 'Yes.' He said, 'This is because of the deficiency of a woman's mind.'"

Even praying or worshipping Allah in a mosque with men is prohibitive to women. According to Islamic teaching the women would defile the mosque and be a distraction to the men during their religious duties.[5]

While striking a woman is forbidden by Christian teaching and frowned upon by the civilized Western World, Muhammad and the Qur'an encourage it. "Men are the maintainers of women because Allah has made some [men] of them to excel others and because they spend out of their property;" surah 4:34 states, "the good women are therefore obedient [the truly devout ones], guarding the unseen [intimacy] as Allah has guarded; and (as to) those [women] on whose part you fear desertion, admonish them, and leave them alone in the sleeping-places and beat [scourge] them; then if they obey you, do not seek a way [of harm] against them; surely Allah is High, Great."

There is one prohibition for wife beating. Muhammad declared, "None of you should flog his wife as he flogs a slave and then have sexual intercourse with her in the last part of the day (hadith 7:62:132)." The implication might be that the husband is to have sex first, then flog his wife. A good beating before intercourse would likely diminish a woman's desire to participate.

According to hadith 7:67:449, Muhammad forbade his followers from beating animals in the face. No such courtesy is afforded Muslim women. Such mistreatment of women is permissible some Muslim scholars say because the Bible states that Job beat his wife. Surah 38:44 erroneously conveys that God told Job to "take in your hand a green branch and beat her with it and do not break your oath ...." There is no such reference in the Bible. Job, according to the Bible, "... was blameless and upright; he feared God and shunned evil" (Job 1:1).

If a Muslim man does beat his wife, as he is expected to do if she displeases him in any way, the Prophet said, "A man will not be asked as to why he beat his wife" (Abu-Dawud hadith 11:2142).

If a woman had the misfortune of being one of Muhammad's wives then she received double punishment for her transgressions. "O wives of the prophet! Whoever of you commits an open indecency, the punishment shall be increased to her doubly; and this is easy to Allah" (surah 33:30). But a wife of the Prophet could also get a *double reward* if she obeyed Muhammad in every way (verse 31).

While a woman could get double the punishment or double the reward, her worth is considered to be only half that of a man. When it came to an inheritance, the male receives twice as much as the female. "Allah enjoins concerning your children:" Muhammad disclosed, "The male shall have the equal of the portion of two females" (surah 4:11). In addition, a woman's testimony was not equal to that of a man. "... and call in to witness from among your men two witnesses; but if there are not two men, then one man and two women from among those whom you choose to be witnesses ..." (surah 2:282). The witness of two women was necessary to equal that of one man.

Jesus, on the other hand, accorded women with nothing but the highest respect and taught His disciples to do likewise. In one of the most poignant stories of the gospels is the encounter Jesus had with the Samaritan woman at Jacob's well near the town of Sychar in Samaria (about 30 miles north of Jerusalem). The Jews of Jesus' era despised the Samaritans and shunned them. Jesus engaged her in friendly conversation and asked her for a drink.

"The Samaritan woman said to him, 'You are a Jew and I am a Samaritan woman. How can you ask me for a drink?'" (John 4:9). Jews would not associate with Samaritans and considered them to be unapproachable.

"Jesus answered her, 'If you knew the gift of God and who it is that asks you for a drink, you would have asked him and he would have given you living water'" (verse 10).

The woman became confused, noticing that Jesus had nothing to use to draw water from the well, so how could He offer her water? Jesus was patient and took the opportunity for a life-saving spiritual lesson.

"Jesus answered, 'Everyone who drinks this water will be thirsty again, but whoever drinks the water I give him will never thirst. Indeed, the water I give him will become in him a spring of water welling up to eternal life'" (verses 13 and 14). Not getting the spiritual analogy, the woman requested this unique water that Jesus offered. Jesus proceeded to reveal her past life to her, much to her astonishment. Although the woman had had five husbands and the man she was now living with was not her husband, Jesus did not condemn her. Instead, He revealed to her the truth of worshipping the only true God.

Jesus declared, "Believe me, woman, a time is coming when you will worship the Father neither on this mountain nor in Jerusalem. You Samaritans worship what you do not know; we worship what we do know, for salvation is from the Jews. Yet a time is coming and has now come when the true worshipers will worship the Father in spirit and truth, for they are the kind of worshipers the Father seeks. God is spirit, and his worshipers must worship in spirit and in truth." (John 4:21-24)

Jesus then disclosed that He was the Messiah that the Samaritans had also been waiting for (John 4:25-26). The woman became overwhelmed with joy and ran into town to announce the arrival of *the Christ* (John 4:25-26, 28-29). There is quite a difference in Jesus' approach to women and that of Muhammad.

Whereas in Islam the man is to dominate and control women and his wife, in Christianity the husband is to provide servant leadership as Christ leads the church. The Apostle Paul made this clear in his letter to the church in Ephesus.

> *For the husband is the head of the wife as Christ is the head of the church, his body, of which he is the Savior. Now as the church submits to Christ, so also wives should submit to their husbands in everything.*
>
> *Husbands, love your wives, just as Christ loved the church and gave himself up for her to make her holy, cleansing her by the washing with water through the word, and to present her to himself as a radiant church, without stain or wrinkle or any other blemish, but holy and blameless. In this same way, husbands ought to love their wives as their own bodies. He who loves his wife loves himself. After all, no one ever hated his own body, but he feeds and cares for it, just as Christ does the church—for we are members of his body. "For this reason a man will leave his father and mother and be united to his wife, and the two will become one flesh." This is a profound mystery—but I am talking about Christ and the church. However, each one of you also must love his wife as he loves himself, and the wife must respect her husband.* (Ephesians 5:23-33)

Paul, following the teaching of Christ, was affirming that husbands and wives should treat each other with mutual respect and love. Husbands, in particular, are called to love their wives just as Christ loves the church, the representation of His body on earth. The Apostle Peter, likewise, called male Christ followers to honor and respect their wives. "Husbands, in the same way be considerate as you live with your wives, and treat them with respect as the weaker partner and as heirs with you of the gracious gift of life, so that nothing will hinder your prayers" (1 Peter 3:7).

In his first letter to the Corinthians, Paul also asserted that, "For the unbelieving husband has been sanctified through his wife, and the unbelieving wife has been sanctified through her believing husband. Otherwise your children would be unclean, but as it is, they are holy" (1 Corinthians 7:14).

Multiple Wives

By revelation from Allah, Muhammad was free to take as many wives as he wanted. "O Prophet!" Allah revealed to Muhammad, "surely We have made lawful to you your wives whom you have given their dowries, and those [slaves] whom your right hand possesses out of those whom Allah has given to you as prisoners of war, and the daughters of your paternal uncles and the daughters of your paternal aunts, and the daughters of your maternal uncles and the daughters of your maternal aunts who fled with you; and a believing woman if she gave herself to the Prophet, if the Prophet desired to marry her—**specially for you, not for the (rest of) believers**; We know what We have ordained for them concerning their wives and those whom their right hands possess in order that no blame may attach to you; and Allah is Forgiving, Merciful (surah 33:50, author's emphasis)." Muhammad could have whatever woman he wanted in marriage and as many wives as he desired and no woman was free to resist or deny him. He had special self-serving dispensation from Allah to do as it pleased him. Partly as a result of this freedom for a Muslim man to almost any woman he wanted, marrying first cousins was and is permissible among Muslims, a practice abhorred in Western culture.

Verse 51 of the same surah certifies Muhammad's freedom of personal indulgence. "You may put off whom you please of them, and you may take to you whom you please," Allah continues, "and whom you desire of those whom you had separated provisionally [like Zayd's wife]; no blame attaches to you; this is most proper, so that their eyes may be cool and they may not grieve, and that they should be pleased, all of them, with what you give them, and Allah knows what is in your hearts; and Allah is Knowing, Forbearing."

Polygamy or the taking of concubines was also practiced by some Mideastern Jews, although it was clearly forbidden by God in the Old and New Testament. It is recorded in Genesis 2:22-23 that God made woman out of the rib of man and that "The man said, 'This is now bone of my bones and flesh of my flesh; she shall be called 'woman,' for she was taken out of man.'"

"For this reason," the Scripture states, "a man will leave his father and mother and be united to his wife, and they will become one flesh" (Genesis 2:24). Now, a man can become *one* only with one woman at a time. To become *one* with multiple women at the same time or through multiple simultaneous marriages is emotionally and spiritually impossible. To convince oneself of this possibility is a complete deception from Satan.

Yahweh, the God of the Jews and Christians detests polygamy. He made this clear through the prophet Malachi.

> *Another thing you do: You flood the Lord's altar with tears. You weep and wail because he no longer pays attention to your offerings or accepts them with pleasure from your hands. You ask, "Why?" It is because the Lord is acting as the witness between you and the wife of your youth, because you have broken faith with her, though she is your partner, the wife of your marriage covenant.*
>
> *Has not the LORD made them one? In flesh and spirit they are his. And why one? Because he was seeking godly offspring. So guard yourself in your spirit, and do not break faith with the wife of your youth.* (Malachi 2:13-15)

Jesus also taught of the importance of a monogamous marriage relationship (Matthew 19:5-6 and Mark 10:7-8). Muhammad advocated multiple and simultaneous marriages. "And if you fear that you cannot act equitably towards orphans, then marry such women as seem good to you, two and three and four ..." (surah 4:3). Of course, if the man felt he could not treat that many wives fairly, then he should only marry one.

Paul also advocated the one wife/one husband directive. "Now the overseer [deacon, elder] must be above reproach, the husband of but one wife, temperate, self-controlled, respectable, hospitable, able to teach, not given to drunkenness, not violent but gentle, not quarrelsome, not a lover of money" (1 Timothy 3:2-3; see also 1 Timothy 3:12; Titus 1:6).

However, Allah (he who Muslims claim is the God of the Bible) sees marriage and fidelity differently. "O Prophet!" disclosed Allah to Muhammad, "why do you forbid (yourself) that which Allah has made lawful for you; you seek to please your wives; and Allah is Forgiving, Merciful (surah 66:1)." Allah is telling Muhammad that he should not withhold himself from having intercourse with all his wives anytime he wanted. In the next verse, Allah annuls any oaths Muhammad might have made concerning such a matter. "Allah indeed has sanctioned for you the expiation [end] of your oaths ...." If any of Muhammad's wives refused his sexual advances, Allah also had a word of warning for them. "Maybe, his Lord, if he divorces you, will give him [Muhammad] in your place wives better than you, submissive, faithful, obedient, penitent, adorers, fasters, widows and virgins" (surah 66:5).

Apparently Muhammad was quite capable of performing his husbandly duties with all his wives. "Anas bin Malik said, 'The Prophet used to visit all his wives in a round, during the day and night and they were eleven in number.' I asked Anas, 'Had the Prophet the strength for it?' Anas replied, 'We used to say that the Prophet was given the strength of thirty (men) ...'" (hadith 1:268).

After twenty-five years of monogamous life with his first wife, Khadija, Muhammad in 620 A.D. (a few days after Khadija's death), married his second wife, Sawda, an elderly widow. The same year, Aisha (or Aishah), the six-year old daughter of Abu Bakr, was betrothed to Muhammad. Three years later he would consummate his marriage with Aisha when she was only nine years old and he was fifty-three.[6, 7, 8] Probably because of the West's distaste for an adult to marry a child, some modern Islamic web sites claim that Aisha was sixteen when Muhammad married her.[9] This contradicts the wealth of historical Islamic records and Aisha herself, who in hadith 7:62:64 is recorded to have said, "that the Prophet married her when she was six years old and he [Muhammad] consummated his marriage when she was nine years old, and then she remained with him for nine years (i.e., till his death)." Ursa also related the same facts in hadith 7:62:88.

In 625, Muhammad married his fourth wife, Hafsah, a young widow of eighteen or twenty years old. Muhammad was fifty-five at the time. A year later he married two more widows, Um Salma and Zaynab.[10, 11, 12]

Muhammad's seventh, eighth and ninth marriages took place in 627 A.D. He married the twenty-year old Juweiriyeh, a captive from the Banu Mustaliq tribe that Muhammad had defeated. He also married Zaynab bint Jarsh and the Jewess, Rayhana.[13, 14, 15] The marriage to Zaynab has also become historically controversial. Zaynab was the beautiful wife of Zayd (or Zaid), Muhammad's adopted son. When Muhammad went to visit one day he inadvertently saw Zaynab scantily clad and from that moment lusted after her.[16] Zayd knew that the Prophet wanted her and offered to divorce his wife so Muhammad could marry her. Muhammad struggled with his covetousness briefly until he got this convenient revelation from Allah giving him the go ahead to fulfill his wanton desire.

> And when you said to him to whom Allah had shown favor and to whom you had shown a favor: Keep your wife to yourself and be careful of (your duty to) Allah; and you concealed in your soul what Allah would bring to light, and you feared men, and Allah had a greater right that you should fear Him. But when Zaid had accomplished his want [or come to the end of his union with] her, We gave her to you as a wife, so that there should be no difficulty for the believers in respect of the wives of their adopted sons, when they have accomplished their want of them; and Allah's command shall be performed.

> There is no harm in the Prophet doing that which Allah has ordained for him; such has been the course of Allah with respect to those who have gone before; and the command of Allah is a decree that is made absolute. (surah 33:37-38)

It was not uncommon in Muhammad's era for fathers without sons (as Muhammad was) to adopt the sons—either minors or adults—of widows. In this surah, it appears that Allah is rewarding Muhammad for his lust and covetousness, and thus setting the example for his followers that might also have adopted sons who were married.

Yahweh, the God of the Jews and Christians says, "You shall not covet your neighbor's house. You shall not covet your neighbor's wife, or his manservant or maidservant, his ox or donkey, or anything that belongs to your neighbor." (Exodus 20:17) The Hebrew word for "neighbor" also stands for an associate, friend, brother, husband or companion.

In 628, at age fifty-eight, Muhammad married Maryam (or Mary the Copt), Um Habeeba and Sufia, his tenth, eleventh and twelfth wives. Maryam was a Christian; Sufia was a Jew taken as a captive and "booty" after Muhammad had her husband and relatives slaughtered. Juweiriyeh and Sufia (or Safiya) were procured by Muhammad for his 7th and 10th wives after he attacked and killed the inhabitants of Khaibar (hadith 5:59:512) and attacked the Bani Mustaliq without warning, killing the men and taking the women and children captive (hadith 3:46:717). In 629, Muhammad married Maimoona, his thirteenth and last wife.[17, 18, 19] Of the thirteen women, eleven were considered his wives, two his concubines.

Divorce

Jesus taught against divorce except in the case where a husband or wife was unfaithful to the bonds of marriage. "Haven't you read," he replied, "that at the beginning the Creator 'made them male and female,' and said, 'For this reason a man will leave his father and mother and be united to his wife, and the two will become one flesh'? So they are no longer two, but one. Therefore what God has joined together, let man not separate" (Matthew 19:4-6). His response was to the Pharisees—Jewish religious leaders—who were trying to trap Him in an interpretation of the Law of Moses. "Jesus replied, 'Moses permitted you to divorce your wives because your hearts were hard. But it was not this way from the beginning. I tell you that anyone who divorces his wife, except for marital unfaithfulness, and marries another woman commits adultery'" (Matthew 19:8-9).

Muhammad, through revelation from Allah, condoned divorce—that is, a man divorcing his wife. "Those who swear that they will not go in to their wives should wait four months; so if they go back, then Allah is surely Forgiving, Merciful. And if they have resolved on a divorce, then Allah is surely Hearing, Knowing .... Divorce may be (pronounced) twice; then keep (them) in good fellowship or let (them) go with kindness ..." (surah 2:226-227, 229). In all this decision-making concerning divorce it is "the men [who] are a degree above [the women]" (verse 228). Women can not divorce their husbands, only husbands can divorce their wives, and for any reason. For the men, "There is no blame on you if you divorce women when you have not touched them [sexually] ... (surah 2:236).

On the surface, Muhammad did promote the concept of reconciliation in matters of divorce. "And if a woman fears ill usage or desertion on the part of her husband," he revealed in . 4:128, "there is no blame on them, if they effect a reconciliation between them, and reconciliation is better, and avarice has been made to be present in the (people's) minds; and if you do good (to others) and guard (against evil), then surely Allah is aware of what you do." Divorce and reconciliation, however, are always on the man's terms. It is the woman who has to beg for forgiveness for disappointing her husband. Hadith 7:62:134 (Bukhari) clarifies this surah. Narrated by Aisha, Muhammad's youthful wife, "It concerns the woman whose husband does not want to keep her with him any longer, but wants to divorce her and marry some other lady, so she says to him: 'Keep me and do not divorce me, and then marry another woman, and you may neither spend on me, nor sleep with me.'"

Aisha, Muhammad's pre-pubescent wife, later recited this verse: "If a woman fears cruelty or desertion on her husband's part (i.e. the husband notices something unpleasant about his wife, such as old age or the like, and wants to divorce her, but she asks him to keep her and provide for her as he wishes) …. 'There is no blame on them if they reconcile on such basis'" (hadith 3:859). Although this sounds like a resolution to divorce it also indicates that the Muslim man is free to divorce his wife for most any reason, including how she looks. It is not uncommon in Muslim societies that as women age their husbands seek more youthful and sexually vibrant mates—after all, Muhammad did.

In a clear distinction, the Bible stresses fidelity with the wife of one's youth. "Drink water from your own well—share your love only with your wife. Why spill the water of your springs in the streets, having sex with just anyone? You should reserve it for yourselves. Never share it with strangers. Let your wife be a fountain of blessing for you. Rejoice in the wife of your youth. She is a loving deer, a graceful doe. Let her breasts satisfy you always. May you always be captivated by her love" (Proverbs 5:15-19, NLT).

According to the Qur'an, a man can divorce his wife without any responsibility for her long-term provision as long as he has not consummated the marriage. It is recommended, however, that he give her something as they separate. "O you who believe! when you marry the believing women, then divorce them before you touch them, you have in their case no term which you should reckon; so make some provision for them and send them forth a goodly sending forth" (surah 33:49).

While Allah makes ready provision for divorce and fully accepts it as part of the normalcy of life, the God of the Bible clearly rejects divorce. "'**I hate divorce**,' says the LORD God of Israel, 'and **I hate a man's covering himself with violence** as well as with his garment,' says the LORD Almighty. So guard yourself in your spirit, and do not break faith" (Malachi 2:16, author's emphasis).

"It has been said," Jesus taught during His discourse during the Sermon on the Mount, "'Anyone who divorces his wife must give her a certificate of divorce.' But I tell you that anyone who divorces his wife, except for marital unfaithfulness, causes her to become an adulteress, and anyone who marries the divorced woman commits adultery" (Matthew 5:31-32).

The Apostle Paul re-emphasized the importance of marriage fidelity and commitment between one man and one woman.

> *Now for the matters you wrote about: It is good for a man not to marry. But since there is so much immorality, each man should have his own wife, and each woman her own husband. The husband should fulfill his marital duty to his wife, and likewise the wife to her husband. The wife's body does not belong to her alone but also to her husband. In the same way, the husband's body does not belong to him alone but also to his wife. Do not deprive each other except by mutual consent and for a time, so that you may devote yourselves to prayer. Then come together again so that Satan will not tempt you because of your lack of self-control.* (1 Corinthians 7:1-5)

In the Apostle Paul's admonitions about marriage, particularly the marriage of a Christian to an unbeliever, he stated, "But if the unbeliever leaves, let him do so. A believing man or woman is not bound in such circumstances; God has called us to live in peace" (1 Corinthians 7:15). That is why Paul felt it was very important that a follower of Jesus Christ not be *yoked* to an unbeliever (2 Corinthians 6:14).

Adultery

Committing adultery—whether by a husband or wife—was prohibited by Jesus, but it was condoned by Muhammad (surah 66:5). In fact, Muhammad promoted it as Allah's will when he lusted after the beautiful Zaynab, the wife of his adopted son, Sayd (surah 33:37-38, noted previously).

Jesus, to the contrary, taught, "You have heard that it was said, 'Do not commit adultery.' But I tell you that anyone who looks at a woman lustfully has already committed adultery with her in his heart" (Matthew 5:27-28).

Muhammad also had a solution for the temptation of lust and the commitment of adultery. "When a woman fascinates [arouses] any one of you," he was heard to say, "and she captivates his heart, he should go to his wife and have an intercourse with her, for it would repel what [lust] he feels." (hadith 2:8:3242 of Sahil Muslim) There is no call for repentance of the sin of lust. Just go have sex with your wife—whether she is willing or not—and thus remove your sexual desires. Remember what Jesus said: "anyone who looks at a woman lustfully has already committed" the sin of "adultery with her in his heart."

Muhammad, the sinful Apostle of Allah, was no exception to lustful desires. "Jabir reported that Allah's Messenger (may peace be upon him) saw a woman, and so he came to his wife, Zainab [the beautiful former wife of Zayd], as she was tanning a leather and had sexual intercourse with her. He then went to his Companions and told them: The woman advances and retires in the shape of a devil, so when one of you sees a woman, he should come to his wife, for that will repel what he feels in his heart' (hadith 2:8:3240, Sahil Muslim). Note that it is the woman's fault and sin for making Muhammad lust after her. But what is the recourse for all those unmarried Muslim men who lust after women and have no wife to relieve themselves? Perhaps they are expected to enter into a quick, but temporary contractual marriage.

In the Gospel of Luke, Jesus further elaborates on the relationship of divorce and adultery. "Anyone who divorces his wife and marries another woman commits adultery, and the man who marries a divorced woman commits adultery" (Luke 16:18). The wise King Solomon said it this way: "Can a man walk on hot coals without his feet being scorched? So is he who sleeps with another man's wife; no one who touches her will go unpunished" (Proverbs 6:28-29).

Can a Muslim man commit adultery and be held accountable? According to the Qur'an it would seem that both male and female adulterers are to be held accountable and punished. Surah 24 begins,

"(This is) a chapter which we have revealed and made obligatory and in which we have revealed clear communications that you may be mindful" (verse 1). The revelation proceeds to explain the consequences of adultery. "(As for) the fornicatress and the fornicator, flog each of them, (giving) a hundred stripes, and let not pity for them detain you from the matter of obedience to Allah ... and let a party of believers witness their chastisement. The fornicator shall not marry any but a fornicatress or idolatress, and (as for) the fornicatress, none shall marry her but a fornicator or an idolater; and it is forbidden to the believers" (verses 2-3).

The equality of the punishment seems straight forward until one reads surah 4:15. "And as for those who are guilty of an indecency [such as adultery] from among your women, call to witnesses against them four (witnesses) from among you; then if they bear witness confine them to the houses until death takes them away or Allah opens some way for them." In reality, women adulterers receive the harsher punishment. In fact, in some Islamic societies that practice shari'a law, the adulterous woman is stoned to death.[20] Also, in many Islamic societies, a woman can not bring testimony against an accused adulterer, but a man's testimony against an adulteress will be accepted.[21]

Murder

Do not murder! The biblical admonition is simple enough but has been the subject of great debates and schisms in the Christian church since the day of Christ. Outside the context of the *just war* or self-defense, the majority of Christians around the world would agree that murder is a sinful act worthy of punishment according to biblical and/or societal laws. To complicate this injunction, Jesus took it a major step forward. "You have heard that it was said to the people long ago, 'Do not murder, and anyone who murders will be subject to judgment.' But I tell you," Jesus declared, "that anyone who is angry with his brother will be subject to judgment" (Matthew 5:21-22a). Jesus is equating unrepentant anger with murder.

However, Jesus' teaching on this subject did not stop there either. Jesus called for and demanded a higher morality for His disciples.

You have heard that it was said, "Eye for eye, and tooth for tooth" (Exodus 21:23-25). *But I tell you, Do not resist an evil person. If someone strikes you on the right cheek, turn to him the other also. And if someone wants to sue you and take your tunic, let him have your cloak as well. If someone forces you to go one mile, go with him two miles. Give to the one who asks you, and do not turn away from the one who wants to borrow from you.* (Matthew 5:38-42)

Muslims reject this type of morality as simplistic and ludicrous. They completely subscribe to the pre-Christ barbarism of retaliatory vengeance of an eye-for-an-eye, life-for-a-life justice. God Almighty, through Jesus Christ clearly repudiated such justice, calling mankind to a much higher plain of responsibility and righteousness. Muhammad, in his form of castigating justice claimed to speak for the same god that Jesus represented. Obviously, he did not. God would not go back on His word and instruction that He cemented in place through His Son, Jesus.

Not only did God reverse His call for *eye for eye* justice, but He called for the followers of His Son to reach for a higher level of response to those that attacked or persecuted them.

You have heard that it was said, "Love your neighbor and hate your enemy." (Leviticus 19:18) But I tell you: Love your enemies and pray for those who persecute you, that you may be sons of your Father in heaven. He causes his sun to rise on the evil and the good, and sends rain on the righteous and the unrighteous. If you love those who love you, what reward will you get? Are not even the tax collectors doing that? And if you greet only your brothers, what are you doing more than others? Do not even pagans do that? Be perfect, therefore, as your heavenly Father is perfec.t. (Matthew 5:43-48)

Muhammad, however, subscribed to the ancient form of retaliatory justice as he revealed in surah 2:178. "O you who believe! retaliation is prescribed for you in the matter of the slain; the free for the free, and the slave for the slave and the female for the female …" In the perverted form of justice that the Qur'an is noted for, one could not just go kill the murderous guilty party. If someone killed your slave, you would not necessarily go and kill the murderer. In the life-for-a-life mentality you more than likely kill one of his slaves—as innocent as he or she might be. The rest of verse 178 also provides another "out" for the guilty party. If the murderer is a person of means, then he might offer the family of the one he murdered *blood money* as a form of restitution.

Surah 17:33 makes it clear that it is Allah that gives the permission for retaliatory killing. "And do not kill any one whom Allah has forbidden, except for a just cause, and whoever is slain unjustly, We have indeed given to his heir authority [to retaliate], so let him not exceed the just limits in slaying; surely he is aided." According to Allah it is okay to take vengeance, but do not take it too far and kill too many. But what about suicide bombers who take innocent life indiscriminately? That type of mass murder, as described previously, falls under the privilege and grace of *jihad*. As it has been pointed out before in the Qur'an and ahadiths, Jews, Christians, pagans and apostates fall into a special unprotected class of past, current and future victims known as *infidels*—all those who refuse to accept Islam as the only way of life. Here, there is no justice for this Islamic prey under the commands of jihad. The *mujahidin* or holy warriors are free to take life wherever, whenever and of whomever they please without clear cause or respect for the innocent—whether female, child or otherwise.

> *There are six things the LORD hates, King Solomon related, seven that are detestable to him: haughty eyes, a lying tongue, hands that shed innocent blood, a heart that devises wicked schemes, feet that are quick to rush into evil, a false witness who pours out lies and a man who stirs up dissension among brothers.* (Proverbs 6:16-19, author's emphasis)

The prophet Isaiah also is quick to reaffirm God's abhorrence of the shedding of innocent blood. "Their feet rush into sin; they are swift to shed innocent blood. Their thoughts are evil thoughts; ruin and destruction mark their ways. The way of peace they do not know; there is no justice in their paths. They have turned them into crooked roads; no one who walks in them will know peace" (Isaiah 59:7-8). Isaiah's words, spoken some twenty-seven centuries ago, might just as well have been directed at today's jihadists, as well as the Muslim clerics and Islamic faithful who remain silent or cheer the mujahidin on in their bloodshed.

God Almighty, the only true God of justice would have this to say: "When you spread out your hands in prayer, I will hide my eyes from you; even if you offer many prayers, I will not listen. Your hands are full of blood; wash and make yourselves clean. Take your evil deeds out of my sight! Stop doing wrong, learn to do right! Seek justice, encourage the oppressed. Defend the cause of the fatherless, plead the case of the widow" (Isaiah 1:15-17). Allah apparently has no such reservations about hearing the prayers of his faithful murderers killing in the *cause of Allah*.

Lying and Deceit

While Muslims worldwide will vehemently deny it, the truth is that Muslims, in general, are masters of deceit and lying and the teachings of their holy prophet condone and encourage it. "Do not give false testimony," Jesus taught His followers (Matthew 19:18). At first glance it would appear that the command of Allah in the Quran would agree: "And do not mix up the truth with the falsehood, nor hide the truth while you know it (surah 2:42)." But the reality and practice of Muslims is much different in both the historic past and the present.

Honesty and truthfulness have been the hallmarks of much of Western society—especially those based in a Judeo-Christian foundation—for two millennia. "However, unlike most religions," author Abdullah Al Araby wrote, "within Islam there are certain provisions under which lying is not simply tolerated, but actually encouraged."[22]) It may be hard for a Westerner to fathom the practice of habitual lying and deceit, but for the Muslim it is easy—especially before an infidel or in a non-Muslim country—to proclaim that "black" is "white" or that "darkness" is "light" or that a "lie" is "truth." Deception and lies roll off some Muslim tongues like some harmless platitude.

The Western world still does not seem to accept this presentation of reality as their diplomats enter into one "agreement" after another with Muslims in the Middle East and elsewhere, accepting their lies as the truth. Relying on or trusting a Muslim to tell the truth when your well-being depends on it, is sort of like trusting that the twenty-foot high bulging, seeping earthen dam you are standing under will not break during the deluge you are witnessing. Even when Muslims are caught in the act of lying, most will deny culpability. They will even go to the extreme of venting anger at your accusations to the point where you begin to believe they must be telling the truth since their passion of resentment has risen so high. Even the taking of an oath in a court of law can come to naught if a Muslim looks to the Qur'an for guidance. "Allah does not call you to account for what is vain [worthless] in your oaths, but He will call you to account for what your hearts have earned …" (2:225). A Muslim can lie under oath and have a clear conscience as long as he believes he was doing it for the cause of Allah.

"There is only cursing [that is to pronounce a curse upon someone], lying and murder, stealing and adultery [says the Lord]; they break all bounds, and bloodshed follows bloodshed. Because of this the land mourns [dries up] and all who live in it waste away; the beasts of the field and the birds of the air and the fish of the sea are dying" (Hosea 4:2-3).

Lying *about* Allah or Muhammad is forbidden. However, a Muslim can deny Allah if one's life depends on it; but cannot lie *about* Allah. "And who is more unjust than he who forges a lie against Allah," Muhammad revealed in surah 6:93, "or says: It has been revealed to me; while nothing has been revealed to him … Give up your souls; today shall you be recompensed with an ignominious chastisement because you spoke against Allah other than the truth …."

Lying was acceptable to Muhammad, unless you were lying about him. "I heard the Prophet saying, 'Ascribing false things to me is not like ascribing false things to anyone else. Whoever tells a lie against me intentionally then surely let him occupy his seat in Hell-fire'" (hadith 2:378).

But Muhammad also said: "He who makes peace between the people by inventing good information or saying good things [though they be lies], is not a liar" (hadith 3:857).

In hadith 32:6303 of Sahih Muslim gives Muslims permission to lie under three circumstances: 1) In the heat of battle; 2) in an effort to bring reconciliation between persons and 3) in the communication between a husband and wife if it brings about a resolution. Other Islamic traditions support telling lies if it is to save one's life; bring about peace or settlement between peoples; influence a woman or when a Muslim is on a journey or mission.[23]

"Muslims believe that war means deception," acknowledged Qur'an scholar and former Muslim, Mark Gabriel, "so lying is an important element of war in Islam .... it's OK to lie to non-Muslims to protect yourself when you are a minority in their country."[24] Muhammad routinely practiced deception during his military campaigns. "When the Prophet .... intended to go on an expedition [of war], he always pretended to be going somewhere else, and he would say: 'War is deception'" (Dawud hadith 14:2631). Muhammad's practice of deception did not stop there. He advocated lying when it came to deceiving his enemies. A long hadith of Bukhari (5:59:369) describes Muhammad's permission for one of his cohorts, Muhammad bin Maslama, to use a lie so that Maslama could deceive an opponent of Muhammad's and kill him. "There is deceit in the hearts of those who plot evil, but joy for those who promote peace" (Proverbs 12:20).

According to Al Araby, "... Muslims' unintentional lies are forgivable and that even their intentional lies can be absolved by performing extra duties ... Muslims can lie while under oath and can even falsely deny faith in Allah, as long as they maintain the profession of faith in their hearts."[25] Christians, on the other hand, can not deny their faith in Christ, not even under persecution or the threat of death. "Whoever acknowledges me before men," Jesus shared with His followers, "I will also acknowledge him before my Father in heaven. But whoever disowns me before men, I will disown him before my Father in heaven" (Matthew 10:33).

Lying in Islam can be conditional. It depends on the reason for one's telling a lie. Iranian Imam Abu Hammid Al-Ghazali (1058-1111 A.D.), One of the greatest Islamic Jurists, theologians and mystical thinkers[26] in the history of Islam had this clarifying insight on when it is permissible to lie. "Speaking is a means to achieve objectives. If a praiseworthy aim is attainable through both telling the truth and lying, it is unlawful to accomplish through lying because there is no need for it. When it is possible to achieve such an aim by lying but not by telling the truth, it is permissible to lie if attaining the goal is permissible."[27] One can deny the truth even when the truth is obvious, as long as it achieves an imagined or stated goal.

A good case of such a denial of reality came when CBS-television aired a story and video on June 19 and 20, 2007 of a humanitarian atrocity discovered in Iraq that was first reported by CBS News chief foreign correspondent Lara Logan on June 18. Members of the U.S. military 82nd Airborne Division, while on patrol in central Baghdad, discovered an orphanage for special needs boys. The twenty-four boys were naked, emaciated, lying on concrete floors and tied by the foot to their cribs. The facility was well stocked with food and brand new clothing, but none of it was being used for the boys.[28]

The American soldiers rescued the boys and took them to a place of safety where they were fed, clothed and received medical attention. Logan marveled at the compassion of the U.S. soldiers and how the children responded so readily to their love and touch. The story and video aired throughout the world, including Iraqi television. "I imagine," Logan wrote in her journal, "that Iraqi people will react with anger and shame. Many will blame the United States for bringing this to them ... For many Americans, that will be hard to comprehend, especially since American soldiers carried these boys in their arms and saved their lives."[29]

So, what was the response of the Iraqi Labor and Social Affairs Minister to all this? Avoiding any responsibility, "he lashed out at the U.S., calling America Iraq's enemy." On CBS Evening News on June 20, 2007 it was reported that: "As CBS News was filming new scenes on Wednesday, the minister was telling the nation these boys are perfectly healthy—and that Logan's report was a lie,"[30]

Anyone who claims to be in the light but hates his brother is still in the darkness. Whoever loves his brother lives in the light, and there is nothing in him to make him stumble. But whoever hates his brother is in the darkness and walks around in the darkness; he does not know where he is going, because the darkness has blinded him. (1 John 2:9-11)

Once again, "dark" is "light" and "lies" are "truth." Such responses from a Muslim are covered under the doctrine of *taqiyya* (*taqeya, taqiya*) or "lying for the faith. A Muslim may tell any lie when they are threatened. In short, a Muslim can lie as a holy duty to deceive and gain an advantage over the unbeliever."[31] Lying to an adversary (whether infidel or fellow Muslim) is acceptable, even though the

Qur'an states, "surely Allah does not guide him who is extravagant, a liar" (surah 40:28).

"Indeed until any non-Muslim comes to realize the degree to which this mentality [of lying] plays out when dealing with many Muslims," wrote Joel Richardson in his book, *Will Islam Be Our Future?*, "it will be only too easy to lose touch with a healthy sense of objectivity. When dealing with someone who is purposefully deceptive, trusting individuals ... are like sheep being led to the slaughter."[32] Author Gabriel would likely agree, for "... those practicing Islam in the United States, Canada, Europe, Australia ... are in the weakened stage [of jihad]. These Muslims are very good at presenting themselves as loving, caring and forgiving people. They compromise any conflict between the image they want to present and what they truly believe.

"They get along with Christians and Jews as if they were brothers. They present Islam to these countries as the answer to all humanity's problems. These Westernized Muslims present their religion as if it stands for mercy, freedom, fairness and reconciliation."[33] Nothing could be further from the truth of Islam's teaching and practice.

"Not a word from their mouth can be trusted;" wrote David, "their heart is filled with destruction. Their throat is an open grave; with their tongue they speak deceit (Psalm 5:9)." While David was talking about his enemies his words ring true for today for anyone who practices lying and deception.

> *"'These are the things you shall do:'"* God revealed to the prophet Zechariah, *"'Speak each man the truth to his neighbor; Give judgment in your gates for truth, justice, and peace; Let none of you think evil in your heart against your neighbor; And do not love a false oath. For all these are things that I hate,' Says the Lord."* (Zechariah 8:16-17, NKJV)

Lying and deceit are primary tools of the devil. Forget not, that "... lying and deceit are a part of the Islamic mind-set," warned Gabriel (34). To which the Apostle John would add: "Many deceivers, who do not acknowledge Jesus Christ as coming in the flesh, have gone out into the world. Any such person is the deceiver and the antichrist" (2 John 7).

> *Jesus said to them, "If God were your Father, you would love me, for I came from God and now am here. I have not come on my own; but he sent me. Why is my language not clear to you? Because you are unable to hear what I say. You belong to your father, the devil, and you want to carry out your father's desire. He was a murderer from the beginning, not holding to the truth, for there is no truth in him. When he lies, he speaks his native language, for he is a liar and the father of lies. Yet because I tell the truth, you do not believe me! Can any of you prove me guilty of sin? If I am telling the truth, why don't you believe me? He who belongs to God hears what God says. The reason you do not hear is that you do not belong to God. (John 8:42-47)*

Conclusion

Muhammad was not a man of high integrity and morality. He was not a righteous man after God's own heart like Noah, Abraham, David or Jesus. He was a sin-laden man in need of repentance and forgiveness for his multitude of sins against God and mankind. He was an opportunist that took advantage of the pagan lifestyle and morals of his day. Although he presented a moralistic law to offset pagan beliefs, his own self-serving way of life was no better than the murderous tribal chiefs of the Arabian Peninsula. He did not improve upon God's revelation that came through Jesus Christ. Instead, he denied the truth and moral code of conduct that was sent by God through Jesus and the Jewish prophets, making a mockery out of the Ten Commandments and all that Jesus Christ stood for and taught.

Freedom From Sin

I was born in the homeland of Christ, the beloved Palestine. We are the so-called "Arabs of the West Bank ...."

But I remember when I was a child, I would soar high in my daydreams in which I was to liberate Palestine. These dreams of liberation always ended up with me being martyred.

... God was my first and last refuge. I prayed and fasted until I was fifteen years old, but what was the result? Did a miracle happen to set us free? Did our homeland return to us? Did God raise our martyrs from the graves? ... Why did death, genocide, banishment, and imprisonment become our destiny and not other nations and peoples? ... I rejected this fate, this destiny, and this God .... So, my life lost its meaning; all morals and principles withered in me .... I committed all the sins and transgressions ...

... *I happened to meet a European young* [Christian] *lady named Tina ... She* [became my] *godly wife, an encouragement toward changing and reflecting God's own image.... I was still leading a sinful life....* My years were spent in slavery to the devil, but in the middle of thorns stood a firm flower with never-ending love—my wife, Tina .... Tina was praying for me. She was asking God to save and rescue me.... God, the true love, does not tempt anyone with evil. God is the source of good, virtue, holiness, and providence. I listened attentively; my heart was thirsty.... Tina wanted me to come to know Christ ... She started to quote all the prophecies that spoke about the Christ. Almost three hundred prophecies ... so I cried out to God, "Let me know the truth. Where is the real and true religion? ... are You still far away from us in the seventh heaven, or have You incarnated and drawn near to us?"

... "Oh, Jesus Christ, if You are really my God and Savior, change my life and turn my black heart into a white one, from a heart full of hatred to a heart full of love, from an unclean heart to a heart full of holiness, purity, and cleanness."... I started to experience a joy that filled my inner being ... My whole life started to change.

... *Now there's a God I am ready to lose everything for; He is all-sufficient for me.*

Khalil
"From the Homeland of Christ"
Into the Den of Infidels, 2003

References

1. *Qur'an*, Muhammad Asad translation. Isamicity.com. Http://www. islamicity.com/Quransearch. Accessed August 10, 2007.
2. Caner, Ergun Mehmet and Emir Fethi Caner. *Unveiling Islam*, 2002. Kregel Publications, div. of Kregel. Inc., pp. 40 and 60.
3. Spencer, Robert. *The Truth About Muhammad, Founder of the World's Most Intolerant Religion*, 2006. Regnery Publishing, Inc., p.33.
4. Almahdy, Dr. Saleem. *Islam Q & A, The Voice of the Martyrs*, April, 2002.
5. Suresh, Fr. Gnana Pragash, *Understanding Islam, Part I*. Society of St. Pius X– Southern Africa, 2001. Http://www.sspxafrica.com/ documents/2001_August/Understanding_Islam.htm. Accessed March 11, 2003.
6. Spencer, pp.170-171.
7. *Muhammad's Wives*. Wikipedia. Http://en.wikipedia.org/wiki/ Muhammad%27s_marriages. Accessed August 17, 2007.
8. Caner & Caner, p.59.
9. *Detail of Marriages of Prophet*. http://www.answering-christianity. com/wives.htm. Accessed February 1, 2007.
10. Caner & Caner, p.56.
11. *Muhammad's Wives*.
12. *Detail of Marriages of Prophet*.
13. Caner & Caner, p.56.
14. *Muhammad's Wives*.
15. *Detail of Marriages of Prophet*.
16. Spencer, p.59-60.
17. Caner & Caner-56.
18. *Muhammad's Wives*.
19. *Detail of Marriages of Prophet*.
20. Spencer, p.174.
21. Ibid, p.67-68.
22. Al Araby, Abddullah, *Lying in Islam*. IslamReview.com. Http://www. islamreview.com/articles/lying.htm. Accessed November 11, 2006.
23. *Lying*. Answering-Islam.com. Http://answering-islam.org.uk/Index/L/ lying. html. Accessed November 2, 2005.
24. Gabriel, Mark A. *Islam and Terrorism*, 2002. Published by FrontLine, a Strang Company, p. 91.

25. Al Araby.

26. Nakamura, Kojiro, *Al-Ghazali, Abu Hamid (1058-1111)*. June 13, 2001 (updated June 6, 2006). Http://www.ghazali.org/articles/gz1.htm. Accessed August 20, 2007.

27. Naqib al-Misri, Ahmad ibn. *The Reliance of the Traveller* (translated by Nuh Ha Mim Keller), 1997. Amana Publications, p.745. Quoted in Http://www.Answering-islam.org.uk/Index/L/lying.html. Accessed November 2, 2005.

28. *Iraqi Orphanage Nightmare*. CBS News, Baghdad, June 18, 2007. Http://www. cbsnews.com/stories/2007/06/18/eveningnews/2946007. shtml. Accessed June 21, 2007.

29. Logan, Lara. *Clinging to Life in a Baghdad Orphanage*. CBS News, June 18, 2007. Http://www.cbsnews.com/stories/2007/06/18/ notebook/2946477.shtml. Accessed June 21, 2007.

30. *Recovering Iraqi Orphans Face Bleak Future*. CBS News, Baghdad, June 20, 2007. Http://www.cbsnews.com/stories/2007/06/20/ eveningnews/2959189. shtml. Accessed June 21, 2007.

31. Keohane, Steve. *Muhammad: Terrorist or Prophet?* BibleProbe.com, 200402007. Http://bibleprobe.com/muhammad.htm. Accessed April 1, 2007.

32. Richardson, Joel, *Will Islam Be Our Future? Chapter 16: Understanding Dishonesty and Deceit in Islam*. Answering-Islam. com. Http://answering-islam.org.uk/Authors/JR/Future/ch16_ understanding_dishonesty.htm. Accessed November 2, 2005.

33. Gabriel, p. 92

34. Gabriel, p. 95.

The Message

CHAPTER 6

God of Love
or God of Hate

Allah is exalted and pleased as he sends people to hell:
this is the fatalistic claim of Islam.

Ergun Mehmet Caner and Emir Fethi Caner
Unveiling Islam, 2002, p. 31

The Bible, both the Old Testament and the New Testament, has much to say about love. Depending on which translation of the Bible you consult, there are between 442 (King James Version) and 763 verses (New Living Translation) on the subject of love. The vast majority deal with God's love for man, man's love for God or man's command to love others (both believers and non-believers).

The Qur'an has little to say about love. Only eighty-four verses use the term love in any capacity. Only a few verses mention "Allah's love" for believers. "If you love Allah," Muhammad states, "then follow me, Allah will love you and forgive you your faults …" (surah 3:31). Or in surah 3:76: "Yea, whoever fulfills his promise and guards against evil—then surely Allah loves those who guard against evil." Allah also loves believers who do good works (surah 3:134), or encourage believers to love other believers.

The Qur'an says little about loving your neighbor and actually preaches against loving your enemy. It clearly states that Allah hates the sinner. "And fight in the way of Allah with those who fight with you, and do not exceed the limits, surely Allah does not love those who exceed the limits [that is, those who are transgressors or sinners] (surah 2:190)." In verse 276 of the same surah, it states, "… Allah does not love any ungrateful sinner." Nor does Allah love the unjust (surah 3:140). Note that Allah not only hates the sin but he hates the sinner also. However, Jesus taught that God loves the sinner, but not the sin and made it a point of his ministry to reach out to sinners—of which "all have sinned" according to the Apostle Paul (Romans 3:23).

Most of the verses on love in the Qur'an speak to what Allah *does not* love. Allah does not love aggressors (surah 2:190), or those who act corruptly (surahs 2:205; 5:64; 28:77), or those who deny the truth (surahs 3:32; 30:45), or evildoers (surahs 3:57, 140; 42:40), those who are self-conceited or boastful (surahs 4:36; 28:76; 31:18; 57:23), those who are not trustworthy (surah 4:107), those who do not do what is right (surahs 5:87; 7:55), those who are wasteful (surahs 6:141; 7:31), those who commit treachery (surah 8:58), those who are arrogant (surah 16:23), those who betray his trust or are unthankful (surah 22:38); and he certainly does not love those who worship idols instead of him (surah 2:165) or love riches (surahs 89:20; 100:8). In that list of whom Allah does not love, it would be hard for anyone to see themselves passing Allah's test of acceptance—even the most devout Muslim.

So what or whom does Allah love? Apparently, Allah has little love to spare. Allah loves only those who do (unspecified) good (surahs 2:195; 3:148; 5:13, 93; 19:96), those who repent (surah 2:222), or those who somehow keep themselves pure or purify themselves (surahs 2:222; 9:108), are patient in adversity (surah 3:146), those who trust in him (surah 3:159), or are careful of their duty to [or conscious of] him (surah 9:4, 7) or those who act rightly (surahs 49:9; 60:8). The only way to be assured of Allah's love is to fight for him. "Surely Allah loves those who fight in His way …" (Muhammad revealed in surah 61:4).

Surah 11:90 implies that repentance *might* bring about Allah's love. "And ask forgiveness of your Lord, then turn to Him; surely my Lord is Merciful, Loving-Kind." While this verse implies that Allah is a source of love, it does not assure the believer that Allah will freely give his love to the repentant believer. The verse also seems to imply that Muhammad has special favor with Allah ("my Lord"). But do other Muslim believers have favor with Allah in receiving his love?

Abandoning one's faith in Allah, while regrettable, is acceptable. Why? It is because Allah will just find someone else to replace you. He will not pursue you and try to win you back. "O you who believe!" the prophet says in surah 5:54, "whoever from among you turns back from his religion [abandons his faith], then Allah will bring a people [forth in your place], He shall love them and they shall love Him, lowly before the believers, mighty against the unbelievers, they shall strive hard in Allah's way and shall not fear the censure of any censurer; this is Allah's grace [favor], He gives it to whom He pleases [wills], and Allah is Amplegiving [infinite], [all-]Knowing."

In contrast, Jesus, in the parable of the lost sheep (Matthew 18:12-14), tells His disciples that God will go after even one lost member of the fold that wanders away.

What do you think? Jesus asked. If a man owns a hundred sheep, and one of them wanders away, will he not leave the ninety-nine on the hills and go to look for the one that wandered off? And if he finds it, I tell you the truth, he is happier about that one sheep than about the ninety-nine that did not wander off. In the same way your Father in heaven is not willing that any of these little ones should be lost.

In the Gospel of John, Jesus expands on the concept of the shepherd who makes sacrifices for his sheep and who goes after those who are not yet in the fold.

I am the good shepherd, Jesus says. The good shepherd lays down his life for the sheep. The hired hand is not the shepherd who owns the sheep. So when he sees the wolf coming, he abandons the sheep and runs away. Then the wolf attacks the flock and scatters it. The man runs away because he is a hired hand and cares nothing for the sheep.

I am the good shepherd; I know my sheep and my sheep know me—just as the Father knows me and I know the Father—and I lay down my life for the sheep. I have other sheep that are not of this sheep pen. I must bring them also. They too will listen to my voice, and there shall be one flock and one shepherd. (John 10:11-16)

It is important to note that Allah's love is conditional, while God's love from the Christian perspective is unconditional. Allah requires that man loves him first or does something for Allah that Allah considers worthy of his love. He *does not* love all people. While Allah demands complete and absolute devotion and love from his followers, he in turn, does not guarantee his love for anyone.

Allah's love is provisional, if it is to be dispensed at all. One must give away his possessions in order to show that he loves Allah (surah 2:177). In surah 3:31, it is clear, that in order to receive Allah's love and forgiveness, one must first love Allah. The powerful message of the New Testament, by contrast, tells us that "while we were still sinners" God loved us (Romans 5: 8). God loves us, His creation, first. And because He loves us, we ought also to love Him.

God is Love

The central theme of the Bible is that *God is love* and He loves those whom He created. Christianity can lay claim to one of the greatest and most reassuring verses of scripture of all the world religions in: "For God so loved the world," Jesus taught His disciples, "that He gave His only begotten Son, that whoever believes in Him should not perish but have everlasting life. For God did not send His Son into the world to condemn the world, but that the world through Him might be saved." (John 3:16-17, NKJV) Imagine! God, the Almighty, the Ruler of the Universe, loved His creation so much, that He decided that the greatest gift He could ever give mankind was to send into the world a human being who was without sin and embodied the complete thought and presence of God; endowed with God's own Spirit, for the eternal and loving purpose of redeeming mankind from its sin which separated it from God and God's love. What an earth-shaking concept that exists in no other religion but Christianity—a concept, which on the surface of man's intellect, seems so preposterous that it could only be true. Man could never have conceived of such an act by any god. Man can only conceive that he must work his way into his god's good graces through fulfilling laws or doing good works which will somehow make him worthy of his god's love and acceptance.

"God loves you! ... Yet in the Qur'an, no such statement is to be found."[1]

John 3:16-17 is such a striking contrast to the message that Muhammad brought to the world. Muhammad, according to the Qur'an was Allah's mouthpiece to condemn the world for not believing in him in the first place. Muhammad was the messenger, procurer and consummator of Allah's hate and wars upon the unbelieving Arabian world (as well as the rest of the world today). Muhammad did not come into the world as Allah's messenger of love and salvation. He came forth as Allah's apostle to persecute those who would not accept the tenets of Islamic faith as laid down by Muhammad.

A thorough search of the Qur'an will not unearth this biblical thesis of God's unmitigated love. In fact, the Qur'anic theme is quite to the contrary. Allah, according to the Qur'an and its messenger, Muhammad, not only hates sin, but he hates the transgressor and all those who do not believe in him.

"Islam is full of discrimination—against women, against non-Muslims, against Christians and most especially against Jews. Hatred is built into the religion.

"The history of Islam, which was my special area of study," wrote Mark Gabriel, "could only be characterized as a river of blood."[2]

One must ask: If God spent so much effort in the Bible and through various messengers in the Bible, as well as His own Son, to convince the world of His unconditional love for mankind, why would He send the opposite message some 600 years later? Was not the message of His love getting through, thus He had to repent and reveal His true feelings of hate for mankind? But God, according to biblical scripture, cannot lie about what He says or what He feels.

The Apostle Paul, in the salutation of his letter to Titus, wrote we have "a faith and knowledge resting on the hope of eternal life, which God, who does not lie, promised from the beginning of time" (Titus 1:2). Similarly, the writer to the Hebrews emphatically stated that "it is impossible for God to lie" (Hebrews 6:18). God *could not* and *would not* go against His covenant of love and salvation that He established through the blood and sacrifice of His dear Son some 600 years prior to the appearance of Muhammad.

The Apostle John, the one that Christ loved, makes it abundantly clear, that God is love, that love is from God and that His love abides with us through Jesus Christ. Muhammad could make no such claim—

that Allah's love abided with him. In fact, his live demonstrated the dead opposite—a life full of hatred and vengeance. The life and times of Muhammad were the antithesis of Jesus and His ministry during His short time on earth.

The Apostle John makes it profusely apparent the purpose and all inclusiveness of God's love.

Beloved, let us love one another, for love is of God; and everyone who loves is born of God and knows God. He who does not love does not know God, for God is love. In this the love of God was manifested toward us, that God has sent His only begotten Son into the world, that we might live through Him. In this is love, not that we loved God, but that He loved us and sent His Son to be the propitiation [atoning sacrifice] *for our sins. Beloved, if God so loved us, we also ought to love one another. No one has seen God at any time. If we love one another, God abides in us, and His love has been perfected in us. . . . And we have known and believed the love that God has for us. God is love, and he who abides in love abides in God, and God in him.* (1 John 4:7-12, 16, NKJV)

The shepherd king, David, in a prayer to his Lord and Almighty God acknowledged, "But you, O Lord, are a compassionate and gracious God, slow to anger, abounding in love and faithfulness" (Psalm 86:15). In another psalm of praise by an unknown writer, the psalmist states that God "is good; his love endures forever" (118:29). Psalm 136, also written by an unknown, exclaims after all twenty-six verses that, "his [God's] love endures forever."

In Psalm 23, David composed one of the most beautiful images of God's faithfulness and love ever written. David, the shepherd boy, whose life was at risk daily from the time he stepped forward on God's center stage to slay the giant known as Goliath. Being anointed king of Israel only increased the threats on his life. Yet he continually praised God and looked to Him for His unconditional love—a love that enveloped a man that frequented the dens of sin, but always returned to God in repentance and humility.

"The Lord is my shepherd, I shall not want. He makes me to lie down in green pastures, he leads me beside quiet waters, he

restores my soul. He guides me in paths of righteousness for his name's sake. Even though I walk through the shadow of death, I will fear no evil, for you are with me; your rod and your staff comfort me. You prepare a table before me in the presence of my enemies. You anoint my head with oil; my cup overflows. Surely [your] goodness and love will follow me all the days of my life, and I will dwell in the house of the Lord forever." (Psalm 23)

David was a man who knew and experienced God's love intimately. Once again, in Psalm 36:5-7, he wrote: "Your love, O lord, reaches to the heavens, your faithfulness to the skies. Your righteousness is like the mighty mountains, your justice like the great deep. O Lord, you preserve both man and beast. How priceless is your unfailing love! Both high and low among men find refuge in the shadow of your wings."

David knew his God and he knew that God was the unswerving source of the unconditional love that he daily sought. Once again, he extols the God he loves.

Praise the Lord, O my soul; all my inmost being, praise his holy name. Praise the Lord, O my soul, and forget not all his benefits—who forgives all your sins and heals all your diseases, who redeems your life from the pit and crowns you with love and compassion, who satisfies your desires with good things so that your youth is renewed like the eagle's. (Psalm 103:1-5)

Such an intimate and assured understanding of God's love seems to have escaped Muhammad's experience. Therefore, as Allah's apostle, he could not assure his followers that they would experience or have a time in their life when they would be assured of Allah's unmitigated love and compassion toward those who believe in him. Its ironic, that all the prophets that Muhammad looked to in the Bible, including Abraham, Moses, Jacob, Noah, David, John the Baptist, Jesus and others, all had an intimate understanding and assurance of God's unconditional love for them. This understanding and experience of a personal love evaded Muhammad throughout his entire lifetime—as it does the followers of Islam today.

The Apostle Paul was so assured of God's love—not only for himself, but for those he called brothers in Christ—that he ended his letters with confident reassurance such as he did in his letter to the church in the wealthy seacoast city of Corinth in ancient Greece.

> Finally, brethren, farewell. Become complete [aim for perfection]. Be of good comfort, be of one mind, live in peace; and the God of love and peace will be with you." (2 Corinthians 13:11, NKJV)

To the church in Ephesus, an ancient large port city in Asia Minor near the Aegean Sea, Paul also guaranteed the faithful that God loved them. This, he was able to do despite the fact that he was in a Roman prison at the time and the city of Ephesus was the location of the Great Temple of Diana (a Greek goddess). The city was overflowing with idol worshippers and the commerce of the city was largely dependent on silversmiths that made icons for the worship of this false god. Yet Paul encouraged this small group of believers with these words: "But because of his great love for us, God, who is rich in mercy, made us alive with Christ even when we were dead in transgressions—it is by grace you have been saved" (Ephesians 2:4).

Toward the end of his first letter to the believers in Corinth, Paul made it clear how important love—God's love—was in his eyes.

> *If I speak in the tongues [languages] of men and of angels, but have not love, I am only a resounding gong or a clanging cymbal. If I have the gift of prophecy and can fathom all mysteries and all knowledge, and if I have a faith that can move mountains, but have not love, I am nothing. If I give all I possess to the poor and surrender my body to the flames, but have not love, I gain nothing.*
>
> *Love is patient, love is kind. It does not envy, it does not boast, it is not proud. It is not rude, it is not self-seeking, it is not easily angered, it keeps no record of wrongs. Love does not delight in evil but rejoices with the truth. It always protects, always trusts, always hopes, always perseveres.*
>
> *Love never fails ....* (1Corinthians 13:1-8a)

God's Love Covenant

It is not enough that God freely expresses and gives His love to all, but His love is a covenant love. It is a love that has been sealed and delivered through the shed blood of Jesus Christ, and no other. Moses, a prophet of God that Muhammad revered, reminded the Israelites, after God rescued them from the slavery of the Egyptians that, God was faithful and they could count on His unfailing love.

Know therefore that the Lord your God is God; he is the faithful God, keeping his covenant of love to a thousand generations of those who love him and keep his commands." (Deuteronomy 7:9)

Likewise, King Solomon as he knelt and prayed before the whole assembly of Israel in front of the altar of the Lord, proclaimed, "O Lord, God of Israel, there is no God like you in heaven or on earth—you keep your covenant of love with your servants who continue wholeheartedly in your way" (2 Chronicles 6:14).

The prophets Nehemiah and Daniel also prayed a similar prayer about God's "covenant of love." (See Nehemiah 1:5; Daniel 9:4.)

God's love is irreversible; it cannot be revoked. In Psalm 89 God, through the Psalmist, expresses His faithfulness to David and his lineage.

My faithful love will be with him, and through my name his horn [strength] *will be exalted. I will set his hand over the sea, his right hand over the rivers. He will call out to me, 'You are my Father, my God, the Rock my Savior.'*

I will also appoint him my firstborn, the most exalted of the kings of the earth.

I will maintain my love to him forever, and my covenant with him will never fail. I will establish his line forever, his throne as long as the heavens endure.

If his sons forsake my law and do not follow my statutes, if they violate my decrees and fail to keep my commands, I will punish their sin with the rod, their iniquity with flogging; but I will not take my love from him, nor will I ever betray my faithfulness. I will not violate my covenant or alter what my lips have uttered. Once for all, I have sworn by my holiness—and I will not lie to David—that his line will continue forever and his throne endure before me like the sun; it will be established forever like the moon, the faithful witness in the sky. (Psalm 89:24-37)

It is important to make a note of the fact that God's love is a **covenant** love—a promise or a contract that cannot be broken (nor will God break it). God's love is *forever* and it *will never fail*. God will not even withhold or violate His covenant of love when one sins against Him. God solidified this love contract with man by sending His only begotten Son into the world to reconcile man with God through the Son's death on the cross.

Unfortunately, for the Muslim believer, Allah offers no such covenant of love or remedy of reconciliation between himself and his followers. Allah's love is conditional; it's reversible and he can withhold his love at anytime for any reason. There is no way for a Muslim to reconcile himself to Allah or to bridge this great divide to assure himself of Allah's love.

Jesus, according to the Gospel of Luke, made it clear to His followers that everyone was important to God. "Are not five sparrows sold for two pennies?" he asked. "Yet not one of them is forgotten by God. Indeed, the very hairs on your head are all numbered. Don't be afraid; you are worth more than many sparrows" (Luke 12:6-7). Again, in verses 22-26 in the same chapter, Jesus affirms God's provision for His children: "'Therefore I tell you, do not worry about your life, what you will eat; or about your body, what you will wear. Life is more than food, and the body more than clothes. Consider the ravens: They do not sow or reap, they have no storeroom or barn; yet God feeds them. And how much more valuable you are than birds! Who of you by worrying can add a single hour to his life? Since you cannot do this very little thing, why do you worry about the rest?"

This love covenant was part of God's plan from the beginning. He reaffirmed it through the institution of the Passover in Egypt. He confirmed it with the Israelites in the Sinai Desert during the forty years of wandering in the wilderness. Then He solidified it for the entire world through the shed blood of His beloved Son, Jesus Christ.

But the ministry Jesus has received is as superior to theirs [the patriarchs of the Old Testament] as the covenant of which

[Jesus] is mediator is superior to the old one, and it is founded on better promises. (Hebrews 8:6)

Jesus Christ is the only mediator, the intermediary through which man can receive God's unconditional love. There is no other go-between; no other agent or liaison. Jesus Christ, crucified, and Him only.

The Sealed Covenant

The Holy Spirit within the Christian seals God's love covenant with him. "Now hope does not disappoint, because the love of God has been poured out in our hearts by the Holy Spirit who was given to us" (Romans 5:5, NKJV).

While God loves us, He loves us for a reason. He loves us because we are His creation, but He also loves us so that we will love Him and share His love with others. Despite His love so freely given, God knows that we are powerless to love others, even with our best efforts and intentions. Therefore, He seals His covenant with those who accept His Son as Lord and Savior, with the inner presence of His Holy Spirit. It is God's presence within the believer that empowers them to act upon and fully share God's unconditional love.

The Apostle Paul proclaimed this when he wrote: "For all the promises of God in Him [Christ] are Yes, and in Him Amen, to the glory of God through us. Now He who establishes us with you in Christ and has anointed us is God, who also has sealed us and given us the Spirit in our hearts as a guarantee [of His covenant]" (2 Corinthians 1:20-22, NKJV).

The eternal reward of accepting the redemptive work of Christ on the cross and receiving Him as your personal Lord and Savior is the adoption into God's family as His very own son or daughter.

"And because you are sons [of God], God has sent forth the Spirit of His Son into your hearts, crying out, 'Abba, Father!' Therefore you are no longer a slave but a son, and if a son, then an heir [to the covenant] of God through Christ" (Galatians 4:6-7, NKJV).

Allah has no sons. Nowhere in the Qur'an is the word *son* used in any connection with Allah. Allah has no sons—spiritual, adopted or otherwise. It is beneath Allah to have such an intimate or personal relationship with mankind. Allah does not even accept "adopted" sons as real sons of his followers. (surah 3:4)

There is no covenant in Islam: no children; no shed blood; no Holy Spirit to seal a covenant.

And the Jews and the Christians say: We are the sons [children] of Allah and His beloved ones. Say: Why does He then chastise you for your faults? Nay, you are mortals from among those whom He has created; He forgives whom He pleases and chastises [causes to suffer] whom He pleases.... (surah 5:18)

What a dim view of one's god. No compassion, no reason as to who Allah will forgive or who he will punish. Allah has no children, so how could he show compassion to those who are so distant and removed from him?

On the other hand, the loving God of the Jews and Christians so loves them that He guides and corrects them when they err or go astray. "My son, do not despise the Lord's discipline and do not resent his rebuke, because the Lord disciplines those he loves, as a father the son he delights in" (Proverbs 3:11-12).

"If you endure chastening, God deals with you as with sons; for what son is there whom a father does not chasten? But if you are without chastening, of which all have become partakers, then you are illegitimate and not sons" (Hebrews 12:7-8, NKJV).

The stark contrast here is this: Allah chastises those whom he hates; God chastises those whom He loves. Why the difference? It is the difference between a distant, detached god and a God who is also a loving Father—a God who has children that He loves and cares about in a very personal, intimate way.

"And you also were included in Christ when you heard the word of truth, the gospel of your salvation. Having believed, you were marked in him with a seal, the promised Holy Spirit, who is a deposit guaranteeing our inheritance until the redemption of those who are God's possession—the praise of his glory" (Ephesians 1:13-14).

There is no place in the theology of Islam for the presence of God's spirit dwelling among and in men. Without the pouring out of God's spirit to dwell within man, there can be no sealing—no assurance—of His love covenant.

"But God demonstrates His own love toward us," the Apostle Paul says, "in that while we were still sinners, Christ died for us" (Romans 5:8, NKJV). The Apostle Paul's statement is all inclusive. No one is left out, since *all* have sinned. God could not have demonstrated any greater love for His human creation than to allow His own perfect Son to be crucified for the sins of all mankind. Allah, on the other hand, is quite selective in whom he decides to accept, for "Allah makes whom He pleases err [sin] and He guides whom He pleases. ." (surah 14:4). Jesus said, "Greater love has no one than this, than to lay down one's life for his friends (John 15:13, NKJV)." While Muhammad was undoubtedly a brave and courageous man in battle, he never laid down his life for another human being. To the contrary, he only took life away from those that opposed him.

Not only does God love us and has established a covenant of His love with us, but in times of trouble we can take refuge in Him. "He who dwells in the shelter of the Most high will rest in the shadow of the Almighty. I will say of the Lord, 'He is my refuge and my fortress, my God, in whom I trust'" (Psalm 91:1-2).

God's Love Reverberated

Jesus Christ, and only He, truly revealed the heart of God. "You have heard that it was said," Jesus commanded, "'Love your neighbor [Leviticus 19:18] and hate your enemy.' But I tell you: Love your enemies and pray for those who persecute you, that you may be sons of your Father in heaven. He causes his sun to rise on the evil and the good, and sends rain on the righteous and the unrighteous. If you love those who love you, what reward will you get?" (Matthew 5:43-46a).

We are **commanded to love** God, but we are also commanded to love others as God loves them. That is the full circle purpose of God loving His children—so that they will love Him and love others.

Moses made this clear to the Israelites during their journey out of the bondage in Egypt.

And now, O Israel, what does the Lord your God ask of you but to fear the Lord your God, to walk in all his ways, to love him, to serve the Lord your God with all your heart and with

*all your soul, and to observe the Lord's commands and decrees
that I am giving you today for your own good?
… For the Lord your God is God of gods and Lord of lords,
the great God, mighty and awesome, who shows no partiality
and accepts no bribes. He defends the cause of the fatherless and
the widow, and loves the alien, giving him food and clothing."*
(Deuteronomy 10:12-13, 17-18)

In an effort to trap Jesus on the issue of love, "One of them [a
Pharisee], an expert in the law, tested him [Jesus] with this question:
"Teacher, which is the greatest commandment in the Law?"

*Jesus replied: "Love the Lord your God with all your heart
and with all your soul and with all your mind"* [Deuteronomy
6:5]. *This is the first and greatest commandment. And the second
is like it: 'Love your neighbor as yourself* [Leviticus 19:18]. *All
the Law and the Prophets hang on these two commandments.*
(Matthew 22:35-40)

As Jesus was nearing the time of His crucifixion He re-emphasized
the commandment to love with a slight twist. "A new command I give
you: Love one another. As I have loved you, so you must love one
another. By this all men will know that you are my disciples, if you
love one another" (John 13:34-35). Notice that Jesus said this is the one
distinguishing trait of His followers by which the rest of the unbelieving
world will know that Jesus was truly sent by God.

Although the Qur'an admonishes Muslims to love Allah, there is no
such commandment in the Qur'an that requires Muslims to love their
neighbors. Who is a neighbor according to Jesus? It is not necessarily
someone who lives nearby. In the Parable of the Good Samaritan (Luke
10:25-37), Jesus demonstrates that the *neighbor* can also be a foreigner,
one who is not of like beliefs, but yet someone that shows mercy to a
complete stranger.

Allah's revelation to Muhammad in surah 60:1 forbids the followers
of Islam to love anyone who is not a believer in Allah. To offer one's
love to someone outside the faith invites Allah's wrath.

Christians, conversely, are called to "Be imitators of God,
therefore," commands the Apostle Paul, "as dearly loved children and

live a life of love, just as Christ loved us and gave himself up for us as a fragrant offering and sacrifice to God" (Ephesians 5:1-2). Followers of Christ are not to withhold love from anyone—friend or foe. Because God has so freely showered us with His love, we ought to share this abundance with others.

The Qur'an, however, orders the followers of Islam to attack and kill its enemies, even if there is no provocation to do so. "True" Muslims are required by Allah, as revealed in the Qur'an, to carry out a one-sided offensive and violent war of attrition against all those who do not accept Allah as God and follow his "commandments."

"O you who believe! fight those of the unbelievers who are near to you and let them find in you hardness [harshness]; and know that Allah is with those who guard (against evil) [or are *Al-Muttaqun* (the pious)]" (surah 9:123). Muhammad believed, taught and commanded the followers of Islam to religiously follow the will of Allah, which he believed was to persecute, plunder and kill all non-believers. "It is not fit for a prophet that he should take captives [of war] unless he has fought and triumphed [or until he has made a great slaughter] in the land" (surah 8:67). Again, this is a harsh contrast to the ministry, life and call of Jesus to His followers. The same god cannot and would not call his followers to seek out and kill unbelievers while at the same time commanding believers to love their enemies.

And let not those who disbelieve think that they shall come in first [that is, can get the better (of the godly)]; surely they will not escape. And prepare against them what force you can [or make ready your strength to the utmost of your power] and horses [of war] tied at the frontier, to frighten [or strike terror] thereby [into the hearts of] the enemy of Allah and your enemy and others besides them, whom you do not know (but) Allah knows them.... (surah 8:59-60)

God's Love is Everlasting

God's love is everlasting because His covenant is everlasting; it never ends. "Give ear and come to me;" said God through the prophet Isaiah, "hear me, that your soul may live. I will make an everlasting covenant with you, my faithful love promised to David" (Isaiah 55:3). Jesus made it clear right before His crucifixion that shedding of His blood would permanently seal God's love covenant with His children (see Matthew 26:28).

Nowhere in the Qur'an does it state that Allah has any kind of covenant with his followers. The word covenant occurs, but only when referencing God's covenant with Moses (surah 7:134), with Abraham (surah 2:124) and with the Israelites (surah 20:80). If one is to assume that Allah was the one making the covenant with Moses, Abraham and the Jews, then surah 9:111 implies that Muslims, by default, have a covenant with Allah. Exactly what kind of covenant is left wide open for interpretation.

> Surely Allah has bought of the believers their persons and their property for this [paradise], that they shall have the garden; they fight in Allah's way, so they slay and are slain; a promise which is binding on Him in the Taurat [Torah] and the Injeel [Gospel] and the Qur'an; and who is more faithful to his covenant than Allah? Rejoice therefore in the pledge which you have made; and that is the mighty achievement. (Surah 9:111)

If, indeed, by the implication in this verse, Allah has made a covenant with his followers, it is a covenant of death—*fight* and *slay*. It is not the blood covenant of God's love that God has bound Himself to with both the Jews and Christians. Muhammad apparently had a very scant understanding of such a covenant as it was prophesied and laid down in both the Old and New Testaments—texts to which Muhammad referred to frequently but had little understanding as to their uniqueness and significance.

Once again, the Apostle Paul made it clear that for those who have accepted Christ it is impossible to be separated from God's love.

> *Who shall separate us from the love of Christ? Shall trouble or hardship or persecution or famine or nakedness or danger or sword? As it is written:*
>
> *For your sake we face death all day long; we are considered as sheep to be slaughtered.* (Psalm 44:22)

> *No, in all these things we are more than conquerors through him who loved us. For I am convinced that neither death nor life, neither angels nor demons, neither the present nor the future,*

*nor any powers, neither height nor depth, nor anything else in
all creation, will be able to separate us from the love of God that
is in Christ Jesus our Lord.* (Romans 8:35-39)

Conclusion

Apparently, if one is to use the Muslim Holy Book, the Qur'an, as
a source text on the issue and relationship of Allah's love for mankind,
it would seem that Allah neither seeks nor desires an intimate love
relationship with his human creation. What love he does have is clearly
conditional—*if you do such and such, then you might be worthy of my
love.* If you are a Muslim you will never be assured of Allah's love. *If,*
after your death, you make it to Paradise, then you can assume that
Allah loves you. Of course, after you die it is too late to change your
outcome with Allah.

Muhammad was forty years old and living in Mecca, Saudi Arabia
when he first believed he had been visited by the angel Gabriel. Twelve
years later, Muhammad and his followers fled to Medina, about 150
miles north of Mecca. It was from Medina that Muhammad and his
forces started their reign of terror against neighboring tribes and
communities. One only needs to read Muhammad's entries to the
Qur'an during this period to get the picture of a bitter, hateful and
vengeful man—the Apostle of Allah. Is it any wonder that Muhammad
conceived of a god that had the same attributes as him?

The Jewish God, Yahweh or Jehovah, is overflowing with
unconditional love. He loves His people, Israel—even if they sin. For
God to include everyone into His family of love, He sent Jesus, His
only begotten Son, to restore mankind into the fellowship of God. God
loves everyone and commands His followers to love everyone with the
love of Christ. This comparison between the two deities could hardly
be more contradictory as one tries to assess the character of God. The
God of the Jews and Christians is loving and kind and desirous of an
intimate, personal relationship with His children—all those whom He
created. The god of the Muslims is unloving and vengeful and wants
to remain distant to those he created. These two portrayals of God are
incompatible and do not depict the same deity. God cannot both love
His creation at the same time He seems disinterested. He cannot desire
a close, personal relationship, yet want to remain at a distance. Nor can

Seeking a God of Love

.... I was the imam [religious leader] of a mosque in the city of Gaza, Egypt. . . .

... I was preaching what they taught me, but inside I was confused about the truth of Islam.

... What confused me the most was that I was told to preach about an Islam of love, kindness and forgiveness. At the same time, Muslim fundamentalists—the ones who were supposed to be practicing true Islam—were bombing churches and killing Christians.

... As a Muslim, I realized I had two options:

• I could continue to embrace the "Christianized" Islam—the Islam of peace, love, forgiveness and compassion, the Islam tailor-made to fit Egyptian government, politics and culture—thereby keeping my job status.

• I could become a member of the Islamic movement and embrace Islam according to the Quran and the teachings of Muhammad. . . .

I went to every interpretation of the Quran trying to avoid jihad and killing non-Muslims, yet I kept finding support of the practice. The [Muslim] scholars agreed that Muslims should enforce jihad [holy war] on infidels (those who reject Islam) and renegades (those who leave Islam).

... I wondered how Allah ... could either contradict himself so much or change his mind so much.

... Allah . . . is not a loving father ....

Islam is full of discrimination ... Hatred is built into the religion.

The history of Islam ... could only be characterized as a river of blood.

Mark A. Gabriel, Ph.D.
Islam and Terrorism, 2002, p.1-5

He claim those He created as His children and at the same time claim to be childless.

References

1. Caner, Ergun Mehmet and Emir Fethi Caner. *Unveiling Islam*, 2002. Kregel   Publications, div. of Kregel. Inc., p.30.
2. Gabriel, Mark A. *Islam and Terrorism*, 2002. Published by FrontLine, a Strang Company, Lake Mary, Florida, p.5.

CHAPTER 7

A Personal God

Seek the LORD while he may be found;
call on him while he is near (Isaiah 55:6).

The Christian and Jewish peoples of the earth have a unique and bonding relationship with their God like no other religion on earth. The Bible enforces and reinforces over and over that they are God's children—people that he dearly loves and for whom He demonstrates His compassion and forgiveness. It is clearly an intimate Father-child relationship. Muhammad could not conceive of such a loving god that would take such a personal interest in him. Therefore, he taught his followers that their god was a god of detachment, one who remained aloof and separated from them. That concept of Allah remains as the core of Islam today.

In the first book of the Bible, in Genesis 6:2, Moses recorded the first reference of God's intimate relationship to His creation when he refers to mankind as "sons of God." This is a very important perception for the theology and belief system of both Jews and Christians. The Hebrew word for *son* used in this verse and throughout the Old Testament means one who is the *builder of the family name*. Those who are Christians and Jews are part of God's holy family. As builders of God's family on earth, Christians and Jews are to imitate their Father-God and His holiness in every way. This sense of belonging to God's family is alien to the Muslims. Allah has no family. He is a harsh and unyielding tyrant-master that takes pleasure in chastening those who attempt to follow his commands.

Moses strengthened this notion of God as Father when he encouraged the Jews during the Exodus from Egypt with these words: "You are the children of the Lord your God ..." (Deuteronomy 14:1). About 250 years later, the word of the Lord came to the prophet Nathan concerning King David and his descendents. The Lord told Nathan to reassure David that his kingdom would be established forever, starting with his son Solomon, and that "I will be his Father, and he shall be My son ..." (2 Samuel 7:14, NKJV). God, through David, established an intimate fatherly relationship with His people that would be strengthened with the advent of Jesus, God's only begotten Son.

In the book of Jeremiah the prophet, God once again promised that He would be Israel's Father. "They will come with weeping; they will pray as I bring them back. I will lead them beside streams of water on a level path where they will not stumble, because I am Israel's father, and Ephraim is my firstborn son" (Jeremiah 31:9).

The God of the Christians and Jews yearns for this intimate, personal relationship with His human creation. King David understood this and wanted his son Solomon to know it and never forget it. "And you, my son Solomon," David recited, "acknowledge the God of your father, and serve him with wholehearted devotion and with a willing mind, for the LORD searches every heart and understands every motive behind the thoughts. If you seek him, he will be found by you; but if you forsake him, he will reject you forever" (1 Chronicles 28:9).

One of the amazing things about Jehovah God is that He desires so much to commune with and "parent" His creation, that He even reveals Himself to those that do not know they are seeking Him. "I revealed myself to those who did not ask for me;" God disclosed to the prophet Isaiah, "I was found by those who did not seek me. To a nation that did not call on my name, I said, 'Here am I, here am I'" (Isaiah 65:1). From the testimonies of converted Muslims to Christianity, this is one of the most common ways that God, the only true God, reveals Himself to seekers of the truth. "The Lord looks down from heaven on the sons of men to see if there are any who understand, any who seek God" (Psalm 14:2). Often, when a Muslim is earnestly seeking the truth of God's existence, he or she will pray that Allah (or sometimes Jehovah God) will reveal himself or the truth of his existence to them. It is important to note that Allah *never* shows up in a vision, dream, revelation or appearance—but Jesus does, every time. That is, because God through His Son Jesus wants and desires that personal relationship. Allah can not and will not reveal himself because he wants to stay detached from those he created, thus, clearly demonstrating once again that Allah is a false god, the figment of Muhammad's vivid imagination or an evil spirit—perhaps Satan himself—who has no desire to adopt mankind into the family of God.

This is My Son

"This is how the birth of Jesus Christ came about: His mother Mary was pledged to be married to Joseph, but before they came together, she was found to be with child through the Holy Spirit (Matthew 1:18)." An unidentified "angel of the Lord" appeared to Joseph in a dream and gave Joseph this assurance: "'Joseph son of David, do not be afraid to take Mary home as your wife, because what is conceived in her is from the Holy Spirit. She will give birth to a son, and you are to give him the name Jesus [i.e. the Lord saves], because he will save his people from their sins.'" (Matthew 1:20- 21)

In the first chapter of Luke, the angel sent to Mary is identified as Gabriel. "In the sixth month, God sent the angel Gabriel to Nazareth, a town in Galilee, to a virgin pledged to be married to a man named Joseph, a descendant of David. The virgin's name was Mary. The angel went to her and said, 'Greetings, you who are highly favored! The Lord is with you.' Mary was greatly troubled at his words and wondered what kind of greeting this might be. But the angel said to her, 'Do not be afraid, Mary, you have found favor with God. You will be with child and give birth to a son, and you are to give him the name Jesus. He will be great and will be called the **Son of the Most High**. The Lord God will give him the throne of his father David, and he will reign over the house of Jacob forever; his kingdom will never end'" (Luke 1:26-33, author's emphasis). Gabriel, the same angel that purportedly visited Muhammad with the revelation of the Qur'an, revealed to Mary that her immaculately conceived child would be the *Son of the Most High* living God. He would also fulfill the prophecy of the ongoing reign of King David.

The great challenge and struggle for the Muslim believer is who is telling the truth? Was it the Gabriel of Luke 1 who delivered the fulfilling prophecy of the Jewish Messiah, the Son of the living God, or the Gabriel of the Qur'an who refuted what he revealed to Mary? The Qur'an also retells the story of Mary's virgin birth of Jesus (surah 19:15-34). However, Muhammad, as Allah's messenger, as it was revealed to him by Gabriel, refers to Jesus' mother as Marium and identifies her as the sister of Aaron (and therefore Moses in verses 27-28) who lived nearly fifteen centuries earlier. Perhaps Allah and his dispatched angel messenger were confused or forgetful as to who actually gave birth to God's promised Messiah. According to Muhammad and every Muslim believer since, Gabriel revealed that Jesus was not God's son. Actually, what is "revealed" is that Jesus is not Allah's son, which is correct, since Allah IS NOT the God of the Jews and Christians.

Over 700 years before the birth of Christ and almost 1300 years before the birth of Muhammad, the prophet Isaiah prophesied: "The people walking in darkness have seen a great light; on those living in the land of the shadow of death a light has dawned.... For to us a child is born, to us a son is given, and the government will be on his shoulders." (Isaiah 9:2, 6a) Isaiah also prophesied that the Messiah would come from the lineage of Jesse, the father of David. This Messiah would be endowed with God's own Spirit—a Spirit of wisdom, understanding, counsel, power, knowledge and fear (reverence) of the Lord God Almighty. He will not judge or apply justice by what he sees or hears but by the heart of righteousness. He will smite the earth and its wicked inhabitants, not with the sword of vengeance, but with the word of God's truth. Righteousness and faithfulness will be his hallmark.

A shoot will come up from the stump of Jesse; from his roots a Branch will bear fruit. The Spirit of the Lord will rest on him—the Spirit of wisdom and of understanding, the Spirit of counsel and of power, the Spirit of knowledge and of the fear of the Lord—and he will delight in the fear of the Lord. He will not judge by what he sees with his eyes, or decide by what he hears with his ears; but with righteousness he will judge the needy, with justice he will give decisions for the poor of the earth. He will strike the earth with the rod of his mouth; with the breath

*of his lips he will slay the wicked. Righteousness will be his belt
and faithfulness the sash around his waist.* (Isaiah 11:1-5)

Muhammad not only did not fit the person in this prophecy, but
he could not hold a candle to the one who was to fulfill it—Jesus
Christ. Muhammad, of course, did not come from the ancestry of
Jesse or King David. Even if he did, it is evident from his life that he
was not bathed in the Spirit of Almighty God—the Spirit of wisdom,
understanding, counsel, power, knowledge and reverence of the only
true living God. His wisdom and understanding of God and His Holy
Word was miniscule and often erroneous. His counsel was frequently
nonsensical and/or barbaric. He could not demonstrate the power of
Almighty God in his midst as all the prophets before him could. His
knowledge of the history that went before him paled by comparison
to the learned of his day or any of the prophets he aspired to from the
Bible. He revered not the God of the Bible but some pagan spirit that
led him and all his followers astray from the true God of creation. And
he did not convert people by the power of his words, but by the power
of his sword.

Isaiah depicted the coming Messiah as a man of righteousness and
peace. He would not even raise his voice in anger, nor so much as crush
a tender reed. He would fulfill the covenant that God had made with
the Jews and point the way to the truth for all non-believers, releasing
them from the bondage of spiritual darkness. Despite Islamic claims
to the contrary, Muhammad did not and could not fulfill any such
characteristics of God's anointed—apostle, prophet or otherwise. He
was not a man of godly righteousness and peace; nor did he fulfill any
covenant with the Jews or lead the unbelieving Gentiles in the way of
truth. When Jesus preached He would frequently say, "Let them who
have ears, hear." He did not bash those who refused his message into
submission with a bloody scimitar, as did Muhammad.

*Here is my servant, whom I uphold, my chosen one in whom
I delight; I will put my Spirit on him and he will bring justice
to the nations. He will not shout or cry out, or raise his voice in
the streets.*

*A bruised reed he will not break, and a smoldering wick
he will not snuff out. In faithfulness he will bring forth justice;*

he will not falter or be discouraged till he establishes justice on earth. In his law the islands will put their hope.

This is what God the Lord says—he who created the heavens and stretched them out, who spread out the earth and all that comes out of it, who gives breath to its people, and life to those who walk on it:

I, the LORD, have called you in righteousness; I will take hold of your hand. I will keep you and will make you to be a covenant for the people and a light for the Gentiles, to open eyes that are blind, to free captives from prison and to release from the dungeon those who sit in darkness. (Isaiah 42:1-7)

The first recognition of Jesus as the Son of God came right after He was baptized in the Jordan River by John the Baptist, and it came from none other than God the Father Himself. "As soon as Jesus was baptized," the Apostle Matthew wrote, "he went up out of the water. At that moment heaven was opened, and he saw the Spirit of God descending like a dove and lighting on him. And a voice from heaven said, 'This is my Son, whom I love; with him I am well pleased'" (Matthew 3:16-17). After baptizing Jesus and witnessing the descending of the Spirit in the form of a dove upon Jesus, John the Baptist also gave testimony that Jesus was indeed the *Son of God* (John 1:34). He would later expand on this witness when he said: "For the one whom God has sent speaks the words of God, for God gives the Spirit without limit. The Father loves the Son and has placed everything in his hands. Whoever believes in the Son has eternal life, but whoever rejects the Son will not see life, for God's wrath remains on him" (John 3:34-36).

The Apostle John also declared that Jesus was the Son of God. "For the law was given through Moses," wrote John, "*but* grace and truth came through Jesus Christ. No one has seen God at any time. The only begotten Son, who is in the bosom of the Father, He has declared *Him*" (John 1:17-18, NKJV). Matthew and John, as well as the other apostles, knew that for Jesus or them to claim that Jesus was God's Son was blasphemy and punishable by death under Jewish law. But that did not deter them from such a belief and proclamation.

After Jesus warned His disciples about the false teaching of the Pharisees and Sadducees, He asked His disciples, "Who do people say that the Son of Man is?" (Matthew 16:13). Some of His followers responded by saying that people were saying that He was John the Baptist, or Elijah, or Jeremiah or one of the other prophets. "'But what about you?' he asked. Simon Peter answered, 'You are the Christ, the Son of the living God'" (Matthew 16:15-16). Peter did not hesitate, even though he knew such a response, if known by the Jewish religious leaders, would mean his certain death.

"Jesus replied, 'Blessed are you, Simon son of Jonah, for this was not revealed to you by man, but by my Father in heaven'" (verse 17). A few days after this confession of faith Jesus took Peter, James and John up on a mountain to pray with Him. As they were praying Jesus was transfigured and Moses and Elijah appeared. "A voice came from the cloud, saying, 'This is my Son, whom I have chosen; listen to him.' When the voice had spoken, they found that Jesus was alone. The disciples kept this to themselves, and told no one at that time what they had seen" (Luke 9:35-36).

When Jesus' teachings became too difficult for some of His followers to accept, many of them deserted Him. Jesus then asked the Twelve, His hand picked disciples, if they wanted to abandon Him also. "But Simon Peter answered Him, 'Lord, to whom shall we go? You have the words of eternal life. Also we have come to believe and know that You are the Christ, the Son of the living God'" (John 6:68-69, NKJV). Despite the wholesale defections from the less committed, Peter remained steadfast in His belief in who Jesus was and the validity of His words.

Perhaps the most often quoted verse of the Bible comes from John 3:16 where Jesus, in response to inquiries from the Pharisee, Nicodemus, tells him, "For God so loved the world that he gave his one and only Son, that whoever believes in him shall not perish but have eternal life." The following two verses continue Jesus' proclamation.

For God did not send his Son into the world to condemn the world, but to save the world through him. Whoever believes in him is not condemned, but whoever does not believe stands condemned already because he has not believed in the name of God's one and only Son. (John 3:17-18)

Once again, Jesus clearly proclaimed Himself to be God's Son. His closest disciples believed it to be so and God Almighty, the Father of heaven and earth confirmed it before witnesses that it was so to the fulfillment of prophecy.

When Jesus was healing people on the Sabbath, the Jewish leaders condemned Him. To which Jesus replied:

Jesus gave them this answer: "I tell you the truth, the Son can do nothing by himself; he can do only what he sees his Father doing, because whatever the Father does the Son also does. For the Father loves the Son and shows him all he does. Yes, to your amazement he will show him even greater things than these. For just as the Father raises the dead and gives them life, even so the Son gives life to whom he is pleased to give it. Moreover, the Father judges no one, but has entrusted all judgment to the Son, that all may honor the Son just as they honor the Father. He who does not honor the Son does not honor the Father, who sent him.

"I tell you the truth, whoever hears my word and believes him who sent me has eternal life and will not be condemned; he has crossed over from death to life. I tell you the truth, a time is coming and has now come when the dead will hear the voice of the Son of God and those who hear will live. For as the Father has life in himself, so he has granted the Son to have life in himself. (John 5:19-26)

The Jewish leaders persisted in their accusations of Jesus' blasphemy for referring to Himself as the Son of God. They sought every opportunity to condemn Him and turn others against Him. During the Feast of Dedication or Hanukkah in Jerusalem, Jesus was once again confronted by the Jews who sought to stone Him on the spot.

Jesus answered them, "Is it not written in your Law, 'I have said you are gods' [Psalm 82:6]? If he called them 'gods,' to whom the word of God came—and the Scripture cannot be broken—what about the one whom the Father set apart as his very own and sent into the world? Why then do you accuse me of blasphemy because I said, 'I am God's Son'? Do not believe me unless I do what my Father does. But if I do it, even though you do not believe me, believe the miracles, that you may know and understand that the Father is in me, and I in the Father." (John 10:34-38)

Even with His gruesome death pending, Jesus maintained His Sonship with God the Father. He refused to deny that heavenly connection even though it meant His assured horrific demise. Common sense would say: *Save yourself, refute this ridiculous claim of being the Son of God. No good can come of it but your painful death.* Jesus knew His origin and to whom He was about to return.

As Jesus and His disciples were on their way to Jerusalem during the Passover feast, He foretold of His coming death.

"Now my heart is troubled, and what shall I say? 'Father, save me from this hour'? No, it was for this very reason I came to this hour. Father, glorify your name!" Then a voice came from heaven, "I have glorified it, and will glorify it again." The crowd that was there and heard it said it had thundered; others said an angel had spoken to him. (John 12:27-29)

Although He knew what was ahead He refused to deny His Sonship with the Father God.

"I have told you these things," Jesus later told His disciples, "so that in me you may have peace. In this world you will have trouble. But take heart! I have overcome the world.

After Jesus said this, he looked toward heaven and prayed: "Father, the time has come. Glorify your Son, that your Son may glorify you. For you granted him authority over all people that he might give eternal life to all those you have given him. Now this is eternal life: that they may know you, the only true God, and Jesus Christ, whom you have sent." (John 16:33-17:3)

Children of the Living God

The Book of Daniel in the Old Testament offers an interesting insight into the God of the Jews and Christians. Daniel had high favor with Belshazzar, King of Babylonia. But the king was murdered and Sixty-two year old Darius the Mede took over the kingdom. In a plot against Daniel, the king's provincial rulers urged the king to issue a decree that anyone who prayed to a god or man other than Darius would be thrown into the lion's den. Daniel, a devout Jew who worshipped the only true God, refused to obey. The king was distraught because he did not want to kill Daniel, but had to comply with his edict. "The king said to Daniel, 'May your God, whom you serve continually, rescue you'" (Daniel 6:16b). Note that the king did not appeal to any pagan god for Daniel's deliverance.

The next morning, the king was anxious to see if Daniel's God had indeed saved him. "Daniel answered [the king's plea], 'O king, live forever! My God sent his angel, and he shut the mouths of the lions. They have not hurt me, because I was found innocent in his [God's] sight ...'" (Daniel 6:21-22). King Darius was overjoyed that Daniel's God had rescued him. "I issue a decree," he wrote to the peoples and nations of his Babylonian empire, "that in every part of my kingdom people must fear and reverence the God of Daniel. 'For he is **the living God** and he endures forever; his kingdom will not be destroyed, his dominion will never end'" (Daniel 6:26, author's emphasis). This was quite a proclamation for a gentile monarch. Darius did not formerly believe in a living, interactive personal God. When Daniel survived the certain death of the lion's den, Darius knew that Daniel's God was alive and personally cared about those who worshipped Him.

Jeremiah warned Israel not to stray and follow the gods and signs of their pagan neighbors. "But the Lord is the true God;" he proclaimed, "he is **the living God,** the eternal King. When he is angry, the earth trembles; the nations cannot endure his wrath (Jeremiah 10:10, author's emphasis)." The Apostle Paul would later reaffirm this call for Jews and Christians to follow the only true living God. "What agreement is there between the temple of God and idols [that are dead]? For we are the temple of **the living God.** As God has said: 'I will live with them and walk among them, and I will be their God, and they will be my people'" [Ezekiel 37:27] (2 Corinthians 6:16, author's emphasis). There is no god like the *living* God—the one and only personal God who takes pleasure in having an intimate Father and son or Father and daughter relationship with His creation.

Once again, the Apostle Paul reiterates the importance of this Father-child relationship by quoting from the prophet Hosea (1:10): "I will call them 'my people' who are not my people; and I will call her 'my loved one' who is not my loved one," and, "It will happen that in the very place where it was said to them, 'You are not my people,' they will be called 'sons of the living God'" (Romans 9:25-26).

How does one procure such a cherished parental relationship with God? Paul spells it out in Galatians 3:26-29. "You are all sons of God through faith in Christ Jesus, for all of you who were baptized into Christ have clothed yourselves with Christ. There is neither Jew nor Greek, slave nor free, male nor female, for you are all one in Christ Jesus. If you belong to Christ, then you are Abraham's seed, and heirs according to the promise." This God of the Jews and Christians wants to have this personal relationship with *all* of His human creation, no matter what the origin of the individual. He clearly separates Himself from Allah who wants no such personal relationship.

There is only one way to be assured of a personal Father-child relationship with the only living God, and that is through faith in Jesus Christ. "The [Holy] Spirit himself [within you] testifies with our spirit that we are God's children. Now if we are children, then we are heirs—heirs of God and co-heirs with Christ, if indeed we share in his sufferings in order that we may also share in his glory" (Romans 8:16-17).

Paul clarifies how an experience with the living God through Christ is different than that of God's expression through the Law of Moses. "You show that you are a letter from Christ, the result of our ministry, written not with ink [of the Law] but with the Spirit of the living God, not on tablets of stone but on tablets of human hearts. . . . He has made us competent as ministers of a new covenant—not of the letter but of the Spirit; for the letter [of the Law] kills, but the Spirit gives life" (2 Corinthians 3:3, 6).

Jesus also made it clear about the type of relationship His followers were to expect and have with God. The only prayer He ever taught His disciples He started by addressing God Almighty as "Our Father ..." (Matthew 6:9).

For those who could not accept the living God as a spiritual father, "Jesus said to them, 'If God were your Father, you would love me, for I came from God and now am here. I have not come on my own; but he sent me'" (John 8:42). Those who do not and can not accept Jesus as the Son of God will never be able to see or accept God as their heavenly Father. That is the conundrum and difficulty that all Muslims face and what keeps them in bondage to Allah, the unseen, non-revealing and impersonal god.

Allah Has No Children

"How great is the love the Father has lavished on us," the Apostle John penned, "that we should be called children of God! And that is what we are! The reason the world does not know us is that it did not know him [Jesus]" (1 John 3:1). Since Allah has no children he is the father to no one. In the Qur'an, the term "father" is only used in the context of a man's relationship to his children. It is never used to describe Allah's relationship to those who worship him. It is forbidden by the faithful to demean Allah with such an earthly association. That Jesus would claim to be the Son of God was preposterous to Muhammad and continues to be unthinkable among Muslims today. Since Muslims draw up short of accusing Jesus of blasphemy, they assert that it was Jesus' apostles that falsely ascribed this *Son of God* association to Him. "And they [Jews and Christians] make the jinn [angels of Allah] associates with Allah, while He created them, and they falsely attributed to Him sons and daughters without knowledge ..." (surah 6:100). Of course, the truth of the matter is that neither Jews nor Christians would ever claim that Allah was the father of Jesus or anyone else among their faithful, because Allah was not and is not their God.

As you discovered in Chapter two, Allah cannot lower himself to have a son. If he can have no son, then he cannot have children. "Allah, the god revealed in the Qur'an, is not a loving Father."[1]) In fact, he is not a father image at all to Muslims. It is beneath Allah to be a father to anyone human. Muslims are therefore spiritual orphans—children of the Creator, but without a father.

To which the Apostle Paul might advise a Muslim believer, "Therefore come out from them and be separate, says the Lord. Touch no unclean thing, and I will receive you. I will be a Father to you, and you will be my sons and daughters, says the Lord Almighty" (2 Corinthians 6:17-18).

In surah 9:30, Muhammad accuses both the Jews and Christians of blaspheming Allah by saying that he has a son and that they are worthy only of death for believing so. "And the Jews say: Uzair [Ezra] is the son of Allah; and the Christians say: The Messiah [Jesus] is the son of Allah;

these are the words of their mouths; they imitate the saying of those who disbelieved before; may Allah destroy them; how they are turned away." Notice that Muhammad is not content with people believing differently than him about God. If their perception of their god is not the same as his, then Allah is called upon to *destroy* them—not love them into his wellspring of faith. On another point, regardless of Muhammad's assertion in this verse, there is no biblical record that the Jews believed that Ezra, a Babylonian exile, who was a scribe and teacher of the Law of Moses, was in any manner considered to be the Son of God (Ezra 7:1-6). This too, would have been blasphemy to the Jew.

Perhaps Muhammad's struggle with a god as a father image related to his personal experience. Muhammad's father died before his birth, and though his grandfather and then his uncle cared for him, he still grew up without a father-son relationship. Is it any wonder then that he could not conceive of a loving Father God who sought a personal relationship with His creation? Muhammad considered himself—and his followers—to be on the low end of the spectrum when it came to Allah's love. "Narrated 'Umar: I heard the Prophet saying, 'Do not exaggerate in praising me as the Christians praised the son of Mary, for I am only a Slave. So, call me the Slave of Allah and His Apostle'" (hadith 4:55:654).

"Islam's god is indeed a master," wrote Silas, "and he can be a kind and forgiving master, but he can not deliver the goods as a God of infinite mercy and love. And this is why there is a dearth of description of Allah being a loving god in the Quran. **Because it is not in Islam's god's nature to be a father**."[2]

In the New Testament, the concept of a slave is used to describe Christians, but in a much different context. The term is used by Jesus and the Apostle Paul to illustrate a servant or serving relationship Christians are to have with God and others. In this respect Jesus set the standard of service. When the apostolic brothers, James and John, requested that they have priority with Jesus in heaven, Jesus gave His disciples a lesson in servant leadership. While the Gentile rulers were tyrant leaders it was not to be the case with those that followed Jesus. "... Instead," Jesus professed, "whoever wants to become great among you must be your servant, and whoever wants to be first must be slave of all. For even the Son of Man did not come to be served, but to serve, and to give his life as a ransom for many" (Mark 10:43-45).

Another reason the notion of Godly Sonship was baffling to Muhammad was that he saw the persecution of Jews as God's punishment. He had no understanding of God's discipline as an expression of His love for His children. "And the Jews and Christians say: We are the sons of Allah and His beloved ones. Say: Why does He then chastise you for your faults? Nay, you are mortals from among those whom He has created; He forgives whom He pleases and chastises whom He pleases; and Allah's is the kingdom of the heavens and the earth and what is between them, and to Him is the eventual coming (surah 5:18)." The writer to the Messianic Hebrews explained God's loving discipline this way: "Endure hardship as discipline; God is treating you as sons. For what son is not disciplined by his father? If you are not disciplined (and everyone undergoes discipline), then you are illegitimate children and not true sons" (Hebrews 12:7-8).

Jesus expressed an even greater vision and purpose of the Father-Son relationship when He explained to His disciples the important difference between being a slave to the Law under the Abrahamic covenant and the freedom to be a part of God's family through faith in Him as God's Son. "Jesus replied, 'I tell you the truth, everyone who sins is a slave to sin. Now a slave has no permanent place in the family, but a son belongs to it forever. So if the Son sets you free, you will be free indeed'" (John 8:34-36).

The Apostle Paul expands on the essential nature of this new God-child relationship. "So you are no longer a slave, but a son; and since you are a son, God has made you also an heir" (Galatians 4:7). It is this freedom in Christ to be a child of God that clearly separates Muslims and Christians and their view of their respective deities. Faith in Christ for a Christian means to fully accept His Sonship as God's only begotten Son and through Him God accepts His followers as His own children. "It is for freedom that Christ has set us free," Paul wrote. "Stand firm, then, and do not let yourselves be burdened again by a yoke of slavery" (Galatians 5:1). Christians, through Christ, can no longer accept the yoke of slavery to sin or enslavement to a tyrannical god. Muslims, because they can not accept this God-child relationship, are trapped in an unrelenting bondage to an oppressive god figure called Allah.

Children Are NOT a Blessing to Allah

In the eyes of Allah children born to his human creation are not a blessing. In fact, children are but a temptation to draw one away from following Allah and his Apostle. "O you who believe! be not unfaithful to Allah and the Apostle, nor be unfaithful to your trusts while you know. And know that your property and your children are a temptation, and that Allah is He with Whom there is a mighty reward" (surah 8:27-28). By contrast, when the disciples of Jesus tried to stop the people from bringing their children before Jesus, Jesus rebuked His disciples. "Jesus said, 'Let the little children come to me, and do not hinder them, for the kingdom of God belongs to such as these'" (Mark 10:14). Jesus and the New Testament teach that children are a cherished treasure from God that He has entrusted to parents.

No such image is portrayed by Allah in the Qur'an. "And let not their [the unbeliever's] property and [the happiness which they may derive from] their children excite your admiration; Allah only wishes to chastise them with these in this world and (that) their souls may depart while they are unbelievers" (surah 9:85). While the God of the Bible calls believers to cherish their children and bring them up in the way of the Lord (Proverbs 22:6), Allah sees them as an instrument of punishment for those that do not follow him.

Once again, in surah 18:46, Allah gives the impression that children are unimportant to him. "Wealth and children are an adornment of the life of this world; and the ever-abiding [which endures forever are] the good works, are [far] better with your Lord in reward and better in expectation [or source of hope]." It is good deeds that count with Allah and what brings one his reward, not the blessing of children.

Children, according to Allah, are also the source of much travail and wickedness. "O you who believe! surely from among your wives and your children there is an enemy to you; therefore beware of them; and if you pardon and forbear and forgive, then surely Allah is Forgiving, Merciful. Your possessions and your children are only a trial, and Allah it is with Whom is a great reward." (surah 64:14-15). It would appear that, not only does Allah not admit to having any children, but that he is jealous of them and that they are dangerous and have evil intent.

The Almighty Living God, however, adores children—children of His creation. "Yet to all who received him [Jesus]," the Apostle John confirmed, "to those who believed in his name, he gave the right to become children of God—children born not of natural descent, nor of human decision or a husband's will, but born of God" (John 1:12-13). Those who follow Christ, the Son of the Living God, have the indisputable right to become and to be called the *children of God*. "For he [God] chose us in him [Christ] before the creation of the world," wrote the Apostle Paul, "to be holy and blameless in his sight. In love he [God] predestined us to be adopted as his sons through Jesus Christ, in accordance with his pleasure and will—to the praise of his glorious grace, which he has freely given us in the One he loves" (Ephesians 1:4-6).

Allah's Creation Is Without Purpose

There is no purpose to Allah's creation and life on earth other than self-serving satisfaction. Two verses in the Qur'an revealed to Muhammad by Allah through Gabriel give the distinct impression that the purpose of Allah's devotees is to travel through life, engaging in pleasures and then they die when the impassionate Allah decides their life is over. When life is over, then will come Allah's judgment. However, he has not given his followers the means to prepare for it, nor to be exempted from it by any other way than a tally of their good deeds outweighing their bad deeds.

Consider the saga of the wandering soul in surah 40:67-68: "He it is Who created you from dust, [and] then from a small life-germ [sperm], [and] then from a clot, then He brings you forth as a child, [and] then [He ordains] that you may attain your maturity, [and] then that you may [grow to] be old—[though some of you (He causes to) die earlier]—and that you may reach an appointed term [of life], and that you may understand. He it is Who gives life and brings death, so when He decrees an affair [to be], He only says to it: Be, and it is."

Surah 57:20 offers another view of the aimless life. "Know that this world's life is only sport and play and gaiety [or a beautiful show] and boasting among yourselves, and vying in the multiplication of wealth and children ... [and] then [in the end, just like a withered plant, your life] becomes dried up and broken down; and in the hereafter is a severe chastisement [or] forgiveness from Allah and [at] (His) pleasure; and this world's life is naught but [a] means of deception." So, after a

Muslim lives this apparent meaningless life on earth, he or she has to stand before Allah and receive his random judgment of one's life on earth based strictly on the scales of good outweighing evil. There is little freedom of choice because Allah will decide how your life should go and when it should end.

Christians, on the other hand, are given a clear picture of their purpose and mission while on earth and the rationale for their creation. The Bible states clearly that those whom God created are called to serve the Lord (Deuteronomy 10:12-13) and worship Him in joy and gladness (Psalm 100:2); to share God's love with others and do no harm (Romans 13:9-10); to be servants (John 12:26) and ambassadors for Christ (2 Corinthians 5:20) with a ministry of reconciliation (2 Corinthians 5:18). To live with Jesus as their example (John 13:14-16; 1 Peter 2:21); always doing that which is good (1 Peter 3:13-17); sharing the Gospel of good news with the world (Matthew 28:19-20; Mark 13:10). Christians are called by God to make the world a better place—sharing, building, restoring, reconciling, forgiving, healing, nurturing, loving; demonstrating mercy and justice—and pointing the lost world to a redeeming, saving knowledge of Jesus Christ. Although Muslims are also called to draw unbelievers to their god, their methods are quite different and diverse (see the section on The Mission).

The God Who Is There

The Christian faith teaches, with the support of its biblical scriptures, that Jehovah God, the Judeo-Christian God of the Old and New Testament, in the person of Jesus Christ and through the ministry and the indwelling presence of the Holy Spirit, changes a human life condition and experience from the inside, out. That is to say, that God chooses to change the heart and soul of man in order to achieve God's intended inner and outer expression of one's faith in Him. "Whoever confesses that Jesus is the Son of God," the Apostle John taught, "God abides in him, and he in God" (1 John 4:15, NKJV).

Those who freely choose to follow Jesus Christ are given an abiding invitation to enter into an intimate personal relationship with God through faith in Jesus. Through Jesus, Christians know the character of their loving God. They know that God loves them so much that He wants to have an "abba" Father or "Daddy" relationship with them

(Romans 8:15). Muslims, on the other hand, are taught that Allah desires no such personal relationship with lowly man and that Allah would not demean himself with such an unclean association. Not only is Allah too high and mighty to leave his thrown to dwell among man, but he would never sully his godhead with such a sinful alliance.

Islam, through the dictates of the Qur'an and the example of Muhammad, seeks to enforce changes upon the outer man in order to bring about inner changes and peace. The history of the world and mankind is at our disposal to demonstrate that such religious enforcement of spiritual law from the outside in has never changed man's inner spirit nor improved his relationship with his god or that with his neighbors.

"… Allah guides whom He pleases to the right path" (surah 2:213). There is no personal, intimate choice in following Allah. It is Allah that chooses whom he wants as his followers. In the world of the Muslim there is no personal choice in accepting the tenets of faith of Islam. Yes, there are adult converts to the faith, but they are far and few between those that are born into Muslim families or children and adult non-believers that are coerced or persecuted into becoming Muslims at the threat of torture or death.

Christianity, on the other hand, as stressed in the scriptures, is a religion of personal choice. One chooses to become a Christian, a follower of Christ, because he or she makes an informed life-changing decision to follow the teachings of Jesus and commit his or her life to His lordship. Yes, there are denominations of the Christian faith that believe in baptizing infants into the faith, but that is not deemed to be binding by other Christian leaders and believers who stress that one can only by knowledge of the truth commit to Christ through an informed, personal decision—a decision that an infant cannot make. By and large, Christians become Christians because they want to, not because someone is threatening to torture them, kill them or their loved ones, rape their daughters, destroy their business or livelihood, or burn down their schools or places of worship—things that happen all too often in the spreading of the Islamic faith.

The central message of the Christian gospel is that: *God loves you and He wants to have a personal, intimate relationship with you.* This message is antithetical to the message of Islam and its prophet,

Muhammad. Allah is distant and far away from the Muslim believer. He is unapproachable and uninterested in an intimate relationship with those who worship him. For the Muslim it is inconceivable and blasphemous to think that Allah would demean himself and walk among his creation. In the Qur'an there are no recordings of Allah acting interpersonally with his creation through healing, deliverance, miracles, or other loving acts toward those he supposedly loves. Whereas, the Bible is full of such loving acts by the Almighty God and Father for the children He created.

Muslims are instructed to call upon Allah as the only true god, but he does not answer. "Surely those whom you call on besides Allah are in a state of subjugation like yourselves; therefore call on them, then let them answer you if you are truthful ... And those whom you call upon besides Him [Allah] are not able to help you, nor can they help themselves" (surah 7:194, 197). Contrast this admonition with the reality of Elijah's confrontation with the prophets of Baal (1 Kings 18). All day long 450 prophets of Baal, the pagan god, sacrificed and cried out to him and pleaded with him to show himself through a miracle, but nothing happened. Elijah taunted them by saying that perhaps their god was asleep, deep in thought or away traveling. Then Elijah made his request of Jehovah God to reveal Himself and He miraculously did just that to prove that He was the only living God. To re-emphasize an earlier point, when Muslims cry out to Allah for truth and to reveal himself, he never does—only Jesus shows up in a dream, vision or visitation.

Unlike Allah's selectivity in whom he will love, the God of the Bible wants all people to love Him because He loves all people. When the Apostle Peter was struggling with the thought of taking the Gospel of Jesus Christ to the Gentiles (the non-Jewish world), God gave him a vision. It took Peter a while to understand it, but he finally received God's truth and His heart for all mankind (see Acts 10:9-23).

The Apostle John stated how important it was for God to express His unreserved love through Christ. "In this the love of God was manifested toward us, that God has sent His only begotten Son into the world, that we might live through Him" (1 John 4:9, NKJV).

Jehovah God revealed himself in the person of Jesus Christ and in so doing invited all of mankind to enter into a personal relationship with Him through faith in Christ Jesus. Then, through the indwelling power of the Holy Spirit, God empowers Christians to live the godly, holy life by initiating life-changing spiritual and soulful change from within. Allah, on the other hand, offers no such opportunity or transforming spirit for his followers. The only "spirit" of God that the Qur'an and Muslims recognize is the angel Gabriel who supposedly ministered to Muhammad. But angels, according to the Bible, are not spirits and have no authority or power to transform the spirit of man. The only hope for the confessing Muslim of Allah's acceptance is to follow the letter of the law of good deeds and allegiance to Allah. This is what Jesus came to do—to set the Jews and all others free from the law. Jesus was not sent to do away with God's law, but to set free those bound by the law and its imprisonment.

For the Muslim there is no room in the Islamic belief system for a personal relationship with Allah. One becomes a Muslim simply by confessing the Shahada, that is the creed that, "There is no god but Allah, Muhammad is the messenger of Allah." That is the simple confession of faith for every Muslim. Once a Muslim, the faithful must adhere to the six doctrines of Islam: There is one god; angels (not the Holy Spirit) do the will of Allah; belief in the Torah, Gospel and the Qur'an; the prophets of Allah (Adam, Noah, Abraham, Moses, Jesus and Muhammad); Allah will judge all mankind and that there is a heaven and a hell for eternal life.[3]

"When Allah is discussed within the Islamic community," wrote the Caner brothers, "the absence of intimacy, atonement, and omnibenevolence becomes apparent. In all the terms and titles for Allah, one does not encounter terms of intimacy."[4] For the Christian, however, intimacy with God is a foregone conclusion based on faith in Jesus Christ. The Apostle Paul illustrated it in this manner. "However, as it is written: 'No eye has seen, no ear has heard, no mind has conceived what God has prepared for those who love him' but God has revealed it to us by his Spirit. The Spirit searches all things, even the deep things of God. For who among men knows the thoughts of a man except the man's spirit within him? In the same way no one knows the thoughts of God except the Spirit of God. We have not received the spirit of the world but the Spirit who is from God, that we may understand what God has freely given us" (1 Corinthians 2:9-12). Muslims have no idea what Allah requires of them other than that stated in the Qur'an.

Christians, on the other hand, through the presence of the indwelling Holy Spirit, have a personal and near to their heart access and insight into God's will for their life.

Historically, by Qur'anic edict, Muslims can only be transformed on the outside through obedience to Allah and good works. But even then, even the most faithful cannot be sure of Allah's full acceptance of them or their worthiness of Paradise. Christians, through the inner witness of the Holy Spirit and their acceptance of the salvation message and the saving work of Christ, have absolute assurance of God's presence in their life and eternal life with Him.

If the Apostle Paul were alive today, he would likely say to the Muslim faithful the same words he spoke to those in the city of Corinth:

The man without the Spirit does not accept the things that come from the Spirit of God, for they are foolishness to him, and he cannot understand them, because they are spiritually discerned. The spiritual man makes judgments about all things, but he himself is not subject to any man's judgment: 'For who has known the mind of the Lord that he may instruct him?' But we have the mind of Christ. (1 Corinthians 2:14-16)

The Apostle Paul, while in prison, wrote to the new Gentile believers in Ephesus to reassure them in their decision to accept Jesus as their Lord and Savior.

But now in Christ Jesus you who once were far away have been brought near through the blood of Christ. For he himself is our peace, who has made the two [the circumcised Jew and the uncircumcised Gentile] *one and has destroyed the barrier* [of the law], *the dividing wall of hostility, by abolishing in his flesh the law with its commandments and regulations. His purpose was to create in himself one new man out of the two, thus making peace, and in this one body to reconcile both of them to God through the cross, by which he put to death their hostility. He came and preached peace to you who were far away* [the Gentiles] *and peace to those who were near* [the Jews]. *For through him we both have access to the Father by   one Spirit.*

Consequently, you are no longer foreigners and aliens, but fellow citizens with God's people and members of God's household, built on the foundation of the apostles and prophets, with Christ Jesus himself as the chief cornerstone. In him the whole building is joined together and rises to become a holy temple in the Lord. And in him you too are being built together to become a dwelling in which God lives by his Spirit. (Ephesians 2:13-22)

For the Christian, the message of the Gospel is that Jesus brought God down to man in the person of the Holy Spirit to dwell within man as a daily witness of God's loving presence with those who accept His saving grace through Christ. The message of the Qur'an and the prophet Muhammad, is that Allah is forever distant and detached from his creation and is too aloof and uninterested in a personal, loving relationship with humankind.

Jesus' promise to those who follow Him is simply this: "And surely I am with you always, to the very end of the age" (Matthew 28:20).

"I am the vine; you are the branches," Jesus taught His followers. "If a man remains in me and I in him, he will bear much fruit; apart from me you can do nothing. If anyone does not remain in me, he is like a branch that is thrown away and withers; such branches are picked up, thrown into the fire and burned" (John 15:5-6).

But "Here is the profound weakness of [Islam] in which there is no genuine connection between God and human being," state the Caner brothers. "Allah guides people into the truth through his messenger Muhammad, but one should never anticipate speaking to Allah personally or relationally."[5]

"Surely my guardian is Allah," revealed Muhammad, "Who revealed the Book [Qur'an], and He befriends the good. And those whom you call upon besides Him are not able to help you, nor can they help themselves" (surah 7:196-197). Muhammad insisted that there was no way to his god Allah except by Allah's choice. He rejected that Allah could have an intermediary such as Jesus or the Holy Spirit. Although he did not intend it to be interpreted this way, Muhammad was indeed correct, because Jesus and the Holy Spirit do not serve Allah, but only Jehovah God, the one and only true and living God.

God, through the prophet Jeremiah, said: "'Am I a God near at hand,' says the Lord, 'And not a God afar off?'" (Jeremiah 23:23). That simple but direct description of the God of the Jews and the Christians says volumes about the difference between the living God and the god of silence of the Muslims. God interacts with His creation; Allah does not.

Shortly after He foretold of the Apostle Peter's betrayal, Jesus sought to reassure His followers. "If you love me," Jesus told His disciples, "you will obey what I command. And I will ask the Father, and he will give you another Counselor [Comforter; i.e. the Holy Spirit] to be with you forever—the Spirit of truth. The world cannot accept him, because it neither sees him nor knows him. But you know him, for he lives with you and will be in you" (John 14:15-17). Aware of His pending crucifixion, Jesus later promised His disciples that He would not leave them alone and without guidance. "But when he, the Spirit of truth, comes, he will guide you into all truth. He will not speak on his own; he will speak only what he hears, and he will tell you what is yet to come. He will bring glory to me by taking from what is mine and making it known to you. All that belongs to the Father is mine. That is why I said the Spirit will take from what is mine and make it known to you" (John 16:13-15).

This indwelling of God's presence within the Christian believer dramatically sets aside the Christian from the Muslim and Christianity from Islam. This established residence of God's presence within the Christian believer in the person of God's Holy Spirit makes Christianity and Islam diametrically opposed to each other. They are theological opposites, having little common ground of faith. It would not be thinkable or possible for a Christian, who truly understood the scriptures of the Bible and had such a personal, intimate relationship with Jesus—the person to whom the believer was indebted to for his personal salvation and eternal guarantee of life everlasting with the Father—to turn and accept the impersonal, detached relationship that Allah offers in Islam.

The only exception, of course, would be for such a believer to be deceived by Satan himself. Satan is the one whom Jesus calls "the father of lies" (John 8:44) and the one who "comes only to steal and kill and destroy" (John 10:10).

Is it possible for a Christian to convert to Islam? Obviously, over the centuries, thousands of "Christians" have freely converted to Islam. But is it possible for a true Bible-believing Christian to go against the teachings and call of Christ and embrace Islam and the anti-Christ teachings of the Qur'an? The hallmark of the Christian faith is the acceptance of Jesus Christ as one's personal Lord and Savior—a decision that establishes an intimate and special relationship between Jesus and the believer. Jesus refers to those in such an intimate relationship as "friend (John 15:14-15)", "brother (Matthew 12:50)", "children of God (Luke 20:36)," "children of the resurrection," (Luke 20:36), "children of light" (John 12:36) and "sons of the Most High" (Luke 6:35). To cement this personal relationship, Jesus promised that He would send the Holy Spirit to dwell within each believer. For a Christian to accept Islam, he or she would have to reject the Holy Spirit of the only true God.

The depth of the personal relationship the Christian has with God is clearly expressed by the Apostle Paul.

And we know that in all things God works for the good of those who love him, who have been called according to his purpose. For those God foreknew he also predestined to be conformed to the likeness of his Son, that he might be the firstborn among many brothers. And those he predestined, he also called; those he called, he also justified; those he justified, he also glorified.

What, then, shall we say in response to this? If God is for us, who can be against us? He who did not spare his own Son, but gave him up for us all—how will he not also, along with him, graciously give us all things? Who will bring any charge against those whom God has chosen? It is God who justifies. Who is he that condemns? Christ Jesus, who died—more than that, who was raised to life—is at the right hand of God and is also interceding for us. Who shall separate us from the love of Christ? Shall trouble or hardship or persecution or famine or nakedness or danger or sword? As it is written:

"For your sake we face death all day long; we are considered as sheep to be slaughtered." (Psalm 44:22)

No, in all these things we are more than conquerors through him who loved us. For I am convinced that neither death nor life, neither angels nor demons, neither the present nor the future, nor any powers, neither height nor depth, nor anything else in all creation, will be able to separate us from the love of God that is in Christ Jesus our Lord (Romans 8:28-39).

Conclusion

Jews and Christians, in particular, are clearly set apart from Muslims in how each views their god and understands their relationship to him. For the Christian, God is a living, interacting presence in one's life—a divine presence that guides, comforts, loves, forgives, redeems and takes personal interest in their wellbeing and eternal destination. For the Muslim, Allah is a distant, impersonal and detached deity that according to the Qur'an and the teaching of Muhammad is really not that interested in the welfare and destiny of his human creation.

This is plainly illustrated by the relationship God establishes in the Bible with those He created, by continually referring to them as His children; a passionate Father-child connection—one that communicates passion and compassion for those He loves. Allah, however, is portrayed and worshipped as a detached, compassionless god who looks upon his creation as nothing more than pawns to be dealt with as he sees fit and without personal interaction.

While the God of the Jews and Christians established a means of personal communication through the indwelling Holy Spirit, Allah provides no such means of communication or means by which to understand his will and guidance. Muslims can pray and pray and never have any sense of Allah's direction for their life. Christians, however, give ready testimony to their prayers being answered and having the security of an inner peace that guides them and comforts them.

Seeking God the Father

Why don't you pray to the God you are searching for? Ask Him to show you His way. Talk to Him as if He were your friend.

I smiled. She might as well suggest that I talk to the Taj Mahal. But then Dr. Santiago said something that shot through my being like electricity .... "Talk to Him," she said very quietly, "as if He were your father."

... No Muslim, I felt certain, ever thought of Allah as his father. Since childhood, I had been told that the surest way to know about Allah was to pray five times a day and study and think on the Quran. . . .

Alone in my room I got on my knees and tried to call Him "Father." But it was a useless effort ....

Hours later I awoke. It was after midnight, my birthday, December 12. I was 54 years old ....

One of my cherished memories was seeing [my father] at work in the study ....

It was always the same with Father. He didn't mind if I bothered him. Whenever I had a question or problem, no matter how busy he was, he would put aside his work to devote his full attention just to me.

... Suppose, just suppose God were like a father. If my earthly father would put aside everything to listen to me, wouldn't my heavenly Father ...?

Shaking with excitement, I got out of bed, sank to my knees on the rug, looked up to heaven and in rich new understanding called God "my Father."

I was not prepared for what happened.

Bilquis Sheikh
I Dared to Call Him Father, 1978, 2003

References

1. Gabriel, Mark A. *Islam and Terrorism*, 2002. Published by FrontLine, a Strang Company, p. 5.

2. Silas, *Islam Has No Father*. Http://www.answering-islam.org/Silas/no_father. htm. Accessed January 14, 2007.

3. Caner, Ergun Mehmet and Emir Fethi Caner. *Unveiling Islam*, 2002. Kregel Publications, div. of Kregel. Inc., p. 145.

4. Caner & Caner, p. 117.

5. Caner & Caner, p. 34.

CHAPTER 8

Forgiveness and Reconciliation

"Come now, let us reason together," says the LORD.
"Though your sins are like scarlet, they shall be as white as snow;
though they are red as crimson, they shall be like wool."
(Isaiah 1:18)

In the preceding chapter it was pointed out briefly that the Qur'an does not lay out any clear plan or purpose for Allah's creation—no means of reconciling sinful man with his god. That, of course, is no surprise, since Allah desires no personal relationship with his creation; no compassionate embrace for those from whom he demands absolute allegiance and adherence to his insurmountable and immeasurable laws. By clear contrast, the Bible and the ministry of Jesus Christ, present a precise plan for mankind to reconcile himself to the God of his creation. While Islam demands that its followers comply with the Islamic law of the Qur'an and ahadiths, the message of Christianity portrays a freedom from the Mosaic Law via the New Covenant with God through faith in Jesus Christ and His saving work of the cross. Muhammad freed no one, but Jesus Christ frees all who will accept His redemptive sacrifice on the Cross of Calvary.

The Nature of Sin

What is sin? Just about any dictionary defines sin as disobeying an acceptable law of God. Muslims would likely concur: That breaking a law of Allah would be sin. The biblical interpretation of sin is perhaps more concise. In the Bible sin is seen as any thought or action that separates one from God—whether one believes in Him or not.

GOD HATES SIN! Jehovah God hates evil doing, but Muhammad, the prophet of Allah, propagated evil doing at every opportunity. "You are not a God who takes pleasure in evil;" wrote the psalmist David, "with you the wicked cannot dwell. The arrogant cannot stand in your presence; you hate all who do wrong. You destroy those who tell lies; bloodthirsty and deceitful men the Lord abhors" (Psalm 5:4-6). God, through an unknown psalmist said: "I will set before my eyes no vile thing. The deeds of faithless men I hate; they will not cling to me" (Psalm 101:3).

Jehovah God of the Jews and Christians hates wrong doing; Allah fosters it. "Since there is no such thing as forgiveness of sins in Islam," author Raza Safa wrote, "Muslims justify their sins. True conviction of sin does not exist in Islam."[1]

Malachi, perhaps the last prophet to the Jews before Christ, chastised the faithless Jews some 400 years before the birth of Jesus. "You have wearied the LORD with your words. 'How have we wearied him?' you ask. By saying, 'All who do evil are good in the eyes of the LORD, and he is pleased with them' or 'Where is the God of justice?'" (Malachi 2:17).

What about the source of sin? Both the Qur'an and the Bible recount the story of the *fall* of Adam and Eve (the Qur'an never uses her name). They both report that it was Satan's temptation that led to the departure from sinlessness. However, the Qur'an states that Adam and his wife repented of their sin in the Garden of Eden (surah 7:23) and that Allah forgave them and set them on the right path (surah 2:37-38). The Bible makes no such declaration of Adam and Eve repenting of their sin, nor of God forgiving them for their transgressions. To the contrary, Adam puts the blame on his wife for his sin and hides his guilt from God. Eve did likewise, but blamed Satan for her sin (Genesis 3:8-13). God then banishes them from the Garden and severely punishes them and all their descendants (Genesis 3:16-23). The Bible and Christian doctrine give credence to the concept that Adam introduced sin to mankind and was the source of *original sin*. The Qur'an makes no such acknowledgement. Muslims, however, do not believe that sin entered the world through Adam's disobedience. They believe in Adam as the first prophet of

Allah. However, they believe that man is basically created good until he sins. The Bible teaches, particularly through the New Testament, that man is born in sin, and if left to his own desires, will continue to sin and separate himself from God. Man's only hope for reconciliation with God is through the redemptive work of Christ on the cross.

What the Qur'an does say is that Allah commanded the angels and Satan (Shaitan or Iblis) to prostrate before Adam and worship him, but Satan refused. "And when We said to the angels: Make obeisance to Adam they did obeisance, but Iblis (did it not). He refused and was proud, and he was one of the unbelievers" (surah 2:34). From a Judeo-Christian viewpoint and biblical teaching, for Jehovah God to command the angels or any other life form to worship anyone other than Him would be outright blasphemy.

"You shall not make for yourself an idol in the form of anything in heaven above or on the earth beneath or in the waters below," God spoke to Moses. "You shall not bow down to them or worship them; for I, the LORD your God, am a jealous God, punishing the children for the sin of the fathers to the third and fourth generation of those who hate me, but showing love to a thousand {generations} of those who love me and keep my commandments" (Exodus 20:4-6).

The Qur'an does state that Satan is the enemy of man (surah 12:5, *et al*); that he misleads and deceives mankind (surah 4:117-121, *et al*) and makes sin attractive (surah 6:43; 15:39). However, with respect to deception and sin, it would seem that Allah is put on the same footing with Satan. Allah, according to the Qur'an (surah 4:142), is a deceiver: "Behold, the hypocrites seek to deceive God—the while it is He who causes them to be deceived ...."[2] It also pleases Allah for him to lead one into sin. "Whomsoever Allah causes to err, there is no guide for him; and He leaves them alone in their inordinacy [overweening arrogance], blindly wandering on" (surah 7:186).

There is no reasoning or justification for Allah's spontaneous and haphazard dealings with his creation. "And they who reject Our communications are deaf and dumb, in utter darkness; whom Allah pleases He causes to err, and whom He pleases He puts on the right way" (surah 6:39). It is Allah, not men and women, that chooses who will sin and who will not. With Allah deceiving and leading whom he pleases into sin, what hope does the Islamic believer have in reconciling himself or herself to their god? If Allah can lead anyone he chooses astray, perhaps he led Muhammad on the wrong path. Furthermore, after Allah leads them into sin, he then tightens his breast and rejects them. "Therefore (for) whomsoever Allah intends that He would guide him aright, He expands his breast for Islam, and (for) whomsoever He intends that He should cause him to err, He makes his breast strait and narrow as though he were ascending upwards; thus does Allah lay uncleanness on those who do not believe" (surah 6:125). After Allah rejects a person there is no way back to him, nor will he send anyone to guide them back on the right path. "Nay! Those who are unjust follow their low desires without any knowledge; so who can guide him whom Allah makes err? And they shall have no helpers" (surah 30:29).

In surah 32:13 Allah's purpose is made clear. It appears that his primary objective for his creation is to fill hell with them. "And if We had pleased We would certainly have given to every soul its guidance, but the word (which had gone forth) from Me was just: I will certainly fill hell with the jinn [spiritual beings] and men together."

The Bible presents Adam and the nature of sin from an entirely different viewpoint. Adam was the archetype of the Christ to come. In Genesis 1:26-27, God makes it clear the nature of Adam and Eve's creation. "Then God said, 'Let us make man **in our image**, in our likeness, and let them rule over the fish of the sea and the birds of the air, over the livestock, over all the earth, and over all the creatures that move along the ground.' So God created man in his own image, **in the image of God** he created him; male and female he created them (author's emphasis)." God made man in His own image. Adam, God's first human creation, was also the son of God (Luke 3:38).

Through Adam sin and death entered the world. "For since death came through a man," the Apostle Paul wrote, "the resurrection of the dead comes also through a man. For as in Adam all die, so in Christ all will be made alive (1 Corinthians 15:21-22)." Jesus, also called the Son of God, was the second and last Adam. "So it is written:" Paul stated, "'The first man Adam became a living being [Genesis 2:7];' the last Adam, a life-giving spirit" (1 Corinthians 15:45).

To the church in Rome, Paul explained this relationship of sin to Adam in this manner: "When Adam sinned, sin entered the world. Adam's sin brought death, so death spread to everyone, for everyone sinned. Yes, people sinned even before the law was given. But it was not counted as sin because there was not yet any law to break. Still, everyone died—from the time of Adam to the time of Moses—even those who did not disobey an explicit commandment of God, as Adam did. Now Adam is a symbol, a representation of Christ, who was yet to come" (Romans 5:12-14, NLT).

The Qur'an repeatedly gives the impression that almighty Allah can be persuaded to lead one into sin and therefore be tempted to do evil toward his creation. Not so with the Almighty God of the Jews and Christians. "When tempted, no one should say, 'God is tempting me.' For God cannot be tempted by evil, nor does he tempt anyone; but each one is tempted when, by his own evil desire, he is dragged away and enticed. Then, after desire has conceived, it gives birth to sin; and sin, when it is full-grown, gives birth to death" (James 1:13-15).

Jesus the Sin Offering

To a world mired hopelessly in sin, the living God spoke these words through the prophet Isaiah: "Seek the LORD while he may be found; call on him while he is near. Let the wicked forsake his way and the evil man his thoughts. Let him turn to the LORD, and he will have mercy on him, and to our God, for he will freely pardon" (Isaiah 55:6-7). God, the God of the Jews and Christians, and not Allah, desires to forgive sin. God, the infinite, living God, proved His great love for mankind in that, *while we were still sinners, Christ died for us.*

"Therefore, since we have been justified through faith, we have peace with God through our Lord Jesus Christ, through whom we have gained access by faith into this grace in which we now stand. And we rejoice in the hope of the glory of God. Not only so, but we also rejoice in our sufferings, because we know that suffering produces perseverance; perseverance, character; and character, hope. And hope does not disappoint us, because God has poured out his love into our hearts by the Holy Spirit, whom he has given us.

You see, at just the right time, when we were still powerless, Christ died for the ungodly. Very rarely will anyone die for a righteous man, though for a good man someone might possibly

*dare to die. But **God demonstrates his own love for us in this:
While we were still sinners, Christ died for us.***

*Since we have now been justified by his blood, how much
more shall we be saved from God's wrath through him."*
(Romans 5:1-9, author's emphasis)

For the Muslim, sadly, there is no sin offering. Allah offers no means
by which the Islamic believer can be reconciled with Allah and set free
from his or her sin. It is a hopeless and unforgiving faith in a hopeless and
unforgiving god. Christians, on the other hand, have a clear and secured
hope in Jesus Christ. "He was delivered over to death for our sins,"
preached and wrote Paul, "and was raised to life for our justification
(Romans 4:25)." In and of himself, man can never be justified and made
right before God. It is only through the substitutionary death of Jesus
Christ, the only Son of the living God, that man, placing his faith in
the sacrificial work of Christ, can be set free from sin and the law of
sin and death.

"For Christ died for sins once for all," the Apostle Peter preached
in his first letter shortly before his own death, "the righteous for the
unrighteous, to bring you to God. He was put to death in the body
but made alive by the Spirit" (1 Peter 3:18). Peter, like Paul, plainly
understood the significance of Christ's substitutionary death in his place
so that he and all those who put their faith in Jesus may be made right
with God. Paul wrote this explanation to the Christians in Rome: "But
the gift is not like the trespass. For if the many died by the trespass of
the one man, how much more did God's grace and the gift that came by
the grace of the one man, Jesus Christ, overflow to the many!" (Romans
5:15). Two verses later he further clarified his spiritual point. "For if,
by the trespass of the one man, death reigned through that one man,
how much more will those who receive God's abundant provision of
grace and of the gift of righteousness reign in life through the one man,
Jesus Christ" (Romans 5:17).

This death on the cross of sin by proxy while clearly part of God's
simple plan for mankind is hard for man to accept and a stumbling block
for many, including Muslims. Man and all Muslims are determined to
work out their own salvation. However, God's principle of personal
salvation is so straightforward: "God made him who had no sin to be

sin for us," Paul told the Corinthians, "so that in him we might become the righteousness of God" (2 Corinthians 5:21). Righteousness before the only true God does not depend on the acts of men and women; it rests upon the saving grace of Jesus Christ and Him only. In this case, both Jews and Muslims share a common mindset and fate—neither can accept this easy road to salvation laid out by Jesus and His heavenly Father. "For just as through the disobedience of the one man [Adam] the many were made sinners, so also through the obedience of the one man [Jesus] the many will be made righteous" (Romans 5:19). Paul's analogy is simple enough: sin entered into the world through one man and it can leave through one man.

Part of the problem is that neither Jews nor Muslims can identify with an advocate, someone who could share in their pain and suffering and understand their need for a savior. "Therefore," wrote the unidentified author of the letter to the Hebrews, "since we have a great high priest who has gone through the heavens, Jesus the Son of God, let us hold firmly to the faith we profess. For we do not have a high priest who is unable to sympathize with our weaknesses, but we have one who has been tempted in every way, just as we are—yet was without sin" (Hebrews 4:14-15). Muhammad could not fill this role, nor any of the prophets or sages before him. Only Jesus Christ, the Son of God.

In chapter nine of the same letter, the writer brings to fruition the role of Jesus' sin offering. "But now he has appeared once for all at the end of the ages to do away with sin by the sacrifice of himself. Just as man is destined to die once, and after that to face judgment, so Christ was sacrificed once to take away the sins of many people; and he will appear a second time, not to bear sin, but to bring salvation to those who are waiting for him" (Hebrews 9:26b-28). Without this sacrifice for sin man has no recourse to reconcile himself to God. He is hopelessly lost in his own wretched despair with no escape from his propensity to sin.

However, for the Christian—the one who truly believes in Christ's sin redeeming sacrifice on the cross—there is always a way back from sin to righteousness and right standing with God. "My dear children, I write this to you so that you will not sin. But if anybody does sin, we have one who speaks to the Father in our defense—Jesus Christ, the Righteous One" (1 John 2:1). When a Christian confesses his or her sin,

Jesus is ever ready to stand before the Father God on their behalf to intercede for their benefit. The Muslim has no such recourse; no such advocate pleading their cause for righteousness before Allah.

Light vs. Darkness

"This is the verdict:" said Jesus, "Light has come into the world, but men loved darkness instead of light because their deeds were evil. Everyone who does evil hates the light, and will not come into the light for fear that his deeds will be exposed. But whoever lives by the truth comes into the light, so that it may be seen plainly that what he has done has been done through God" (John 3:19-21). Muslims, it would seem, love the darkness. They are forbidden to read or even possess a Bible—the only source of God's truth which holds out a hope of salvation for them. Likewise, the Bible is banded in the wide majority of Muslim controlled countries. A Christian is prohibited from entering Mecca or its environs at any time for any reason. In other words, both truth and light—the light of God's word—are banded from the life of the Muslim. Muslim imams and their followers fear the truth and are blinded by the light of the Gospel. Darkness only gives way to more darkness.

In John 8:12, Jesus affirms that "I am the light of the world. Whoever follows me will never walk in darkness, but will have the light of life." The revelation of Allah in surah 5:15-16 would appear to confirm Jesus' words. "O followers of the Book [Bible]! Indeed Our Apostle has come to you making clear to you much of what you concealed of the Book and passing over much; indeed, there has come to you light and a clear Book from Allah; With it Allah guides him who will follow His pleasure into the ways of safety and brings them out of utter darkness into light by His will and guides them to the right path."

Historically and biblically, Jesus exemplified the revelation knowledge and light of Almighty God. Wherever He went, multitudes, including Jewish religious leaders, marveled at His godly wisdom and enlightenment. The same cannot be said of Muhammad. For the most part, Jews, Christians and pagans of his era were not impressed or moved by Muhammad's words, life examples or tactics. While Muhammad claimed that the Bible (the *Taurat* or Torah and *Injeel* or Gospel) was revealed to Jews and Christians by Allah, it is apparent by his life, words and deeds that he believed little in what was revealed in the *Book* or Bible. In particular, the life and teachings of Jesus Christ, which Muhammad claimed to supersede, was in direct contradiction to what Muhammad taught and exemplified.

"The man who walks in the dark," Jesus said, "does not know where he is going. Put your trust in the light while you have it, so that you may become sons of light .... I have come into the world as a light, so that no one who believes in me should stay in darkness" (John 12:35b-36a, 46). While God the Father sent Jesus to be *the light of the world*, it would appear—by the sole criterion of his deeds—that Muhammad was sent by Allah to usher in a new dominion of darkness. Whereas the message of Jesus brought freedom, the message of Muhammad returned to bondage all those who followed it.

Shortly before he was crucified upside down, the Apostle Peter wrote a letter to the persecuted Christians in the Roman provinces that now make up present-day Turkey. "But you are a chosen people," he reminded them, "a royal priesthood, a holy nation, a people belonging to God, that you may declare the praises of him who called you out of darkness into his wonderful light" (1 Peter 2:9). The lost, through the ministry of Christ's followers, were being called out of the darkness of oppression into the wondrous light of redemptive freedom. Contrast this independence with the slavery and subjugation that the message of Islam brought to the peoples of the Middle East and continues to present to the world today.

"In him was life," the Apostle John wrote of Jesus, "and that life was the light of men. The light shines in the darkness, but the darkness has not understood" (John 1:4-5). It is ironic, as this scripture points out, but the ones who actually live in spiritual darkness are the ones who have the most difficult time seeing the light of truth.

"Furthermore, since they did not think it worthwhile to retain the knowledge of God, he gave them over to a depraved mind, to do what ought not to be done. They have become filled with every kind of wickedness, evil, greed and depravity. They are full of envy, murder, strife, deceit and malice. They are gossips, slanderers, God-haters, insolent, arrogant and boastful; they invent ways of doing evil; they disobey their parents; they are senseless, faithless, heartless, ruthless. Although they know

God's righteous decree that those who do such things deserve death, they not only continue to do these very things but also approve of those who practice them." (Romans 1:28-32)

It is no great surprise, however, that Muslims have a hard time exiting their spiritual darkness in order to come into the light of spiritual truth. If they can not accept the idea of a savior who can redeem them from their sins, how could they ever come to the light of God's forgiveness? "For he has rescued us from the dominion of darkness," Paul wrote from his prison cell in Rome, "and brought us into the kingdom of the Son he loves, in whom we have redemption, the forgiveness of sins" (Colossians 1:13-14). A person who can not receive the reality of God's redemptive grace and forgiveness offered to them will not likely to be set free from their spiritual and emotional bondage to darkness and evil.

Muslims are not alone in their life of darkness. All people live in sin and spiritual darkness according to Christ and His apostles until they acknowledge the free gift of salvation in Jesus Christ that God sent into the world over 2,000 years ago. "For you were once darkness," Paul again wrote from prison, "but now you are light in the Lord. Live as children of light (for the fruit of the light consists in all goodness, righteousness and truth) and find out what pleases the Lord. Have nothing to do with the fruitless deeds of darkness, but rather expose them" (Ephesians 5:8-11).

"Now if we died with Christ, we believe that we will also live with him. For we know that since Christ was raised from the dead, he cannot die again; death no longer has mastery over him. The death he died, he died to sin once for all; but the life he lives, he lives to God.

In the same way, count yourselves dead to sin but alive to God in Christ Jesus. Therefore do not let sin reign in your mortal body so that you obey its evil desires." (Romans 6:8-12)

Allah, the Compassionless God

Allah was always compassionate to Muhammad but not to those who rejected Muhammad, including women, children, Jews, Christians, Arab poets or anyone who was a dissenter to his message.[3] The saga of

Muhammad's uncle, Abu Lahab, is a good example of the compassionless Allah. Abu Lahab refused to accept Muhammad as a prophet. Shortly after a public confrontation Muhammad received a revelation from Allah cursing Lahab for his objection to Muhammad's message.[4,5] The response is an entire five verse surah. "Perdition overtake both hands of Abu Lahab, and he will perish. His wealth and what he earns will not avail him. He shall soon burn in fire that flames, and his wife, the bearer of fuel, upon her neck a halter of strongly twisted rope" (surah 111:1-5).

God, in the revealed person of Jesus Christ, expressed nothing but love and compassion for the spiritually lost—the unbeliever. "But you, O Lord," David prayed, "are a compassionate and gracious God, slow to anger, abounding in love and faithfulness" (Psalm 86:15). Allah, as expressed through Muhammad, had nothing but hatred and contempt for those who failed to see the truth of his message. By comparison, Jesus, in the Gospel of Luke, told His disciples the allegory of the ungrateful son, popularly known as the parable of the *Prodigal Son* (Luke 15:11-32). The father had two sons, Jesus said. The younger wanted his inheritance from his father now so that he could go off and live a life of debauchery and sinfulness apart from the father. He squandered all his money and became destitute. Finally, he realized the error of his ways and started on his journey home. "But while he was still a long way off, his father saw him and was filled with compassion for him; he ran to his son, threw his arms around him and kissed him" (verse 20).

The tale, of course, is a metaphor for the compassion and love God has for the lost—those who initially reject Him and His saving grace through Christ. Rather than God rejecting them because of their sin or lack of belief in Him, He is overjoyed when just one such sinner comes to Him in faith—faith in Jesus Christ.

Then there was the miracle of the *loaves and fishes* or the feeding of the five thousand (Mark 6:30-44). When Jesus tried to retire to a quiet place, five thousand men and an unreported number of women and children gathered around Him. "When Jesus landed [on the shore] and saw a large crowd, he had compassion on them, because they were like sheep without a shepherd …" (verse 34). As He preached the word of God to them the day grew late and the people were hungry but without food. When all was assessed there were only five loaves of bread and two fish among them. But God, through the faith and compassion of Jesus performed a miracle that fed them all with more left over than what they had at the beginning. A similar example of Allah's compassion for his followers can not be found in the Qur'an.

Not only is Allah without compassion, but he provides no means by which a transgressor can be reconciled with him. Surah 3:56 clearly states, "Then as to those who disbelieve, I will chastise them with severe chastisement in this world and the hereafter, and they shall have no helpers."

"And certainly," Allah revealed to Muhammad in surah 6:94, "you have come to Us alone as We created you at first, and you have left behind your backs the things which We gave you, and We do not see with you your intercessors about whom you asserted that they were (Allah's) associates in respect to you; certainly the ties between you are now cut off and what you asserted is gone from you." Surah 10:18 makes it clear that Allah does not recognize any intercessor in heaven or on earth on the behalf of his faithful. If they sin, they are on their own with no recourse other than facing Allah's judgment.

However, the God of the Jews and Christians does provide a means of redemption through the shed blood of Christ. "Who will bring any charge against those whom God has chosen?" The Apostle Paul taught. "It is God who justifies. Who is he that condemns? Christ Jesus, who died—more than that, who was raised to life—is at the right hand of God and is also interceding for us" (Romans 8:33-34). Allah, on the other hand, denies that there can be any intercessor standing before him. "Or have they taken intercessors besides Allah? Say: what! Even though they did not ever have control over anything, nor do they understand. Say: Allah's is the intercession altogether; His is the kingdom of the heavens and the earth, then to Him you shall be brought back" (surah 39:43-44).

Finally, Allah informs the faithful in surah 40:18, "And warn them of the day that draws near, when hearts shall rise up to the throats, grieving inwardly; the unjust shall not have any compassionate friend nor any intercessor who should be obeyed." Allah made it obvious that Muhammad was no more than an apostle (surah 3:144) and was in no position or authority to intercede before Allah for anyone. Compared to Jesus and the importance of His role for mankind, Muhammad was of little significance.

Forgiveness and Reconciliation

While Allah can forgive sin if he so pleases—if he's not too busy leading his believers astray—he can not redeem the sinner. Without a source or means of redemption, the only hope of salvation that a Muslim has available is that his inclination for sinning does not outweigh his accumulation of good deeds. But then, again, that may not be good enough to satisfy Allah. According to surah 5:54, Allah gives grace only *to whom he pleases.* Jehovah God gives grace to all those who receive Jesus Christ as Lord and Savior (John 1:17; Romans 5:15).

For a sinner—and all people are sinners—to live in sin without the hope of redemption and forgiveness only keeps them in bondage to sin. If there is no hope to be set free from sin, then why stop sinning? The shepherd-king, David, understood this; for he considered himself chief among the sinners.

Blessed is he whose transgressions are forgiven, whose sins are covered.

Blessed is the man whose sin the LORD does not count against him and in whose spirit is no deceit.

When I kept silent, my bones wasted away through my groaning all day long. For day and night your hand was heavy upon me; my strength was sapped as in the heat of summer. Selah

Then I acknowledged my sin to you and did not cover up my iniquity. I said, "I will confess my transgressions to the LORD"—and you forgave the guilt of my sin. Selah. (Psalm 32:1-5)

David had an intimate, personal relationship with God long before Jesus, the redeemer, was revealed. He understood that his God could and would forgive him for his sins and that as long as he did not conceal them from the living God, He was just and merciful and would relieve him of the burden of his iniquities. His guilt that he carried for his sin was removed as long as he confessed his transgressions to the Lord. With the revelation and ministry of Christ, God made it clear that He would not condemn anyone for their sin as long as they confessed it and accepted the redeeming work of His Son. "Therefore, there is now no condemnation for those who are in Christ Jesus," the Apostle Paul taught, "because through Christ Jesus the law of the Spirit of life set me free from the law of sin and death. For what the law was powerless to do in that it was weakened by the sinful nature, God did by sending his own Son in the likeness of sinful man to be a sin offering. And so he condemned sin in sinful man, in order that the righteous requirements of the law might be fully met in us, who do not live according to the sinful nature but according to the Spirit" (Romans 8:1-4).

Jesus taught all those who would listen how important it was to be set free from sin. It was essential to become an heir to the Kingdom of God. "To the Jews who had believed him, Jesus said, 'If you hold to my teaching, you are really my disciples. Then you will know the truth, and the truth will set you free,' … Jesus replied, 'I tell you the truth, everyone who sins is a slave to sin. Now a slave has no permanent place in the family, but a son belongs to it forever. So if the Son sets you free, you will be free indeed'" (John 8:31-32, 34-36). Freedom from sin was and is vital to accepting one's sonship with the Father in heaven.

Where the Spirit of the Lord Jesus Christ is, there is freedom from sin. "But whenever anyone turns to the Lord, the veil is taken away," Paul wrote in his second letter to the church in Corinth. "Now the Lord is the Spirit, and where the Spirit of the Lord is, there is freedom. And we, who with unveiled faces all reflect the Lord's glory, are being transformed into his likeness with ever-increasing glory, which comes from the Lord, who is the Spirit" (2 Corinthians 3:16-18). Key to this transformation that Paul talked about is the daily confession of sin, accepting God's forgiveness and receiving the redemptive work of the Cross. The Apostle John decreed it in this manner:

This is the message we have heard from him and declare to you: God is light; in him there is no darkness at all. If we claim to have fellowship with him yet walk in the darkness, we lie and do not live by the truth. But if we walk in the light, as he is in the light, we have fellowship with one another, and the blood of Jesus, his Son, purifies us from all sin.

If we claim to be without sin, we deceive ourselves and the truth is not in us. If we confess our sins, he is faithful and just and will forgive us our sins and purify us from all unrighteousness. If we claim we have not sinned, we make him out to be a liar and his word has no place in our lives. (1 John 1:5-10)

Unlike the believers of the Islamic faith, it is not by any works of righteousness that deliver a Christian from sin. It is purely by the generous grace of God through faith in His Son, Jesus Christ. It is an act of faith, not works, which redeems one from sin. "Therefore," Paul wrote to the church in Rome, "since we have been justified through faith, we have peace with God through our Lord Jesus Christ, through whom we have gained access by faith into this grace in which we now stand. And we rejoice in the hope of the glory of God" (Romans 5:1-2). In his letter to the Galatians, Paul emphasized the necessity and role of Christ's crucifixion to one's deliverance from sin and the sinful nature. "I have been crucified with Christ and I no longer live, but Christ lives in me. The life I live in the body, I live by faith in the Son of God, who loved me and gave himself for me'" (Galatians 2:20).

Sins Remitted or Unforgiven

According to former Muslim and author Raza Safa, who converted to Christianity, "… not a single Muslim in the world can tell you boldly that his sins are forgiven and that he has eternal life."[6] When it comes to forgiveness there are two great stumbling blocks for the Muslim. First, they can not conceive of a compassionate, forgiving god that would redeem them from their sins here and now, rather than at the *judgment* after their death. Second, they can not fathom and refuse to accept that a man, any man, could be sacrificed as a sin offering for anyone, much more for the good of all mankind. Over 700 years before the birth of Jesus, Isaiah prophesied about the coming Messiah's mission. "But he was pierced for our transgressions, he was crushed for our iniquities; the punishment that brought us peace was upon him, and by his wounds we are healed" (Isaiah 53:5).

Muslims, like Christians and Jews, are to abstain from all sin and wickedness. However, when a Muslim sins, the only way back into Allah's grace is through repentance and good deeds. Repentance does not obliterate the sin or wipe it from the mind of Allah. The sin, though confessed and repented of, is still added to Allah's ledger of bad deeds.

Also, it is not clear in the Qur'an or ahadiths what actually constitutes sin other than blaspheming or defaming Allah or Muhammad. Sin—whatever can be determined as such—must then be overcome by an appropriate good deed—if that can also be determined. The Muslim faithful never have absolute assurance that any confession of sin earns Allah's unconditional forgiveness and their slate is wiped clean for that offense. Christians, on the other hand, have a blood covenant with God through the sacrifice of Christ that guarantees them of an absolute forgiveness for any sin they commit. "My dear children," the Apostle John proclaimed, "I write this to you so that you will not sin. But if anybody does sin, we have one who speaks to the Father in our defense—Jesus Christ, the Righteous One" (1 John 2:1). Christians may rest assured, that when they commit a sin, if they confess it to God and seek forgiveness of both God and the one offended, they are made right with God because of Jesus' shed blood and His intercession before God on their behalf.

"And [there are] others [who] have confessed their faults, they have mingled a good deed and an evil one; [it] may [well] be [that] Allah will turn to them [and accept their repentance] (mercifully); surely Allah is Forgiving, Merciful" (surah 9:102). Note that forgiveness for a Muslim's sins, even if confessed, is not a sure thing with Allah. He may forgive them, He may not—no one knows for certain. It may well be that Allah will forgive their faults or it may well be that he will not. For the Jew and Christian there is no doubt about God's forgiveness. "Praise the Lord, O my soul, and forget not all his benefits—who **forgives all your sins** and heals all your diseases, who **redeems your life from the pit** and crowns you with love and compassion" (Psalm 103:2-4, author's emphasis). In distinct contrast, Allah is selective in what he might forgive. "And whatever affliction befalls you," Muhammad revealed in surah 42:30, "it is on account of what your hands have wrought, and (yet) He pardons most (of your faults)."

In Isaiah 43:25, God, through the prophet Isaiah, makes it clear that His intentions are complete and unmitigated forgiveness for sin, to the extent that He will not even bring them to remembrance ever again. "I, even I, am he who blots out your transgressions, for my own sake, and remembers your sins no more" (Isaiah 43:25).

David, the author of Psalm 103, made it clear that the true nature of his God and the God of the Jews and Christians was that of a compassionate and forgiving God that permanently removed the sins of those who transgressed against Him. "The Lord is compassionate and gracious," David wrote, "slow to anger, abounding in love. He will not always accuse, nor will he harbor his anger forever; he does not treat us as our sins deserve or repay us according to our iniquities. For as high as the heavens are above the earth, so great is his love for those who fear him; as far as the east is from the west, so far has he removed our transgressions from us" (Psalm 103:8-12). What a contrast to the god of the Muslims. Allah is an angry, vengeful god, who is indecisive about forgiveness and waits until after a believer's death to determine their degree of righteousness. Jehovah, the living God of the Judeo-Christian faiths is a compassionate, forgiving God who withholds His anger in exchange for unreserved love—a love that removes sin forever from the repentant transgressor.

Allah is not a forgiver and a redeemer of souls. He only offers a brief respite from his eventual retribution for one's sinfulness. "And if Allah had destroyed men for their iniquity," Muhammad revealed, "He would not leave on the earth a single creature, but He respites them [gives them a breather] till an appointed time; so when their doom will come they shall not be able to delay (it) an hour nor can they bring (it) on (before its time)" (surah 16:61). Allah may offer temporary forgiveness on earth; however, no Muslim can be sure he or she has actually received it. The only thing they know for sure is that their deeds—good and bad—will be judged *after* their death when there is no hope of reconciliation.

It does appear that Allah offers to bargain on sin. "If you shun the **great sins** which you are forbidden, We will do away with your **small sins** and cause you to enter an honorable place of entering" (surah 4:31, author's emphasis). As a counter balance, does this mean if a Muslim commits a great sin, then his or her small ones will not be forgiven? And what is a great sin, and what is a small sin? Is the jihadist suicide bomber who murders innocent people committing a *great* sin? Not so, according to the Qur'an and the teaching of Muhammad. Instead, he is awarded the highest honor by Allah. To God Almighty of the Jews and

Christians, sin is sin. No sin is weighed greater than another, other than the sin of blasphemy against the Holy Spirit (Matthew 12:31).

"What shall we say, then?" Paul asked rhetorically, "Shall we go on sinning so that grace may increase? By no means! We died to sin; how can we live in it any longer? Or don't you know that all of us who were baptized into Christ Jesus were baptized into his death? We were therefore buried with him through baptism into death in order that, just as Christ was raised from the dead through the glory of the Father, we too may live a new life" (Romans 6:1-4).

Remember, Allah is in the sin business, not the forgiveness enterprise. "… Allah **makes whom He pleases err** and He guides whom He pleases …" (surah 14:4, author's emphasis). How can any Muslim ever be sure that he is not being directed by Allah to do evil? But then, if he is doing evil, then it must be Allah's will. If forgiveness is to come, one might have to wait for it until Allah is good and ready to dispense it. "Except those who are patient and do good; they shall have forgiveness and a great reward" (surah 11:11). But how long must one wait? Not a single Muslim could tell you, other than Allah's judgment will be certain at the end of their life. Once again, in surah 6:39, Muhammad disclosed, "And they who reject Our commandments are deaf and dumb, in utter darkness; **whom Allah pleases He causes to err** [sin], and whom He pleases He puts on the right way" (author's emphasis). So, the rationale would be, if one is sinning it must be Allah's fault. It is his guidance and direction for one's life and can not be resisted because it is by Allah's good pleasure and he is responsible. The God of the Christians and Jews hates sin—all sin. He can not be tempted to lead someone astray, nor does He cause anyone to sin (James 1:13).

Jehovah God, speaking through the prophet Isaiah once again, promised that all transgressors would be delivered and set free from sin by the sacrificial death of His Son. "Therefore I will give him a portion among the great, and he will divide the spoils with the strong, because he poured out his life unto death, and was numbered with the transgressors. For he bore the sin of many, and made intercession for the transgressors" (Isaiah 53:12). This forgiveness of sin, Jeremiah prophesied, would come through a personal knowledge of a personal God that would bear witness to one's own spirit, that indeed they had received God's forgiveness. "'No longer will a man teach his neighbor, ог а man his brother, saying, *Know the Lord*, because they will all know me, from the least of them to the greatest,' declares the Lord. 'For I will forgive their wickedness and will remember their sins no more'" (Jeremiah 31:34).

Three disciples of Christ and authors of biblical epistles shared this redemptive truth with their fellow Christians. The Apostle Peter wrote, "He himself bore our sins in his body on the tree, so that we might die to sins and live for righteousness; by his wounds you have been healed. For you were like sheep going astray, but now you have returned to the Shepherd and Overseer of your souls "(1 Peter 2:24-25). The Apostle Paul wrote to the church in Ephesus that, "In him we have redemption through his blood, the forgiveness of sins, in accordance with the riches of God's grace that he lavished on us with all wisdom and understanding" (Ephesians 1:7-8). The unknown author of the letter to the Hebrews penned, "How much more, then, will the blood of Christ, who through the eternal Spirit offered himself unblemished to God, cleanse our consciences from acts that lead to death, so that we may serve the living God! (Hebrews 9:14).

All three, as did the other Apostles and early disciples of Jesus, undoubtedly knew what it meant to be redeemed by the sacrifice of Jesus. They all lived under the Law of Moses and oppressive guilt, but now had been set free by a merciful and loving God.

The Apostle Paul, in his very thorough letter to the Christians in Rome, set forth the contrast between this new found freedom in Christ and the sinful nature of man.

> *Those who live according to the sinful nature have their minds set on what that nature desires; but those who live in accordance with the Spirit have their minds set on what the Spirit desires. The mind of sinful man is death, but the mind controlled by the Spirit is life and peace; the sinful mind is hostile to God. It does not submit to God's law, nor can it do so. Those controlled by the sinful nature cannot please God.*
>
> *You, however, are controlled not by the sinful nature but by the Spirit, if the Spirit of God lives in you. And if anyone does not have the Spirit of Christ, he does not belong to Christ. But if Christ is in you, your body is dead because of sin, yet your spirit is alive because of righteousness. And if the Spirit of him who*

raised Jesus from the dead is living in you, he who raised Christ from the dead will also give life to your mortal bodies through his Spirit, who lives in you. (Romans 8:5-11)

Two verses that many Christians memorize to remind them of this substitutionary sacrifice of Christ are Romans 5, verses 7 and 8, were Paul states that, "Very rarely will anyone die for a righteous man, though for a good man someone might possibly dare to die. But God demonstrates his own love for us in this: While we were still sinners, Christ died for us."

Observing the Law of Works

The Law of Moses handed down to the Jews by Yahweh, the God of the Jews, like any religious law, was a series of you *shall* and *shall not* do what God commands. The Law was impossible to keep, for all men were sinful and weak. "Clearly **no one is justified before God by the law**," Paul wrote to the church in Galatia, "because, 'The righteous will live by faith [Habakkuk 2:4]'" (Galatians 3:11, author's emphasis). To the Christians in Rome, Paul offered this observation: "The law was added so that the trespass might increase. But where sin increased, grace increased all the more, so that, just as sin reigned in death, so also grace might reign through righteousness to bring eternal life through Jesus Christ our Lord" (Romans 5:20-21).

By contrast, the law of good and evil reign supreme in Islamic teaching. Only good works can offset evil deeds and not the saving grace of Allah. "And (as for) those who believe and do good deeds, these are the dwellers of the garden; in it they shall abide" (surah 2:82). Once again, in the same surah, Muhammad reveals the benefits of good deeds. "And spend in the way of Allah and cast not yourselves to perdition with your own hands, and do good (to others); surely Allah loves the doers of good" (surah 2:195).

According to the Bible, however, sinful man can never do enough good deeds to offset his sinfulness. God knew that from the very beginning of time. God sought a man that would answer His call to righteousness. "The people of the land practice extortion and commit robbery;" God spoke through the prophet Ezekiel, "they oppress the poor and needy and mistreat the alien, denying them justice. I looked for a man among them who would build up the wall and stand before me in the gap on behalf of the land so I would not have to destroy it, but I found none" (Ezekiel 22:29-30). God wanted an intercessor; someone to stand in the gap and take on the burden of sin of mankind, but none was blameless enough to answer the call. About one hundred years earlier, the prophet Isaiah revealed what would be God's ultimate solution for man's redemption. "He saw that there was no one, he was appalled that there was no one to intervene; so his own arm worked salvation for him, and his own righteousness sustained him. He put on righteousness as his breastplate, and the helmet of salvation on his head; he put on the garments of vengeance and wrapped himself in zeal as in a cloak" (Isaiah 59:16-17). In order to redeem man from his own sinful destruction, God would extend His *own arm* in the person of His Son to bring about salvation for His children.

God's eventual solution for mankind's sinful separation from Him was to bring about redemption and reconciliation by His own hand. Once again, through the prophet Isaiah, God revealed His loving intent. "But now, this is what the Lord says—he who created you, O Jacob, he who formed you, O Israel: 'Fear not, for I have redeemed you; I have summoned you by name; you are mine. When you pass through the waters, I will be with you; and when you pass through the rivers, they will not sweep over you. When you walk through the fire, you will not be burned; the flames will not set you ablaze. For I am the Lord, your God, the Holy One of Israel, your Savior'" (Isaiah 43:1-3a). A few verses later in the same chapter, God revealed that no one else would be able to bring about this deliverance; this redemptive reconciliation of His creation with Him. "'I, even I, am the Lord, and **apart from me there is no savior**. I have revealed and saved and proclaimed—I, and **not some foreign god** among you. You are my witnesses,' declares the Lord, 'that I am God. Yes, and from ancient days I am he. No one can deliver out of my hand. When I act, who can reverse it?" (Isaiah 43:11-13, author's emphasis)

For the Old Testament Jew there was only one hope for removing the curse of the law (as illustrated in Deuteronomy 28), and that was to offer an animal sacrifice—to shed the blood of a warm-blooded animal. However, it was the high priest that had to make the sacrifice; the sinner could not come before God and do it. God's plan all along was to set the stage to end the blood sacrifice of the law once and for all with the shed blood of the Lamb of God, His only begotten Son, Jesus Christ. "When you were dead in your sins and in the uncircumcision of your sinful nature," the Apostle Paul proclaimed to the church in the Greek city of Colossae, one hundred miles west of Ephesus, "God made you alive with Christ. He forgave us all our sins, having **canceled the written code** [the law], with its regulations, that was against us and that stood opposed to us; he took it away, nailing it to the cross" (Colossians 2:13-14, author's emphasis).

To the Galatians, Paul declared, "Christ redeemed us from the **curse of the law** by becoming a curse for us, for it is written: 'Cursed is everyone who is hung on a tree'" [Deuteronomy 21:23] (Galatians 3:13, author's emphasis). Christ did not do away with the Law of Moses; He only put to death the curse for not keeping the law. "Do not think that I have come to abolish the Law or the Prophets;" Jesus told His listeners, "I have not come to abolish them but to fulfill them. I tell you the truth, until heaven and earth disappear, not the smallest letter, not the least stroke of a pen, will by any means disappear from the Law until everything is accomplished" (Matthew 5:17-18).

In many of his letters to the churches in Asia Minor, Paul hammered home the point that because of Christ's sacrifice, those who would accept it by faith were no longer under the curse of the law. There was no amount of good works that could redeem a person from sin and the law of consequences. "For when we were controlled by the sinful nature," Paul wrote, "the sinful passions aroused by the law were at work in our bodies, so that we bore fruit for death. But now, by dying to what once bound us, we have been released from the law so that we serve in the new way of the Spirit, and not in the old way of the written code" (Romans 7:5-6). No longer would it suffice for the blood of goats and bulls to be shed for a sin sacrifice. God, through Christ, had made a new and everlasting covenant with mankind through the shed blood of His Son. "But the ministry Jesus has received is as superior to theirs as the covenant of which he is mediator is superior to the old one, and it is founded on better promises" (Hebrews 8:6).

This new covenant concept was not an easy one for the Jew to accept. Even Paul, a devout Jew, struggled with it from time to time. "We know that the law is spiritual;" he confessed, "but I am unspiritual, sold as a slave to sin. I do not understand what I do. For what I want to do I do not do, but what I hate I do. And if I do what I do not want to do, I agree that the law is good. As it is, it is no longer I myself who do it, but it is sin living in me. I know that nothing good lives in me, that is, in my sinful nature. For I have the desire to do what is good, but I cannot carry it out. For what I do is not the good I want to do; no, the evil I do not want to do—this I keep on doing" (Romans 7:14-19).

Despite his pitiful struggle, Paul understood God's redemptive plan and each time he fell captive to sin he would turn to the saving work of his Lord and Savior, Jesus Christ. "So I find this law at work:" Paul admitted to the young Christians in Rome, "When I want to do good, evil is right there with me. For in my inner being I delight in God's law; but I see another law at work in the members of my body, waging war against the law of my mind and making me a prisoner of the law of sin at work within my members. What a wretched man I am! Who will rescue me from this body of death? Thanks be to God—through Jesus Christ our Lord!" (Romans 7:21-25a).

For the Muslim faithful there is no deliverance, no respite from the law of Allah and his judgment. Only good works offer any hope of reconciliation with Allah. The law reigns supreme for Muslims. Failure to keep the law can only be offset by good deeds. "Allah originates the creation, then reproduces it, then to Him you shall be brought back. And at the time when the hour shall come the guilty shall be in despair. And they shall not have any intercessors from among their gods, and they shall be deniers of their associate-gods" (surah 30:11-13). There is no mediator for the sinful Muslim; none that can plead his case before Allah and no assurance of ever being reconciled with Allah in this life or the next.

It is by faith—faith in Jesus Christ—that a person is justified, not by works or the law. "It was not through the law that Abraham and his offspring received the promise that he would be heir of the world," preached Paul, "but through the righteousness that comes from faith. For if those who live by the law are heirs, faith has no value and the promise is worthless, because law brings wrath. And where there is no law there is no transgression. Therefore, the promise comes by faith, so that it may be by grace and may be guaranteed to all Abraham's offspring—not only to those who are of the law but also to those who are of the faith of Abraham. He is the father of us all" (Romans 4:13-16, NIV).

Muslims, as do Jews and Christians, claim to be descendents of Abraham. If God, through the revelations of Jesus and his Apostles, revealed that redemption from sin came through the righteousness of faith, by God's grace, why would he take it back through a new revelation through Muhammad, that salvation or redemption from personal sin can only come through man's best efforts at good works, or by following the law?

"Therefore," Paul continues, "since we have been justified through faith, we have peace with God through our Lord Jesus Christ, through whom we have gained access by faith into this grace in which we now stand. And we rejoice in the hope of the glory of God" (Romans 5:1-2).

"The sting of death is sin," wrote the Apostle Paul, "and the power of sin is the law. But thanks be to God! He gives us the victory through our Lord Jesus Christ" (1 Corinthians 15:56-57). Without the sweet sacrifice of Christ that brought redemption and reconciliation with God, Christians would be no better off than those that follow the dictates of Islam. "So I say," penned Paul in his letter to the church in Galatia, "live by the Spirit, and you will not gratify the desires of the sinful nature. For the sinful nature desires what is contrary to the Spirit, and the Spirit what is contrary to the sinful nature. They are in conflict with each other, so that you do not do what you want. But if you are led by the Spirit, you are not under law .... But the fruit of the Spirit is love, joy, peace, patience, kindness, goodness, faithfulness, gentleness and self-control. Against such things there is no law. Those who belong to Christ Jesus have crucified the sinful nature with its passions and desires. Since we live by the Spirit, let us keep in step with the Spirit" (Galatians 5:16-18; 22-25).

The Apostle Paul spent much of his effort in his sixteen chapter letter to the Christians in Rome thoroughly explaining the nature of the law and sin and how believers in the saving work of Christ were set free from the law of sin and death. "The mind of sinful man is death, but the mind controlled by the Spirit is life and peace; the sinful mind is hostile to God. It does not submit to God's law, nor can it do so. Those controlled by the sinful nature cannot please God" (Romans 8:6-8).

Paul further revealed that keeping the law did not make one righteous before God. "Now we know that whatever the law says," he articulated, "it says to those who are under the law, so that every mouth may be silenced and the whole world held accountable to God. Therefore no one will be declared righteous in his sight by observing the law; rather, through the law we become conscious of sin. But now a righteousness from God, apart from law, has been made known, to which the Law and the Prophets testify. This righteousness from God comes through faith in Jesus Christ to all who believe. There is no difference, for all have sinned and fall short of the glory of God, and are justified freely by his grace through the redemption that came by Christ Jesus" (Romans 3:19-24).

A few verses later, Paul proclaimed, "For we maintain that a man is justified by faith apart from observing the law …. Do we, then, nullify the law by this faith? Not at all! Rather, we uphold the law" (Romans 3:28, 31). It is no longer the law that dictates the actions of the Christian; it is the Spirit of God living within each believer. "For sin shall not be your master," Paul wrote three chapters later, "because **you are not under law**, but under grace" (Romans 6:14, author's emphasis).

No Plan of Salvation

Salvation comes from confession of faith, not by works.

Allah offers no plan of redemption or salvation; no freedom of choice in what one chooses to believe. The Muslim lives in a constant state of anxiety, never knowing that his deeds will be good enough before Allah to assure him of everlasting life in heaven. He lives strictly by the law, the Qur'anic law as Allah supposedly revealed to Muhammad one verse at a time, and often at times when it benefited Muhammad and his objectives.

"In Islam," the Caner brothers revealed in their book, *Unveiling Islam*, "it is hoped that salvation is earned through one's good works…. There is no security for the believer of Islam."[7]

Not one Muslim who has died or who now lives knows his fate for sure after death. "So no soul knows what is hidden [after death] for them of that which will refresh the eyes; a reward for what they did. Is he then who is a believer like him who is a transgressor? They are not equal" (surah 32:17-18). These two verses must be confusing to a

Muslim. If a believer in Allah is not like a transgressor, then all Muslim believers must be sinless and all sinners are non-Muslim. However, even the most spiritually uninformed know that all men are sinners through and through. No one is perfect and without sin—no one except Jesus Christ the Son of God. Yet, Muhammad promises his followers in verses 19 and 20 that those who do (unspecified) good will abide in paradise, while those who do (unspecified) evil will abide in hell. Despite his unqualified proclamation, not even Allah's Apostle knew where he would spend eternity. Upon the death of a faithful Muslim, 'Uthman bin Maz'un, the one who nursed 'Uthman during his declining days, asked the Prophet what 'Uthman's post death future might be.

"But who else is worthy of [honor] (if not 'Uthman)?"

To which Muhammad replied, "As to him, by Allah, death has overtaken him, and I hope the best for him. By Allah, though I am the Apostle of Allah, yet I do not know what Allah will do to me [after I die]" (hadith 5:58:266). Muhammad had no clue and no hope of eternity, even though he was Allah's chosen Apostle—the one who was to deliver Allah's final message to all mankind; a message not of salvation, but of hopelessness.

"If you ask a Muslim what will happen to him when he dies," Reza Safa wrote, "he will answer, 'Only God knows!'

"Muslims do not have assurance of salvation ... the word *salvation* is unknown to them."[8]

Muhammad never sacrificed his life for anyone. As a result, Muslims live in their sin until the day they die, hoping that when they appear before Allah in the hereafter, their good deeds will outweigh their bad ones and tip the scale in their favor. But they can never be assured of their salvation in this life, and in the next life. If their good deeds measure up to be insufficient, it's just too late and their soul will burn in the eternal fires of hell.

By comparison, all those who call upon the name of Jesus Christ are assured of their salvation. "Although he was a son, he learned obedience from what he suffered and, once made perfect, he became the source of eternal salvation for all who obey him" (Hebrews 5:8-9).

"Salvation [to rescue; deliver; bring to safety]," the Apostle Peter boldly preached before the Sanhedrin in Jerusalem, "is found in no one else [other than Jesus Christ], for there is no other name under heaven given to men by which we must be saved" (Acts 4:12).

Sadly, for the Muslim believer in Allah, there is no salvation and no reconciliation with him. "And We have made every man's actions to cling to his neck," Allah revealed to Muhammad, "and We will bring forth to him on the resurrection day a book which he will find wide open: Read your book; your own self is sufficient as a reckoner against you this day. Whoever goes aright, for his own soul does he go aright; and whoever goes astray, to its detriment only does he go astray; nor can the bearer of a burden bear the burden of another, nor do We chastise until We raise an apostle" (surah 17:13-15). Every bad deed and every good deed that a Muslim performs during his or her life will go with them to the grave. Allah will then review them from his book on the day of resurrection and weigh the good against the bad. There is no grace; no forgiveness. Every believer in Allah will stand spiritually naked before Allah waiting upon his judgment. There will be no intercessor; no mediator before Allah on behalf of the faithful. Only their works will be judged.

A Muslim's success or failure in life is based solely on his or her works—good or bad. "Why is it so important that Muslims do what Allah wants?" wrote author and former Muslim, Dr. Mark Gabriel. "It's because Islam is a religion of works. Entrance to Paradise (heaven) must be earned. The sad part is that Muslims can never have assurance of salvation."[9]

Once a bad deed is done there is no going back to redeem it, nor is there anyone who will intercede before Allah for them. "... are there for us then any intercessors so that they should intercede on our behalf?" Muhammad asked in surah 7:53. "Or could we be sent back so that we should do (deeds) other than those which we did? Indeed they have lost their souls, and that which they forged has gone away from them." Once a Muslim dies there is no hope for them. Nor is there any hope for them while they are alive. The only hope is that their good deeds over shadow their bad deeds.

Even Muhammad was uncertain about his future after death. "Say: I am not the first of the apostles, and I do not know what will be done with me or with you [by Allah]: I do not follow anything but that which is revealed to me, and I am nothing but a plain warner" (surah 46:9).

"Surely," Muhammad revealed, "they who believe and do good deeds and keep up prayer and pay the poor-rate they shall have their reward from their Lord, and they shall have no fear, nor shall they grieve" (surah 2:277). While the Qur'an talks about Allah's mercy toward believers, it says very little about Allah's grace (cf. surah 3:31). To receive Allah's love and mercy, a believer must follow the law—the law of good deeds, charity and prayer. Although Christians are called to the same godly ideals, it is in response to their salvation at the hands of a loving, forgiving God, not a performance in order to gain God's favor. Those who come to God through Christ know that their sins are too great; that they are too weak to retain God's favor without the shed blood of Christ covering their sins and their sinfulness. Without Christ, no one has the authority or the mediation to approach God for forgiveness and reconciliation. Islam provides for no such approach to Allah, and while Christ is presented in the Bible as God's sinless Son, the Qur'an presents Allah's "messenger," Muhammad, as a murderous, sin-laden human being with many imperfections—so imperfect that he tried to commit suicide several times and sought to kill his followers. Something Jesus never did; never considered and never would, because he loved God, his Father, he loved life and he loved everyone—his followers and even those who sought to kill him.

The essence of the message of the New Testament is that God so loved the world that He sent His only Son to redeem it; to save it from its own sinful destruction. In a dream God revealed to Joseph that his wife to be, Mary, was with child. "She will give birth to a son, and you are to give him the name Jesus, because he will save his people from their sins" (Matthew 1:21). Jesus was sent by God to save people from their sins. Muhammad, on the other hand, was apparently sent by Allah to destroy them.

"And the measuring out on that day [of judgment] will be just;" Muhammad proclaimed in surah 7:8-9, "then as for him whose measure (of good deeds) is heavy [exceeding his bad deeds], those are they who shall be successful [in entering paradise]; and as for him whose measure (of good deeds) is light, those are they who have made their souls suffer loss because they disbelieved in Our communications."

Jesus came to destroy the works of the devil. Muhammad, it seems, to implement them. The Apostle John wrote:

> *Dear children, do not let anyone lead you astray. He who does what is right is righteous, just as [Jesus] is righteous. He who does what is sinful is of the devil, because the devil has been sinning from the beginning. The reason the Son of God appeared was to destroy the devil's work. No one who is born of God will continue to sin, because God's seed remains in him; he cannot go on sinning, because he has been born of God. This is how we know who the children of God are and who the children of the devil are: Anyone who does not do what is right is not a child of God; nor is anyone who does not love his brother.* (1 John 3:7-10)

No one can earn or work toward God's salvation. "For it is by grace you have been saved, through faith—and this not from yourselves, it is the gift of God—not by works, so that no one can boast" (Ephesians 2:8-9). To be saved means to be justified in the eyes of God—to be determined and declared innocent and accepted by God—by faith with guaranteed results of eternal life as opposed to a Muslim working out acceptance by Allah but never being sure of their final destination. "Therefore," Paul affirmed, "since we have been justified through faith, we have peace with God through our Lord Jesus Christ, through whom we have gained access by faith into this grace in which we now stand. And we rejoice in the hope of the glory of God" (Romans 5:1-2).

God's plan of salvation is rather simple and available to anyone—Muslim, Jew, Hindu, Buddhist, or atheist; anyone—who would call upon the name of Christ. "That if you confess with your mouth, 'Jesus is Lord,' and believe in your heart that God raised him from the dead," the Apostle Paul proclaimed, "you will be saved. For it is with your heart that you believe and are justified, and it is with your mouth that you confess and are saved … for, 'Everyone who calls upon the name of the Lord will be saved'" (Romans 10:9-10, 13).

Freedom

To live a life of freedom—true spiritual and emotional freedom—one must appropriate it by faith in Jesus Christ. There is no other road to this freedom except through a personal relationship with Christ that brings one into an intimate relationship with the living God of the Jews

231

and Christians. No other religion offers such an opportunity, such a release from bondage.

> *You are all sons of God through faith in Christ Jesus, for all of you who were baptized into Christ have clothed yourselves with Christ. There is neither Jew nor Greek, slave nor free, male nor female, for you are all one in Christ Jesus. If you belong to Christ, then you are Abraham's seed, and heirs according to the promise.*
>
> *What I am saying is that as long as the heir is a child, he is no different from a slave, although he owns the whole estate. He is subject to guardians and trustees until the time set by his father. So also, when we were children, we were in slavery under the basic principles of the world. But when the time had fully come, God sent his Son, born of a woman, born under law, to redeem those under law, that we might receive the full rights of sons. Because you are sons, God sent the Spirit of his Son into our hearts, the Spirit who calls out, "Abba, Father." So you are no longer a slave, but a son; and since you are a son, God has made you also an heir.* (Galatians 3:26-4:7)

Freedom—true freedom—is unique to Judeo-Christian theology. It does not exist in the Islamic faith or among Muslims. "… to earn this religious freedom Muslims believe they must deprive religious freedom to others," wrote the Caner brothers in their book, *Unveiling Islam*.[10] When Jesus returned to His hometown of Nazareth early in His ministry, he opened the scroll of the prophet Isaiah (61:1) and read these words that described His coming as the Messiah. "The Spirit of the Sovereign LORD is on me, because the LORD has anointed me to preach good news to the poor. He has sent me to bind up the brokenhearted, to proclaim **freedom** for the captives and release from darkness for the prisoners" (Luke 4:18, author emphasis). Since time began, man has been in bondage to sin and separated from God. The Jews sacrificed animals in an effort to free them from their sins. Muslims labor at what they perceive to be "good works" to overshadow their sinful nature. Christians freely, without sacrifice or works, receive by the grace of God, forgiveness of their sins through the sacrifice of Christ and are set free from the bondage of sin and spiritual death.

"For we know," Paul preached in his letter to the new Christians in Rome, "that our old self was **crucified with him** so that the body of sin might be done away with, that we should no longer be slaves to sin—because anyone who has died has been freed from sin" (Romans 6:6-7, author's emphasis).

"In him," Paul wrote to the Ephesians a few years later, "and through faith in him we may approach God with freedom and confidence" (Ephesians 3:12). It is this freedom in Christ; freedom from the sinful nature, that believers in Christ can approach God through an intimate, personal experience that no other religion offers the believer. "It is for freedom that Christ has set us free," Paul penned to the Galatians. "Stand firm, then, and do not let yourselves be burdened again by a yoke of slavery" (Galatians 5:1). While physical slavery is confining and sometimes painful, it is spiritual and emotional imprisonment that wears on the hearts and souls of men and women and keeps mankind living under oppression and tyranny. The precepts of Islam present neither the philosophy nor reality of spiritual freedom or physical freedom. While slavery has been outlawed and abandoned in Western cultures, it is still a much practiced human indignity in much of the Muslim world today.

Slavery, at one time or another, has been the bane of most societies for millennia. The great difference is that Western cultures that are centered on Judeo-Christian principles are free to correct and redeem their sinful errors and have done so. Muslim cultures, on the other hand, have continually practiced slavery for fourteen centuries and have no prohibition against it in concept or teaching. "You, my brothers," Paul stated in his letter to the church in Galatia, "were called to be free. But do not use your freedom to indulge the sinful nature; rather, serve one another in love" (Galatians 5:13). Christians are called—and have always been called—to set people free from bondage, not to enslave them.

"Live as free men," the Apostle Peter insisted, "but do not use your freedom as a cover-up for evil; live as servants of God" (1 Peter 2:16). True Christianity is a religion of freedom—not freedom to gratify personal wants and desires, but freedom to serve Almighty God and those whom He loves. Islam, as revealed by Muhammad and taught by Islamic clerics, is a religion of oppression that seeks to take away the freedom of individuals, cultures, societies and countries and forcefully make them submit to the perceived law of Allah. There is no freedom of choice; no exercise of free will permitted. The Apostle Peter warned about false prophets that would seek to enslave what God had set free. "They promise them freedom," Peter wrote, "while they themselves are slaves of depravity—for a man is a slave to whatever has mastered him" (2 Peter 2:19).

The final goal of freedom in Christ for the Christian is not just to be separated from sin, but to secure a place in heaven with God. "But now that you have been set free from sin and have become slaves to God, the benefit you reap leads to holiness, and the result is eternal life. For the wages of sin is death, but the gift of God is eternal life in Christ Jesus our Lord" (Romans 6:22-23). Paul, an apostle of Jesus Christ, who before his reproach by Christ and his conversion, was a frequent persecutor and murderer of Christians, was no stranger to sin. He considered himself to be a leader among sinners, yet set free through Christ from his sinful nature and eternal damnation.

Heaven or Paradise

For the Muslim faithful who are successful in passing through Allah's judgment, they are awarded paradise, a place of personal, hedonistic pleasures: young virgin women and boys; sex; wine; servants and complete aggrandizement of personal indulgence. Paradise, however, apparently is just for men. Women (virgin women) are only mentioned with respect to meeting the sexual and other needs of Allah's chosen men. "And convey good news to those who believe and do good deeds, that they shall have gardens in which rivers flow; whenever they shall be given a portion of the fruit thereof, they shall say: This is what was given to us before; and they shall be given the like of it, and they shall have **pure mates** in them, and in them, they shall abide" (surah 2:25, author's emphasis).

Surely those who guard (against evil) shall be in gardens and bliss, rejoicing because of what their Lord gave them, and their Lord saved them from the punishment of the burning fire. Eat and drink pleasantly for what you did, reclining on thrones set in lines, and We will unite them to large-eyed beautiful ones [houris].

And (as for) those who believe and their offspring follow them in faith, We will not diminish to them aught of their work; every man is responsible for what he shall have wrought. And We will aid them with fruit and flesh such as they desire. They shall pass therein from one to another a cup wherein there shall be nothing vain nor any sin. And round them shall go boys of theirs as if they were hidden pearls. (surah 52:17-24)

Apparently, for the Muslim man who reaches paradise, anything goes. All the lust and sin that was forbidden to him on earth will now be freely available to him. The central theme of paradise for the Muslim male who is fortunate enough to enter it is the overwhelming availability of *houris*—young, voluptuous virgins with full breasts and large dark eyes.

And you shall not be rewarded except (for) what you did. Save the servants of Allah, the purified ones. For them is a known sustenance, fruits, and they shall be highly honored, in gardens of pleasure, on thrones, facing each other. A bowl shall be made to go round them from water running out of springs, white, delicious to those who drink. There shall be no trouble in it, nor shall they be exhausted therewith. And with them shall be those [houris] who restrain the eyes, having beautiful eyes; as if they were eggs carefully protected. (surah 37:39-49)

The men of paradise are free to engage the houris whenever they feel like it. They are pure and no man or jinni has ever had sex with them. In [the garden] shall be those [maidens] who restrained their eyes; before them neither man nor jinni [invisible beings] have touched them" (surah 55:56). The houris are there in paradise for one reason: to serve the needs of the Muslim man. "Then We have made them virgins, loving, equals in age, for the sake of the companions of the right hand" (surah 56:36-38).

"Thus (shall it be), and We will wed them with Houris pure, beautiful ones" (surah 44:54). Jesus said that there will be no marriage in heaven, but that everyone "will be like the angels in heaven" (Matthew 22:30). Jesus, in responding to the Sadducees (the Jewish religious leaders who did not fully accept the doctrine of the resurrection of the dead) on the issue of marriage in heaven, stated: "But those who are considered worthy of taking part in that age and in the resurrection from the dead will neither marry nor be given in marriage, and they will no longer die; for they are like the angels. They are God's children, since they are children of the resurrection" (Luke 20:35-36).

There appears to be one slight glitch with this journey to paradise. It seems, according to surah 19:70-72, that *every* Muslim goes to hell initially. "Again We do certainly know best those who deserve most to be burned [in hell] therein. And there is not one of you but shall come to it; this is an unavoidable decree of your Lord. And we will deliver those who guarded (against evil), and We will leave the unjust therein on their knees" (surah 19:70-72). So, despite Allah's plea to make sure the believer's good deeds exceed his bad deeds, in the end it makes no difference to Allah; he's going to send you to hell anyway.

Heaven and the Jihadist

There is one sure way, according to the teaching of Muhammad, for the Muslim to reach paradise. The jihadist or holy warrior has special favor with Allah. To kill Allah's enemies—that is all non-Muslims—is the only guaranteed way to paradise. "The Prophet said ... 'Paradise has one-hundred grades which Allah has reserved for the Mujahidin [holy warriors] who fight in His Cause" (hadith 4:52:48, narrated by Abu Huraira).

Abdullah Al Araby, writer for the Islam Review, confirms that, "The only assurance a Muslim has of going to Paradise is through fighting for the cause of spreading Islam (Jihad), and being martyred in the process"[11] The Caner brothers also concur: "Eternal security is further based on a Muslim's hatred toward enemies of Allah."[12]

Both the Qur'an and the ahadith also agree that it is the jihadist, the one who murders for the *cause of Allah*, and not the doer of good deeds, who will be awarded paradise without Allah passing judgment. "Therefore let those [who] fight in the way of Allah, who sell this world's life for the hereafter; and whoever fights in the way of Allah, [whether] he be slain or be he victorious, We shall grant him a mighty reward" (surah 4:74).

"The Prophet said, 'Nobody who dies and finds good from Allah (in the Hereafter) would wish to come back to this world even if he were given the whole world and whatever is in it, except the martyr who, on seeing the superiority of martyrdom, would like to come back to the world and get killed again (in Allah's Cause).' Narrated Anas: The Prophet said, 'A single endeavor (of fighting) in Allah's Cause in the afternoon or in the forenoon is better than all the world and whatever is in it'" (hadith 4:52:53, narrated by Anas bin Malik).

Not only are jihadists, including the suicide bombers of the world, granted a free pass to paradise, but according to a number of Islamic sources, including one cited by the Caner brothers, jihadists enter a palace in paradise where there are "seventy couches made of gold and emerald on which lay virgins, untouched by man prepared for their bridegrooms."[13]

The ones who are assured an abode in hell are not the murderous mujahidin, but those who reject Allah. "And (as to) those who disbelieve in and reject My communications, they are the inmates of the fire, in it they shall abide" (surahs 2:39; 5:10; 9:63).

> *Now a man came up to Jesus and asked, "Teacher, what good thing must I do to get eternal life?" "Why do you ask me about what is good?" Jesus replied. "There is only One who is good. If you want to enter life, obey the commandments." "Which ones?" the man inquired. Jesus replied, "Do not murder, do not commit adultery, do not steal, do not give false testimony, honor your father and mother, and love your neighbor as yourself."* (Matthew 19:16-19)

Muslims have had a long history of not loving their neighbors or being at peace with those nearby. To the contrary, they have had a long sorted and bloody history of murder, adultery, rape, thievery, deception, lies and hatred for their neighbors. This is certainly not a résumé that would get one into the heaven of Jehovah God.

The Reward of Righteousness

For those who accept the righteousness of God through faith in Jesus Christ *there is* a rich reward. "The wicked is driven away in his wickedness," declared King Solomon: "but the righteous hath hope [a refuge] in his death" (Proverbs 14:32, KJV). That *hope* after death for the righteous in Christ is everlasting life with the Father and His Son,

Jesus Christ. No other religion on the face of the earth offers this hope; this assurance of eternal life in Heaven. "The prospect of the righteous is joy, but the hopes of the wicked come to nothing," proclaimed Solomon (Proverbs 10:28).

This everlasting heavenly reward brings the ultimate peace to the believer in Christ. "Those who walk uprightly enter into peace; they find rest as they lie in death" (Isaiah 57:2). The follower of Allah and his prophet Muhammad have no such peace and reassurance of their final resting place. They can only hope that their good deeds (that are mostly unspecified in the Qur'an) will outweigh their bad deeds at the final reckoning *after* death.

"What the wicked dreads will overtake him;" Solomon wrote, "what the righteous desire will be granted. When the storm has swept by, the wicked are gone, but the righteous stand firm forever" (Proverbs 10:24-25). Once the final tally of deeds—good and bad—is in, there is no going back after death to right wrongs and tilt the scales in one's favor. After death, what's done is done and one's judgment shall be accordingly. Only the righteous in Christ will be able to breathe easily.

"The truly righteous man attains life," Solomon penned once again, "but he who pursues evil goes to his death. The Lord detests men of perverse heart but he delights in those whose ways are blameless. Be sure of this: The wicked will not go unpunished, but those who are righteous will go free …. The desire of the righteous ends only in good, but the hope of the wicked only in wrath" (Proverbs 11:19-21, 23).

> *You have said, "It is futile to serve God. What did we gain by carrying out his requirements and going about like mourners before the Lord Almighty? But now we call the arrogant blessed. Certainly the evildoers prosper, and even those who challenge God escape."*
>
> *Then those who feared the LORD talked with each other, and the LORD listened and heard. A scroll of remembrance was written in his presence concerning those who feared the LORD and honored his name.*
>
> *"They will be mine," says the LORD Almighty, "in the day when I make up my treasured possession. I will spare them, just as in compassion a man spares his son who serves him. And you will again see the distinction between the righteous and the*

wicked, between those who serve God and those who do not." (Malachi 3:14-18)

"For my Father's will," Jesus told His disciples, *"is that everyone who looks to the Son and believes in him shall have eternal life, and I will raise him up at the last day."* (John 6:40)

Conclusion

One of the core beliefs of the Christian is that he has been redeemed from his sin by the shed blood of Christ and has been made righteous in the eyes of God, his heavenly Father. This redemption from sin and reconciliation with God is alien to the Muslim believer. Allah does not want to redeem his creation, nor can he redeem it. He is not interested in reconciliation between himself and those who follow him.

The Christian faith, through Christ's work of redemption, offers hope—the only source of hope—to all mankind to be made right with Almighty God. Islam offers no hope, only hopelessness and despair. There is no assurance for the Muslim believer, who is taught to live by Allah's law, that he or she could ever please Allah enough or do enough good deeds to warrant his favor at the time of judgment after death. The Christian, however, is taught that it is by faith—faith in Christ, not deeds, that one is saved from everlasting fire and promised eternal life with the heavenly Father.

Freedom from Bondage

When I heard the gospel for the first time in my life, an awful fear began to grow within me, a doubt, a voice of warning. What if I were wrong? What if Muhammad was not sent by God?... I was afraid of God, afraid of resisting Muhammad, afraid of Islam.

Throughout my years as a practicing [radical Shiite] Muslim and strong follower of Islam, I had learned a tremendous respect for and fear of Muhammad and God. To reject Muhammad and the religion of Islam was to reject God. To deny God means the wrath of God, which would result in judgment to the pits of hell.

The history of Islam has shown that a Muslim who converts to Christianity or any other religion will pay a high price, especially those who are raised in strict Muslim homes. At the least, he will lose everything and everyone whom he loves. At worst, he will lose his life.

... The more I became fascinated with the truth of Christianity, the more fear increased in my mind.... I became afraid of the dark.... I had nightmares often, and I woke up in the middle of the night filled with fear.

Even after my conversion, I was not instantly free from the fear of Islam. One night shortly after my conversion I had an encounter with the spirit of fear in my room ... it seemed as though some awful sort of being who was full of darkness was standing over my head. Suddenly, I felt something heavy and dreadful land on my chest.

I realized that I was not dreaming, but that I was confronting demonic forces. I knew the only way to defeat those beings was to rebuke them and call upon the name of Jesus....

I knew that if I rebuked Satan in Jesus' name, he had no choice but to leave. But when I tried to open my mouth, I was unable to speak. My jaw was frozen, and I could not utter a word. I did not give up, though; I kept calling upon the name of Jesus in my mind. It was not long before my jaws were loosened, and I shouted the name of Jesus as loud as I could. The moment Jesus' name was uttered from my mouth, I was set totally free. Glory to His name. Since that time I have not feared Islam.

Reza F. Safa
Inside Islam, 1996
p. 93-94

References

1. Safa, Reza F. *Inside Islam: Exposing and Reaching the World of Islam*, 1996. Charisma House, p. 81.
2. *Qur'an*, Muhammad Asad translation. Isamicity.com. Http://www. islamicity.com.
3. Keohane, Steve. *Muhammad: Terrorist or Prophet?* BibleProbe.com, 200402007. Http://bibleprobe.com/muhammad.htm. Accessed April 1, 2007.
4. Ibid.
5. Spencer, Robert. *The Truth About Muhammad, Founder of the World's Most Intolerant Religion*, 2006. Regnery Publishing, Inc., p. 74.
6. Safa, p. 81.
7. Caner, Ergun Mehmet and Emir Fethi Caner. *Unveiling Islam*, 2002. Kregel Publications, div. of Kregel. Inc., p. 31.
8. Safa, p. 80.
9. Gabriel, Mark A. *Islam and Terrorism*, 2002. Published by FrontLine, a Strang Company, p. 27.
10. Caner & Caner, p.35.
11. Al Araby, Abdullah, *Nothing in Common*. IslamReview.com. http://www.islamreview.com/articles/nothingincommon.shtml. Accessed November 11, 2006.
12. Caner &Caner, p. 35.
13. Caner and Caner, p. 193.

The Mission

CHAPTER 9

Sacrificial Service or Sacrificial Murder

The universalism of Islam, in its all-embracing creed,
is imposed on the believers as a continuous process of warfare,
psychological and political, if not strictly military. . .
The Jihad, accordingly, may be stated as a doctrine of a
permanent state of war, not continuous fighting.

Majid Khadduri
War and Peace in the Law of Islam© 1955, p.64

"Christians & Jewish martyrs say; 'I will die for what I believe.' A Muslim martyr says; 'you will die for what I believe.'"[1] The underlying principle and foundation of Christianity is love: God's love for His human creation; Jesus' expression of God's love by His sacrifice on the cross for all mankind and His commandment to all His followers to love everyone—fellow believers, non-believers and even enemies. Muslims, however, are taught and called by the teachings of the Qur'an and Islam's revered prophet, Muhammad, to hate all those who oppose Islam—not only to hate, but to kill and annihilate *all* infidels and secure the world for Allah.

This latter religious dogma and mindset is difficult for the Western mind, and particularly those bathed in the teachings of Christ, to comprehend and absorb. However, it is this dramatic and fundamental difference that is essential for the non-Muslim world to grasp if it is to

245

come to grips with and neutralize this rapidly expanding ideology that threatens the free world and all that it cherishes.

While hate and murder are not alien to Western culture and history, it is hard for most to fathom that one's religion calls for them to hate someone or kill them just for the sake of doing so, or because they do not believe the way you do. But that is the relentless and unparalleled dictate of Islam and its religious leaders, whether housed in Iran, England or the United States. It is the common thread that holds the religion together—hate in the name and *cause of Allah*.

The Common Ground of Persecution

One thing Islam and Christianity do have in common is persecution. However, the commonality is in the word and concept only, not in how it is played out in one's faith. Christ's ministry and teaching in the New Testament call for Christians to sacrifice their life for another. "Greater love has no one than this, than to lay down one's life for his friends," Jesus taught His followers (John 15:13, NKJV).

Jesus was the shining example of such sacrifice for His disciples. "The reason my Father loves me," He told them, "is that I lay down my life—only to take it up again. No one takes it from me, but I lay it down of my own accord. I have authority to lay it down and authority to take it up again. This command I received from my Father" (John 10:17-18). While Jesus' ultimate sacrifice was in obedience to God, it was also His personal choice. He *did not* have to go to the cross, but He did in obedience to His Father in heaven and out of love for all mankind.

This call for Christians to sacrifice takes on many forms. Christians are called to sacrifice their money, property, time and talents in service to others or in meeting the needs of those less fortunate. But Christians are also called, like Jesus, to make the ultimate sacrifice, if necessary, for the cause of their faith. Although, in developed and free societies it is hard to comprehend the need for such sacrifice in today's world, the truth is, that Christians all over the world give their lives daily at the hands of others who persecute them and kill them just because they are peace-loving Christians. Christians are also called to take their faith to the definitive test. When faced with persecution or even death, they are not to deny their faith or their Lord and Savior, Jesus Christ.

Muslims are also called to sacrifice, but from a quite different perspective and for a much different purpose. While they are called to be charitable within their own circles, they are not required to sacrifice their goods or resources for the sake of helping non-Muslims. If they are persecuted or threatened with death, the teaching and example of Muhammad gives them permission, if it will spare their life, to deny Allah. They are not called to lay down their life for someone else. But the jihadists—which can be any Muslim who takes the teaching of Muhammad seriously—are called to sacrifice their lives—not to save others—but, in so doing, to take the lives of others.

Love the Brethren

During His brief ministry on earth, Jesus taught His followers many things. One teaching, however, seems to stand out among all others. Right before Jesus told Peter that he would deny knowing Jesus, Jesus gave His disciples what He considered His most important command after that of loving God. "A new command I give you: Love one another," Jesus instructed. "As I have loved you, so you must love one another. By this all men will know that you are my disciples, if you love one another" (John 13:34-35). In a world of so much hate—then, now and in the future—Jesus knew that there would be one thing that would set His followers apart from all others: How they share His love with each other. It was not that they were to love each other exclusively, but rather, out of this love they would be able to love others and thus distinguish themselves among all the peoples of the earth. He later reaffirmed this commandment. "As the Father has loved me, so have I loved you. Now remain in my love …. My command is this: Love each other as I have loved you" (John 15:9, 12).

In the Qur'an and the teachings of Muhammad, the concept of unconditional love is only vaguely implied and does not extend beyond fellow believers in Allah. Not even Allah offers his adherents unconditional love. Allah only loves the doers of good (surah 2:195), those that trust him (surah 3:159) and fight for him (surah 61:4), but he does not love sinners (surah 3:57). Except for the command to love Allah, the theology of love is glaringly absent from the Qur'an. In fact, there are more verses in the Qur'an that tell believers what or who Allah *does not* love than there are stating what Allah *does* love.

Followers of Islam are called to love Allah before he will love them (surahs 3:31, 5:54). Whereas, the theme throughout the Bible is that God loved us, His creation, before we loved Him. Once again, this verse of scripture bears repeating: *For God so loved the world that he gave his one and only Son, that whoever believes in him shall not perish but have eternal life. For God did not send his Son into the world to condemn the world, but to save the world through him* (John 3:16-17). Jehovah God's love is unconditional and extended toward those who do not love or acknowledge Him. Allah's love comes to the believer only after a Muslim expresses love toward Allah; and Allah's love is *only* for the believer, no one else.

"No one has ever seen God," the Apostle John admitted, "but if we love one another, God lives in us and his love is made complete in us" (1 John 4:12). While God is invisible, He expresses His love for His children by how those that believe in Him love one another. This is the most common way that people see the love of God in their lives, is through the love shared with them by others.

"If anyone says, 'I love God,' yet hates his brother," John continued, "he is a liar. For anyone who does not love his brother, whom he has seen, cannot love God, whom he has not seen. And he has given us this command: Whoever loves God must also love his brother" (1 John 4:20-21).

Love the Unbeliever

Not only is the overall concept of love fleeting in the Qur'an, but in no uncertain terms it surely does not extend to non-believers—either by Allah or any of his followers. All those who are not Muslim are seen as adversaries and enemies of Allah and Islam. "Allah's Apostle said, 'I have been ordered to fight with the people till they say, 'None has the right to be worshipped but Allah,' and whoever says, 'None has the right to be worshipped but Allah,' his life and property will be saved by me except for Islamic law, and his accounts will be with Allah, (either to punish him or to forgive him) (hadith 4:196).'" Unlike Christianity, there is no concept within Islam to love the unbeliever into the fold of believers. Rather, the command is to persecute them, fight them and kill them.

Even in the Old Testament, the word of God to the Jews was to love people and not seek to do them harm. "Do not seek revenge or bear a grudge against one of your people, but love your neighbor as yourself. I am the Lord" (Leviticus 19:18). Even foreigners (who were non-believers) were to be treated with love. "The alien living with you must be treated as one of your native-born. Love him as yourself, for you were aliens in Egypt. I am the Lord your God" (Leviticus 19:34). Again, in Deuteronomy 10:19, Moses instructed the Jews "... to love those who are aliens, for you yourselves were aliens in Egypt."

Jesus not only commanded His disciples to love their enemies but to also pray for those who persecuted them. "You have heard that it was said, 'Love your neighbor and hate your enemy.' But I tell you: Love your enemies and pray for those who persecute you, that you may be sons of your Father in heaven. He causes his sun to rise on the evil and the good, and sends rain on the righteous and the unrighteous. If you love those who love you, what reward will you get? Are not even the tax collectors doing that?" (Matthew 5:43-46). Jesus wanted His followers to stand out in a world of hate and sin. Telling someone to love their enemy was an unheard of and seemingly ridiculous request considering the environment in which He and his followers lived. To command one to love his enemies was bad enough, but to pray for them also seemed a step too far. But that was Jesus' example that was His godly uniqueness that no one could match before Him, during His era or in the future. Neither Muhammad, nor anyone in history, could hold a candle to Jesus, His teaching, or His mission.

When a rich man asked Jesus what he must do to inherit eternal life, Jesus was succinct. "Jesus replied, 'Do not murder, do not commit adultery, do not steal, do not give false testimony, honor your father and mother,' and 'love your neighbor as yourself'" (Matthew 19:19). While the term *neighbor* meant someone close by, it did not necessarily mean someone who was a fellow believing Jew or Christian. A similar command was not and could not be given by Muhammad to his followers because Muhammad practiced the opposite of what Jesus taught and required of His disciples.

When a Pharisee, who was an expert in the Law of Moses, inquired of Jesus, "Teacher, which is the greatest commandment in the Law?" Jesus gave him a reply similar to that of the rich man.

Jesus answered: "'Love the Lord your God with all your heart and with all your soul and with all your mind.' This is the first and greatest commandment. And the second is like it: 'Love your neighbor as yourself.' All the Law and the Prophets hang on these two commandments" (Matthew 22:36-40).

The Apostle Paul, taking his example from Jesus and Proverbs, advanced Jesus' teaching even further. "On the contrary: 'If your enemy is hungry, feed him; if he is thirsty, give him something to drink. In doing this, you will heap burning coals on his head' [Proverbs 25:21-22]. Do not be overcome by evil, but overcome evil with good' (Romans 12:20-21).

Paul further instructed the Roman Christians to:

Let no debt remain outstanding, except the continuing debt to love one another, for he who loves his fellowman has fulfilled the law. The commandments, "Do not commit adultery," "Do not murder," "Do not steal," "Do not covet," and whatever other commandment there may be, are summed up in this one rule: "Love your neighbor as yourself." Love does no harm to its neighbor. Therefore love is the fulfillment of the law. (Romans 13:8-10)

Not long after Paul founded the church in Galatia, a small group of Jewish Christians tried to convince the new faithful that they needed to follow certain aspects of Jewish law in order to be fully followers of Christ. Paul, of course, vehemently rejected such notions and wrote a stern letter to the members of the young church.

You, my brothers, were called to be free, but do not use your freedom to indulge the sinful nature; rather, serve one another in love. The entire law is summed up in a single command: "Love your neighbor as yourself." If you keep on biting and devouring each other, watch out or you will be destroyed by each other. (Galatians 5:13-15).

In this last sentence, Paul pointed out the result and consequence of failing to love one another—whether fellow believers or unbelieving neighbors.

Love Your Enemy

Where Christianity and Islam really separate on the issue of love is with respect to the treatment of real or perceived enemies. Christ taught His disciples to love their enemies, no matter who they were; Muhammad, however, led murderous raids and commanded his followers to kill non-believers wherever they could be found (surah 2:191, 193, et al). Among treasured Islamic scriptures there are whole *books* comprising hundreds of verses inciting the faithful to fight and kill non-believers for the cause of Allah. Islam is not a peaceful religion!

On December 18, 2005, *The Australian* quoted from the fiery sixty page script of one of Islam's leaders, Sheikh Mukhlas of Indonesia.

> You who still have a shred of faith in your hearts, have you forgotten that to kill infidels and the enemies of Islam is a deed that has a reward above no other ....
>
> Aren't you aware that the model for us all, the Prophet Mohammed and the four rightful caliphs, undertook to murder infidels as one of their primary activities, and that the Prophet waged jihad operations seventy-seven times in the first ten years as head of the Muslim community in Medina?[2]

The rantings of a madman? Perhaps, for these are the words of Sheikh Mukhlas of Indonesia, the one responsible for the Bali bombing of 2002. He might be deemed an Islamic madman had he not truthfully cited the Prophet of Islam, Muhammad, as his inspiration and example. For Muhammad was indeed all that Mukhlas proclaimed: a murderer of infidels and a frequent wager of war against those who refused to accept Islam. So what has changed in Islam's approach to the non-believer over fifteen centuries? Nothing!

"You shall not murder" is Jehovah God's commandment to His followers in the Old Testament (Exodus 20:13). The Qur'an, on the other hand, *commands* the faithful to "kill" and "slaughter" ALL non-believers, i.e., ALL non-Muslims, including Muslims deemed to be unfaithful adherents to Islam. Jesus expanded on this Old Testament commandment by teaching His followers that, "You have heard that it was said to the people long ago, 'Do not murder, and anyone who murders will be subject to judgment.' But I tell you that anyone who is angry with his brother will be subject to judgment (Matthew 5:21-

22a). Here, Jesus associates anger with murder. It is the precursor to the act of killing. Hatred of Jews, Christians and non-Muslims, in general, reigns supreme among many Muslims. Despite this Qur'an-sanctioned hatred, Christians are not to follow that example and retaliate. Instead, they are to always follow the example of Christ and Him only.

A Christian martyr, on the other hand, is one who dies at the hands of another while refusing to deny his or her faith in Christ or in the protection of the innocent. A Christian who deliberately takes another's life without just cause is a murderer. On the other hand, an adherent to the Islamic faith and its prophet Muhammad, is declared a martyr if he is slain in the course of slaying "the enemies" of Allah. Allah, according to Muhammad and the Qur'an, rejoices in this type of martyrdom. While the martyr following the way of Christ takes no life but willingly lays down his own for the sake of Christ, the Muslim martyr achieves his lofty goal by killing others, including innocent people.

Muhammad rejoiced and delighted in seeing his enemies tortured, beheaded and enslaved. It was Allah's will for the unbelievers, he would claim. Jesus would and does rejoice and take delight in one enemy soul repenting and coming to eternal glory with Him and the Father. Jesus called upon God and His followers to bless His enemies and pray for those who persecute His followers. Muhammad cursed and called upon Allah to curse his enemies and commit them to hell.

Paul, in expressing this new philosophy of Jesus said, "Very rarely will anyone die for a righteous man, though for a good man someone might possibly dare to die" (Romans 5:7). His point was that Jesus, a sinless and righteous man, not only chose to die for those that might be considered good, but also for those who were vile sinners through and through. Again, such a concept is not to be found or espoused in the Qur'an or anywhere else in Islamic belief or teaching. According to Islam, the unrepentant sinner or non-believer is worthy of nothing less than *severe chastisement* or death.

Even the wise King Solomon saw the folly of killing just for the sake of killing.

> *My son, if sinners entice you, do not give in to them. If they say, "Come along with us; let's lie in wait for someone's blood, let's waylay some harmless soul; let's swallow them alive, like the grave, and whole, like those who go down to the pit; we*

will get all sorts of valuable things and fill our houses with plunder; throw in your lot with us, and we will share a common purse"—*my son, do not go along with them, do not set foot on their paths; for their feet rush into sin, they are swift to shed blood.* (Proverbs 1:10-16)

As it was pointed out in chapter 8, sacrificial murder—that is sacrificing one's life while taking the lives of others (combatants or non-combatants)—is the only assured way that a Muslim has of getting to heaven or Paradise. "Christ's 'Martyrdom' on the cross," wrote author James Arlandson, "means that Christians do not have to die in a holy war to be quaranteed heaven."[3] As televised images and reports from the Middle East and elsewhere in the Muslim world reveal, certain Muslims have no reservations about sacrificing their own children or the children of others in the so-called *cause of Allah.*[4]

However, the Apostle Paul taught that the followers of Jesus should see themselves as *living sacrifices* for the cause of Christ—not as martyrs who kill others, but as saints called to sacrifice all for the sake of others. "Therefore, I urge you, brothers, in view of God's mercy, to offer your bodies as living sacrifices, holy and pleasing to God—this is your spiritual act of worship. Do not conform any longer to the pattern of this world, but be transformed by the renewing of your mind" (Romans 12:1-2a).

The question must be asked by any serious seeker of spiritual truth: Has the once forgiving, loving God as revealed by and through Jesus Christ—who died an agonizing death on the cross for the atonement of the sins of all mankind—changed His mind a scant 600 years after Christ's death, that it was all for nothing and that revenge, murder and mayhem are the only ways to convince the world that He loved them and wanted a relationship with Him? The Apostle Peter reaffirmed Jesus' teaching that the way to God's heart was to be loving and compassionate, even to one's enemies. "Finally, all of you, live in harmony with one another," Peter preached, "be sympathetic, love as brothers, be compassionate and humble. Do not repay evil with evil or insult with insult, but with blessing, because to this you were called so that you may inherit a blessing" (1 Peter 3:8-9).

Prophet of Change

Jesus was the last and only true prophet of change. As the Son of God, He completely and truthfully revealed the passion, character and heart of God to the human race. Muhammad had no special link or claim to insight with God. Jesus' revelation of God, His Father, was consistent, loving and built upon the message and prophesies of the Old Testament. The message that Muhammad brought to mankind were inconsistent, diabolical, hateful, murderous and self-serving of his power hungry, depraved and domineering mentality.

Muhammad financed his armies and raids on his neighbors by sacking the towns and plundering his "enemy." He also collected revenue through the tax assessed upon non-believers and taking mostly women and children into captivity and selling them as slaves. During his lifetime as Allah's Apostle/Prophet, Muhammad led twenty-seven raids or battles against those who refused to submit to him and sent his armies out on forty-seven more without him.[5] Not exactly the messenger of peace that God sent six centuries prior in the person of Jesus Christ. Perhaps God decided that his Son had failed in his mission in drawing people to Himself through the salvation message and decided that it would be better to coerce them into His kingdom through oppression and murder.

"When your Lord revealed to the Angels: I am with you, therefore make firm those who believe. I will cast terror into the hearts of those who disbelieve," Allah revealed to Muhammad. "Therefore strike off their heads and strike off every fingertip of them. This is because they acted adversely to Allah and His Apostle; and whoever acts adversely to Allah and His Apostle—then surely Allah is severe in requiting (evil)"(surah 8:12,13). This is certainly not the image of the loving, compassionate and forgiving Jehovah God of the Jews and Christians. "They ask you about the windfalls," Allah instructed Muhammad. "Say: The windfalls are for Allah and the Apostle. So be careful of (your duty to) Allah and set aright matters of your difference, and obey Allah and His Apostle if you are believers" (surah 8:1). Whatever plunder there was, 20% went to Allah and Muhammad, his kin, the needy and orphans, and the remaining 80% could be divided among his raiders (surah 8:41).

"Mohammedanism has produced an enslaved personality. 'Its Koran demands intellectual slavery,'" preached the popular missionary Methodist bishop, Charles Galloway, in the chapel of Emery College in Georgia in 1898, "'Its harem requires domestic slavery; its state implies and enforces both religious and a civil slavery.' The Koran puts a premium upon war, offering the highest rewards to those who slay the greatest number of infidels. Mohammed's cardinal principle, the end justifies the means, consecrated every sort of persecution and violence .... The citizen is the slave of the [Islamic] state; he has no rights to be respected. Mohammedanism is an absolute despotism, the most gigantic engine of intolerance and persecution the world ever saw .... In every land swept by this heartless despotism it has left a tale and trail of blood.'"[6]

Jesus brought forth a world-changing attitude toward others with a very simple principle: "... love your neighbor as yourself" (Matthew 19:19). If one is loving others as he is loving himself, how can he then hate or murder someone? "You have heard that it was said," Jesus preached during the Sermon on the Mount, "'Eye for eye, and tooth for tooth' (Exodus 21:24; Leviticus 24:20; Deuteronomy 19:21). But I tell you, Do not resist an evil person. If someone strikes you on the right cheek, turn him the other also" (Matthew 5:38-39).

Again, a few verses later He repeated the concept.

You have heard that it was said, "Love your neighbor and hate your enemy." But I tell you: Love your enemies and pray for those who persecute you, that you may be sons of your Father in heaven. He causes his sun to rise on the evil and the good, and sends rain on the righteous and the unrighteous. If you love those who love you, what reward will you get? Are not even the tax collectors doing that? (Matthew 5:43-46)

This model of kind and benevolent treatment of ones enemies was an unheard of proposal during the time of Jesus (or any time prior) and continues to be to this day. It is hard enough loving those close to you without being called to love those who are out to do you harm. But that is what made Jesus the unique and radical change merchant. He presented the inconceivable as plausible and with God's help it was possible to accomplish. Muhammad brought forth nothing new under the sun. He preached hate which was the accepted norm for his time and for all the history that went before him.

Once again, Jesus said:

> But I tell you who hear me: Love your enemies, do good to those who hate you, bless those who curse you, pray for those who mistreat you ... If you love those who love you, what credit is that to you? Even "sinners" love those who love them ... But love your enemies, do good to them, and lend to them without expecting to get anything back. Then your reward will be great, and you will be sons of the Most High, because he is kind to the ungrateful and wicked. (Luke 6:27-28, 32-33, 35)

The Apostle Paul, who before his conversion to Christianity was its primary persecutor as the Pharisee, Saul of Tarsus, embraced this teaching of Jesus. He wrote to the Roman Christians:

> Bless those who persecute you; bless and do not curse. Rejoice with those who rejoice; mourn with those who mourn. Live in harmony with one another. Do not be proud, but be willing to associate with people of low position. Do not be conceited.
>
> Do not repay anyone evil for evil. Be careful to do what is right in the eyes of everyone. If it is possible, as far as it depends on you, live at peace with everyone. Do not take revenge, my friends, but leave room for God's wrath, for it is written: "It is mine to avenge; I will repay," says the Lord. (Romans 12:14-19)

For those who did not and will not follow His teaching on love, Jesus had some stern words of rebuke.

> Jesus said to them, "If God were your Father, you would love me, for I came from God and now am here. I have not come on my own; but he sent me. Why is my language not clear to you? Because you are unable to hear what I say. You belong to your father, the devil, and you want to carry out your father's desire. He was a murderer from the beginning, not holding to the truth, for there is no truth in him. When he lies, he speaks his native language, for he is a liar and the father of lies. Yet because I tell

the truth, you do not believe me! Can any of you prove me guilty of sin? If I am telling the truth, why don't you believe me? He who belongs to God hears what God says. The reason you do not hear is that you do not belong to God. (John 8:42-47)

A Call to Charity and Servanthood

Christians are called to practice charity and servanthood toward all people, believers and non-believers alike. "Share with God's people who are in need," Paul commanded. "Practice hospitality" (Romans 12:13). Some translations of the Bible imply that this verse applies to those in Christ, others, including the *New International Version* quoted here give the verse a seemingly broader context of all God's people, that is His human creation. Jesus certainly did not discriminate when it came to meeting the spiritual and material needs of those around Him, whether they were Jews or Gentiles. "If your enemy is hungry," Solomon wrote, "give him food to eat; if he is thirsty, give him water to drink. In doing this, you will heap burning coals on his head, and the Lord will reward you" (Proverbs 25:21-22). Solomon was not saying that such acts of charity would bring harm to one's enemy, but rather, such compassion would soothe the hatred one's enemy harbored against them.

Charity in Islam is typically practiced among Muslims, from Muslim to Muslim, and rarely toward those outside the faith.

A case in point can be illustrated from the December, 2004 Indian Ocean earthquake and tsunami. There were an estimated 280,000 deaths with almost 80% in Indonesia, a country with an 88% Muslim population. Yet, the overwhelming majority of aid 96.3% came from Western countries or non-Muslim countries, corporations, Christian and Jewish organizations, churches and synagogues and numerous other Western and non-Muslim charitable organizations. Yes, some Muslim countries and charitable organizations offered assistance (3.7% of the total), but it paled by comparison to the response of the non-Muslim world. That should not be surprising, since there are no verses in the Qur'an telling Muslims to give to anyone outside their faith. The United States alone pledged over $900 billion or 18.9% of the world total.[7]

In another example of charity, generous Americans set an all-time giving record in 2006 of nearly $300 billion.[8] They responded readily and overwhelmingly, whether the need was for disaster aid in their own country (such as for hurricane Katrina) or the tsunami in Southeast Asia, or for poor and needy wherever they lived. Some sardonic individuals would say that is because America and Americans are the wealthiest in the World. That may be so, but the reality is, Americans and their country do not have to be so generous, but they are and have been since the country was founded on biblical principles 400 years ago.

The reality of the 2006 giving record is that only 1.3% of all monies donated were from what was termed *mega gifts*. The majority (65%) of what Americans gave came from households with incomes less than $100,000.[9] Mostly, it is the hard working American taxpayer and retiree that gave the greater persentage of their available dollars and resources to those in need. The remainder of the money came from corporate or private foundations.

The wide majority of Americans have always operated on the biblical principle stated in Proverbs 3:28: "Do not say to your neighbor, 'Come back later; I'll give it tomorrow'—when you now have it with you." Jesus took this admonition a step further, remember, by telling the rich man to "sell your possessions and give to the poor, and you will have treasure in heaven. Then come, follow me" (Matthew 19:21). Jesus even advocated to "Give to the one who asks you, and do not turn away from the one who wants to borrow from you" (Matthew 5:42). The early church took Jesus' teaching on charity to heart and pooled their possessions so they would have more to give to those in need (Acts 2:44-45; 4:32-35).

However, despite Jesus' fervent teaching on the matter of charity, even His Apostles had to be reminded of the level of service to which they were called.

Also a dispute arose among them as to which of them was considered to be the greatest. Jesus said to them, "The kings of the Gentiles lord it over them; and those who exercise authority over them call themselves Benefactors. But you are not to be like that. Instead, the greatest among you should be like the youngest, and the one who rules like the one who serves. For who is greater, the one who is at the table or the one who serves? Is it not the one who is at the table? But I am among you as one who serves. You are those who have stood by me in my trials. And I confer on you a kingdom, just as my Father conferred one on me, so that you may eat and drink at my table in my kingdom and sit on thrones, judging the twelve tribes of Israel. (Luke 22:24-30)

The Apostle Peter summed up this type of service very simply in his first circular letter to the Christian faithful who were being persecuted in the Roman provinces. "It is better, if it is God's will," he wrote, "to suffer for doing good than for doing evil" (1 Peter 3:17). Suffering for doing good, Peter was noting, comes at the bidding of man; suffering for doing evil is the judgment of God.

Conclusion

There is a clear and concise difference in how Christians and Muslims are to treat those who do not believe as they do. In both circles the faithful are to be charitable with their brethren in the faith. But that is where the similarity stops. Christ called His followers to give to those who were the enemies of His disciples—to love them and pray for them—even as they were being persecuted by them.

Muslims, however, are not called to such a gracious extension of love and charity. To the contrary, they are called to persecute and kill all those who refuse to see life their way and follow Allah. In each case, the adherents of Christianity and Islam are light and dark examples of their respective religions. They are images in the flesh of the unseen God and Allah.

My Beautiful Lord

In Pakistan, many Christians like Azra Bibi bear the double burden of poverty and persecution .... Her family, the only Christians in this Muslim community, spent each day doing back-breaking labor making hundreds of bricks.

"I am not educated. I liked to watch the other children going to school. I wanted to be a teacher of the Word of God, but my mother only earned $1.14 per day. My father died and we lived hand to mouth ....

"The kiln owner wouldn't allow us to go to church so my mother always told the owner, 'We are going to see our relatives,' or 'We are going to the market ....'

"The neighbors never liked it when we played the worship songs and many times tried to stop us. They tried to offer us many things, trying to convert us to Islam. Mother strongly refused all their offers, telling them, 'I have Jesus in my heart. There is no need for anything else ....'

"One day my mother asked me, 'Azra, please get some flour and let's make some chapatti [Pakistani bread].' We went outside to the community oven and met Mai Jana, an old Muslim lady who worked at this oven .... she became very aggressive and said, 'You Christian dogs, take your flour and get away from here. Your prophet was a Jewish dog.' My mother became very angry and replied, 'You can call me a Christian dog but never ever call our prophet these kinds of words.'

"Mai Jana stood up and started beating my mother. Other ladies joined in. They beat my mother very badly until she started bleeding. They also beat me .... Some Muslim men showed up and took us to the office of Malik Saleem Khokhar, the brick kiln owner ....

"It was about 10 p.m. when the brick kiln owner called for my mother. His assistant, Muhammad Akram, took her away. . . .

"Mother never came back .... For ten days I was locked in that room. My mother's friend ... said, 'The night Muhammad Akram took your mother to the kiln owner, they violated her and then chopped her body to pieces. They burned her body in the kiln.' I wept and I prayed. I was alone in this world.

... "Muhammad Akram [a seventy-year old man] often came to my room. He kept trying to convert me to Islam. I told him, 'My God is an alive God. How can I leave the alive God and accept your faith?' He decided to force me to marry him ....

"... the day my marriage was supposed to take place, the pastor came with [$1,100 to pay her debt]. They paid the money to the kiln owner, but Muhammad Akram was very angry. He beat and injured the pastor, but I was still set free.

"Wow, what a moment! I cried before my Lord, 'I am released! I am free! I can go where I want to go. Oh Jesus, I thank You. Oh my beautiful Lord, You heard my prayers.'"

Azra Bibi
The Voice of the Martyrs
February, 2007, p. 3-5

References

1. Keohane, Steve. *Muhammad: Terrorist or Prophet?* BibleProbe.com, 200402007. Http://bibleprobe.com/muhammad.htm. Accessed April 1, 2007.

2. *The Australian*, December 18, 2005. Accessed February 1, 2007 (Posted on: http://www.jihadwatch.org/archives/2005/12/009459.html).

3. Arlandson, James M. *Does Islam Improve on Christianity?* Answering-Islam.org. Http://answering-islam.org.uk/Authors/Arlandson/fruit_inspection.htm. Accessed November 2, 2005.

4. Winston, Emanuel A., July 17, 2001. *Abomination: The Sacrificing of Children*. Http://www.tzemach.org/fyi/docs/Winston/july17-01.htm. AccessedMarch 12, 2003.

5. Keohane.

6. Galloway, Bishop Charles B. *Christianity and the American Commonwealth*,1898, p. 26-27. Reprinted in 2005 by American Vision, Inc.

7. *Tsunami: Funds Pledged by Country*. Http://www.nationmaster.com. Accessed May 31, 2007.

8. *U.S. Sets Charitable Giving Record*. MSNBC.com, June 25, 2007. Http://www.Msnbc.msn.com/id/19409188. Accessed June 25, 2007.

9. *U.S. Charitable Giving Reaches $295.02 Billion in 2006*. Giving USA Foundation, June 25, 2007.

CHAPTER 10

Winning Souls

Satan wants to disseminate his plans and ideas among
humans and entice them to follow him radically.
If Satan also gives these human beings social, political
or religious status, they will become vessels for him to
use against the church and the plan of God.

Reza F. Safa
Inside Islam, 1996, p. 15

Christians, out of the joy and peace of knowing Jesus, want to share
their faith with others—to bring them into the saving knowledge
of Jesus Christ, their Lord and Savior. According to the Qur'an and
the traditions of Islam, Muslims are called to share their religion by
subduing and conquering those who do not believe as they, and thus
rule the world. Christians, by stark contrast, are called as followers of
Jesus to save the world by leading each person one by one, to salvation
from their evil intentions—not by coercion or persecution, but by a
gentle persuasion and revealing of what they believe to be the truth
about God.

The tradition and history of Islam is a bloody one, rife with
continuous harassment, persecution, subjugation and killing of non-
believers or infidels. Christianity, of course, is not absolved of dark
periods in its history—the Crusades, the Reformation, the Inquisition,
colonization and slavery to name a few. However, the tenets of faith of
Christianity and the teaching of Jesus do not support such historical
aberrations from the truth of the Gospels. When Christians act in
ways contrary to Jesus' way, they have His teaching to bring them

back to humble repentence. On the other hand, the violent activities of the Muslim faithful are fully supported by Islamic teaching that has not changed since the inception of Islam nearly fourteen hundred years ago.

Proselytize Through Love & Service
or Through Coercion & Violence

In surah 2:256, Muhammad proclaimed that *there is no compulsion in religion* or *no coercion in matters of faith.*[1] The implication and understanding is that there is to be no forcing of one to believe one way or the other. Yet, the Qur'an and ahadiths are full of Muhammad's proclamations to harass, persecute and kill ALL those who refused to accept Islam as their belief and Allah as their God or Muhammad as their prophet. For example, in the very same surah, Muhammad readily contradicts himself (and thus, the word of Allah) in verse 193 when he advocates, "Fight with them [the unbelievers] until there is no persecution, and religion should be only for Allah ...."

Although this verse has been cited before, surah 9:5 commands faithful Muslims to "Fight and slay the Pagans wherever you find them, and seize them, beleaguer them, and lie in wait for them in every stratagem (of war); but if they repent, and establish regular prayers and practice regular charity, then open the way for them: for Allah is Oft-forgiving, Most Merciful." Further, surah 4:89 states, "Those who reject Islam must be killed. If they turn back (from Islam), take (hold of) them and kill them wherever you find them ...." This does not sound like a merciful god with a merciful approach to evangelism. *Accept what I believe or I will kill you*, appears to be the evangelical cry of Islam.

Furthermore, where the teaching of Christianity is to befriend others, including non-believers, the teaching of Muhammad prohibits faithful Muslims from even making friends with Christians or Jews (surah 5:51). In surah 47:4, Muhammad even advocates extreme hostility and cruelty toward infidels. "So, when you meet those who disbelieve, smite (their) necks till when you have killed and wounded many of them, then bind a bond firmly (on them)", that is take them as captives. It needs to be pointed out once again, that this *is not* an isolated teaching in the Qur'an or ahadiths, but rather the rule of Islamic law. It is a harsh and unforgiving religion and any Muslim believer that says differently is either deceived or is practicing deception.

"The fruit of the righteous is a tree of life, and he who wins souls is wise" (Proverbs 11:30). To *win souls*, as is the common phraseology in Christian circles, has nothing to do with coercion, intimidation or persecution. Christianity is a personal religion requiring a personal decision without the heavy-handedness of another "guiding" the way. Christians are to freely share the gospel of Jesus Christ and then let the Holy Spirit convict the person of the truth of what was shared. Most Christians that share their faith are "seed planters"—sowing their faith and letting God do the salvation work.

Since there is no plan of salvation—rescuing souls from the pit of hell—within Islamic theology, there is no plan to calmly, lovingly and patiently share one's faith as a testimony to an unbeliever. It is, despite, Muhammad's proclamation, a faith by compulsion. A faith that coerces and brow beats one into believing a lie—a lie that draws people away from the true saving message of Jesus Christ.

Jesus made it very clear on how His message was to be disseminated. The unsaved were to be reached and converted by the Gospel being preached: "As you go, preach this message: 'The kingdom of heaven is near.' Heal the sick, raise the dead, cleanse those who have leprosy, drive out demons. Freely you have received, freely give" (Matthew 10:7-8). No where in the Qur'an does it tell Muslims to *preach* the Islamic message to the unbeliever. Not only were the disciples of Jesus to preach the message of salvation, but they were to imitate Jesus through acts of healing and deliverance. Muhammad never healed anyone, nor could he command his followers to follow such a compassionate example.

"And this gospel of the kingdom will be preached in the whole world as a testimony to all nations," Jesus told His disciples, "and then the end will come" (Matthew 24:14). The Apostle Mark recorded in his gospel, "Then the disciples went out and preached everywhere, and the Lord worked with them and confirmed his word by the signs that accompanied it" (Mark 16:20). The "signs" Mark was referring to were the miracles of healing and deliverance performed through the disciples as they exercised their faith. No such documentation has ever been forthcoming for those that follow the teachings of Muhammad.

This preaching of the Gospel by the disciples of Jesus was a fulfillment of Old Testament prophecy. "Their voice goes out into all the earth, their words to the ends of the world. In the heavens he has pitched a tent for the sun" (Psalm 19:4). However, the disciples could not fully preach the Gospel until Christ's crucifixion and resurrection had been accomplished. "He told them, 'This is what is written: The Christ will suffer and rise from the dead on the third day, and repentance and forgiveness of sins will be preached in his name to all nations, beginning at Jerusalem'" (Luke 24:46-47). Even the Apostles, His closest companions, did not fully understand the purpose of Jesus' mission until after he died and was resurrected and appeared to them once again.

In his letter to the Colossians (Greek gentiles), Paul illustrated his full comprehension of this gospel.

"We always thank God, the Father of our Lord Jesus Christ, when we pray for you, because we have heard of your faith in Christ Jesus and of the love you have for all the saints—the faith and love that spring from the hope that is stored up for you in heaven and that you have already heard about in the word of truth, the gospel that has come to you. All over the world this gospel is bearing fruit and growing, just as it has been doing among you since the day you heard it and understood God's grace in all its truth" (Colossians 1:3-6). Later in the same chapter, he continued. "Once you were alienated from God and were enemies in your minds because of your evil behavior. But now he has reconciled you by Christ's physical body through death to present you holy in his sight, without blemish and free from accusation—if you continue in your faith, established and firm, not moved from the hope held out in the gospel. This is the gospel that you heard and that has been proclaimed to every creature under heaven, and of which I, Paul, have become a servant" (Colossians 1:21-23).

Sheep or Goats?

One of Christ's greatest portrayals on how His disciples were to spread the message of the Gospel was recorded in 25th chapter of Matthew. It is commonly referred to as the parable of the *Sheep and Goats* or how reaching out to strangers or the non-believer is as if one were serving Christ. Please note, that the Greek word used for "stranger" in the following verses is the same as that for foreigner or alien.

When the Son of Man comes in his glory, and all the angels with him, he will sit on his throne in heavenly glory. All the nations will be gathered before him, and he will separate the people one from another as a shepherd separates the sheep from the goats. He will put the sheep on his right and the goats on his left.

Then the King will say to those on his right, "Come, you who are blessed by my Father; take your inheritance, the kingdom prepared for you since the creation of the world. For I was hungry and you gave me something to eat, I was thirsty and you gave me something to drink, I was a stranger and you invited me in, I needed clothes and you clothed me, I was sick and you looked after me, I was in prison and you came to visit me."

Then the righteous will answer him, "Lord, when did we see you hungry and feed you, or thirsty and give you something to drink? When did we see you a stranger and invite you in, or needing clothes and clothe you? When did we see you sick or in prison and go to visit you?"

The King will reply, "I tell you the truth, whatever you did for one of the least of these brothers of mine, you did for me."

Then he will say to those on his left, "Depart from me, you who are cursed, into the eternal fire prepared for the devil and his angels. For I was hungry and you gave me nothing to eat, I was thirsty and you gave me nothing to drink, I was a stranger and you did not invite me in, I needed clothes and you did not clothe me, I was sick and in prison and you did not look after me."

They also will answer, "Lord, when did we see you hungry or thirsty or a stranger or needing clothes or sick or in prison, and did not help you?"

He will reply, "I tell you the truth, whatever you did not do for one of the least of these, you did not do for me."

Then they will go away to eternal punishment, but the righteous to eternal life. (Matthew 25:31-46)

As a part of their mission of disseminating the Gospel of Christ, Christians are to perform acts of charity and compassion. When Christian missionaries enter a country they usually do not head right for the pulpit and start preaching. More than likely they first carry out acts of mercy and compassion to demonstrate to the people that they are not there to threaten them or cause them any harm. They bring medical supplies, food, clothing, literature; they build schools, medical clinics and hospitals; they teach agriculture and self-sufficiency and they become a caring and giving part of the community.

The "Great Commission" or the Great Slaughter

After His resurrection and before He ascended into heaven, Jesus conveyed to His disciples what has become to be known in the Christian world as the "Great Commission"—the command to make disciples throughout the world. "Then Jesus came to them and said, 'All authority in heaven and on earth has been given to me. Therefore go and make disciples of all nations, baptizing them in the name of the Father and of the Son and of the Holy Spirit, and teaching them to obey everything I have commanded you. And surely I am with you always, to the very end of the age'" (Matthew 28:18-20). This was not a radical call to war or oppression of the masses, but a call to share the *good news* of salvation and God's redemptive love.

By contrast, as Muhammad lay dying, he commanded his followers to purge the Arabian Peninsula of non-believers. Also, at the end of his life, as Muhammad was reflecting on his "career" he was quoted as saying: "I have been sent with the shortest expressions bearing the widest meanings, and I have been made victorious with terror ...." (hadith 4:52:220). Jesus, of course, never harbored such claims of aggression toward anyone or any country or people.

"You are the **salt of the earth**," Jesus instructed His followers during the Sermon on the Mount. "But if the salt loses its saltiness, how can it be made salty again? It is no longer good for anything, except to be thrown out and trampled by men. You are the **light of the world**. A city on a hill cannot be hidden. Neither do people light a lamp and put it under a bowl. Instead they put it on its stand, and it gives light to everyone in the house. In the same way, let your light shine before men, that they may see your good deeds and praise your Father in heaven"

(Matthew 5:13-16, author's emphasis). Jesus wanted His disciples to be set apart from all others as a pure example of God's love for His creation. During the time of Jesus and throughout history, salt has been a necessary ingredient and commodity for the nations and peoples of the world. Jesus wanted His disciples to be the "necessary ingredient" from which others would draw the life of God. He wanted them to be a light in the midst of a dark world of sin so that all people would be drawn to Him and His heavenly Father. The disciples of Jesus then and now are to be shining examples of a compassionate, forgiving God who wants everyone to share eternal life with Him. The same cannot be ascribed to Allah, his apostle, or his followers.

Through the Christian's personal relationship with their saving God and the joy of their salvation, they have the desire to see others share in the same discovery. As the Apostle Paul wrote to the Philippians:

"For it is God who works in you to will and to act according to his good purpose. Do everthing without complaining or arguing, so that you may become blameless and pure, children of God without fault in a crooked and depraved generation, in which you shine like stars in the universe as you **hold out the word of life**—*in order that I may boast on the day of Christ that I did not run or labor for nothing.* (Philippians 2:13-16, author's emphasis)

It is through the internal working of the Holy Spirit within Christians that they are motivated to share God's grace and mercy. Muslims have no such internal witness of their unseen god and therefore are not motivated from within but from the controlling, oppressive environment in which they live and are brainwashed from birth to death. It is impossible to share life out of the darkness of one's soul. Muhammad could not do it, nor have any of his followers since. "Do not repay anyone evil for evil," admonished Paul.

Be careful to do what is right in the eyes of everybody. If it is possible, as far as it depends on you, live at peace with everyone. Do not take revenge, my friends, but leave room for God's wrath, for it is written: "It is mine to avenge; I will repay," says the Lord. On the contrary: "If your enemy is hungry, feed him; if he is thirsty, give him something to drink. In doing this, you will heap burning coals on his head." Do not be overcome by evil, but overcome evil with good. (Romans 12:17-21)

The Apostle Paul, in keeping with the message of Christ, reminded the Christians in Rome, who were under extreme persecution from the Romans, to *live at peace with everyone* no matter what the cost. Not only to live at peace, but to extend the grace and mercy of God to their enemies. This was also impossible for Muhammad to do and for his followers. If one does not follow a god of compassion, mercy and forgiveness, it is not likely that you are going to be able to demonstrate anything different.

"Cain's spirit," wrote former devout Muslim, Reza Safa, "is the kind of spirit that Satan uses to come against the righteous man. This kind of religious spirit is an open door for demonic influence. This religious spirit is hateful, vengeful, murderous and bloodthirsty. It is resentful, unforgiving and does not know mercy."[2] Cain, a son of Adam and Eve, was banished from Eden to live in the Land of Nod (Genesis 4:16) which was east of Eden. "You will be a restless wanderer on the earth," God told Cain (Genesis 4:12b). Many biblical scholars place the Land of Nod (Hebrew for wandering or vagrancy) in the Middle East, perhaps in Iran. If so, it should not be a great surprise that the murderous spirit of Cain still survives to this day in the Middle East. Remember also from chapter one the curse of Ishmael from whom Arab Muslims claim their parentage. God told Abraham and Sarah that Ishmael would "be a wild donkey of a man; his hand will be against everyone and everyone's hand against him, and he will live in hostility toward all his brothers" (Genesis 16:12).

Such hostility is brought forth by Muhammad in many surahs such 60:1.

O you who believe! Do not take My enemy and your enemy for friends: would you offer them love while they deny what has come to you of the truth, driving out the Apostle and yourselves because you believe in Allah, your Lord? If you go forth struggling hard in My path and seeking My pleasure, would you manifest love to them? And I know what you conceal and what you manifest; and whoever of you does this, he indeed has gone astray from the straight path. (surah 60:1)

The God of the Jews and Christians, however, calls upon those who believe in Him to live at peace with one another. "Finally, all of you, live in harmony with one another; be sympathetic, love as brothers, be compassionate and humble," the Apostle Peter reminded the Christians throughout the Roman provinces. "Do not repay evil with evil or insult with insult, but with blessing, because to this you were called so that you may inherit a blessing. For, 'Whoever would love life and see good days must keep his tongue from evil and his lips from deceitful speech. He must turn from evil and do good; he must seek peace and pursue it. For the eyes of the Lord are on the righteous and his ears are attentive to their prayer, but the face of the Lord is against those who do evil'" (1 Peter 3:8-12). Christians are called unequivocally to do good at every opportunity; to *seek peace and pursue it*—to be peacemakers in a world at war with itself.

A few verses later, Peter again called the new Christians to pursue goodness regardless of the outcome. "Who is going to harm you if you are eager to do good? But even if you should suffer for what is right, you are blessed. 'Do not fear what they fear; do not be frightened.' But in your hearts set apart Christ as Lord. Always be prepared to give an answer to everyone who asks you to give the reason for the hope that you have. But do this with gentleness and respect, keeping a clear conscience, so that those who speak maliciously against your good behavior in Christ may be ashamed of their slander. It is better, if it is God's will, to suffer for doing good than for doing evil" (1 Peter 3:13-17). Christians are called to do good deeds for others and to speak in love. Compare that to the hostile acts and words of hate that spew forth from the Muslim regions of the world.

The Apostle Paul, like his Savior, Jesus, put it into agrarian terms that his hearers would understand. "Do not be deceived: God cannot be mocked. A man reaps what he sows. The one who sows to please his sinful nature, from that nature will reap destruction; the one who sows to please the Spirit, from the Spirit will reap eternal life. Let us not become weary in doing good, for at the proper time we will reap a harvest if we do not give up. Therefore, as we have opportunity, let us do good to all people, especially to those who belong to the family of believers" (Galatians 6:7-10). It is a simply analogy: one can only harvest what one plants. Planting wheat seed will not yield a harvest of melons. Sowing hate will not produce love. Sowing acts of mercy and love, while they may not always produce a reciprocating response, will never yield hate unless it is in the darkened and deceived mind and spirit of the recipient. Eventually, love wins out and when it is sowed continuously, it *will* yield a crop of similar genome.

The Bloody Century

After Muhammed settled in Medina, the remainder of the seventh century became a bloody one as the Muslims sought to spread their new found influence and conquest outside the Arabian Peninsula. Although Muhammad had planned and/or led numerous raids against his enemies while in Mecca, beginning in 624 A.D., Muslim violence in the name of Allah escalated. During the remainder of that century, Muslim faithful marched in no less than one hundred battles, raids and conquests. Muslim influence and domination quickly spread throughout the Arab world of the Middle East, as well as North Africa, the Mediterranean and parts of south central Asia. Pagans, Jews and Christians were systematically exiled from their homeland, converted or murdered.[3, 4]

The brutality of the Muslim advance is well illustrated in The Battle of the Trench in 627 against the Jewish Banu Qurayzah tribe of Medina. After their conquest and surrender, Muhammad left their fate up to one of his warriors. The warrior suggested that all the Jewish men should be beheaded and their wives and children taken captive. This sounded fair to Muhammad and he had all 800-900 Jewish men systematically so dispatched with himself actively participating in the beheadings.[5]

Such vicious treatment of the captives of war effectively wiped out all Jewish resistance in the area. Such treatment of the captives of war was largely practiced then, as it is now, by the Islamic world. It is firmly supported by Allah's revelation to Muhammad.

When you sought aid from your Lord, so He answered you: I will assist you with a thousand of the angels following one another:

When your Lord revealed to the angels: I am with you, therefore make firm those who believe. I will cast terror into the hearts of those who disbelieve. Therefore strike off their heads and strike off every fingertip of them.

This is because they acted adversely to Allah and His Apostle; and whoever acts adversely to Allah and His Apostle—then surely Allah is severe in requiting (evil). (surah 8:9, 12-13)

Fighting is ordained for Muslims by Allah and his Apostle as the primary method of spreading the "gospel" of Islam. "Fighting is enjoined on you," Muhammad revealed from Allah, "and it is an object of dislike to you; and it may be that you dislike a thing while it is good for you, and it may be that you love a thing while it is evil for you, and Allah knows, while you do not know" (surah 2:216). That is, fighting the enemies of Allah—which are ALL non-believers—is required or commanded for all Muslims by Allah and his Apostle. Of course, when one is victorious there is booty to be procured from the vanquished and the faithful wanted to know how it should be distributed. Not unexpectedly, Muhammad shared this self-serving revelation from his god. "They ask you about the windfalls [of battle]. Say: The windfalls are for Allah and the Apostle. So be careful of (your duty to) Allah and set aright matters of your difference, and obey Allah and His Apostle if you are believers" (surah 8:1).

One of the surest ways to rally the faithful into battle is to abase, dehumanize and demonize your non-believing foe. Muhammad was quite adept at securing Allah's revelation and approval when it came to suppressing his enemies. "Surely the vilest [most hated] of animals in Allah's sight are those who disbelieve, then they would not believe" (surah 8:55). In addition to referring to Jews as pigs and apes, non-believers as a whole are dehumanized in the sight of Islam's god and its prophet.

"Surely those who disbelieve from among the followers of the Book [the Jews] and the polytheists [the Christians] shall be in the fire of hell, abiding therein; they are the worst of men" (surah 98:6). Islam demonizes all non-believers, thus fostering the justification for mistreatment, deprivation and murder. For the true follower of Islam, such persecution of the non-believer is only advancing their already determined destiny of hell and therefore not only justified but the carrying out of Allah's judgment. "O Prophet! Urge the believers to war;" Allah commanded Muhammad, "if there are twenty patient ones of you they shall overcome two hundred, and if there are a hundred of you they shall overcome a thousand of those who disbelieve, because they are a people who do not understand" (surah 8:65).

Two years after Muhammad and his military junta fled to Medina in 622, Muhammad mapped out a very aggressive plan of oppression and military conquest of his neighbors. While Muhammad and his followers were in Mecca he was somewhat more conciliatory toward Jews and other non-believers in the hope they would convert to his theology. However, after being run out of Mecca Muhammad developed a much more hostile approach toward conversion—convert or die.

In 624 Muhammad orchestrated his first major battle against the Quraysh Jews of Mecca in the Battle of Badr. It gave him the opportunity to take out his vengeance on the tribe that rejected him. He was ruthless, ordering the beheading of those who survived the carnage.[6, 7] In the same year, emboldened by his victory over the Quraysh, Muhammad led a campaign of terror against the Bani Qainuqa (aka Bani Qaynuqa) Jews of Medina, expelling any survivors from their homeland.[8, 9] Such raids became the primary way in which Muhammad financed the expansion of Islam and kept his warriors happy with plundering the vanquished.

The following year, the Quraysh who had fled to fight another day were bent on revenge and had amassed around 3,000 warriors. In the ensuing Battle of Uhud (a mountain near Mecca) the Quraysh were successful in defeating Muhammad's forces. But Muhammad would not accept defeat and once again he would carry out his revenge upon the Quraysh.[10] With his vengeance against the Jews running high, Muhammad also exiled the Jewish Banu Nadir tribe from Medina.[11]

Three years after the massacre of the Banu Qurayzah, Muhammad, with 10,000 Muslim warriors, conquered Mecca. He ordered the slaughter of all who resisted. The Ka'bah (or Ka'aba), the site of idol worship in Mecca, was established as the center of Islam.[12] A year later, the remaining Arabic tribes, fearing Muhammad's wrath, accepted Islam. Now Muhammad could turn his attention to his war against Christians.

The death of Muhammad in 632 did not halt the Muslim advance. The bloody post mortem campaigns began a reign of terror that brought the conquest of the Middle East and beyond. Abu Bakr, Muhammad's faithful friend, was elected the first Caliph or Islamic leader. Under his direction and the caliphs that would follow him the brutal expansion of Islam continued throughout the rest of the seventh century with the conquests of Bahrain, Oman, Yemen, Iraq, Damascus, Syria, Jerusalem, Egypt, Persia and bold invasions into Western Russia, Asia Minor, North Africa, the Island of Cyprus, Sicily and the siege of Constantinople in 677.[13] The battles were mostly land grabbing offenses to expand the reaches of Islam. There was no quarter given. Accept Islam or die.

The first one hundred years of Islam's attacks and conquering raids throughout the Middle East and beyond would set the stage for centuries of bloody conquests to follow. The 8th Century would see Islam expanding its empire with attacks on the Berbers of North Africa; the conquest of Spain; invasion of Constantinople; the Battle of Tours in France and a century of battles and revolts throughout the Islamic region. By the end of the 11th century the Muslim vanguard had conquered the holy city of Jerusalem, the Middle East and the Mediterranean countries. In an effort to regain this formerly controlled Christian territory, the first of the Crusades was launched in 1095.

The pattern of Islamic barbarity continues into the modern era and the 21st century. According to Steve Keohane,[14] from 1970-2000, "there were 43,721 terrorist attacks worldwide; 113,425 people were killed. Over 82,126 injured. Over 90% of these barbaric acts were committed by Muslims."

Conclusion

It is clear that the two dominating religions of the world—Islam and Christianity—have very divergent ideas on how to win converts to their religious beliefs. Christians are called to share Christ out of their personal experience and passion for their Lord and Savior. Muslims are called to advance the cause of Islam by any means necessary, including violence, oppression, subjugation and murder.

While the call to peaceful evangelism is made clear through the teaching of Christ and the instruction of the New Testament, it is also very clear that the holy book of Islam and the teaching of its prophet commands Islam to be spread by violence, not peace, and not from an inner witness of a compassionate, merciful god.

Christianity is not free of an imperialistic and sometimes violent past. The clear difference is this: the Muslim holy book and its prophet command the Islamic people to commit violence; the Bible and Jesus command Christians to go forth in peace and love.

Hatred for Joy

My name is Idris Miah [of Bangladesh]. I was a good Muslim man, but I knew a bad Muslim man named Abu Bakkar Sidhikki who would often get drunk. No one in our village liked him, but what Abu eventually did made us hate him: he became a Christian ....

The village leaders met and decided that what he did was so bad that we would have to kick him out of our village and burn down his house. We formed a group of twenty-five men and went to his house. We were sneaking up to his house to take him by surprise.

As we got closer we could hear him praying. He was actually praying for our whole village. He was asking Jesus to forgive everyone in the village. He said Jesus should forgive us because we did not know what we were doing. This made us angry because we thought we knew what we were doing. Then all twenty-five of us rushed to his house to apprehend him, but there was an invisible force that would not let any of us enter his house to drag him out. We all became scared and everyone ran back to his own house.

When I got home I could not sleep. I kept thinking about Abu's prayer. He said we did not know what we were doing. Was it true? Was he right? Finally, at 3:00 A.M. I could not wait any longer. I went back to Abu's house and said, "Who is Jesus?"

He told me how Jesus gave his life for sinners and how I could be saved. After three hours of this, I asked Jesus to forgive me and I surrendered my life to him. Jesus saved me!

I rushed home to my house and shared what happened to me with my wife and she also became a Christian along with my [four] children ....

I have the joy of Jesus in my heart. I give my life and my family to Jesus. I hope this gift is acceptable to my Lord.

"Hatred Traded for Happiness"
Jesus Freaks
dc Talk and The Voice of the Martyrs
1999

References

1. *Qur'an*, Muhammad Asad translation. Isamicity.com. Http://www. islamicity.com. Quransearch. Accessed August 10, 2007.

2. Safa, Reza F. *Inside Islam: Exposing and Reaching the World of Islam*, 1996. Charisma House, p. 16.

3. *Islamic History (Chronology)*. Http://www.barkati.net/English/ chronology.htm. Accessed January 30, 2007.

4. Spencer, Robert. *The Truth About Muhammad, Founder of the World's Most Intolerant Religion*, 2006. Regnery Publishing, Inc., chapters 6-8.

5. Spencer, pp. 129-130.

6. *Islamic History.*

7. Spencer, pp. 103-106.

8. *Islamic History*

9. Spencer, pp. 111-112.

10. Spencer, pp. 117-119.

11. *Islamic History.*

12. Spencer, pp. 146, 149.

13. *Islamic History.*

14. Keohane, Steve. *Muhammad: Terrorist or Prophet?* BibleProbe.com, 200402007. Http://bibleprobe.com/muhammad.htm. Accessed April 1, 2007.

CHAPTER 11

Treatment of Non-believers
or Infidels

*In the end, the Muslim, both externally and internally,
must passionately hate those who stand against
the expansion of Allah's cause.*

Ergun Mehmet Caner and Emir Fethi Caner
Unveiling Islam, 2002, p. 36

While the Qur'an seems obsessed with Allah's retribution toward the "infidels" or "unbelievers,"notably Jews and Christians, the Bible mentions God's vengeance against those who do not believe rather sparingly. In the Old Testament, non-Jews are mostly referred to as the "uncircumcised." In the New Testament, the term, "Gentile" replaces the reference to a non-Jew. Rather than retribution, the God of the Bible first seeks to bring the lost into His kingdom through acts of love and mercy and the testimony of His Son, Jesus Christ.

While the Apostle Paul warned the Corinthians not to be "yoked together with unbelievers," he was not advocating that the Corinthians disassociate themselves from the non-believers around them or to cause them any harm (2 Corinthians 6:14a). Instead, he was calling upon them to guard their new faith from the temptations of the Greek pagans they were living among and not fall once again into the bondage of spiritual darkness. "For what do righteousness and wickedness have in common? Or what fellowship can light have with darkness (verse 14b)?"

To the Ephesians, Paul wrote, "Let no one deceive you with empty words, for because of such things God's wrath comes on those who are disobedient. Therefore do not be partners with them. For you were once darkness, but now you are light in the Lord. Live as children of light (for the fruit of the light consists in all goodness, righteousness and truth) and find out what pleases the Lord. Have nothing to do with the fruitless deeds of darkness, but rather expose them (Ephesians 5:6-11)." Christians were not and are not called to oppress those who do not believe as they believe, but instead, they are to shine the light of the Gospel in the midst of spiritual darkness and expose non-believers to the truth of the Gospel of Jesus Christ. The rule, Jesus taught His disciples in the art of relating to others was, "Be merciful, just as your Father is merciful" (Luke 6:36).

The principle laid down by Jesus was to show mercy and extend God's love to all people, whether they were fellow Christians or not. Because God is love and it was He that first loved His creation, those that choose to follow Him through faith in Jesus Christ, in turn have His love to share with others, including non-believers. The Apostle John wrote it down this way.

Dear friends, let us love one another, for love comes from God. Everyone who loves has been born of God and knows God. Whoever does not love does not know God, because God is love. This is how God showed his love among us: He sent his one and only Son into the world that we might live through him. This is love: not that we loved God, but that he loved us and sent his Son as an atoning sacrifice for our sins ....

If anyone acknowledges that Jesus is the Son of God, God lives in him and he in God. And so we know and rely on the love God has for us.

God is love. Whoever lives in love lives in God, and God in him. (1 John 4:7-10, 15-16)

Muslims, however, not sure that their god Allah loves them, have no well-spring of inner love to share with others. Since their god offers no personal relationship; no father-child identity, there is no sense of God's caring embrace. When the well is empty there can be no satisfying of the thirsty soul—whether it be your own or someone else's.

Hatred of the Jews and Unbelievers

Ever since the Jews of Arabia refused to accept Muhammad as a prophet of their God, the followers of Islam have been repeatedly conditioned—that is, brainwashed—into a livid hatred of them and Christians by association. Much of the hatred is generated and fomented on absolute fabrications that have no basis in fact or history. Take, for example, an essay written by Muhammad Al-Munajjid.[1] The author claims to draw his information from the Jewish Talmud to justify, "Why do we hate the Jews? We hate them for the sake of our Lord, we hate them for the sake of Allah because they slandered Allah and they killed and slandered his prophets." The Talmud, first of all, is the written record of Jewish oral law and its subsequent discussions and expounding by rabbinic leaders. There are two versions: the Palestinian (compiled sometime during the 4th century) and the Babylonian (compiled around 500 A.D.). While the Talmud helped refine or resolve certain legal issues of the Torah, it did not supersede that which was handed down through Moses.

Among the outlandish things that Al-Munajjid claims are in the Talmud are:

- The sperm of a non-Jew is like the sperm of an animal.
- Every Jew has to do his utmost to prevent all other nations from having any possessions on earth ....
- If God had not created the Jews, there would be no blessing on earth.
- The souls of the Jews are dear to God ... all other souls ... are devilish souls ....
- The Jew is not at fault if he attacks the honour of a non-Jewish woman ... the non-Jewish woman is considered to be an animal ....
- The Jews have the right to rape non-Jewish women.
- Fornication with a non-Jew, whether male or female is not punishable, because they (non-Jews) are the descendants of animals.
- That God is not infallible ....
- ... that the rabbis have authority over God ....
- ... that God consults the rabbis on earth when there is a problem for which He cannot find a solution in heaven.
- ... that the teaching of the rabbis cannot be undone or changed, even by the command of God.

281

In the highly acclaimed and award winning documentary, *Obsession: Radical Islam's War Against the West*, a segment shows a Muslim production for Arab television promoting the common belief among Arab Muslims that Jewish pastries for the Jewish religious holiday of Purim are made with the blood of sacrificed young Christian boys.[2] This is confirmed by no less than the Saudi government.[3]

To the non-Muslim West, all this hyperbole and fallacy might be laughable if not for the realization that Muslims worldwide gobble this misinformation up as the truth, thus giving their already mistrust of the Jews further justification for their hatred of them.

"O Prophet!" Allah revealed to Muhammad, "Strive hard against the unbelievers and the hypocrites and be unyielding to them; and their abode is hell, and evil is the destination" (surah 9:73). This commandment of Allah is quite a contrast to the commandments of Jesus for His followers to love the non-believer and reach out to them by sharing the Gospel of good news.

"Fight those who do not believe in Allah, nor in the latter day, nor do they prohibit what Allah and His Apostle have prohibited, nor follow the religion of truth, out of those who have given the Book, until they pay the tax in acknowledgment of superiority and they are in a state of submission. (surah 9:29). This Qur'anic verse commands that Muslims must fight against four groups of people: those who do not believe in Allah; those who do not believe in the last day; those who do what Allah and Muhammad prohibit; and those who do not submit to Islam as the true religion.

"Those who believe fight in the way of Allah, and those who disbelieve fight in the way of the Shaitan [Satan]. Fight therefore against the friends of the Shaitan; surely the strategy of the Shaitan is weak" (surah 4:76). NOTE: In the Islamic world, it is the Jews and Christians who are portrayed as devils or agents of Satan and the United States, in particular, as "The Great Satan." In the Islamic mind and teaching there is no room for parity with the West or the non-Muslim; no compromise; no mercy; no conciliation.

"Whoever is the enemy of Allah and His angels and His apostles and Jibreel [Gabriel] and Meekaeel [Michael], so surely Allah is the enemy of the unbelievers" (surah 2:98). *All* non-believers are enemies of Allah, and whoever is an enemy of Allah is an enemy of Islam, and whoever is an enemy of Islam is an enemy of every Muslim. Therefore, it only makes sense to the Muslim faithful that Allah would call upon them to kill the unbelievers (surah 9:5). No such open-ended command exists in the Bible for any of God's people to indiscriminately kill their enemies or those who do not believe as they do.

The Qur'an calls upon all Muslims not to befriend Jews and Christians (surah 5:51). It further tells the Muslim faithful that the Jews are cursed because of their unbelief (surah 5:78). Thus, this gives even further rationalization for Muslims to hate Jews and Christians by association since they follow the Jewish Messiah and support the validity of the Jewish existence. Proverbs 3:29-30, written by Solomon, reprimands the followers of Jehovah God to "not plot harm against your neighbor, who lives trustfully near you. Do not accuse a man for no reason—when he has done you no harm." Jews have attempted to live at peace with their Muslim neighbors in the Middle East for centuries and in Israel for the last sixty years, but to no avail. Just like the Muslims of Muhammad's era, the Muslims for eons have persecuted the Jew in their midst and then point the finger at the Jew claiming they were the aggressor.

The Muslim psychology is supported by their holy book. "Abasement [degradation or humiliation] is made to cleave to [the unbelievers] wherever they are found, except under a covenant with Allah and a covenant with men, and they have become deserving of wrath from Allah, and humiliation is made to cleave to them; this is because they disbelieved in the communications of Allah and slew the prophets unjustly; this is because they disobeyed and exceeded the limits"(surah 3:112). Anything is justified when it comes to the treatment of Jews and other non-believers. The goal is to demean and persecute the unbeliever until only Muslims exist.

The Qur'an commands that the followers of Allah must continue to fight against the infidels until there is only one religion and that is Islam. "And fight with them [the unbelievers] until there is no more persecution and religion should be only for Allah; but if they desist, then surely Allah sees what they do" (surah 8:39).

According to Muhammad, there were three options for non-believers: they could convert to Islam; they could remain as Jews or

Christians but pay an annual non-believer tax or *jizya*; or die for there unwillingness to submit to the heavy hand of Islam.

While Islam forbids its followers to pay or charge interest, it is okay to extort money from infidels or suppress them with usury to gain the upper hand. The God of the Jews and Christians forbids such tactics (see Ezekiel 22:12, et al).

Good Samaritan

While Muslims are called to oppress non-believers until they submit to Islam, Jesus taught His followers that they should strive for a much higher moral ground. In Luke 10:25-37, Jesus tells the parable of the Good Samaritan to His disciples as an illustration of their call to service. The life example was prompted by a question from a Jewish man who was an authority on the Law.

"'Teacher,' he asked, 'what must I do to inherit eternal life?'"

"'What is written in the Law?'" Jesus replied. "'How do you read it?'"

"He answered: 'Love the Lord your God with all your heart and with all your soul and with all your strength and with all your mind'; and, 'Love your neighbor as yourself'" (verses 25b-27).

Jesus was impressed. "'You have answered correctly,' Jesus replied. 'Do this and you will live?'" (verse 28).

However, the man was not content because "he wanted to justify himself, so he asked Jesus, 'And who is my neighbor?'" (verse 29). The Greek word, plēsiŏn, used here for *neighbor* refers to someone who is *close by* or a *countryman* who is near. The man asked out of an attitude of testing Jesus, rather than really wanting to know. But Jesus took it as a teachable moment, not only for the man of the Law but for His disciples.

"In reply Jesus said: 'A man was going down from Jerusalem to Jericho, when he fell into the hands of robbers. They stripped him of his clothes, beat him and went away, leaving him half dead. A priest happened to be going down the same road, and when he saw the man, he passed by on the other side. So too, a Levite, when he came to the place and saw him, passed by on the other side'" (verses 30-32). To illustrate His story, Jesus used the priest as an example of the pious Jewish religious community who were great at thumping their chests in their outward display of righteousness but failed to address the needs of God's people. Jesus selected the Levite as an example of one who was in charge of God's holy temple and the sacrifices therein. As men of faith and understanding of the Law they both should have known their responsibility to reach out to the man, but they did not.

"But a Samaritan," Jesus continued, "as he traveled, came where the man was; and when he saw him, he took pity on him. He went to him and bandaged his wounds, pouring on oil and wine. Then he put the man on his own donkey, took him to an inn and took care of him. The next day he took out two silver coins and gave them to the innkeeper. 'Look after him,' he said, 'and when I return, I will reimburse you for any extra expense you may have (verses 33-35).'" The Samaritan was on the opposite end of the societal ladder among the Jews. Samaritans of the era were natives of Judah and the region of Israel that became known as Samaria. They were descendants of Syrians and were despised by the Jews as being unclean and were subsequently shunned. It was a Samaritan woman that Jesus ministered to and opened her eyes to the truth of the living God (John 4). It was the region of Samaria to which some of the disciples of Jesus fled and preached the Gospel when Saul of Tarsus (who would later convert to Christianity and become the Apostle Paul) was persecuting the young church (Acts 8).

Since the victimized man was traveling through the mountains from Jerusalem to Jericho it is possible that the man was a fellow Jew, but Jesus does not disclose that because it is not germane to His parable. In any case, of the three potential men that could have easily helped the injured man, it was not the two representatives of the religious community, but the hated and ostracized Samaritan. He not only took the time to stop and help, but he went the extra mile to bring the victim to a place of safety and healing and paid for the needed services.

It should be obvious, but Jesus asked the student of the Law, "'Which of these three do you think was a neighbor to the man who fell into the hands of robbers?'

"The expert in the law replied, 'The one who had mercy on him (verses 36-37a).'"

Jesus simply replied, "Go and do likewise" (verse 37b).

The disciples of Jesus are called to acts of mercy and to serve those in need, whether they are fellow believers, non-believers or the despised of society. The Samaritan did not believe as the Jews and did not live under the Law which commanded among other things to *love your neighbor as yourself* (Leviticus 19:18). However, he responded out of compassion for his fellow man, not out of religious law.

"For the LORD your God is God of gods and Lord of lords, the great God, mighty and awesome, who shows no partiality and accepts no bribes," Moses instructed the Hebrews. "He defends the cause of the fatherless and the widow, and loves the alien, giving him food and clothing" (Deuteronomy 10:17-18). The God of the Jews and Christians does not discriminate when it comes to people in need. All are the same in His sight, children of the heavenly Father. Christians are called to such sacrificial service on a daily basis and demonstrate it worldwide through millions of missionaries, aide workers, agriculturalists, para-church ministries and churches throughout the world, often in the most threatening and unpleasant environments. Compare that outreach to the words of Muhammad to his dedicated followers.

Muhammad is the Apostle of Allah, and those with him are firm [and unyielding] of heart against the unbelievers [deniers of the truth], [yet full of] compassionate [mercy] among themselves [or towards one another] …. (Surah 48:29)

The New Testament Bible and the ministry of Jesus was and is all about reconciling sinners and non-believers with the God who loves them. On the other hand, the Qur'an and the testimony of Muhammad in the Qur'an is much about oppressing, murdering, enslaving, or, at the very least, distancing one from those who do not believe in Allah.

Again, a Pharisee, a student of the Law, asked Jesus, "Of all the commandments, which is the most important?"

"The most important one," answered Jesus, "is this: 'Hear O Israel, the Lord our God, the Lord is one. Love the Lord our God with all your heart and with all your soul and with all your mind and with all your strength' [Deut. 6:4-5]. The second is this: 'Love your neighbor as yourself. There is no commandment greater than these" (Mark 12:28-31; Matt. 22:34-40). There is not a greater commandment from God; not a greater response of man toward man then the expression of God's love.

"Let no debt remain outstanding," the Apostle Paul wrote, "except the continuing debt to love one another, for he who loves his fellowman has fulfilled the law ... and whatever other commandment there may be, are summed up in this one rule: 'Love your neighbor as yourself' [Lev. 19:18]. Love does no harm to its neighbor. Therefore love is the fulfillment of the law" (Romans 13:8-10). Two chapters later, Paul reaffirmed this commitment. "Each of us should please his neighbor for his good, to build him up ... Accept one another, then, just as Christ accepted you, in order to bring praise to God" (Romans 15:2, 7).

Cruel and Unusual Punishment

Man seems to have an unhealthy capacity to exercise any level of cruelty toward his fellow man. Atrocities have been well documented in various holy books and historical records. They are usually seen as aberrations of humanity that are condemned by one's god or the general society. One can easily recall from recent history the diabolical acts of inhumanity of Adolf Hitler and the Third Reich; the Sudanese and other African massacres; the Communist Chinese purge of hundreds of millions of Christians and other religious groups; the butchery of Cambodia's Pol Pot or North Korea's starvation prisons. The list is, perhaps, endless. Most such atrocities are committed by what society would determine are men with demented minds—sadists or ones possessed with evil. Few, if any, would be described as sane men following the dictates of their holy book or religious beliefs.

Unfortunately, that does not hold true for Muslims who commit heinous crimes against humanity. More often then not, they are following the dictates of their holy scriptures and their revered prophet, Muhammad. The call for the followers of Islam to mistreat and persecute non-believers is escalated in the Qur'an to a call for the *enemies of Allah* to suffer beheadings and amputations. Beheadings have been the hallmark of the Islamic faith since it was founded by Muhammad. "The punishment of those who wage war against Allah and His apostle," revealed Muhammad, "and strive to make mischief in the land is only this, that they should be murdered or crucified or their hands and their feet should be cut off on opposite sides or they should be imprisoned ... And (as for) the man who steals and the woman who steals, cut off their hands as a punishment for what they have earned, an exemplary punishment from Allah ..." (surah 5:33, 38).

Lopping off heads seems to be one of the favorite blood sports of Islamic terrorists, particularly in the Middle East—now and in centuries past. As it has been cited before, Muhammad commanded his followers to *strike off* the heads and finger tips of the enemies of Allah (surahs.8:12-13; 47:4). While other societies—notably the French—have, in the past, used beheading as a form of capital punishment, it usually came after a formal trial to determine guilt. Not so in the realm of Islam. There is no trial; no determination of guilt required. The victim just has to be declared an *enemy of Allah.* Who is an enemy of Allah?—Anyone who does not accept him as their god or Muhammad as the prophet of their god. No dreadful crime against humanity needs to be committed—only that one is an apostate or a non-believer.

Slavery

The act of enslaving someone is a horrendous act of dehumanization. Unfortunately it has been practiced by societies and various religious groups, including Christians, Jews and Muslims throughout the centuries. Slavery is no longer condoned in Judeo-Christian or free world circles, but still exists in many Muslim-dominated societies. Just watch the evening news or read the communiqués of organizations like Release International or The Voice of the Martyrs and you will realize that slavery still prevails, not only in the well-publicized Sudan, but in other African countries, the Middle East, Southeast Asia, and elsewhere in the Muslim world.

"From the days that Muhammad drew his sword to rob and conquer non-Muslims to this very day," Silas wrote, "Muslims have been taking non-Muslims, and even other black Muslims, as slaves.

"Muslims were enslaving black Africans long before any slave ships sailed for the New World."[4]

Muhammad was an undeniable proponent of slavery as attested to by verses in the Qur'an (surahs 4:24; 23:6; 33:50; 70:29-31, et al). The euphemism used in the Qur'an for a slave is *those whom your right hand possesses.* In addition to the Qur'an there are numerous ahadiths that record that not only did Muhammad own slaves but he supported his followers in owning slaves, many of whom were women taken as captives from their conquered foe. It is known that at least two of Muhammad's wives were women that he had taken captive from tribes he had gained victory over. One particular female of exceptional beauty, the twenty-year old Juweiriyeh (a.k.a. Javeria or Juwayriya) was taken captive in a raid upon the Arab Banu al-Mustaliq tribe in 627 A.D.[5]

Best-selling author, Robert Spencer, wrote in his book, *The Truth About Muhammad*, that, "From a twenty-first-century perspective [slavery] is one of the most problematic aspects of Muhammad's status as 'an excellent model of conduct': the treatment of women as war prizes, with no consideration of their will ... in the Islamic world it is particularly hard to eradicate [slavery] because of the prophetic sanction it has received."[6]

No Punishment for Killing an Infidel

Within Islamic culture and law there is a certain prescribed forgiveness for murder that carries no punishment. It comes straight from the teachings of Muhammad and is recorded in the ahadith.

"The legal regulations of Diya (Blood-money) and the (ransom for) releasing of the captives, and the judgment that no Muslim should be killed in Qisas (equality in punishment) for killing a Kafir (disbeliever) (hadith 9:83:50)." *Qisas* is the retaliatory *eye for an eye* justice system within Islam. While killing a Kafir is acceptable under any circumstance, the killing of a fellow Muslim is not. "Allah's Apostle said, 'The blood of a Muslim who confesses that none has the right to be worshipped but Allah and that I am His Apostle, cannot be shed except in three cases: In Qisas for murder, a married person who commits illegal sexual intercourse and the one who reverts from Islam (apostate) and leaves the Muslims'" (hadith 9:83:17).

There are a lot of crazy people on the planet, but Islam seems to have a disproportionate share and all of them quoting the Qur'an or their holy prophet as the justification for their mindless barbarism. Take the example of Mohammed Taheri-azar. On March 3, 2006, the Iranian national and graduate of the University of North Carolina drove his rented Jeep Cherokee into a crowd of nine students in an attempt to kill them all. Was he angry with them? Had they abused or otherwise mistreated him? Did he even know them? The answer is "no" to all three. His reasoning was quite basic from his viewpoint. "Allah gives permission in the Quran," he wrote in a letter to the ABC television affiliate in Durham, North Carolina, "for the followers of Allah to attack those who have raged war against them, with the expectation of eternal paradise in case of martyrdom and/or living one's life in obedience of all of Allah's commandments found throughout the Quran's 114 chapters."[7] He was quick to add that, "I did not act out of hatred for Americans, but out of love for Allah instead."

According to Muhammad and the Qur'an, unbelievers (infidels or *kafir*) are considered an *open enemy* of Allah, Muhammad, Muslims and Islam (surah 4:101) and worthy only of *disgraceful chastisement* (humiliation and suffering) from Allah to be carried out by Allah's faithful (surah 4:102).

Apostasy

Allah leads people into unbelief (surah 4:88), then he commands that those that disbelieve must be killed (surah 4:89).

"What is the matter with you, then," Muhammad exclaimed, "that you have become two parties about the hypocrites, while Allah has made them return (to unbelief) for what they have earned? Do you wish to guide him whom Allah causes to err? And whomsoever Allah causes to err, you shall by no means find a way for him.

"They desire that you should disbelieve as they have disbelieved, so that you might be (all) alike; therefore take not from among them friends until they fly [flee] (their homes) in Allah's way; but if they turn back [to enmity], then seize them and kill them wherever you find them, and take not from among them a friend or a helper." (surah 4:88-89)."

In contrast, Jesus taught His disciples that if one believer left the fold and became spiritually lost, they were to go after him and rescue him and bring him back into the kingdom of God.

"What do you think?" Jesus asked His disciples. "If a man owns a hundred sheep, and one of them wanders away, will he not leave the ninety-nine on the hills and go to look for the one that wandered off? And if he finds it, I tell you the truth, he is happier about that one sheep than about the ninety-nine that did not wander off. In the same way your Father in heaven is not willing that any of these little ones should be lost" (Matthew 18:12-14). Instead of going after someone who has left the faith in an effort to kill them, Jesus recommended that those who leave should be won back with care and compassion.

There are many examples in the ahadith of how Muslims are to deal with apostates. Here is one such instruction:

> Narrated 'Ikrima: Some Zanadiqa (atheists) were brought to 'Ali and he burnt them. The news of this event reached Ibn 'Abbas who said, "If I had been in his place, I would not have burnt them, as Allah's Apostle forbade it, saying, *Do not punish anybody with Allah's punishment (fire).* I would have killed them according to the statement of Allah's Apostle, *Whoever changed his Islamic religion, then kill him.*" (hadith 9:84:57)

The following verse 58 also recorded the killing of a Jew who converted to Islam and then converted back to Judaism and that, "This is the judgment of Allah and His Apostle."

A few verses later, the fate of an apostate is once again reaffirmed ... No doubt I heard Allah's Apostle saying, "During the last days there will appear some young foolish people who will say the best words but their faith will not go beyond their throats (i.e. they will have no faith) and will go out from (leave) their religion as an arrow goes out of the game. So, wherever you find them, kill them, for whoever kills them shall have reward on the Day of Resurrection." (hadith 9:84:64)

In the preceding hadith, not only is the Muslim to kill the apostate, but he will receive a special reward on the Day of Resurrection— otherwise known euphemistically as the *incentive clause.*

"Surely," Muhammad reaffirmed, "those who disbelieve and die while they are disbelievers, these it is on whom is the curse of Allah and the angels and men all" (surah 2:161).

According to Silas, a frequent contributor to the web site, Answering-Islam, "Muslims living in the Mideast have no problem with the concept of putting apostates to death. But to Muslims living in the West it is an embarrassing Islamic edict.... A close examination of the Quran, Hadith, and Sirat [Sirah or written stories of Muhammad] will show that indeed, the punishment for leaving Islam, either under an Islamic government, or not, was execution."[8]

There are thousands of modern day martyrs who have been killed because they turned away from Islam and embraced Christianity. In Somalia, a country that is nearly 100% Sunni Muslim, Ali Mustaf Maka'il, a 22-year old college student was shot in the back and killed on September 7, 2006, shortly after he converted to Christianity. He had harmed no one.[9]

In today's world, however, the killing of apostates is not limited to Muslim countries. In Australia, for instance, a Muslim medical doctor stabbed his wife to death because their seventeen-year old daughter became a Christian.[10] Why did he kill his wife and not his daughter? It is because, in the Muslim household it is the wife who is responsible for the guidance and welfare of the daughters. These are only two of the thousands of "honor killings" that occur throughout the Muslim world every year in order to take revenge on a Muslim or their family when they choose to leave Islam.

> "O Prophet! Strive hard against the unbelievers [deniers of the truth] and the hypocrites [those who pretend religious devotion to Allah] and be unyielding to them," Allah revealed to Muhammad, "and [if they do not repent] their abode is hell, and evil is the destination. They [the hypocrites] swear by Allah that they did not speak [anything wrong], and certainly they did speak [denying the truth], the word of unbelief, and disbelieved after their [surrender to] Islam, and they had determined upon what they have not been able to effect, and they did not find fault [with the Faith] except because Allah and His Apostle enriched them out of His grace; therefore if they repent, it will be good for them; and if they turn back, Allah will chastise them with a painful chastisement [great suffering] in this world and the hereafter, and they shall not have in the land any guardian or a helper [to give them comfort]." (surah 9:73, 74).

Remember, in hadith 9:83:17 previously cited in this chapter, that Muhammad, in the name of Allah, granted that a Muslim or Muslims may take the life of one who has murdered someone, committed adultery or has left the faith. "He who disbelieves in Allah after having believed," Muhammad declared, "not he who is compelled while his heart is at rest on account of faith, but he who opens (his) breast to disbelief—on these is the wrath of Allah, and they shall have a grievous chastisement" (surah 16:106). Here, a crafty distinction is presented. A Muslim can deny his faith without being an apostate if he feels compelled to do so before his enemy, while at the same time in his heart he confesses Allah. However, a Muslim who truly turns from Allah is to be killed.

Conclusion

There are clearly two divergent methods of dealing with infidels or unbelievers and apostates or those that leave the faith of Islam or Christianity. In Islam and its teachings, infidels and apostates can not be tolerated and must be eliminated for the sake of Allah. The Qur'an and the recorded sayings or teachings of Muhammad are quite clear on this issue. There are no modifications or exceptions—infidels and apostates are to be killed if they refuse to convert or re-convert to Islam. Non-believers, not apostates, can escape the death penalty (on occasion) if they submit to paying the oppressive poll tax or *jizya*.

Christians, however, are called to reach out to the unbeliever, not to persecute them. If a Christian leaves the faith, he or she is free to do so, but Jesus advised His disciples that they should make an effort to rescue the lost member of the fold, rejoicing with the Father in heaven at the return of one of His children.

Following the Light

Our hatred toward Christians took the form of harassment and assaults against them on the streets [of Egypt], but they answered our assaults with disgusting meekness. We responded by being more aggressive against them, and we started to plan how we could torture and intimidate them. According to the Koran, all their belongings were to be considered a "gift" from God to the Muslims (Surah 59:7).

I started reading the Gospel of Matthew [to build a case against the Christians] and already stumbled, even before I finished the first chapter .... I saw that they traced the genealogy of Christ back to David. I thought they were crazy.

I found the Bible speaking about what we did with Christians as if it recorded the present events. I read what the Bible said about persecution, humiliation, and murder—our idea of obeying God ....

Our life was full of violence, cruelty and terrorism. This was not our normal behavior. We felt if we did not act this way, we would not be obedient to Allah. Allah had stated in the Koran how we were to treat the infidels, whether People of the Book, polytheists, or false Muslims.

I prayed, "If you are the God of Muslims, take out everything from my mind except Islam, and if You are the God of the Christians, give me some light to follow."

I felt God was encircling me with evidences, and I had no way to reject Christ's call for me to follow Him. I never stopped reading the Bible; it became a friend of mine. The more I read, the more I tasted its sweetness.

I saw the door of my room open, a man with long hair and a heavy beard, and a pillar of white light radiating beside him. I heard him calling me, "Stand up; the Christ wants you."

Paul
The Voice of the Martyrs
December, 2003, p. 8-9

References

1. Al-Munajjid, Muhammad. *The True Nature of the Enmity Between the Muslims and the Jews.* Http://www.alminbar.com/khutbaheng/9022. htm. Accessed December 3, 2006.

2. *Obsession: Radical Islam's War Against the West* (Documentary). Trinity Home Entertainment, 2007.

3. *Saudi Government Daily: Jews Use Teenagers' Blood for 'Purim' Pastries.* The Middle East Media Research Institute, *Special Dispatch Series—No. 354,* March 13, 2002. Http://memri.org/bin/opener.cgi? Page=archives&ID=SP35402. Accessed May 23, 2007.

4. Silas, *Slavery in Islam.* Http://answering-islam.org.uk/Silas/slavery. htm. Accessed October 4, 2007.

5. Spencer, Robert. *The Truth About Muhammad, Founder of the World's Most Intolerant Religion,* 2006. Regnery Publishing, Inc., p. 134.

6. Ibid, pp. 133-134.

7. *Muslim: I Attacked 'Out of Love for Allah.'* WorldNetDaily.com, March 15, 2006. Http://www.worldnetdaily.com/news/article. asp?ARTICLE_ID=49276. Accessed March 16, 2006.

8. Silas, *The Punishment for Apostasy from Islam.* Http://answering-islam. org.uk/Silas/apostasy.htm. Accessed February 7, 2007.

9. Ireland, Michael. *Convert from Islam to Christianity Killed.* WorldNetDaily.com, September 16, 2006. Http://www.worldnetdaily. com/news/article.asp? ARTICLE_ID= 52004. Accessed September 16, 2006.

10. *Muslim Stabs Wife When Daughter Becomes Christian.* WorldNetDaily. com, October 14, 2006. Http://www.worldnetdaily.com/news/article. asp?ARTICLE_ID= 52437. Accessed October 14, 2006.

Advance of Islam
in the 21st Century

CHAPTER 12

World Outlook

We don't shy away from declaring that Islam is
ready to rule the world . . .
We must prepare ourselves to rule the world ...

Mahmoud Ahmadinejad
President of Iran
January 5, 2006

Hadith 9:83:26 (Volume 9, Book 83, Number 26), narrated by Abu Huraira, says: "That he heard Allah's Apostle saying, 'We (Muslims) are the last (to come) but (will be) the foremost (on the Day of Resurrection)." Christianity and Islam are on a collision course with diametrically opposed objectives. Christianity peacefully seeks to bring the personal salvation message of Jesus Christ to the world and free people from sin and bondage. Islam seeks to conquer the world by violence and oppression, force everyone to submit to Islam and the teachings of Muhammad and live a life of subjugation and bondage or die.

"This is Islam's demographic moment and they have to make the most of it," claimed Mark Steyn in his stark reality book, *America Alone*.[1] His premise, backed with statistics, is that Muslim birthrates far exceed that of Western developed countries. At the same time the birthrate of the majority of those countries is below what is required to replace their dying populations. Thus, Muslims are rapidly replacing the native populations of the countries that they are immigrating to.

Former devout Shiite Muslim and author, Reza Safa, asserted that, "In the Islamic nations, other religions do not have the right to exist.

The few people who practice other religions are under tremendous oppression. They are routinely incarcerated and executed."[2]

In their best selling book, *Unveiling Islam*, brothers Ergun and Emir Caner, former Muslims and now Christian theologians, wrote: "Therefore, jihad (holy war) is completed only when the entire world is placed under the submission of Allah and when his laws reign supreme."[3]

Just watch or read the world news. Daily, the majority of the stories center on terrorist attacks or persecutions by Muslims against other Muslims or non-Muslims everywhere in the world. The Muslim world is both exploding and imploding worldwide with no end in sight.

In February, 2007, *Parade*, a Sunday morning newspaper insert, made the following observations:

> There are more than 70 countries ruled by dictators who exercise arbitrary authority over their citizens and who cannot be removed from power through legal means. These tyrants suppress the freedoms of speech and religion, and the right to a fair trial. Some also commit torture, execute opponents and starve their own people.[4]

Parade's list is dominated by Muslim-controlled countries. Topping the list at number one is Sudan (85% Muslim) led by the butcher of Dafur, Omar Al-Bashir, who has driven (at last count in 2006) over 5.3 million mostly Christian Sudanese from their homeland. Of the top ten, there are six Muslim-led or Muslim-dominated countries (there would be seven if not for the military intervention in Iraq). Number three is Iran (99% Muslim), led by two maniacal sociopaths and religious and political madmen, Ayatollah Sayyid Ali Khamenei and President Mahmoud Ahmadinejad. Saudi Arabia (100% Wahhabi Muslim), is the financier of terrorism worldwide, led by King Abdullah who controls the world's wealthiest oil reserves, comes in at number five.

Rounding out the top ten is number eight, Uzbekistan (88% Muslim), led by President Islam Karimov who has committed countless human rights abuses and murders throughout this former satellite country of the Soviet Union. Right behind Uzbekistan is Libya (100% Muslim) under the control of cultural Muslim fanatic, Muammar Al-Qaddafi, who seized leadership in 1969 and has become one of the leaders in state-sponsored Islamic terrorism throughout the globe. Syria (90% Muslim) ranks number ten. Led by Bashar Al-Assad, the country is a well-known supplier and conduit of military arms and terrorists throughout the Mideast region.

In case any of these six Muslim countries should falter and have a humanitarian change of heart, there are five more Muslim-controlled countries waiting in the "wings" of the next ten "Worst Dictators." They are the small African country of Eritrea (80%), Pakistan (97%), Ethiopia (65%), Egypt (94%) and Cameroon (55%).

"Up to 250 million Christians worldwide will face persecution and repression in 2007, simply for following Jesus Christ .... But persecution is growing fastest of all in the Islamic world," reported persecution watchdog, Release International.[5]

"Governments in even moderate Muslim countries often fail to safeguard the rights of their Christian minorities. Abuses suffered by Christians include kidnapping, forced conversion, imprisonment, church destruction, torture, rape and execution.[6]

"... One of the world's worst abusers of religious freedom is Saudi Arabia, guardian of Islam's holiest sites Mecca and Medina," RI disclosed. "Saudi forbids all other religions. A Muslim found 'guilty' of converting to Christianity could face the death sentence for apostasy. And anyone who leads a Muslim to Christ faces jail, expulsion or execution."[7]

According to Release International CEO, Andy Dipper, Saudi Arabia "is a government that hands out the death sentence to its own citizens who want nothing more than the freedom to choose their own faith. And while Saudi bans all Christian literature, it spends billions of dollars each year propagating Islam around the world."[8]

The Myth of the "Moderate Muslim

When the West looks at Islam it tends to see the adherents of the faith in terms of *black and white*: they are either "radical" or "peaceful", "terrorist" or "non-terrorist", "fundamentalist" or "moderate." However, in the Muslim world, among Islamic clerics and the teachings of the Qur'an and the prophet Muhammad, there is *only* one form of Islam—radical and fundamental. ALL Muslims are called to believe in the fundamental (basic, original, elemental) truths of their faith as embodied in the Qur'an and the teachings of their prophet, Muhammad. There are no exceptions or deviations permitted. Unlike the Christian faith, in which there are many interpretations of scripture and the teachings of Jesus that have resulted in numerous denominations over the centuries, Islam is seen as one size fits all and all must believe in the same things. Hence, the ongoing blood baths between Islamic sects, such as the Sunni versus the Shi'a, etc. Each believes that they and they only are the followers of true Islam.

In religion, a fundamentalist is one who takes the holy scriptures of their faith literally as the divinely inspired and infallible word of their god. Christian fundamentalists, for example, believe that the Bible—in every detail—is the divinely inspired word of God and is free from any human error. Although fundamentalist Christians are sometimes ridiculed, they are not typically persecuted or murdered, nor do they assault non-fundamentalist Christians. It is different within Islam. *All* Muslims are called to believe in the Qur'an as the undeniable and infallible word of Allah as revealed through Muhammad—despite the fact that there are numerous historical errors and contradictions throughout the Qur'an. Historical or scientific proof aside, the Qur'an cannot be disputed or challenged. Therefore, all Muslims are called to and commanded to follow a fundamentalist faith of Islam. There can be no moderation or moderate Muslims, only fundamentalists or "radical" believers. "Moderate" Muslims, if the West chooses to use such a moniker, in the reality of the Muslim world, do not exist. If they do in practicality, they are viewed as *akafir* or infidels just like the rest of the unbelievers outside Islam.

Almost a year after the September 11, 2001 terrorist attack there was still no massive repentant outcry from the Muslim clerical community throughout the world. No repudiation of the terrorists or their dastardly acts. Six years later, America still waits. Instead, six years later, despite overwhelming evidence to the contrary, the vast majority of Muslims in the United States and worldwide believe that the terrorist attacks were either carried out by Israel or the United States. The Pew Research Center survey, *Muslim Americans*, released May 22, 2007, found that only 40% of Muslims living in the U.S. thought that the September 11 attacks were carried out by Arab Muslims.[9] In the rest of the world it is worse. Only 35% of Muslims living in Germany believe the terrorists were Muslim. In Egypt, 32 ; Turkey, 16 and Pakistan, only 15% thought Muslims did it.

In the West a pitiful handful of Muslim clerics, scholars and leaders weakly protest to pacify the ignorant non-Muslim, that the jihad terrorist has "hijacked" their religion; that the murderous mujahidin around the world do not represent "true" Islam. If that were so, then why is it that there are not thousands of "moderate" Muslims living free in the United States, England and elsewhere running to enlist in the military of those countries to fight against this radical element that is "hijacking" their faith? Why are there not tens of thousands or millions of Muslims everywhere rising up in voice and action to stop this radical disease that is sweeping the world? Why are there not sermons spewing forth from the mosques; lectures from Muslim academia condemning the actions of the jihadists? Why is the Muslim media throughout the world not only silent on this issue but actively inflaming and encouraging the jihadists to fight on? Why? Because the jihadists are not alone in their misfit theology. It is not their theology to hijack. It is the theology imbedded deep in the heart and core of Islam as preached in their Qur'an, by Muhammad, their imams and scholars worldwide and is lying dormant or not so dormant like a cancer in the deep, dark bowel of every Muslim soul.

"If a band of Americans," wrote noted author and columnist, William F. Buckley, Jr., "proclaiming their devotion to the faith, assaulted a Muslim center, we would not need to wait very long for disavowals by Christian leaders. When John Brown [the Kansas abolitionist] carried his faith to unreasonable lengths, we hanged him [in 1859]. What we are waiting for ... is an apology from Muslim leaders ... an explicit disavowal, as contrary to acceptable teachings of the Koran, of the acts of the terrorists."[10]

Mark Steyn, author of *America Alone*, wrote that "the most prominent 'moderate Muslims' would seem to be more accurately designated as apostate or ex-Muslims ... It seems likely that the beliefs of Mohammed Atta [leader of the September 11, 2001 attack on America] are closer to the thinking of most Muslims ...."[11]

Ibn Warraq (pseudonym), author of *Why I Am Not a Muslim*, believes there are moderate Muslims but that Islam, itself, is *not* moderate.[12] Interviewed on Australian Radio National a month after the attack on the World Trade Center in New York, Warraq stated that, "Both [President George W.] Bush and [Prime Minister] Tony Blair are the two leaders who have introduced religion into political life, and now they're the ones who refuse to use the word 'Islam' when talking about terrorism. They just won't understand what is happening; they will repeat the same old mistakes. If they cannot analyze the situation and see that Islam is the motivating factor behind all this [the September 11, 2001 attack], then how on earth are they going to tackle the problem?"[13]

On June 18, 2006, *The New York Times* published an interview with two home bread "rising star" converts to Islam, Sheik Hamza Yusuf (formerly Mark Hanson of San Francisco) and Imam Zaid Shakir (formerly Ricky Mitchell of Georgia). They were lauded for their establishment of the first Islamic seminary in the United States. Touted as moderate and "modern middle ground" Muslims, they have established a considerable following among American college age youth. While their message might be considered by many—both inside and outside Islam—as a watered-downed, Westernized version of Islamic beliefs, their goal is clear.[14]

Shakir was candid about his dream of America being an Islamic country ruled by Islamic law, "not by violent means," of course, he said, "but by persuasion." And what example in the Muslim world can he point to where there is Islamic law that is not applied with violence? None! Unless, of course, he equates "persuasion" with violence or violence as a form of persuasion.

"Every Muslim," Shakir commented, "who is honest would say, I would like to see America become a Muslim country. I think it would help people, and if I didn't believe that, I wouldn't be a Muslim. Because Islam helped me as a person, and it's helped a lot of people in my community."

If the Muslim "youth" riots in France in 2006 are to be an example of an expression of Muslim modernity, the Western world should take notice. "… Al Qaida and its allies are literally battling the Crusaders every day in Europe," the World Tribune.com reported in October, 2006. "And so far, Europe isn't doing so well."[15] Thousands of Muslim youths orchestrated by terrorist leaders such as al Qaida are creating chaos or *intifada* (terror or violent uprising) throughout France. Their nightly rampages throughout France in the fall of 2006 resulted in assaults and injuries to 2,500 French police officers. "European law enforcement sources say France could be a model for other countries. The most worried are Britain and the Netherlands."[16]

Political Correctness Until Death Do Us Part

Political Correctness destroyed any hopes of continued War on Terror coalition efforts with the United States in the Middle East. At the beginning of 2007 Washington insiders gave up on further coalition efforts with Western European countries and the expansion of the war effort in the Middle East. According to Lyric Wallwork Winik, "many of the leaders in Western Europe are unwilling to antagonize their growing Muslim populations by taking on Islamic radicals or siding with an increasingly unpopular U.S."[17]

Even in Israel, political correctness is threatening the very survival of the Jewish state. With the U.S. thirst for peace in the Middle East and hopefully in the Western world, President George W. Bush and Secretary of State Condoleezza Rice and other U.S. dignitaries have been working both above and below ground to coerce Israel into giving into more and more concessions requested by the Palestinians in order for them to give their blessing of peace. However, just as in the time of the Jewish prophets Jeremiah and Ezekiel, the leaders of Israel cry, "peace, peace" when there is no peace (Jeremiah 6:14; Ezekiel 13:10).

"From the least to the greatest," Jeremiah prophesied, "all are greedy for gain; prophets and priests alike, all practice deceit. They dress the wound of my people as though it were not serious. 'Peace, peace,' they say, when there is no peace. Are they ashamed of their loathsome conduct? No, they have no shame at all; they do not even know how to blush" (Jeremiah 6:13-15).

About two decades after Jeremiah's prophesy, the prophet Ezekiel proclaimed these words from God:

Therefore this is what the Sovereign Lord says: Because of your false words and lying visions, I am against you, declares the Sovereign Lord. My hand will be against the prophets who see false visions and utter lying divinations. They will not belong to the council of my people or be listed in the records of the house of Israel, nor will they enter the land of Israel. Then you will know that I am the Sovereign Lord.

Because they lead my people astray, saying, "Peace," when there is no peace, and because, when a flimsy wall is built, they cover it with whitewash, therefore tell those who cover it with whitewash that it is going to fall. (Ezekiel 13:8-11a)

This wave of political correctness and appeasement of terrorists by the United States and others that is being imposed upon Israel is destroying the morale and lives of the Jews in Israel. Since the Gaza strip was ceded to the Palestinians in 2005, Israel has been under constant attack by Palestinian terrorists.

"Yesterday we had our first Suicide Bomber in [the town of] Eilat, killing three," wrote messianic Jew, Jerry Golden, in his January 30, 2007 newsletter from Jerusalem, *The Golden Report* ....[18] "In today's Jerusalem Post we see his mother telling everyone how proud she is of her son …. Moslems are bringing her flowers and other presents and thanking their god Allah for her son for killing Jews. In Gaza today they are once again dancing in the streets and passing out candy while waving a picture of this Islamic murderer. With such a people there can never be peace, it is either victory or defeat, and losing for us is not an option."

And what was Israel's politically correct response according to Golden? That the bombing was not that bad, since it only killed Jews and not tourists. "Don't worry; [the] bombing was far from the hotels," the Tourism Minister was quoted as saying.

Perhaps Israel and its leaders and the leaders of the free Western world would fair well to heed the words of the Old Testament prophet Zechariah.

This is the word of the Lord concerning Israel. The Lord, who stretches out the heavens, who lays the foundation of the earth, and who forms the spirit of man within him, declares: "I am going to make Jerusalem a cup that sends all the surrounding peoples reeling. Judah will be besieged as well as Jerusalem. On that day, when all the nations of the earth are gathered against her, I will make Jerusalem an immovable rock for all the nations. All who try to move it will injure themselves. On that day I

will strike every horse with panic and its rider with madness,"
declares the LORD. "I will keep a watchful eye over the house
of Judah, but I will blind all the horses of the nations. Then the
leaders of Judah will say in their hearts, 'The people of Jerusalem
are strong, because the LORD Almighty is their God."

"On that day I will make the leaders of Judah like a firepot
in a woodpile, like a flaming torch among sheaves. They will
consume right and left all the surrounding peoples, but Jerusalem
will remain intact in her place.

"The LORD will save the dwellings of Judah first, so that
the honor of the house of David and of Jerusalem's inhabitants
may not be greater than that of Judah. On that day the LORD
will shield those who live in Jerusalem, so that the feeblest among
them will be like David, and the house of David will be like
God, like the Angel of the LORD going before them. On that
day I will set out to destroy all the nations that attack [come
against] *Jerusalem."* (Zechariah 12:1-9)

Ibn Warraq, who was living and teaching in London during the
1970s was in favor of cultural diversity or "multiculturalism" at the
time—another outgrowth of political correctness. "But I now realize
that we have gone too far, in that we have emphasized the differences
which has [sic] been disastrous for the community. Not only have we
emphasized the differences," Warraq asserted, "we have accepted totally
false representations of what the West is. Every ill in the world, including
the Third World of course, has been attributed to the wicked West ….
Of course slavery and the Muslims were deeply implicated in the slave
trade. Islam was an Imperialist religion which destroyed Christianity
in the Near East, yet nobody mentions those facts."[19]

According to the French publication, *Journal Chretien* [Christian],
political correctness (or bending over backwards until it hurts) is getting
out of hand.[20] Some banks are dropping the "piggy" bank because of
the fear of losing Muslim customers who view pigs as unclean. German
butchers that offer pork sausage are having their wiener displays spat on
by passing Muslims. Muslim taxi cab drivers in many cities in Europe
refuse to pick up passengers with dogs, even if it is a service animal for
the blind or hearing impaired. This backlash of resistance spread to the

United States in early 2007, where Muslim cab drivers in Minneapolis and elsewhere refused to take fares with dogs or carrying alcohol.[21] Also in Minneapolis and elsewhere in the United States, Muslim cashiers are causing a lot of consternation for customers and employers of food stores by refusing to handle food items that contain pork.[22, 23]

Some state members of the European Union are permitting Muslims to implement shari'a (Muslim religious) law with its own judicial system.

"Islam is slowly but surely taking a grip on the European culture," wrote journalist Wolfgang Polzer in the *Journal*. "Traditional values, customs and judicial standards are gradually customized to meet Muslim requirements."[24]

In Britain, where many of the Muslim immigrants are of Somali origin, a Somali form of cultural shari'a is unofficially allowed in many parts of the country. In many cases it has become the alternative law for Somali and other Muslims to that of British criminal law.[25] One young Somali man, Aydarus Yusuf, interviewed by the *London Telegraph*'s Legal Editor, Joshua Rozenberger, said that he felt more obligated to the Somali cultural law than to that of his new country. "Us Somalis," Yusuf is quoted as saying, "wherever we are in the world, we have our own law. It's not sharia, it's not religious—it's just a cultural thing."[26] Faizul Aqtab Siddiqi, a Muslim lawyer and principal of Hijaz College Islamic University in Britain predicted that within a decade there will be a formal network of shari'a courts throughout Britain. That should usher in the collapse of British society as the world knows it.

In Germany, with 3.5 million Muslims and 40% of them believing that the German constitution is incompatible with Islam, it is only a matter of time before the once staid and proud Germanic people succumb to Islamofication.[27]

In Britain, the rapidly growing younger Muslim populace is sounding more radical than the more senior Muslims. An early 2007 survey of Muslims in Britain, titled "Living Together Apart: British Muslims and the Paradox of Multiculturalism" and reported in *the Jerusalem Post*, reveals that 40% of younger Muslims (age 16-24) would prefer Islamic Shari'a law to that of British law. Only 17% of Muslims fifty-five or older would favor such a change.[28] 36% of the younger group believed that anyone that converted from Islam to another religion should be put to death. In this same youth group, 74% wanted women to wear the veil in public and 37% want Islamic schools.

The more frightening statistic: 13% of young Muslims "admired" terrorist groups like al-Qaida that fought against the West. Sound immaterial? In Britain's 2001 census there were an estimated 1.6 million Muslims living in Britain. With young Muslims the fastest growing demographic in England, a 13% favorable view of terrorism translates into tens of thousands of young British Muslims who just might see themselves carrying out an act of terror against Britain or other Western countries.

At the same time, the survey disclosed that 84% of all Muslim respondents felt they were being treated fairly by the Brits. Yet 58% felt all the world's problems could be blamed on the West.

The politically correct conclusion of the survey's author, Munira Mirza: The British and their government policies were to blame for the Muslims feeling as they do and that the Brits should make more concessions to make Muslims feel at home. Meanwhile in the land of the "Queen Mum," the second most popular name for newborn boys in the past year was Muhammed or anyone of thirteen other variations of the prophet of Islam's name.[29] By next year it is expected to be the number one boy's name for newborns in staid old England.

In the United States, as in Canada and Western Europe, in the guise of political correctness and cultural diversity, Muslim imams are being invited to pray before federal and state legislatures. Ignorance by political leaders has run amok in the United States and elsewhere. The majority of legislators are under the misguided assumption that Muslims pray to the same god as the Jews and Christians. Muslim imams, of course, think they do also, as the invocation of Imam Mohamad Joban before the Washington state legislature on March 3, 2003 can attest. Imam Joban's opening remarks (prayer) started with:

> *We open this session of House of Representatives in the name of Allah, the one God of Abraham, God of Moses, God of Jesus, and God of Muhammad, peace be upon them all .... We ask Allah or God to bless the state of Washington so it may continue to prosper and become a symbol of peace and tranquility for people of all ethnic and religious backgrounds. We pray that*

Allah may guide this House in making good decisions for the people of Washington ....[30]

Allah is in no way, shape or form the God of Abraham, Moses or Jesus. He may be the god of Muhammad, but he is not the god of *anyone* in the Bible. Only two legislators declined to participate in the imam's prayer and they were highly ridiculed to the point where they were forced to apologize to the imam and the Muslim community. Of course, Americans are still waiting for a Muslim apology for the September 11, 2001 attacks on their nation.

In April, 2007, the Texas state Senate committed a similar blunder by inviting Imam Yusuf Kavakci, a known supporter of the Iranian butcher, Ayatollah Khomeini and other "radical" Muslim leaders. He opened by reciting the *fatehah* or first chapter (surah) of the Qur'an like so many imams do.[31]

> In the name of god, Allah, the beneficent, the merciful. All praise is for Allah, our lord, the lord of the worlds, the compassionate, the merciful, master of the day of judgments. Oh, god, Allah, you alone we worship, and you alone we call on for help. Oh, Allah, guide us to the straight path, the path of those whom you have favored, **not of those who have earned your wrath or of those who have lost the way**. Our lord, have mercy on us from yourself and guide us in our efforts, strivings and works. (article emphasis)[32]

Ignorance also ran amok among Texas legislators that day. They no doubt missed the fact that this was not a universal prayer to the God of the Jews and Christians. This was a prayer to Allah, the god of the Muslims only. First, the *us* in this prayer is **not** a universal, all inclusive *us*, as in *all who were present* or all mankind. The *us* are the Muslims, as in *Allah, you alone we worship*. No one worships Allah except the Muslim faithful. Only Muslims pray that Allah will guide *them* on the straight path. Everyone else is on the crooked or wrong path. Allah favors only Muslims, no one else. Only non-Muslims or infidels—those worthy only of death—are *those who have earned* [Allah's] *wrath or of those who have lost the way.* So, what this imam was praying is what every Muslim prays when they pray the *fatehah*, and that is for the protection of Muslims and the destruction of infidels. When will America and the West wake-up from their politically correct stupidity?

Apparently, not any time soon. At the Democratic National Committee winter meetings on February 2, 2007, Imam Husham Al-Husainy led the faithful Democrats in the same surah 1 prayer, essentially praying for their conversion to Islam. It was reported that *heads* [were] *bowed reverently.*[33]

Follow the Leader?

While Europe crumbles under the demands of Islam, Canada and the United States, both of which take great pride in their cultural diversity-political correctness jargon and pandering, are hot on the heels of their European cousins.

In the United States it is hard to get a handle on the exact number of Muslims living in the country. Popular estimates range widely from 1.6 million, upwards to 8 million. A U.S. Department of State *Fact Sheet* published in 2001 projected that by 2010 the Muslim population in America will exceed the Jewish population (currently estimated at 5.2 million) and thus become the second largest faith in the country.[34] The same *Fact Sheet* projected that there were 2,000 mosques in the United States. An estimated 30% of mosque attendees are new converts to Islam.[35] There are no studies that reveal current numbers, but with the rapidity of mosque construction in the U.S., the number today is certainly significantly higher. One source, *The Jewish Exponent*, claims that the Muslim population in the U.S. in 2007 already exceeds the U.S. Jewish population, making Muslims the second largest religious group in America.[36]

The annual growth rate of the Muslim population in America is estimated to be 6% compared to 0.9 % for the total U.S.[37] Two-thirds of U.S. Muslims hold college degrees and are considered affluent. And here's a real sobering statistic: While 67% of the adult American population is **over** forty years old, the same age of adult American Muslims is **under** forty years old. Nearly 40% of American Muslims are between ages of eighteen and twenty-nine, while only 14.1% of all Americans are in this age bracket. In addition, only 1% of American

Muslims are age 65 or older, compared to the U.S. population with 27.2%.

A Pew Research Center poll of American Muslims released in May, 2007, disclosed that 65% of U.S. Muslims are foreign born and 56% are in the eighteen to thirty-nine age bracket.[38] While Muslims in France, Germany, Great Britain and Spain earn far less than their European counterpart, the wages of Muslims in America are almost identical to other Americans.

In 2007, the U.S. Department of Homeland Security (DHS) made available $24 million to beef up facility security for non-profit organizations "deemed high-risk for a potential international terrorist attack." Who was one of the first non-profit groups to take advantage of the grants? Muslim mosques! Almost immediately following the announcement of the availability of the grants, the Council on American-Islamic Relations (CAIR), posted the following "Action Alert" on its website: "ACTION REQUESTED: All eligible 501(c)(3) American mosques and other Islamic institutions are urged to begin the application process to receive training and to purchase equipment such as video cameras, alarm systems and other security enhancements."[39]

At the same time that the European Union is actively investigating European mosques for complicity in Islamic terrorism, the U.S. is granting mosques in the United States free taxpayer monies to improve their security. This, despite the fact, that since the terrorist attack on America, there has been no investigation of U.S. mosques for possible ties to Islamic terrorists. The initial intent of the DHS grants was to provide improved security for churches and synagogues that are often targets of Islamic terrorists who see them as centers of worshiping infidels. Although there have been no incidents of terrorism toward U.S. mosques, there have been some U.S. mosques implicated in terrorist plots. The Dar al-Hijrah Islamic Center in Washington, D.C., for example, was the source of spiritual guidance and fake identification for some of the September 11, 2001 hijackers.[40]

CAIR, on the other hand, has proven ties to terrorism and is a foreign funded spin-off of a Hamas terrorist front group. Several CAIR executives have been convicted of terrorist activities. Amazingly, however, members of the Washington-based organization sit on the U.S. Federal Bureau of Investigation (FBI) advisory board. As a result, the FBI rarely conducts a raid in a Muslim community without CAIR approval.[41]

Hate Crimes and Terroristic Threats du Jour

Since the late 1970s, the United States and European countries have become obsessed with "hate crimes" legislation. A hate crime, at least in the U.S., is defined as any crime (in an oral, physical or other manner) that is perpetrated against a person or group because of their race, religion, ethnicity or sexual orientation. The web of inclusion as to the type of incident that qualifies as a "crime" or the group to be protected seems to expand almost yearly.[42] A seemingly companion law that exploded out of the September eleventh attack is the "terroristic threats" crime enacted throughout the country. In Pennsylvania, for instance, according to the Crimes and Offenses Statute 2706, "A person commits the crime of terroristic threats if the person communicates, either directly or indirectly, a threat to: 1. commit any crime of violence with intent to terrorize another; 2. cause evacuation of a building, place of assembly, or facility of public transportation; or 3. otherwise cause serious public inconvenience, or cause terror or serious public inconvenience with reckless disregard of the risk of causing such terror or inconvenience."[43]

Apparently there is some disparity in the application of these two relatively new crime classifications. Muslims and Muslim clerics, in particular, seem to be exempt from these statutes, whether in Pennsylvania or anywhere in the U.S. Muslim clerics can spew forth hate speeches from their mosques toward those they consider to be infidels or apostates—whether individuals or groups—with impunity and without fear of retribution.

Muslim imams (preachers) can even issue *fatwas* (religious rulings) calling for the murder of an infidel or apostate without fear of arrest or prosecution in the U.S. or Europe.

On the other hand, the focus of recent hate crimes legislation would seek to make it a crime if a Christian pastor, teaching from the scriptures of the Bible, were to convey to his or her congregation the sin or evil of practicing homosexuality.

In our politically correct society where local and federal officials appear to cower in fear of Muslim retaliation, victims of Muslim vitriol and death threats appear to be devoid of civil rights. A case in point are the death threats hurled at Somali author and U.S. resident, Ayaan Hirsi Ali, who wrote the highly controversial and inflammatory (from a Muslim viewpoint) exposé, *Infidel*, on the horrors of Islam and life in Somalia.

In America, one is free to believe what they want to believe and even publicly express their opinion without fearing for their life. However, some Muslim clerics and leaders living in America do not believe in freedom of speech when it comes to things critical of Islam. But do not try to shut them up when they are denigrating America, Christians or Jews. For them, it's their right and their duty in a free country.

When Hirsi Ali was invited to talk at the University of Pittsburgh in Johnstown, Pennsylvania in April, 2007, area Islamic leaders tried to block the effort. They were unsuccessful and the lecture proceeded much to the displeasure of Imam Fouad ElBayly, the Egyptian born president of the Johnstown Islamic Center. "She has been identified as one who has defamed the faith," exclaimed ElBayly. "If you come into the faith, you must abide by the laws, and when you decide to defame it deliberately, the sentence is death."[44]

Such *fatwas* (religious proclamations) are not new to Hirsi Ali. She routinely received such death threats in the Netherlands where she served briefly as a member of the Dutch parliament. She fled to the U.S. when the Dutch decided they could no longer protect her. Now, in Pennsylvania and elsewhere in the United States, our citizens and guests are suppose to be protected from such death threats. But was Imam ElBayly charged with a "terroristic threat" against Hirsi Ali? No. However, if a non-Muslim in America made such a public death threat, they would be arrested immediately. Unfortunately, Hirsi Ali had to flee the U.S. in the fall of 2007 when the American government refused to continue her personal security when the Dutch government dropped it.[45]

ElBayly's viewpoint of those defaming Islam is not an uncommon one for Muslim clerics throughout the world, including the United States. Just because they come to America does not make them more peaceful and accepting, nor does it change their radical perspectives of their religion.

This also trickles down to the faith's adherents in America, as a Letter to the Editor of the *Lansing* [Michigan] *State Journal* should illustrate. Posted by JihadWatch.org, the letter is written by Muslim faithful, Nazra Quraishi.

Islam is not only a religion, it is a complete way of life …. The Quran and prophet Muhammad's words and practical application of Quran in life cannot be changed.

Islam is a guide for humanity, for all times, until the day of judgment. It is forbidden in Islam to convert to any other religion. The penalty is death. There is no disagreement about it.

Islam is being embraced by people of other faiths all the time. They should know they can embrace Islam, but cannot get out. This rule is not made by Muslims; it is the supreme law of God.[46]

Syrian born Wafa Sultan who left her faith of Islam decades ago and is now a U.S. citizen and a vociferous critic of the horrors of Islam would certainly take the misguided Ms. Quraishi to task. Sultan strongly insists that President Bush is sadly mistaken and uninformed for referring to Islam as a "religion of peace."

"If you are not familiar with Islamic culture, how can you claim Islam is a peaceful religion?" Sultan rhetorically asked.[47] "I believe he undermines our credibility by saying that," Sultan added. "We came from Islam, and we know what kind of religion Islam is."

Only six days after the September 11 attack, President Bush proclaimed before the Islamic Center of Washington, D.C., "The face of terror is not the true faith of Islam. That's not what Islam is all about. Islam is peace. These terrorists don't represent peace. They represent evil and war."[48] With all due respect to the President, all of Islam represents *evil and war*.

On the other side of the world, two Australian Christian pastors were convicted of "hate crimes" for quoting the Qur'an (accurately) to their congregation during a lecture on the differences between Christianity and Islam.[49] Pastors Danny Nalliah and Daniel Scot were charged and convicted under the 2002 "Victorian Religious and Racial Tolerance Act" in Australia. The Victorian Supreme Court upheld their appeal but referred it back to the lower court for yet another trial. Finally, after spending over $500,000 defending their right to free speech and religious freedom, the pastors were exonerated.[50] Similar laws, of course, have been passed in much of Europe, Canada and the United States, and you can bet the Muslims will take full advantage of them to stifle any criticism or exposure of truth about Islam.

Adding Insult to Injury

The rampant political correctness and cultural diversity in America is going to kill it just like it is killing much of Europe and eventually Canada. How much more can it be demonstrated that this political-cultural nonsense has gone astray than at the memorial service for the 32 slain Virginia Tech students and staff in Blacksburg, Virginia on April 17, 2007? Although America is decidedly Christian in heritage and practice and the vast majority of Americans claim to be Christians, the memorial service gave center stage to Allah and a Muslim cleric who invoked words of the Qur'an which were meaningless to the grieving masses in attendance.[51] Not even the avowed Christian, President George W. Bush or the Christian minister at the podium invoked the name of Jesus. How insensitive and politically *incorrect* can we be by not invoking the aid and healing of the One to whom this country owes much for its existence and prosperity? How many Muslims were among the slain at Virginia Tech? None!

If a similar attack occurred in a Muslim country—which it does on a daily basis—you could bet your entire fortune and that of the entire planet that a Christian minister would not be invited nor allowed to share the podium with a Muslim imam.

How are Christians and other *infidels* treated in Muslim countries like Iran, Iraq, Saudi Arabia, Indonesia, Sudan and in dozens of other countries under Islamic control? How about in Iraq where the U.S. and coalition forces have been since early in 2003? With all that protection and scuttle-butt about freedom and democracy, the minority religion of Christianity should be flourishing, right? Quite to the contrary. Tens of thousands of Iraqi Christians are fleeing their homeland because their churches are being bombed, homes burned, their women raped and their men and children killed by their intolerant Muslim neighbors. Some are allowed to stay if they pay the Qur'an-mandated *jizya* or protection tax—a tax which guarantees Iraqi Christians a subservient existence and second class citizenship.[52]

Reverse Assimilation

Previous waves of immigration to America from places like Germany, Italy, Spain, Norway, Nigeria, Japan, Mexico and numerous other countries resulted in America's famed "melting pot" of cultures and beliefs—an assimilation into one multi-cultural, multi-ethnic population seeking freedom and prosperity. The wave of Muslim immigration into Europe, Canada, Australia, the United States and elsewhere comes with a decided and dramatic difference. The vast majority of Muslims do not seek nor want to be assimilated into their host country. They do not and will not give up any aspect of their culture or religion. In fact, as most Western countries touting their liberalized cultural diversity are discovering, Muslims demand that the societies around them assimilate into their religious, social, cultural, political and legalistic views. Freedom of expression is to be suppressed. Scientific research and discovery is to be guided only through Islamic dictates. All morality and religious thought and expression is to be according to the Qur'an and the teachings of Muhammad.

"Everywhere one looks in Europe," wrote religious and political commentator and author, Cal Thomas, "there are signs that free people are prepared to surrender without a fight to those who would place them in bondage."[53] In England and other European countries, the historical truth about the Holocaust during World War II and the Crusades of the 11th century are being withdrawn by school districts because such history might offend the growing Muslim populations. Everywhere one looks in Europe there are signs of appeasement and concessions toward Muslims in the hopes that the radical fringe will disappear. "The sacrifice of truth," Thomas stated in his April 7, 2007 column, "in favor of propaganda for fear of violence is the first step on the road to enslavement."

"One of the consequences of Europe's growing secularization," continued Thomas, "is its jettisoning of the moral and theological concept of evil ...."

"The world is on fire, but Britain and much of the rest of Europe are not paying attention ... but its enemies are noticing. And while

Europe's enemies arm themselves for war, they regard the European attitude toward them as unilateral surrender."

Nationally syndicated talk show host, Rusty Humphries, has been following closely the Muslim rise in Britain and the Western world. After recording a Muslim rally in front of the London Central Mosque on June 22, 2007, where three thousand Muslim adherents cheered Islamic leaders preaching the downfall of Britain, Humphries bemoaned that both the United Kingdom and the United States had three vulnerabilities making them susceptible to a Muslim takeover: loss of border control, inability to say 'no' and a lack of assimilation by Muslims.[54]

Author and journalist Mark Steyn penned: "When they want to, Islamists can assimilate at impressive speed. So we have fire-breathing imams milking Euro-welfare and litigious lobby groups with high rent legal teams. Neither of these are features of Arab life. Rather, they illustrate how adept Islam is at picking and choosing what aspects of Westernization are useful to it."[55]

Islamic and non-Islamic propaganda machines aside, "it is a fantasy to imagine that the world's two largest faiths [Christianity and Islam] are in any meaningful sense the same," proclaimed Boston University Department of Religion chairman, Stephen Prothero, "or that interfaith dialogue between Christians and Muslims will magically close the divide between them."[56]

While individual Muslims may give the appearance of integrating into and adapting to Western society, the ultimate goal as expressed by Muslim clerics and leaders and quietly held to by the Muslim faithful, is not assimilation into Western culture at any level, but to unhinge the stability of it and weaken it to meet the prescribed Islamic takeover.

Although Christians are being forced to give-up every vestige of their faith in the public arena, Muslims are being allowed to force their religion down the politically correct, multi-cultural throats of American society. Muslims across the country are pressuring public schools to recognize their holidays. In Montgomery County, Maryland, for instance, schools will recognize three religious holidays: Rosh Hashanah, Christmas and Easter. Muslims, however, want the schools to recognize Eid ul-Fitr, the end of Ramadan.[57]

In some Chicago area schools, certain Christmas traditions are being threatened because they are "offensive" to Muslims. This is on the heels of the controversial elimination of Jell-O and pork from school menus because it violates Muslim dietary restrictions.[58] Why Jell-O? Because the gelatin used often comes from tissues or bones of pigs and other animals.

At airports across the U.S., Muslim taxicab drivers are demanding and getting special foot bath stations installed so they can wash their feet before their ritual five-times-a-day prayers to the benevolent Allah.[59]

In Bed With the Enemy

According to excerpts posted on April 24, 2007 for Joseph Farah's *G2 Bulletin* report, California Democratic Representative, Tom Lantos, who chairs the House Foreign Affairs Committee, wants to see "a predominantly Muslim country [Kosovo] in the very heart of Europe."[60]

Rep. Lantos' reasoning for such a creation apparently goes like this: "Just a reminder to the predominantly Muslim-led governments in this world that there is yet another example that the United States leads the way for the creation of a predominantly Muslim country in the very heart of Europe. This should be noted by both responsible leaders of Islamic governments, such as Indonesia, and also the jihadists of all color and hue. The United States' principles are universal, and, in this instance, the United States stands foursquare for the creation of an overwhelmingly Muslim country in the very heart of Europe."

Rep. Lantos and others in Washington still do not get it. Appeasement is not the way to the heart of the Muslim faithful. They could care less about the United States condoning the establishment of a Muslim country in Europe. They already have declared that *all* of Europe will be under the control of Muslims—jihadists and their ilk—by the middle of this century. They could care less about a tiny little section known as Kosovo. They are already well on their way to the Islamofication of much of the twenty-seven member European Union, including Austria, Belgium, Bulgaria, Cyprus, Czech Republic, Denmark, France, Germany, Hungary, Italy, Malta, Netherlands, Sweden, and the United Kingdom. France has all but surrendered to the Islamic invaders with one concession after another. With a birth rate significantly below what is needed to replace the proud but dying French and a fertility rate that is only one-quarter of that of the immigrating Muslims, France does not stand a chance against Muslim domination within the next generation or two.

America's entrance into the Islamic *boudoir*, unfortunately, does not stop with tiny Kosovo. According to Ze'ev Schiff, correspondent for the online Israeli news service, *Haaretz.com*, in April, 2007, newly appointed U.S. Defense Secretary Robert Gates announced during his visit to Israel that the well-groomed forward thinkers in Washington had decided to sell JDAMs (Joint Direct Attack Munition or "smart bombs") to Saudi Arabia. "Pilots and other experts say this type of bomb 'can be aimed through a window,'" reported Schiff.[61] This follows on the heels of the U.S. selling the Saudis AWACs (Airborne Warning and Control System), a system that "provides superior surveillance capabilities," according to the U.S. aircraft manufacturer, Boeing. The U.S. has also sold advanced F-16 fighter jets to Saudi Arabia and Harpoon missiles to Egypt.

It has been well documented by U.S. and Israeli intelligence that the Saudis are the main financial backers of Islamic jihadists worldwide. They are also the biggest exporters of their form of radical Islam (known as Wahhabism) to the West, including the United States. In the United States and throughout Europe they fund the building of mosques from which vehement hatred of the West is preached. They are also major backers of madrassahs (Islamic religious schools) in the United States and other Western countries—schools that teach the most radical form of Islam. The Wahhabi sect of Islam is the most extreme form of Islam in the world and calls for "warfare between Islam and all *akafir* (infidels) who do not worship Allah."[62]

America's benevolence ignores the disclosure by many Western analysts of the indisputable fact that "Saudi-born Osama bin Laden's popularity in the [Saudi] kingdom along with the Saudi citizenship of fifteen of the nineteen September eleventh hijackers. Saudi Arabia backed bin Laden's mujahedin [holy warriors] twenty years ago, which fought the Soviet Union in Afghanistan and spawned militants involved in insurgencies around the world."[63]

How extensive is the Saudi kingdom's worldwide reach? On March 27, 2002, The Middle East Media Research Institute in Washington, D.C.

published a "Special Dispatch Series" on an article that appeared in the Saudi government English weekly *Ain Al-Yaqeen* on March 1, 2002.[64] The piece details how thorough the Saudi king and royal family have spread their brand of Wahhabi Islam throughout the world.

"… The determination of the Kingdom to support Islam and Islamic institutions to the best of its ability was evident from the formation of the Kingdom by King Abdul Aziz but it was only when oil revenues began to generate real wealth that the Kingdom could fulfill its ambitions of spreading the word of Islam to every corner of the world, of assisting Muslim countries less well endowed economically and of alleviating the suffering of Muslim minorities wherever they might live." While the total financial contribution by the royal family is unknown, the article indicates that it is likely to be in the hundreds of millions or perhaps billions in U.S. dollar equivalents.

"The cost of King Fahd's efforts in this field has been astronomical, amounting to many billions of Saudi Riyals [at 3.75 to the U.S. dollar]," the article continued. Worldwide this has translated into 210 Islamic centers, more than 1500 mosques, 202 colleges and nearly 2,000 schools strictly for educating Muslim children. Included are Islamic institutions in such places as Fresno, California; New Brunswick, New Jersey; East Lansing, Michigan; Los Angeles; Toledo, Ohio; Chicago and Washington, D.C.

According to U.S. terrorism experts, an estimated 80% of the mosques in the United States are funded and controlled by the Saudis.[65] "Mosques," stated terror expert, Steve Emerson, "have tended to serve as safe havens and meeting points for Islamic terrorist groups."

Islamic research institutes funded by the royal family have crept into such prestigious American institutions of higher learning as American University in Washington, D.C., Duke University, Howard University, John Hopkins University, Georgetown University, Syracuse University and many other institutions of higher learning. To demonstrate their infinite capacity for compassion toward the U.S. after the September 11, 2001, attacks, the Saudis shortly thereafter pledged one billion U.S. dollars—not for the victims of the attacks, but—to evangelize American college campuses and prisons in order to gain more terrorist converts to their radical brand of Islam. Establishment of such institutes and mosques is much more wide spread across Europe where Islam is rapidly gaining a solid foothold. What do you think the chances might be of America establishing Christian or Jewish schools, institutions and churches or synagogues in Muslim countries? Absolutely none!

From the viewpoint of Jim Jubak, Senior Markets Editor for *MSN Money*, it is the oil wealth of the Saudis that is controlling the U.S. economy and not the Federal Reserve.[66] It is easy to see his point. Among OPEC (Organization of Petroleum Exporting Countries) members, Saudi Arabia is the only major producer with excess production capacity. According to the U.S. Energy Information Administration, for the first quarter of 2007, the U.S. had imported an average of 1.356 million barrels of crude oil per day from the Saudis.[67] At $65.00 per barrel that comes to $29 billion the U.S. could shell out to the Saudi royal family in 2007, which would fund an awful lot of their brand of Islam in the U.S. and elsewhere. However, the U.S. is not the only Saudi customer. In 2007, Saudi Arabia was pumping out 8.5 million barrels a day and has the capacity to go to 11 million if it needs to. Even at 8.5 million, that is over $200 billion (at $65/barrel) going into the Wahhabi Saudi terrorist chest. Needless to say, that is one country that does not know the meaning of deficit spending, trade deficit or national debt.

Certain Democrats in the U.S. Congress seem to be particularly disposed to appeasement and surrender to Islamic terrorists. Not only do they want to cut and run from Iraq with their tails between their legs, but apparently some want to aid and abet the enemy as well. In December, 2006, the Palestinian news website, Maannews, reported that officials of the Palestinian terrorist group, Hamas, met with high-ranking members of the Democratic Party at an undisclosed location in Europe.[68] "… the Democrats expressed an understanding with the Hamas principle of not recognizing Israel and applauded Hamas' willingness to accept a long-term cease-fire with the Jewish state in exchange for an Israeli withdrawal to what is known as the pre-1967 borders," wrote WorldNetDaily Jerusalem correspondent, Aaron Klein. Hamas, of course, along with the PLF (Palestine Liberation Front) have had a decades-long battle with Israel using a variety of terrorist tactics, the most recent of which is lobbing rockets into Jewish neighborhoods from the recently "liberated" West Bank.

Such spineless concessions and recognition of terrorists by U.S. politicians is met with extreme giddiness and glee by the terrorists. "This is why American Muslims will support the Democrats," gloated Jihad Jaara, a senior member of the Al Aqsa Martyrs Brigades, "because there is an atmosphere in America that encourages those who want to withdraw from Iraq."[69] And support the Democrats they do, by an overwhelming majority. According to a 2007 Pew Research Center, only a scant 14% of U.S. registered Muslim voters voted for President George W. Bush in the 2004 presidential election, while 71% voted for the Democratic challenger, John Kerry.[70] Not surprisingly, 70% of Muslims want more government in their lives and 59% want the government to control public and private morality.

Most Democrats and a few Republicans in the U.S. Congress believe that a withdrawal from Iraq will take away the goal of the insurgents—the defeat of the Americans. Quite to the contrary, in a war with terrorists, and particularly Muslim terrorists, a withdrawal would be seen only as a total defeat for the U.S. and the West and further embolden terrorist tactics. Muhammad Saadi, senior leader of the West Bank's Islamic Jihad, in commenting on a potential withdrawal of American forces from Iraq, said that it would "prove the resistance is the most important tool and that this tool works. The victory of the Iraqi revolution will mark an important step in the history of the region and in the attitude regarding the United States."[71]

Conclusion

Western civilization is experiencing the greatest unabashed assault against its freedom and way of life that it has ever known. At the same time, it is this love of freedom that is giving the enemies of it unlimited opportunities to denigrate the peoples of the West, and Christians and Jews in particular, in a politically correct, multi-cultural, cultural diversity mixture of devilish darkness. While the European Union countries are floundering under a demographic Muslim assault, Canada and the United States are not far behind.

Muslims mean business—not just "radical" Muslims, but all those who follow the faith of Muhammad. The West, its governing bodies, news media, educational institutions and security forces appear to be oblivious to the threat that is mounting and that will change the way

Westerners experience the world and life around them. Time is short and without wisdom and understanding a nation perishes.

Liibaan's Martyrdom:
A Transformed Life of Humility

Liibaan Ibraahim Xasan (Liban Ibrahim Hassan) was shot dead in Muqdisho (Mogadishu), apparently because of his Christian activities in the Somali capital.

While growing up, Liibaan had listened to Christian radio broadcasts both in Somali and in English. In 1982, at the age of about 13, he read Sigmund Freud's "Dreams", which disturbed him so much that he began to suffer from insomnia. Traditional solutions—visits to sheikhs, reading the Qur'an etc.—did not cure him. An expatriate Christian gave him a New Testament and suggested that he read the first letter of John. During the mid-1980s Liibaan struggled over deep theological and spiritual issues as he read the Bible in Italian and English. He also read Italian devotional books on the epistles of Paul. He prayed for God to show him the right path.

Liibaan became dissatisfied with Islam for a variety of reasons. He wondered why it was necessary always to pray to God in Arabic, a foreign language. He wondered why it was necessary to face Mecca when praying. Ethical issues also troubled him, particularly the fact that the Qur'an, he believed sanctioned polygamy and abuse of women.

Finally, in 1985, Liibaan decided that only the Bible could be true and not the Qur'an. He decided that the first thing he must do as a follower of Jesus Christ was to practice humility. (Humility is not normally considered a desirable trait in Somali culture.) Liibaan's friends began to notice a change in him the following year, and he told them about his new faith. In 1990 he sent off for a Somali New Testament. "Please be aware that if you send me [this book] you will be sending me the greatest gift that can be given to a human," he wrote.

... In December 1992 Liibaan's wife decided to join her husband in following Jesus Christ and was baptized.

The civil war in Somalia provided Liibaan with many opportunities to witness. While working in the hospital, medical staff noticed that he had a totally different attitude from the other workers. He did not differentiate between patients based on their clan. He showed sympathy and concern for people; working as a nurse's aide in the operating room was not just a job for Liibaan.

He used to have religious discussions with a sheikh who had been badly wounded. Later, he donated blood for this man, and after the sheikh had recovered Liibaan told him to listen to the Somali Christian radio broadcasts. In due course the sheikh wrote to the radio station to request Christian Scriptures and a correspondence course.

... He encouraged numbers of people to study the Scriptures and some of them embraced Christianity. The scattered Christians of Muqdisho met in his home and he pastured them.

... Such a bold Christian stance made him notorious in a country which is almost 100% Muslim. In 1993 Islamic radicals criticized his activities in newspaper articles.

On the morning of 21 March 1994, two gunmen were waiting for Liibaan on the sandy road near his office ... they ambushed him and shot him at close range ....

It is not known who killed him, but it is most likely that the motives were religious. Many Muslims believe that it is their duty to kill an apostate themselves if the state fails to uphold the sharia and that God will reward them for it.

Liibaan: A Somali Martyr
Source: Answering-Islam.org

References

1. Steyn, Mark, *America Alone: The End of the World as We know It*, 2006. Regnery Publishing, Inc., p. 19.

2. Safa, Reza F. *Inside Islam: Exposing and Reaching the World of Islam*, 1996. Charisma House, p. 21.

3. Caner, Ergun Mehmet and Emir Fethi Caner. *Unveiling Islam*, 2002. Kregel Publications, div. of Kregel. Inc., p. 70.

4. Wallechinsky, David, *The World's 10 Worst Dictators*. Parade, February 11, 2007. According to the article, the "annual list is drawn in part on reports from Human Rights Watch, Amnesty International, Reporters Without Borders and the U.S. State Department."

5. *250m Christians to Face Persecution in 2007—Rising Fastest in Islamic World*. Release International Press Release, December 31, 2006. Http://www.releaseinternational.org.

6. Ibid.

7. Ibid.

8. Ibid.

9. *Muslim Americans: Middle Class and Mostly Mainstream*. Pew Research Center, May 22, 2007, p. 51.

10. Buckley, Jr., William F. *Are We Owed an Apology?* Townhall.com, August 19, 2002. Http://www.townhall.com/columnists/wfbuckley/printwfb 20020819.shtml. Accessed August 21, 2002.

11. Steyn, p. 88.

12. *Ibn Warraq: Why I Am Not A Muslim*. The Religion Report, ABC Radio National (Australia), October 10, 2001. Http://www.abc.net.au/rn/talks/8:30/relrpt/stories/ S386913.htm. Accessed May 22, 2007.

13. Ibid.

14. Goodstein, Laurie, *U.S. Muslim Clerics Seek a Modern Middle Ground*. The New York Times, June 18, 2006.

15. *Ongoing 'Intifada' in France Has Injured 2,500 Police in 2006*. World Tribune.com, October 27, 2006. Http://www.worldtribune.com/worldtribune/WTARC/2006/eu_france_10_27.html. Accessed October 27, 2006.

16. Ibid.

17. Winik, Lyric Wallwork, *Intelligence Report: Coalition in Collapse*, Parade, February 18, 2007, p. 18.

18. Golden, Jerry, *It Doesn't Look Good, but God is in Control.* The Golden Report, January 30, 2007. Http://www.thegoldenreport.com. Accessed May 15, 2007.

19. *Ibn Warraq: Why I Am Not A Muslim.*

20. Polzer, Wolfgang, *Islam is Taking a Grip on Europe.* Journal Chretien, March 10, 2007. Http://www.spcm.org/Journal/spip. php?page=imprimir_articulo&id_article=7249. Accessed March 12, 2007.

21. *Muslim Cabbies Tell Airport They Won't Bend in Alcohol Dispute.* Associated Press, February 28, 2007.

22. *Target Shifts Muslims Who Won't Ring Up Pork to Other Tasks.* Associated Press, March 18, 2007.

23. Serres, Chris and Matt McKinney (Minneapolis Star Tribune). *Some Muslim Cashiers Refuse to Handle Pork Products.* SanLuisObispo.com., March 13, 2007. Http://www.sanluisobispo.com/mld/sanluisobispo/ news/nation/16897385.htm. Accessed March 16, 2007.

24. Polzer.

25. Rozenberg, Joshua, *Sharia Law is Spreading as Authority Wanes.* London Telegraph, November 29, 2006. Http://www.telegraph.co.uk. Accessed November 29, 2006.

26. Ibid.

27. Polzer.

28. Paul, Jonny, *40% of Young UK Muslims Want Shari'a.* Jerusalem Post Online Edition, January 30, 2007. Accessed June 4, 2007.

29. Nugent, Helen and Nadia Menuhin, *Muhammad is No 2 in Boy's Names.* Times Online, June 6, 2007. Http://timesonline.co.uk/tol/ news/article 1890354.ece? Accessed June 6, 2007.

30. *Lawmakers Snub Imam's Opening Prayer.* WorldNetDaily.com., March 4, 2003. Http://www.worldnetdaily.com/news/Article. asp?ARTICLE_ID= 31350. Accessed March 5, 2003.

31. *Pro-Khomeini Imam to Pray Before Texas Senate.* WorldNetDaily. com., April 4, 2007. Http://www.worldnetdaily.com/news/Article. asp?ARTICLE_ ID–55031. Accessed April 4, 2007.

32. *Texas Senate Prayer Excludes Christians.* WorldNetDaily.com., April 5, 2007. IIttp://www.worldnetdaily.com/news/Article.asp?ARTICLE_ ID= 55049. Accessed April 5, 2007.

33. *Imam Leads Democrats in Prayer of Conversion.* WorldNetDaily.com., February 3, 2007. Http://www.worldnetdaily.com/news/Article.asp? ARTICLE_ ID= 54085. Accessed February 3, 2007.

34. *Fact Sheet: Islam in the United States*. U.S. Department of State, International Information Programs, 2001. Http://usinfo.state.gov/usa/islam/fact2.htm. Accessed February 13, 2003.

35. *American Muslims Demographic Facts*. Allied Media Corp., 2007. Http://www.allied-media.com/AM/default.htm. Accessed June 6, 2007.

36. Schwartzman, Bryan, *U.S. Muslim Population Tops Jews, Says Scholar*. The Jewish Exponent, April 12, 2007. Http://www.jewishexponent.com/article/12673. Accessed June 6, 2007.

37. *American Muslims Demographic Facts*.

38. *Muslim Americans: Middle Class and Mostly Mainstream*, pp. 15-19.

39. *Mosques Awarded Homeland Security Grants*. WorldNetDaily.com, May 25, 2007. Http://www.worldnetdaily.com/news/article.asp?ARTICLE_ID=55859. Accessed May 25, 2007.

40. Ibid.

41. Ibid.

42. *Hate Crimes Fact Sheet*. The Civil Rights Coalition for the 21ˢᵗ Century, July 14, 2005. Http://www.civilrights.org/press_room/press-release/hate-crimes-fact-sheet.html.

43. *Pennsylvania Consolidated Statutes: Crimes and Offenses (Title 18), Chapter 27. Assault*. Http://members.aol.com/StatutesP8/18PA2706.html. Accessed May 22, 2007.

44. Acton, Robin, *Furor Over Author Ayaan Hirsi Ali's Visit Stirs Debate on Religious Freedom*. Pittsburgh Tribune-Review, April 22, 2007. Http://pittsburghlive.com/x/pittsburghtrib/news/rss/print_503977.html. Accessed May 22, 2007.

45. *Threatened Islam Critic Forced to Leave U.S.* WorldNetDaily.com, October 2, 2007. Http://www.worldnetdaily.com/news/article.asp?ARTICLE_ID=57933. Accessed October 2, 2007.

46. *Islam or Death*. Lansing State Journal (Letter to the Editor). Posted by JihadWatch.org, July 5, 2006. Http://www.jihadwatch.org/archives/2006/07/012109print.html. Accessed May 22, 2007.

47. Moore, Art. *Bush Empowering Terrorists, Charges Vocal Muslim Critic*. WorldNetDaily.com, November 18, 2006. Http://www.worldnetdaily.com/news/article.asp?ARTICLE_ID= 52962. Accessed November 18, 2006.

48. Ibid.

49. *Pastors' Convictions for Quoting Quran Overturned*. WorldNetDaily.com, December 28, 2006. Http://www.worldnetdaily.com/news/article.asp? ARTICLE_ ID= 53526. Accessed December 28, 2006.

50. *Case Over 'Vilifying' Islam Settled.* WorldNetDaily.com, July 21, 2007. Http://www.worldnetdaily.com/news/article.asp?ARTICLE_ ID= 56786. Accessed July 21, 2007.

51. *University Convocation Told of Allah, Not Jesus.* WorldNetDaily. com., April 17, 2007. Http://www.worldnetdaily.com/news/article. asp?ARTICLE_ID=55252. Accessed April 18, 2007.

52. *Iraqi Christians Forced to Pay 'Protection Tax.'* WorldNetDaily. com., April 18, 2007. Http://www.worldnetdaily.com/news/article. asp?ARTICLE_ID=55261. Accessed April 18, 2007.

53. Thomas, Cal, *Europe is Learning to Surrender All Over Again.* Syndicated column, April 7, 2007.

54. Moore, Art, *Muslims Declare Sovereignty Over U.S., UK.* WorldNetDaily. com., July 10, 2007. Http://www.worldnetdaily.com/ news/article.asp? ARTICLE_ ID= 56503. Accessed July 10, 2007.

55. Steyn, p. 84.

56. Prothero, Stephen, *True or False: The Major Religions Are Essentially Alike.* Newsweek, July 9, 2007.

57. Pierson, Drew. *Pushing for a Muslim School Holiday.* The Prince George's Sentinel, October 2, 2007. Http://www.thesentinel. com/293311113118001. php. Accessed October 2, 2007.

58. Caputo, Angela. *First Jell-O, Now Santa.* Sun Times, September 28, 2007. Http://www.suntimes.com/news/metro/578734%2CCST-NWS-oaklawn28. article. Accessed October 2, 2007.

59. Unruh, Bob. *Muslim Footbaths Spark Another Fight.* WorldNetDaily. com., October 2, 2007. Http://www.worldnetdaily.com/news/article. asp? ARTICLE_ ID= 57935. Accessed October 2, 2007.

60. *Why is U.S. Pushing European Muslim State?* Joseph Farah's G2 Bulletin.

    Http://www.worldnetdaily.com/news/article.asp?ARTICLE_ ID=55354. Accessed April 24, 2007.

61. *Arabia.* Haaretz.com, April 20, 2007. Http://www.haaretz.com/hasen/ objects/pages/PrintArticlcEn.jhtml?itemNo=850746. Accessed April 20, 2007.

62. Caner & Caner, p. 167.

63. *Royals Pump 'Billions' Into Global Islam.* WorldNetDaily.com., March 29, 2002. Http://www.worldnetdaily.com/news/article.asp?ARTICLE_ ID=26987. Accessed March 29, 2002.

64. *Saudi Government Paper: "Billions Spent by Saudi Royal Family to Spread Islam to Every Corner of the Earth.'* The Middle East Media Research Institute, *Special Dispatch Series—No. 360*, March 27, 2002.

Http://memri.org/bin/opener.cgi? Page=archives&ID=SP36002. Accessed May 23, 2007.

65. *Muslim Americans: Middle Class and Mostly Mainstream.*
66. Jubak, Jim, *U.S. Economy's Fate in Saudi Hands.* Jubak's Journal, June 5, 2007. Http://articles.moneycentral.msn.com/Investing/ JubaksJournal/DoYouTrustTheSaudis.aspx? Accessed June 5, 2007.
67. *Crude Oil and Total Petroleum Imports Top 15 Countries.* Energy Information Administration, U.S. Department of Energy, May 30, 2007.
68. Klein, Aaron, *Hamas Confirms Meeting With Group of Democrats.* WorldNetDaily.com, December 10, 2006. Http://www.worldnetdaily. com/news/Article.asp?ARTICLE_ID=53312. Accessed December 10, 2006.
69. Ibid.
70. *Muslim Americans: Middle Class and Mostly Mainstream.*
71. Klein.

CHAPTER 13

Jihad in the 21st Century and the Call for Islamic Domination

We will map 29 sensitive sites in the United States
and give the information to all international
terror organizations.... We have a strategy drawn up for the
destructionof Anglo-Saxon civilization.

Hassan Abassi
Head of the Iran's Revolutionary Guards'
Center for Doctrinaire Affairs
June 17, 2004

I t's not black (the bomber) and white (the rest of us); there's a lot of murky shades of gray in between: the [Islamic] terrorist bent on devastation and destruction prowls the streets, while around him are a significant number of people urging him on, and around them a larger group of cock-sure young male co-religionists gleefully celebrating mass murder, and around them a much larger group of "moderates" who stand silent at the acts committed in their name, and around them a mesh of religious and community leaders openly inciting treason against the state, and around them another mesh of religious and community leaders who serve as apologists for the inciters, and around them a network of professional identity-group grievance-mongers adamant that they're the real victims, and around them a vast mass of elite opinion in the media and elsewhere too squeamish about ethno-cultural matters to confront reality, and around them a political establishment desperate to pretend this is just a managerial problem that can be finessed away with a few new laws and a bit of community outreach.

It's these insulating circles of gray—the imams, lobby groups, media, bishops, politicians—that bulk up the loser death-cult and make it a potent force. And way out at the end of this chain of shades of gray is the general population …. That's how great nations die—not by war or conquest, but bit by bit, until one day you wake up and you don't need to sign a formal instrument of surrender because you did it piecemeal over the last ten years. (Mark Steyn, *America Alone: The End of the World As We Know It*).[1]

Anyone in the non-Islamic world who thinks that Islamic terrorism will melt away is either ignorant of Islam's ultimate goals, blinded by political correctness, or choosing to ignore the wealth of evidence presented before them. Islamic aggression will not go away or subside until one of two things happen: 1. Islam succeeds in converting the world or Islam is converted to Christianity; 2. Islam defeats and destroys the West or non-Islamic countries destroy and conquer Islam. According to the Qur'an, a believer in the Islamic faith cannot be a moderate Muslim; he can only be a 100 % believer in Allah and his way. There is no middle ground. If there is a middle ground on which to stand, then one cannot truly be a Muslim but is classified with the infidels or non-believers.

"Five [now seven] years after September 11," wrote Robert Spencer, "there are still no organized, comprehensive programs in American mosques and schools to teach against the jihad ideology or confront the elements of Muhammad's life that today fuel jihadist violence and subversion."[2]

Polluting the Minds

It all starts with an indoctrination of misinformation, deception and lies. The "Special Report" on Islam in America that was published by *Newsweek* on July 30, 2007 is a prime example. The feature article, *American Dreamers*, written by lead Newsweek correspondent, Lisa Miller, put a politically correct spin on the "most affluent, integrated, politically engaged Muslim community in the Western world."[3] This was followed by an article by two Muslims, titled: *The Ideals We Share*. They start their piece with this deceptive paragraph:

It's strange that the United States and the Muslim world so often seem to be in conflict. The more you know about America's basic ideals and those of classical Islam, the more similarities you see. For one thing, both the country and the religion were founded on the principle that individual freedom is a God-given, inalienable right. For another, they share a central belief in the strength that comes from embracing diversity.[4]

The next paragraph continued with: "The Muslim world grew in much the same way America would, a thousand years later. As Islam spread from its birthplace in Western Arabia, its community of followers—the *umma*—expanded into an increasingly diverse collection of cultures, peoples and nations." They make it sound like Islam is such a benevolent, peaceful way of life that every wise person should embrace and extol it.

Perhaps Rauf and Khan were smoking something *heavy* when they wrote this, or perhaps they expect Americans to be smoking something when they read it. Islam shares absolutely none of the fundamental ideals and values of most Americans. The religion was neither founded upon, nor embraces the concept of *individual freedom* and has no comprehension of *God-given, inalienable* rights (which, by the way, is uniquely Christian and biblically based). Furthermore, Islam does not embrace cultural diversity; not even close to that ideal. This is yet another example that Muslims in the United States and throughout the world strategically plan to play on the complete ignorance of the West when it comes to Islam, Islamic beliefs and the Muslim worldwide agenda. The U.S. liberal media, of course, is only too willing to play the fool.

Then there are Capitol Hill political leaders like Ohio Democratic congresswoman Marcy Kaptur who declared: "One could say that Osama bin Laden and these non-nation-state fighters with religious purpose are very similar to those kind of atypical revolutionaries that help cast off the British crown."[5] Comparing favorably in the same breath the founders of America with the butcher of Saudi Arabia is vulgar and obscene. Rep. Kaptur appears to be a product of the American school system that is devoid of pure American history. Rep. Kaptur went on to say that she felt that Americans of faith understood that these terrorists were just trying to better the lives of Muslims and "their actions are acts of sacred piety ...."

One might expect such remarks from the first Muslim elected to the U.S. Congress, Representative Keith Ellison, the Democrat from Minnesota, whose radical views were quick to surface, too. Before a group of Minnesota atheists, Rep. Ellison told them that President Bush's response to the September 11 attacks reminded him of Hitler's response to communist Russia after the burning of the Reichstag parliament building in Berlin in 1933.[6] No doubt, President Bush is on the hot seat for the war in Iraq and the War on Terror, but comparing a U.S. president to the diabolical megalomaniac Adolph Hitler is on the level of treasonous "free" speech.

"Islam, in the West," wrote Abdullah Al Araby in the online *Islam Review*, "is fighting its battle of acceptance and legitimacy. Muslim activists are working fervently trying to improve Islam's image. Their goal is to create an environment in which Islam can be easily propagated .... This tool is telling Christians that **Islam and Christianity have a lot in common.**"[7] Christians have nothing in common with Muslims, Al Araby declared.

Among the political material coming from America's own educational system is this definition of jihad from the University of Southern California: *Jihad should not be confused with Holy War; the latter does not exist in Islam nor will Islam allow its followers to be involved in a Holy War. The latter refers to the Holy War of the Crusaders.*[8] *Jihad* has ALWAYS meant a holy war against non-believers within Muslim circles. It is repetitive theology throughout the teachings of Muhammad and the clerics of Islam of the past and present.

Many universities now have Islamic departments that offer a Westernized version of Islam that feeds Islamic mush to unsuspecting young minds. At the University of North Carolina, for instance, incoming freshmen are required to read *Approaching the Qur'an: The Early Revelations.*[9] Muslim "activists" are not just after college students, they are after all students from kindergarten on up.

In England, a new government study released in the summer of 2007 proposed that the once prim and proper universities of Britain implement Islamic studies *for all students*.[10] It should be no great surprise that the good ole chap who was the author of the report was a *British* Muslim who is a senior research fellow at the Islamic Foundation in England. Could Christian ministers recommend that courses in Christianity be taught to all university students? Not a chance! Just one more nail in the Islamofication coffin for the Brits.

The American educational system, however, is nipping at the heals of the British with Islam forcing its way into the educational system across the country. It is safe to say, that if your community has a significant Muslim population, your educational system is either experiencing threats of Islamofication or it will. For a decade, perhaps longer, Muslims have been subtly assaulting the U.S. educational system with Islamic influence—from educational materials to class activities to re-writing Muslim history to make it more pleasant for Western consumption. They have found school superintendents and boards of education all too willing to cooperate.

One outraged teacher of seventh graders in the Byron Union School District in California where Islam was being crammed down the throats of students exclaimed: "We can't even mention the name of Jesus in the public schools, but ... they teach Islam as the true religion, and students are taught about Islam and how to pray to Allah."[11] The district was just following the educational standards that all schools in California must follow that were adopted by the California State Board of Education in 1998. The *standards* included a thorough indoctrination into the religion of Islam. Six months later the Thomas More Law Center filed a suit against the district on behalf of concerned parents. Among other things, in the study of Islam, students were being required to dress like Muslims, recite the Five Pillars of Faith, chant prayers to Allah, and memorize parts of the Qur'an and play a dice game on *jihad*.[12]

You might be tempted to say, *Well, that's California*. However, the Islamic assault on American education is occurring coast to coast. The incidents are too numerous to try and cover in this chapter. To illustrate the intensity of the Islamic educational attack, the American Textbook Council published its findings in a 2003 report, *Islam and the Textbooks*.[13] They found that the new wave of world history textbooks (many with sections on Islam written or edited by Muslims) had great distortions of the truth about Islam. The thirty-five page report is both revealing and troubling and should be read by every American citizen with children in school.

While young minds are being corrupted by Islamic lies, religious minds are not immune to deception either. On August 13, 2007, on Netherlands television program *Network*, Catholic bishop, Tiny Muskens, suggested that to ease the tensions between Muslims and Christians that Christians should start referring to God as Allah.[14] Why not go right to the heart of the matter and call Satan, Jehovah God, and be done with the ruse? Muskens claims that God does not mind what He is called. Apparently he has not read the Bible lately, or maybe not at all.

The Politically Correct War on Terror

Let's start with the definitions: *terror* is an emotion; it's fear. One cannot war against an emotion—unless you are trying to overcome it by telling yourself that there is "no fear, except fear itself." Now, if the West was declaring war on *terrorists* that would be a little more accurate; and if it declared war on *Islamic terrorists*, then that would be precise. However, the West and the United States in particular either has a hard time identifying the enemy, or as a result of political correctness, refuses to do so.

The U.S. Department of Homeland Security *Muster Module: Briefing Notes* of January, 2004, has this definition for a terrorist:[15]

The violent true believer is defined as an individual who is committed, or appears to be committed, to an ideology or belief system that advances the killing of oneself and as a legitimate means to further a particular goal. Terrorists who are violent true believers are our greatest concern.

Following immediately after this definition are the following *briefing Key Points*:

• Not all violent true believers are Muslim.
• The majority of Muslims are not terrorists and believe violence is against the teaching of the Qur'an.

There are certain misconceptions and fallacies in the *Briefing Notes* that make the western world—and the United States in particular—vulnerable to enemy attack:

First, when it comes to Islam, there are *only* true believers. All other believers—whether Westerners, secular Muslims or Muslims ignorant of their faith—are considered as *kafir* or infidels. According to the teachings of the Qur'an and Muhammad, those that are *kafir* are worthy of only two things: complete submission to Allah and Islam or death.

Second, **all** true believers of Islam, by edict of the Qur'an and Muhammad, *must* carry out acts of violence against infidels if Islam is to spread and conquer the world as Allah commands it to do so.

Third, while it can be loosely stated that, *not all violent true believers are Muslim*, the fact remains that an overwhelming majority of terrorists worldwide are indeed Muslims. Throughout the world, whether in Iraq and the Middle East, Pakistan, Indonesia, Malaysia, the Philippines or elsewhere, *true believers* of the teachings of Muhammad are savagely attacking and murdering all classifications of infidels from all types of ethnic and religious backgrounds. A British intelligence report, for instance, that was released in 2007, claimed that an estimated 200 million Christians in sixty countries will face persecution coordinated by al-Qaida alone.[16]

Fourth, that violence is not taught in the Qur'an is a great fabrication. Muhammad's life after moving his Islamic movement to Medina in Saudi Arabia was one of continuous violence against all who opposed him. The revelations in the Qur'an from his Medina period are very violent and command the followers of Islam to oppress and murder anyone who refuses to believe in Allah and take up the cause of Islam. Muslim clerics who repeatedly tell westerners that Islam is a religion of peace are liars. Muslims who believe their religion does not teach violence are ignorant of their faith or are deluding themselves about Islam's true tenets of belief in order to make their life in the West more palatable.

If Americans think that the Department of Homeland Security is protecting them against terrorism, they need to reassess their knowledge of the department's activities. On May 8, 2007, in order to show that we are *equal opportunity* in the *War on Terror*, Homeland Security

Secretary Michael Chertoff invited four U.S. Muslim leaders to an agency meeting to get their input on how to fight Islamic terrorism.[17] Of course the phrase *Islamic terrorism* was a no-no since that is offensive to Muslims, as is *Islamist terrorists*, or *Muslim terrorists*, or *jihadists*. So, the meeting dealt with *homegrown radicalism*.

The Western world is once again guilty of ignoring, and in many cases aiding and abetting its enemy as it did in the 1930s. As Nazi Germany was rising to prominence under its charismatic leader, Adolf Hitler, the rest of Europe and the United States turned a blind eye and a deaf ear to the cries of the oppressed. Ignoring reality, much of the world of that time chose to overlook the true designs of Nazism and its maniacal leader.

At its peak, Nazism captured the allegiance of over five million people at the start of World War II.[18] Islam, on the other hand, commands the allegiance of 1.5 billion or more adherents to the Qur'anic theology of violence. Yet, Michael Chertoff, U.S. Secretary of the Department of Homeland Security, in an August 10, 2006 staff memo, referred to Islamic terrorists as "extremists" as though they are an aberration of Islam.[19]

On December 11, 1941, Adolph Hitler declared war on the United States of America. President Franklin D. Roosevelt reciprocated with a declaration of war against Germany with these words: "Never before has there been a greater challenge to life, liberty and civilization."[20] Five days later at a cabinet meeting, German Hans Frank, a Nazi provincial leader in Poland, stated: "Gentlemen, I must ask you to rid yourselves of all feeling of pity. We must annihilate the Jews wherever we find them and wherever it is possible in order to maintain there the structure of the Reich as a whole ...."[21]

Nearly sixty years later, on September 11, 2001, once again, war was declared on America—not by a handful of radical Islamic jihadists, but by the world of Islam. While the politically correct stand in the West is that this murder of thousands of innocent civilians was the task of a band of terrorists, Muslims worldwide danced in the streets and their imams proclaimed Allah's judgment on America from thousands of Mosques in both the East and the West. Clearly, the Islamic world saw the attack as a victory for Allah, not the demented act of a few extremists.

Hans Frank's blood thirsty declaration on behalf of the Nazi Party in 1941 is eerily echoed by Muhammad in the Qur'an: "And kill them [Christians and Jews] wherever you find them, and drive them out from whence they drove you out ..." (surah 2:191).

Political correctness, when it comes to Islam and Muslims, is not confined to the United States. It reigns throughout Western Europe and Canada as well. Afraid that government officials might alienate European Muslims, a classified European Union handbook instructs officials to not use terms like "jihad," "Islamic" or "fundamentalist" when referring to Muslims.[22]

In 2006, the European Union publicly suggested that the phrase "Islamic terrorism" be mollified with the phrase "terrorists who abusively invoke Islam."[23]

Gerald Batten, a member of the British Parliament in 2007, recoiled at such political speak. "This type of newspeak," he complained, "shows that the EU refuses to face reality. The major world terrorist threat is one posed by ideology and that ideology is inspired by fundamentalist jihadi Islam."[24]

Back in Washington, the War on Terror is being stymied by Secretary Chertoff and others in the Department of Homeland Security who insist that Islam is not the enemy; that Islam is a religion of peace and that it is only a handful of extremists that are distorting true Islam. DHS field agents are told repeatedly that the majority of Muslims do not believe in violence. Customs and Border Protection agents—the ones that are suppose to keep terrorists out of the U.S.—have been told that "violence is against the teachings of the Quran."[25] Whoever wrote this has not read the Qur'an.

Invite a Death Squad to Lunch

Council on American-Islamic Relations (CAIR) founder, Omar Ahmad, at a Muslim meeting in Fremont, California in 1998, reportedly stated that Islam was not in America to be equal to any other faith, but to become dominant. The Qur'an, he asserted, should be the highest authority in America and Islam the only accepted religion on earth.[26] CAIR is strategically headquartered in Washington, D.C. and has more than a little influence on American politics and terrorist investigations. CAIR is a known offshoot of the now defunct Islamic Association for

Palestine which was founded by Hamas radical, Mousa Abu Marzook.[27] It also has ties to the Muslim Brotherhood or Brotherhood which was created in Egypt in 1928. The Brotherhood is responsible for much of the terrorist attacks worldwide and includes such infamous groups as al-Qaida.

On June 4, 2007, CAIR, along with the Islamic Society of North America (headquartered in Plainfield, Indiana, just southwest of Indianapolis) and the North America Islamic Trust were named as "unindicted co-conspirators" in a plot to fund the Hamas terrorist organization.[28] On their website, CAIR identifies themselves as "a Muslim civil liberties and advocacy group" with a "vision to promote justice and mutual understanding."[29] The three core goals of the organization are "enhancing understanding of Islam, promoting justice and empowering American Muslims."

CAIR claims to have affiliates in ninteen states with more than thirty active chapters in the United States and Canada. It boasts of having high influence in high places. "CAIR officials have met or regularly meet with U.S. presidents, members of the administration, members of congress, governors, mayors, members of state legislatures, county commissioners and others.... CAIR regularly meets with law enforcement officials at the national, state and local levels.... CAIR has conducted diversity/sensitivity training on Islam and Muslims for the FBI, U.S. Armed Forces, several local and state law enforcement agencies, and many U.S. corporations." It sounds like they have the U.S. just about covered in every arena.

The U.S. Department of Homeland Security and the FBI, of course, are cooperating with CAIR to bolster their influence and agenda. On June 21, 2006, the DHS obliged members of CAIR with a behind the scenes tour of security operations at Chicago O'Hare, the nation's busiest airport. Despite the fact that several CAIR executives have been convicted on terrorist-related charges, "U.S. Customs and Border Patrol agents were asked to describe for CAIR representatives various features of the high-risk passenger outlook system," reported WorldNetDaily.[30]

"... Brian Humphrey, Customs and Border Patrol's executive director of field operations, assured CAIR officials that agents ... undergo a mandatory course in Muslim sensitivity training," reported the online news service. "The course teaches agents that Muslims believe jihad is an 'internal struggle against sin' and not holy warfare." This politically correct definition of jihad goes against the wisdom and scholarship of well-known former Muslims who define jihad as Muslim terrorists do. Mark A. Gabriel, Ph.D. (*Islam and Terrorism*), former professor at the prestigious Muslim Al-Azhar University in Cairo, Egypt, defines jihad as a "holy war; fighting those who resist Islam." The Caner brothers, Drs. Ergun and Emir (*Unveiling Islam*), classify jihad as "holy fighting." And former devout Muslim, Reza F. Safa (*Inside Islam*), describes jihad as a "Holy War."

It is uncomfortable to know, that while the U.S. DHS was giving a known terrorist affiliate behind the scenes tour of airport security, the British, at the same time, were trying to bust up a Muslim terrorist plot to blow up U.S. airplanes in Britain.[31]

"'Isn't that nice of CBP [Customs and Border Patrol],' one agent said, 'to provide a group like CAIR with a guided, behind-the-scenes tour of our customs facilities, explaining how programs designed to catch Muslim terrorists work.'" CAIR, of course, enthusiastically declared that it was looking forward "to continuing the relationship with U.S. Customs and Border Protection offices ... in order to eliminate problems for Muslim travelers." No doubt they are.

CAIR, it might be noted, also conducts the Department of Homeland Security's "sensitivity training" for Immigration and Customs Enforcement officers and superiors.

CAIR, funded by Saudis, also conducts similar training for the U.S. military.

The Covenant

If you cannot clearly identify who your enemy is, how can you locate and fight him? Michael F. Scheuer, who was head of the CIA's bin Laden unit, has stated that, "We are losing in Iraq and Afganistan because the political leaders in both parties—and their politically correct acolytes in the media, the academy and the general officer corps—refuse to square with the American people about the enemy's motivation."[32] Scheuer believes the enemy's war against the West is driven by the Islamic faith and what it teaches. "It's strategically important," commented Middle

East scholar Daniel Pipes, "for the U.S. and its war allies to accurately identify the enemy."[33]

This may be hard to do when even the U.S. Secretary of State, Condoleezza Rice, seemed confused about the role of Islam and terrorism in the Middle East when she referred to the notorious Islamic terrorist group, Hamas, as a "resistance movement" during her press conference in London on January 18, 2007.[34] With key figures in the War on Terror like Chertoff and Rice mudding the waters with political correctness when identifying the enemies of the free world, the West has a long battle ahead of it.

It should be comforting and reassuring to the members of Hamas, that despite their avowed destruction of Israel and their venomous hatred of the U.S., that they are viewed as no more than a *resistance movement* by U.S. officials. And just what are they resisting? Peace? Freedom? Democracy? Justice?

The Hamas tenets of belief have not changed one iota since the Hamas covenant was drafted on August 18, 1988. In the Preamble to the Covenant, the intent of Hamas is made clear.

> The covenant of the Islamic Resistance Movement (Hamas) reveals its face, presents its identity, clarifies its stand, makes clear its aspiration, discusses its hopes, and calls out to help it and support it and to join its ranks, because our fight with the Jews is very extensive and very grave, and it requires all the sincere efforts. It is a step that must be followed by further steps; it is a brigade that must be reinforced by brigades upon brigades from this vast Islamic world, until the enemies are defeated and Allah's victory is revealed.[35]

Hamas, like other Islamic terrorist groups, believe that it is they that are the *true believers* and followers of Islam. It is they who adhere to every precept of Muhammad and the Qur'an. It is Islam and Islam only that permeates every aspect of daily life and reason. **Article One** of the Covenant makes that unambiguous.

> The Islamic Resistance Movement: Islam is its way. It is from Islam that it derives its ideas, concepts, and perceptions concerning the universe, life, and man, and it refers to Islam's

judgment in all its actions. It is from Islam that it seeks direction so as to guide its steps.

There are thirty-six Articles of the Covenant, but just a few will give you an idea of where members of this *resistance movement* stand and what they call **all** Muslims to embrace. **Article Two** expands upon the first:

The Islamic Resistance Movement is one of the wings of the Muslim Brotherhood in Palestine. The Muslim Brotherhood movement [founded in 1928 by Hasan Al-Banna] is a global organization and is the largest of the Islamic movements in modern times. It is distinguished by its profound understanding and its conceptual precision and by the fact that it encompasses the totality of Islamic concepts in all aspects of life, in thought and in creed, in politics and in economics, in education and in social affairs, in judicial matters and in matters of government, in preaching and in teaching, in art and in communications, in secret and in the open, and in all other areas of life.

Article Three calls upon all Muslims who are loyal to Allah to raise the banner of military jihad against the filthy, impure and evil unbelievers worldwide.

Article Six specifies that Muslims are to raise the banner of jihad over all of Palestine, including Israel.

Article Seven claims that the "movement" and its "jihad" is worldwide and must be accepted and supported by all Muslims.

Article Eight delineates the Movement's motto: Allah is its goal, the Prophet its model to be followed, the Koran its constitution, Jihad its way, and death for the sake of Allah its loftiest desire.

Article Nine states that without Islam everything is evil and out of order and must be corrected by whatever means necessary in order to establish the dominance of Islam.

Article Ten asserts that "no effort in upholding the truth and eradicating falsehood" will be spared.

In **Article Eleven** all of Palestine (including Israel) is claimed as an Islamic Waqf or Islamic religious endowment, that is, the right of Muslims because it was once conquered by Muhammad. Because Islamic law and tradition says it is theirs, it is theirs. This, despite there is no historical fact to lay credence to such a claim other than the fact they stole it from the Jews who had lived there for thousands of years.

Article Thirteen states that all "peace" initiatives or solutions for Palestine are null and void before they are even implemented because they "stand in contradiction to the principles of the Islamic Resistance Movement" and that the only solution is for its members to "wage jihad in order to raise the banner of Allah over the homeland." The last paragraph of this Article concludes with: "There is no solution to the Palestinian problem except by jihad."

Despite this clear-cut stance, U.S. diplomats and political leaders in Washington truly believe that they will be able to broker a genuine peace between Israel and the Palestinians. They believe, as some blinded Israeli leaders believe, that if Israel will just give up some land for a Palestinian state that the terrorist appetite will be sated. Nothing could be further from the truth.

Article Fifteen begins, "The day the enemies conquer some part of the Muslim land, jihad becomes a personal duty of every Muslim. In the face of the Jewish occupation of Palestine, it is necessary to raise the banner of jihad …. It is necessary to instill the spirit of jihad in the nation, engage the enemies and join the ranks of the jihad fighters."

Clearly, Hamas, as do other Islamic groups, believe that they and their Islamic beliefs are the only answer to the world's chaos and its moral, social, economic and political ills. Through their distorted mindset and the corrupted teachings of their Prophet and scriptures they intend to use violence and persecution to bring order out of chaos, holiness out of immorality, peace out of murder and political stability out of disorder and corruption.

Islam and World Destruction

As mentioned in the Introduction, one of the most frightening developments of the post-Cold War with the Soviet Union, is the rapid rise of the Muslim population in Russia. The birth rate of Russia's ethnic Slavic population has plummeted to 1.28 births per woman—way below the replacement rate of 2.1 births. "From a population peak in 1992 of 148 million," wrote author Mark Steyn, "Russia will be down below 130 million by 2015, thereafter dropping to perhaps 50 or 60 million by the end of the century."[36] At the same time Russia's Muslim population has skyrocketed to 25 million, with Muslim woman giving birth to 6-8 children on average.

By 2015, Russia's military will be dominated by Muslims.[37] Another fallout of the end of the Cold War is that Russia still has a lot of nuclear technology and nuclear arsenal, much of which is unprotected or unaccounted for. With Islam's clearly stated objective of world domination, mixing a Muslim-dominated powerful military with nuclear technology and supply will not bode well for the free world. And how does a dying country keep its hopes of survival alive? "You've got nuclear know-how," commented Steyn, "which a lot of ayatollahs and dictators are interested in."[38]

"We [the United States] are living in a dream world," wrote veteran investigative journalist, Philip V. Brennan, "caught up in a fantasy that is turning into a nightmare. No matter what the reality, we shield ourselves from it by ignoring any facts that might jolt us into living in the real world.

"We are engaged in a war," Brennan continued, "in a struggle where the enemy can be counted in the tens of millions, located in every corner of the globe. We fight the battles in this war [on terror] as if they were separate and distinct events, having no connection with the wider conflict of which they are a part. It's a case of treating the symptoms while ignoring the disease that causes them.

"… even though we don't comprehend the reality of this world war, our enemies know exactly what it's all about."[39]

Ibn Khaldun (1332-1406 A.D.), considered by Muslim scholars to be one of Islam's greatest intellectuals, saw *jihad* as Islam's obligation of aggression to bring about conversion and world domination. Quoted in a number of sources, Khaldun stated, "The other religious groups did not have a universal mission, and the holy war was not a religious duty for them, save only for the purposes of defense . . . in the Muslim community, the holy war [jihad] is a religious duty, because of the universalism of the Muslim mission and (the obligation to) convert everybody to Islam either by persuasion or by force .... Islam is under obligation to gain power over other nations."[40, 41, 42]

"Those are not words of openness, tolerance, and democracy," commented author and Islam and jihad expert, Robert Spencer. "And they are still widely held in the Muslim world."[43]

"Most think [jihad] is a form of religious war," stated N. S. Rajaram, "something like the Crusades. This comparison is altogether inadequate, for the war is only the beginning. Jihad should be seen as a complete political and economic system that often includes selective genocide and slavery."[44]

Outspoken Wafa Sultan, a Syrian immigrant in the United States, who turned away from Islam twenty-seven years ago at age twenty, said on Al Jazeera Arab television in February, 2006, that, "I don't believe you can reform Islam," because its scriptures are immersed in violence and human rights violations.[45]

Our Way or the Death Way

The Muslim cleric, Sheikh Omar Bakri Muhammad, living in London at the time, gave this searing comment in the April 18, 2004 edition of Lisbon, Portugal's *Publica* magazine: "We don't make a distinction between civilians and non-civilians, innocents and non-innocents. Only between Muslims and unbelievers. And the life of an unbeliever has no value. It has no sanctity."[46]

In the award winning documentary, *Obsession: Radical Islam's War Against the West*, it was stated that an estimated 10-15% of Muslims worldwide support the jihadist agenda of murder and annihilation of Jews and Christians and non-Muslims in general (47). This percentage agrees with the 2007 Pew Research Center survey of Muslims in the United States where 13% said that they support the acts of suicide bombers.[48] If one takes the most commonly quoted figure of 1.5 billion Muslims in the world and an estimated six million in America, that makes 150-225 million Muslims in the world and 780,000 in the U.S. that favor the religious war of jihad as a means to Islam's world domination. A much wider circle of Muslims, it was pointed out in the film, hate the West, America and Israel, in particular, and yearn for their destruction. These estimates, it should be pointed out, do not exclude women and children who are also schooled in the terror of jihad—children as young as three years old are taught to kill and be suicide bombers in many Islamic circles.

In case one needs to be reminded, it only takes one, just one nut case with a dirty nuclear bomb and a pension for Allah's glory in the midst of a major city to wreak havoc and kill millions of citizens. How many are planning just that, one will never know until the first one is detonated.

For over fourteen hundred years Islam has always demonstrated that it is an ideology of violence and oppression—an ideology, not just of a few fanatics, but of the entire body of believers. Why, on earth, in the 21st century, would anyone in the West believe that the core teachings of Islam and the beliefs of its faithful adherents have changed for modern day consumption?

"Islam," asserted former devout Muslim, Reza F. Safa, "is beginning to retrieve its former status as a world power, a power which appropriates new territories by force, fear, war and bloodshed."[49]

In 1979, only six months after his return to Iran after fifteen years in exile, Iran's revered holy leader, Ayatollah Khomeini, was widely quoted as saying: "The governments of the world should know that Islam cannot be defeated. Islam will be victorious in all the countries of the world, and Islam and the teachings of the Koran will prevail all over the world."[50, 51]

"To take Khomeini's declaration lightly," stated Safa, "is to be ignorant of the history of Islam and its accomplishments. We must realize that Islam has been, and today is, a potent political and economic force in the world."[52]

Over a century ago, the noted missionary bishop of Methodism, Dr. Charles B. Galloway, made the following comments about Islam in a speech at Emory College in Georgia.

Mohammedanism has produced an enslaved personality. "It's Koran demands intellectual slavery; its harem requires domestic slavery; its state implies and enforces both religious and a civil slavery." The Koran puts a premium upon war, offering the highest rewards to those who slay the greatest number of infidels. Mohammed's cardinal principle, that the end justifies the means, consecrated every form of deception and lying, and encouraged every sort of persecution and violence … The citizen is the slave of the state; he has no rights to be respected. Mohammedanism is an absolute despotism, the most gigantic engine of intolerance and persecution the world ever saw ... In every land swept by this heartless despotism it has left a tale and trail of blood.[53]

The Terror of Jihad

A popular book—at least in Islamic circles—published in Pakistan in 1979, *The Qur'anic Concept of War*, by Pakistani Brigadier General S. K. Malik, has raised some eyebrows in the West with this quote: "Terror struck into the hearts of the enemies is not only a means, it is the end in itself. Once a condition of terror into the opponent's heart is obtained, hardly anything is left to be achieved. It is the point where the means and the end meet and merge. Terror is not a means of imposing decision upon the enemy; it is the decision we wish to impose upon him."[54]

The politically correct in the West, parroting Islamic clerics, proclaim the Muslim terrorists are from the radical fringe and not true Muslims. In a September, 2006 article on suicide bombers, it was stated, "In public, the U.S. government has made an effort to avoid linking the terrorist threat to Islam and the Quran while dismissing suicide terrorists as crazed heretics who pervert Islamic teachings."[55] Western governments, despite overwhelming evidence to the contrary, are reticent to link Islamic terrorism with Islam and its teachings.

"But internal Pentagon briefings," cited the same article, "show intelligence analysts have reached a wholly different conclusion after studying Islamic scripture and the backgrounds of suicide terrorists. They've found that most Muslim suicide bombers are in fact students of the Quran who are motivated by its violent commands—making them, as strange as it sounds to the West, 'rational actors' on the Islamic stage .... 'Suicide in defense of Islam is permitted, and the Islamic suicide bomber is, in the main, a rational actor,' concludes a recent Pentagon briefing paper titled, *Motivations of Muslim Suicide Bombers.*"[56]

Mark Gabriel, former radical Muslim and professor of Islamic history at the prestigious Al-Azhar University in Cairo, Egypt, was searching for truth. "I went to every interpretation of the Quran trying to avoid jihad and killing non-Muslims, yet I kept finding support of the practice. The [Muslim] scholars agreed that Muslims should enforce jihad on infidels ...."[57]

The Caner brothers would concur. "… Islam does in fact have an essential and indispensable tenet of militaristic conquest …. Military warfare is an absolute necessity if Allah is to be honored and worshipped."[58] There is an absolute necessity for the Muslim to participate in jihad. "The alliance of Muhammad, Allah, war and victory eternally intermingles the idea of struggle with the shedding of blood," noted the Caners. "The parallel between military victory and the will of Allah is key in understanding that Islam at its core desires both physical and meta-physical victory, and the use of force is not only acceptable, but it is commendable."[59]

Hadith 1:35 stresses the importance of jihad and subsequent martyrdom. "The Prophet said, 'The person who participates in (Holy battles) in Allah's cause and nothing compels him to do so except belief in Allah and His Apostles, will be recompensed by Allah either with a reward, or booty (if he survives) or will be admitted to Paradise (if he is killed in the battle as a martyr). Had I not found it difficult for my followers, then I would not remain behind any sariya going for Jihad and I would have loved to be martyred in Allah's cause and then made alive, and then martyred and then made alive, and then again martyred in His cause.'"

"The Hadith makes it transparent that jihad has as its primary characteristic a bloody struggle involving military battles."[60] Jihad is not an inner spiritual struggle of the individual in an effort to achieve holiness like Muslim leaders and the political pundits would like the Western World to believe. It is an ongoing military conflict in an all-out effort to destroy the perceived and Muhammad "revealed" enemies of Allah—the infidel, the non-believing world and more concretely, the Jew and Christian.

"The promise of eternal security is the ultimate motive behind the passion for Allah in the eager young Muslim warrior. He follows the footsteps of the messenger Muhammad, who fought for the cause of Allah. He is obeying the noble words of the Qur'an and Hadith, which legitimize his use of the sword. And if he is killed in battle, he achieves the desire of his heart—Allah's guarantee of a spot at the highest level of Paradise."[61]

Participating and being killed (martyred) during jihad is the only assurance the Muslim has of receiving Allah's forgiveness and securing a place in heaven for eternity.

"And if you are slain in the way of Allah [during jihad] or you die, certainly forgiveness from Allah and mercy is better than what they [the unbelievers] amass. And if indeed you die or you are slain, certainly to Allah shall you be gathered together" (surah 3:157-158).

Jihad: Coming to a Place Near You

"It's only a matter of time," wrote Baltimore Sun correspondent, James E. Goodby.[62] "That's what the experts say when asked whether a terrorist organization might detonate an atom bomb in an American city." Scare tactics? Unfortunately, not likely. Perhaps, beyond scary when you consider that it does not even have to be someone from a recognized terrorist organization. It could be any Muslim who adheres to the tenets of faith of Muhammad; a Muslim sympathizer or your neighbor next door.

In the publisher's review of Graham Allison's sobering book, *Nuclear Terrorism*, it is stated that, "if policy makers in Washington keep doing what they are currently doing about the [nuclear] threat, a nuclear terrorist attack on America is likely to occur in the next decade. And if one lengthens the time frame, a nuclear strike is inevitable.

"... The choice is ours: to grab this beast by the horns or to be impaled on those horns. We do not have the luxury of hoping the problem will go away ...."[63]

In the latter part of September, 2007, residents of southern part of Macomb County, Michigan (which includes the northern suburbs of Detroit) found their car windshields with fliers advocating violence against Jews and Christians. "Kill Jews and Christians if they don't believe in Allah and Mohammad," the fliers promoted. "Fight those who do not believe."[64]

"I really don't know what it means other than suggesting violence to Jews and Christians," commented Detective Sgt. Paul Jesperson of the Sterling Heights police department. It should be noted that only Paris has a larger Arab population outside the Middle East than Michigan with over 300,000.[65] As pointed out in the previous chapter, Muslims are now the fastest growing religion in the United States, replacing the Jews as the second largest religious body in the country.[66]

According to the 2007 Pew Research Center study, 19% of Muslims living in the United States are not concerned about "the rise of Islamic extremism around the world."[67] It got worse when U.S. Muslims were asked about "the rise of Islamic extremism in the United States." A whopping 34% said they were not too concerned or concerned at all. The study provided an even scarier statistic. Among U.S. Muslims age eighteen through twenty-nine, an incredible 26% said that suicide bombing can always be justified. Another 15% in that age bracket said that it could be often or sometimes justified.[68]

Indeed, Islamic terrorist cells and compounds are growing by leaps and bounds within the U.S. A now dated *Islamic Terrorist Network* map of 2002-03 pinpoints dozens of such camps in Massachusetts, New York, Maryland, Washington, D.C., Virginia, North Carolina, Florida, Ohio, Michigan, Indiana, Illinois, Missouri, Oklahoma, Texas, Colorado, Arizona, California, Oregon and Washington.[69]

One such camp, Islamberg, in the Catskill Mountains of New York is inhabited by a paramilitary group tied to radical Islamic cleric Sheikh Mubarak Ali and boasts 5,000 members in more than two dozen compounds or *hamaats* or *jamaats* across the U.S. The sheikh's stated objective "is to 'purify' Islam through violence."[70] Other Mubarak Ali hamaats have been located in Maryland, Virginia, Pennsylvania, South Carolina, Georgia, Tennessee, Colorado, Oklahoma, California and Washington.[71]

The hamaat at Islamberg is mostly populated by African-American males from the Northeast. "The group seeks to counter 'excessive Western influence on Islam' through any means necessary, publicly embracing the ideology that violence is a significant part of its quest to purify Islam. The enemies of Islam, the group says, are all non-Muslims and any Muslim who does not follow the tenets of fundamentalist Islam as detailed in the Quran.[72] It's bad enough when your foreign enemy sets up camp in your backyard, but even more unsettling when born and bred Americans join their numbers.

Shortly after the September 11 attack, American Daniel Pipes, the Director of the Middle East Forum and a worldwide authoritative journalist on the Middle East, penned: "The Muslim population in this country is not like any other group, for it includes within it a substantial body of people—many times more numerous than the agents of Osama bin Ladin—who share with the suicide hijackers a hatred of the United States and the desire, ultimately, to transform it into a nation living under the strictures of militant Islam. Although not responsible for the atrocities in September, they harbor designs for this country that warrant urgent and serious attention."[73]

In July, 2007, the National Intelligence Council, an amalgam of all U.S. intelligence agencies, published its *National Intelligence Estimate: The Terrorist Threat to the US Homeland*. According to the Council, the "National Intelligence Estimates (NIEs) are the Intelligence Community's (IC) most authoritative written judgments on national security issues ...."[74]

Among their findings and concerns in the brief report:

• We are concerned ... that ... international cooperation may wane as September 11 becomes a more distant memory and perceptions of the threat diverge.

• Al-Quaida is and will remain the most serious terrorist threat to the Homeland.

• ... we judge that the United States currently is in a heightened threat environment.

•... al-Quaida will continue to try to acquire and employ chemical, biological, radiological, or nuclear material in attacks and would not hesitate to use them if it develops what it deems is sufficient capability.

• We assess that the spread of radical ... Internet sites, increasingly aggressive anti-US rhetoric and actions, and the growing number of radical, self-generating cells in Western countries indicate that the radical and violent segment of the West's Muslim population is expanding, including in the United States.

While Muslim terrorists are setting up camp in Mexico and throughout much of Latin America,[75] FBI analysts have stated that "al-Qaida is aggressively recruiting black Americans for suicide operations against the homeland ...."[76]

In the meantime, the oil-pumping Saudis are stepping up their hate-filled speech and publications within their U.S. mosques, according to the Center for Religious Freedom in Washington, D.C. In the year-long investigation by the human rights group released in January, 2005, the Center found numerous incidents and publications in Saudi-funded mosques on American soil that promoted the aggressive hatred of Jews and Christians and instructed Muslims that they were in an enemy land of non-believers.[77] Hatred is "being mainstreamed within our borders through the efforts of a foreign government, namely Saudi Arabia, [and] demands our urgent attention," the report warned.

Jesus' Return and the Mahdi (12th Imam)

"True" Muslims believe that the End Times will be sparked by a military clash of Armageddon proportions between Muslims and Zionists Jews, Trinitarian Christians and the Far Eastern Orientals. They believe this is foretold in the Qur'an (surah 21:95-98).

> Hence, it has been unfailingly true of any community whom We have ever destroyed that they [were people who] would never turn back [from their sinful ways] until such a time as Gog and Magog are let loose [upon the world] and swarm down from every corner [of the earth], the while the true promise [of resurrection] draws close [to its fulfillment]. But then, lo! The eyes of those who [in their lifetime] were bent on denying the truth will stare in horror, [and they will exclaim:] "Oh, woe unto us! We were indeed heedless of this [promise of resurrection]!—nay, we were [bent on] doing evil!" [Then they will be told:] "Verily, you and all that you [were wont to] worship instead of God [Allah] are but fuel of hell: that is what you are destined for.[78]

In this passage, Muslims believe that Gog and Magog are the Zionist Jews, Trinitarian Christians or polytheists, the idol worshippers and anyone else left that is not a Muslim.[79] The Muslim Web site, Answering-Christianity, claims that Allah has ordained that Muslims will fight all these people in the End Times. However, in the Old Testament of the Bible, Gog is identified as "the chief prince of Meshech and Tubal" (Ezekiel 38:2; likely areas in central Asia) and Magog represents the barbarous nations to the north of Israel (Ezekiel 39). Gog will lead a "great horde" against Israel (Ezekiel 38:4). His army will also include those from Persia, Cush and Put or Phut (verse 5). Today, those areas would include North Africa, much of the Middle East and much of Asia Minor—all dominated by Muslims. In the New Testament, in chapter 20 of the book of Revelation, Gog and Magog are symbolic of the Antichrist—those nations and peoples who have rejected Jesus Christ.

> *When the thousand years are over, Satan will be released from his prison and will go out to deceive the nations in the four corners of the earth—Gog and Magog—to gather them for battle. In number they are like the sand on the seashore. They marched across the breadth of the earth and surrounded the camp of God's people, the city he loves. But fire came down from heaven and devoured them. And the devil, who deceived them, was thrown into the lake of burning sulfur, where the beast and the false prophet had been thrown. They will be tormented day and night for ever and ever.* (Revelation 20:7-10)

Although Muslims believe that the battle of Armageddon will be fought between them and essentially the rest of the world, Allah has given them no assurance that they will win it. Interestingly, they believe that Jesus, not the promised Mahdi, will return to defeat the Antichrist and all evil on the earth.[80] In referring to the Last Days, Muhammad told his followers that when Jesus returned he would "break the cross" or do away with the Christians and "kill the pigs" or annihilate the Jews. "Narrated Abu Huraira: Allah's apostle said, 'The Hour will not be established until the son of Mary (i.e. Jesus) descends amongst you as a just ruler, he will break the cross, kill the pigs, and abolish the Jizya tax. Money will be in abundance so that nobody will accept it (as charitable gifts)." (Bukhari hadith 3:43:656) The Dawud hadith 37:4310 records a similar statement by Muhammad. Furthermore, Muhammad claimed that when Jesus returns He will judge people, not by the truth of the Gospel and personal salvation through Christ, but by the law of the Qur'an. "Allah's Apostle said 'How will you be when the son of Mary (i.e. Jesus) descends amongst you and he will judge people by the Law of the Quran and not by the law of the Gospel.'" (hadith 4:658) In both biblical accounts of Gog and Magog, however, God stands against them and destroys them.

The president of Iran, Mahmoud Ahmadinejad, has an apocalyptic mind-set. He has made no secret of his belief that he has a role to play in the End Times and has a maniacal desire to bring about Armageddon and ushering in the return of the Mahdi. He believes he has been called to bring about the cataclysmic destruction of the world, which according Shiite Muslim lore, will result in the return of the 12th Imam or Muslim Messiah or Mahdi. In his invective speech before the United Nations in September, 2006, Ahmadinejad's most important words were lost on the non-Muslim world as he invoked the return of the Mahdi.

"I emphatically declare that today's world, more than ever before, longs for just and righteous people with love for all humanity; and above all longs for the perfect righteous human being and the real savior who has been promised to all peoples and who will establish justice, peace and brotherhood on the planet. Oh, Almighty God, all men and women are your creatures and you have ordained their guidance and salvation. Bestow upon humanity that thirsts for justice, the perfect human being promised to all by you, and make us among his followers and among those who strive for his return and his cause."[81]

Now, what does Ahmadinejad and Islam have to do with righteousness, love, peace, justice and brotherhood? Muslims do not believe that *all* humanity is the same or that all peoples should be treated with equality and justice. The purpose of the Mahdi is not to bring salvation to the lost but, rather, to usher in an age of world destruction so that only Muslims will inherit the earth. "Ahmadinejad," according to WorldNetDaily, "is on record as stating he believes he is to have a personal role in ushering in the age of the Mahdi. In a Nov. 16, 2005, speech in Tehran, he said he sees his main mission in life as to 'pave the path for the glorious reappearance of Imam Mahdi, may Allah hasten his appearance.'"[82] The Iranian mad-Mahmoud is bent on world destruction, and if no one stops him soon, he will have the nuclear capability to do just that. There is one obstacle that he sees in his way: America.

However, the leadership in America is questionable as to whether it is up to the task. On October 4, 2007 in a White House interview with Al Arabiya, a Mideast Muslim news agency, President George W. Bush emphatically stated to the Muslim correspondent, Elie Nakouzi, that "I believe in an Almighty God, and I believe that all the world, whether they be Muslim, Christian, or any other religion, prays to the same God. That's what I believe. I believe that Islam is a great religion that preaches peace …"[83] The 2008 presidential race in America is no more reassuring. In October, 2007, the clear Democratic front runner, Senator Hillary Clinton, received a resounding endorsement from Middle East Muslim terrorists. "The Iraqi resistance is succeeding," gushed one terrorist leader, "Hillary and the Democrats call for withdrawal. Her popularity shows that the resistance is winning and that occupation is losing. We just hope that she will go until the end and change the American policy, which is based on oppressing poor and innocent people."[84]

America, you have your work cut out for you and it looks like a long, hard road ahead. God save America!

Conclusion

Islam has always been a religion of aggression and oppression. With demographics in its favor and modern technology enhancing the propensity of its sincerest advocates to wage war it has become a militaristic front to contend with of mammoth proportions. If the Jews and Christians were indeed an oppressive, warring people as Islamic adherents claim, then the warriors of Islam would not stand a chance. But the reality is, that Jews and Christians and the peoples of the free world do, indeed, prefer to live at peace with their fellow human beings. Qur'an-thumping, Muhammad-believing Muslims do not. They can not even live among each other without killing themselves. Muhammad and the Qur'an make it abundantly clear to every Muslim: Islam must be spread by violence and everyone must be a Muslim or die. They will try to corrupt the minds of any free people they cannot kill by infiltrating every aspect of their lives. The irony is that the free world societies abide by constitutions that are all too friendly and permissive and meet the objectives and provide the means to the end for those that truly adhere to the tenets of Islam. Political correctness and cultural diversity pushes in the West are the Muslim's dream come true to further foment their brand of religious, political, social and cultural revolution.

Because of Jesus

My name is Petrus Kristian [of Indonesia]. I am the oldest son of Pastor Ishak Kristian, who was burned to death a few months ago. It happened on October 10, 1996. At 11:30 A.M., about twenty people came and surrounded the church. My father, the pastor, tried calming those angry people, but they did not move away from the church. My father went into the house and prayed with six other people, including the rest of my family.

Thirty minutes later, about 200 people came on foot bringing many kinds of tools. They started smashing the church building and parsonage. Six of the people in the house, including my father, ran and hid in a room at the back of the house. The other person hid upstairs where he was safe. Some of those angry people saw them and told them to get out of the room. Since they did not leave, the people started burning the building.

One of those seven people, Didit (a church worker) ran through the fire and escaped. My father, mother, sister, cousin, and a church worker were trapped in the house and burned to death.

During the fire, the local police did not take any action, probably because they were afraid of the mob ....

The night before the funeral, a local government official apologized. He advised me not to take revenge. He also said that the incident might be my family's fate. (This is Muslim teaching—the will of Allah)

At first, I was really disappointed because I lost all of my beloved people. But this made me realize that material things around me are not eternal or worth loving. After the fire, most of our congregation became stronger in faith.

Because we have Jesus, it is not difficult to be a Christian, although there are many oppressions.

Petrus Kristian
"It Is Not Difficult to Be a Christian"
Jesus Freaks
dc Talk and The Voice of the Martyrs
p. 199

References

1. Steyn, Mark, *America Alone: The End of the World As We Know It*. Regnery Publishing, Inc., 2006, pp. 196-197.

2. Spencer, Robert. *The Truth About Muhammad, Founder of the World's Most Intolerant Religion*, 2006. Regnery Publishing, Inc., p. 193.

3. Miller, Lisa, *American Dreamers*, Newsweek, July 30, 2007, p. 25.

4. Rauf, Imam Feisal Abdul and Daisy Khan, *The Ideals We Share*. Newsweek, July 30, 2007, p. 32-33.

5. *Congresswoman Compares Osama to U.S. Founders*. WorldNetDaily. com, March 6, 2003. Http://www.worldnetdaily.com/news/article. asp?ARTICLE_ ID=31381. Accessed March 6, 2003.

6. *Muslim Congressman Compares Bush to Hitler*. WorldNetDaily. com, July 13, 2007. Http://www.worldnetdaily.com/news/article. asp?ARTICLE_ID=56656. Accessed July 13, 2007.

7. Al Araby, Abdullah, *Nothing in Common*. Islam Review. Http://www. islamreview.com/articles/nothingincommon.htm. Accessed November 11, 2006.

8. *Jihad*. USC-MSA Compendium of Muslim Texts: Islamic Glossary. Http://www.usc.edu/dept/MSA/reference/glossary/term.JIHAD.html. Accessed August 18, 2007.

9. *Conservative Students vs. Liberal Professors*. Associated Press, December 26, 2004.

10. *Islamic Education for All*. WorldNetDaily.com, August 2, 2007. Http:// www.worldnetdaily.com/news/article.asp?ARTICLE_ID=56973. Accessed August 2, 2007.

11. Lynne, Diana, *Islam Studies Spark Hate Mail, Lawsuits*. WorldNetDaily.com, January 16, 2002. Http://www.worldnetdaily. com/news/article.asp? ARTICLE _ID=26074. Accessed January 17, 2002.

12. Lynne, Diana, *District Sued Over Islam Studies*. WorldNetDaily. com, July 2, 2002. Http://www.worldnetdaily.com/news/article. asp?ARTICLE_ID= 28146. Accessed July 2, 2002.

13. Sewell, Gilbert T., *Islam and the Textbooks*. American Textbook Council, 2003. Http://www.historytextbooks.org/islam.

14. *Bishop Urges Christians to Call God 'Allah.'* WorldNetDaily.com, August 16, 2007. Http://www.worldnetdaily.com/news/article. asp?ARTICLE_ID= 57178. Accessed August 16, 2007.

15. *Muster Module: Briefing Notes. Interviewing Violent True Believers*, January, 2004, Department of Homeland Security. Http://wnd.com/images2/DHS_ briefing.jpg. Accessed February 10, 2007.

16. *Al-Qaida Cited in Persecution of 200 Million Christians.* WorldNetDaily. com, June 2, 2007. Http://www.worldnetdaily.com/news/article.asp? ARTICLE_ID=55968. Accessed June 2, 2007.

17. Kuruvila, Matthai Chakko, *Security Agency Enlisting Muslims to Rebut Radicals.* San Franciso Chronicle, June 5, 2007. Http://www.sfgate.com/cgi-bin/article.cgi?File=/c/a/2007/06/05/MNGPOQ7IRT1.DTL. Accessed June 6, 2007.

18. *Lesser Known Facts of WWII Pre-War to 1939, 1940.* Http://members.iinet. net.au/~gduncan/facts.html. Accessed May 14, 2007.

19. *DHS Employee Communications: Message from Secretary Chertoff to All DHS Employees*, August 10, 2006. Http://wnd.com/images2/Chertoffmemo. jpg. Accessed February 10, 2007.

20. *The History Place—Holocaust Timeline.* Http://www.historyplace.com/worldwar2/holocaust/timeline.html. Accessed May 14, 2007.

21. Ibid.

22. *EU Guidebook: Don't Link Islam With Terror.* WorldNetDaily.com, March 31, 2007. Http://www.worldnetdaily.com/news/article.asp?ARTICLE_ID= 54954. Accessed March 31, 2007.

23. Ibid.

24. Ibid.

25. *Chertoff's 'Islam PC' Rankles Fed Officials.* WorldNetDaily.com, February 10, 2007. Http://www.worldnetdaily.com/news/article.asp?ARTICLE_ID= 54164. Accessed February 10, 2007.

26. Gardiner, Lisa, *American Muslim Leader Urges Faithful to Spread Islam's Message.* San Ramon Valley Herald, July 4, 1998.

27. *Feds Name CAIR in Plot to Fund Hamas.* WorldNetDaily.com, June 4, 2007. Http://www.worldnetdaily.com/news/article.asp?ARTICLE_ID=56009. Accessed June 5, 2007.

28. Ibid.

29. *25 Facts About CAIR: Did You Know?* Council on American-Islamic Relations. Http://www.cair.com/factsaboutcair.asp. Accessed June 6, 2007.

30. *Controversial Muslim Group Gets VIP Airport Security Tour.* WorldNetDaily.com, August 18, 2006. Http://www.worldnetdaily.com/news/article.asp?ARTICLE_ID=51573. Accessed August 18, 2006.

31. Ibid.

32. *Chertoff's 'Islam PC' Rankles Fed Officials.*

33. Ibid.

34. *Roundtable With Traveling Press: Secretary Condoleezza Rice*, January 18, 2007, London, England. U.S. Department of State. Http://www. state.gov/secretary/rm/2007/79038.htm. Accessed May 15, 2007.

35. *The Covenant of the Islamic Resistance Movement—Hamas.* The Middle East Media Research Institute, Special Dispatch Series—No. 1092, February 14, 2006.

36. Steyn, p. 27.

37. Mainville, Michael, *Muslim Birthrate Worries Russia.* The Washington Times, November 21, 2006. Http://www.washingtontimes.com/ world/20061120-115904-913r.htm. Accessed June 1, 2007.

38. Steyn, p. 29.

39. Brennan, Philip V., *All Middle Eastern Battles Part of Global War of Jihad.* NewsMax.com, August 9, 2006. Http://www.newsmax.com/ archives/2006/8/8/191356.shtml. Accessed March 12, 2007.

40. Trifkovic, Srdja, *Faith, Logos, and Antichrist: A Post Scriptum on Regensburg.* Chronicles Magazine, December 26, 2006. Http://www. chroniclesmagazine.org. Accessed January 4, 2007.

41. Rajaram, N. S., *A Challenge to Islamic Correctness* (a book review of *The Legacy of Jihad: Islamic Holy War and the Fate of Non-Muslims* by Andrew Bostom), American Thinker, September 9, 2005. Http://www. americanthinker.com. Accessed June 4, 2007.

42. Spencer, Robert, *Islam and Democracy: Saad Eddin Ibrahim and Ibn Khaldun*, Jihad Watch, November 26, 2003. Http://www.jihadwatch. org. Accessed June 4, 2007.

43. Ibid.

44. Rajaram

45. Watanabe, Teresa, *Islam Fatally Flawed, Says Voice From Corona via Al Jazeera.* Los Angeles Times, March 13, 2006. Http://latimes.com/news/ local/la-me-sultan13mar13,0,1829473. Accessed March 13, 2006.

46. *Muslim Cleric Says Attack on London "Inevitable."* JihadWatch.org. Http://www.jihadwatch.org/archives/2004/04/001611.html. Accessed July 14, 2007.

47. *Obsession: Radical Islam's War Against the West* (Documentary). Trinity Home Entertainment, 2007.

48. *Muslim Americans: Middle Class and Mostly Mainstream.* Pew Research Center, May 22, 2007, p. 54.

49. Safa, Reza F. *Inside Islam: Exposing and Reaching the World of Islam*, 1996. Charisma House, p. 12.

50. Brennan.

51. Safa, pp. 14-15.

52. Safa, p. 15.

53. Galloway, Bishop Charles B. *Christianity and the American Commonwealth*, 1898, pp. 26-27. Reprinted in 2005 by American Vision, Inc., Powder Springs, Georgia.

54. Sahni, Ajai, *War and the 'Deluge' of Terror*. Asia Times, March 26, 2003. Http://www.atimes.com/atimes/Middle_East/EC26AK03.html. Accessed June 4, 2007.

55. *Suicide Bombers Follow Quran, Concludes Pentagon Briefing*. WorldNet Daily.com, September 27, 2006. Http://www.worldnetdaily. com/news/article.asp?ARTICLE_ID=52184. Accessed September 28, 2006.

56. Ibid.

57. Gabriel, Mark A. *Islam and Terrorism*, 2002. Published by FrontLine, a Strang Company, p. 5.

58. Caner, Ergun Mehmet and Emir Fethi Caner. *Unveiling Islam*, 2002. Kregel Publications, div. of Kregel. Inc.. pp. 184-185.

59. Ibid, p. 190.

60. Ibid, p. 36.

61. Ibid, p. 36.

62. Goodby, James E., *U.S. Must Take Offensive Against Nuclear Terrorism*. Baltimore Sun, February 4, 2007. Http://www. baltimoresun.com/news/opinion/oped/ bal-op.nuketerror04feb,1,10995 87. Accessed May 15, 2007.

63. Allison, Graham, *Nuclear Terrorism: The Ultimate Preventable Catastrophe*, 2004. Henry Holt and Company. Publisher's review. Accessed May 15, 2007.

64. Wilczynski, Gordon. *Anti-Jewish, anti-Christian Fliers Found on Cars*. The Macomb Daily, September 28, 2007. Http:www.macombdaily. com/stories/092807/loc_fliers001.shtml. Accessed October 1, 2007.

65. *Mich*[igan] *Has Largest U.S. Muslim Population*. Psychiatry News 40(2):13.Http://pn.psychiatryonline.org/cgi/content/full/40/2/13-b. Accessed October 1, 2007.

66. Schwartzman, Bryan. *U.S. Muslim Population Tops Jews, Says Scholar*. Jewish Exponent, April 12, 2007. Http:www.jewishexponent.com/ article/12673. Accessed October 1, 2007.

67. *Muslim Americans: Middle Class and Mostly Mainstream*, p. 52.

68. *Muslim Americans: Middle Class and Mostly Mainstream*, p. 54.

69. *Islamic Terrorist Network in America* (map), 2002-2003. Http://www. somebodyhelpme.info/Terrorist_network_map.gif. Accessed May 17, 2007.

70. *Probe Finds Terrorists in U.S. "Training for War."* WorldNetDaily.com, February 17, 2006. Http://www.worldnetdaily.com/news/article.asp? ARTICLE_ID=48868. Accessed May 13, 2007.

71. Williams, Paul, *Radical Muslim Paramilitary Compound Flourishes in Upper New York State.* Canada Free Press, May 11, 2007. Http://www. canadafreepress.com/2007/paul-williams051107.htm. Accessed May 13, 2007.

72. *Probe Finds Terrorists in U.S. "Training for War."*

73. Pipes, Daniel, *The Danger Within: Militant Islam in America*, November, 2001. Http://www.danielpipes.org/pf.php?id=77. Accessed June 15, 2007.

74. *National Intelligence Estimate: The Terrorist Threat to the US Homeland*, July, 2007. National Intelligence Council, Washington, D.C.

75. Farah, Joseph, *Islam on March South of the Border*. WorldNetDaily. com, June 7, 2005. Http://www.worldnetdaily.com/news/article. asp?ARTICLE_ID=44636. Accessed June 7, 2005.

76. *Al-Qaida Recruiting Black Bombers*. WorldNetDaily.com, May 21, 2007. Http://www.worldnetdaily.com/news/article.asp?ARTICLE _ID=55796. Accessed May 21, 2007.

77. *Report: Saudis Spread Hate Through U.S. Mosques*. WorldNetDaily. com, January 29, 2005. Http://www.worldnetdaily.com/news/article. asp?ARTICLE_ID=42603. Accessed January 29, 2005.

78. *Qur'an*, Muhammad Asad translation. Isamicity.com. Http://www. islamicity.com/Quransearch. Accessed August 10, 2007.

79. *The End Times Battles in Islam*. Answering-Christianity.com. Http:// www.answering-chritianity.com/end_of_times_battles_in_islam.htm. Accessed July 28, 2006.

80. *The Signs of Armageddon (The End Times Battles) in Islam*. Answering-Christianity.com. Http://www.answering-christianity.com/ signs_of_Armageddon.htm. Accessed June 8, 2007.

81. *Iran Leader's U.N. Finale Reveals Apocalyptic View*. WorldNetDaily. com, January 29, 2005. Http://www.worldnetdaily.com/news/article. asp?ARTICLE_ID=42603. Accessed January 29, 2005.

82. Ibid.

83. *Interview of the President by Al Arabiya*, The White House, October 4, 2007. Http://www.whitehouse.gov/news/releases/2007/10/20071005- 5.html. Accessed October 8, 2007.

84. *It's Official: Terrorists Endorse Hillary in '08*. WorldNetDaily.com, October 7, 2007. Http://www.worldnetdaily.com/news/article. asp?ARTICLE_ID=57970. Accessed October 8, 2007.

CHAPTER 14

Sound the Trumpet

*. . . men of Issachar, who understood the times
and knew what Israel should do. . .*
(1 Chronicles 12:32)

S atan is using people of Islamic faith to persecute those of the blood covenant, whether they are Christians or Jews, because Satan, in the name of Allah, despises the only true God and Jesus whom he could not corrupt. He has blinded Muslims to the truth with his hatred of Christ. Is it any wonder that those who follow the Islamic faith do so only because they were born into a Muslim family; were persecuted into doing so or are ignorant of its tenets of faith? The fulfillment of Ishmael's legacy as the seed of a woman of bondage and whose descendents would be *against everyone* has been fulfilled and capitalized on by Satan's continued bondage-inducing hold on the people of Islam. Until they are set free in Christ, they will forever persecute and be adversaries of those of the only true blood covenant—Jews by heritage and Christians through Jesus' sacrifice on the cross.

"Because the church has failed to understand Islam, the Islamic people have not been stirred or touched by the gospel of Jesus Christ. They remain in darkness of a fanatical religion which forces them to have faith in a god who is unreachable, untouchable and unknowable."[1]

Sound the Alarm

We must make "the most of every opportunity, because the days are evil," stated the Apostle Paul (Ephesians 5:16). While the peoples of the earth have always known periods of darkness and evil, the evil of today envelops the earth in impending doom. "Blow the trumpet in Zion;

sound the alarm on my holy hill," declared the prophet Joel. "Let all who live in the land tremble, for the day of the Lord is coming" (Joel 2:1). In generations of the past the enemies of free and just peoples were easily definable and locatable. They were British, Spanish, French, Germans, Japanese, Russians, Vietnamese, the Mongol hordes, etc. They were countries, political entities and armies with clearly defined leaders and battle lines. Their armies numbered in the thousands; maybe a million or two. Today's enemy is everywhere, in every culture and country, driven by a religious fanatical fervor and with numbers in the tens of millions, perhaps hundreds of millions and threatens the existence of the entire earthly population. It is mostly an army of individuals who recognize no boundaries, no political entity, no justice and no sane leadership other than their holy book and dead prophet.

When the Jews of the Old Testament were facing an enemy, it was up to the priests, the religious leaders to sound the alarm to warn the people. "The sons of Aaron, **the priests, are to blow the trumpets**. This is to be a lasting ordinance for you and the generations to come," commanded Moses. "When you go into battle in your own land against an enemy who is oppressing you, sound a blast on the trumpets. Then you will be remembered by the Lord your God and rescued from your enemies" (Numbers 10:8-9, author's emphasis). Where are the *men of Issachar* in the church and synagogues today? Where are the *priests* or pastors and rabbis sounding the alarm? Christianity and Judaism and the entire free world are under a merciless attack by Satan himself while they debate the similarities of Islam and Christianity and Judaism, or whether the mullahs are correct when they say Islam is a religion of peace or whether God is Allah or Allah is God. For some, they will cry out "peace, peace" as the scimitar strikes their bowed neck.

We Are at War!

There, it's been said. It is politically incorrect; it smacks of cultural insensitivity; it may be offensive to some, but it is a correct and inescapable conclusion. But it is not a war that will be won by traditional military means. It is a war that will only be won by God Himself—if His people will hear the sound of the trumpet and respond as they should. "Wherever you hear the sound of the trumpet," the prophet

Nehemiah told the people of Judah, "join us there. Our God will fight for us!" (Nehemiah 4:20).

The trumpet or rams horn played a very significant role in the life of the Jewish people. The trumpet sound announced God's presence; (Exodus 19:17-19) called the people to worship; (2 Chronicles 5:13) heralded a warning (Joel 2:15) and sounded the cry of battle (Job 39:24-25). This battle is the Lord's but He needs His faithful servants to speak the truth, but so far they have remained mostly silent. They have not called upon Him to intervene and show the way to victory.

Where should the Judeo-Christian faithful start to prepare for this war? The prophet Joel provides a not so subtle clue. "Blow the trumpet in Zion, declare a holy fast, call a sacred assembly" (Joel 2:15). Prayer and fasting would be a good place to start. All the wisdom of God must come to bare in this conflict. "Oh, my anguish, my anguish! I writhe in pain," cried the prophet Jeremiah. "Oh, the agony of my heart! My heart pounds within me, I cannot keep silent. For I have heard the sound of the trumpet; I have heard the battle cry" (Jeremiah 4:19).

The prophet Ezekiel was called of God to be a watchman for the house of Israel (Ezekiel 3:17; 33:7). The watchmen of the people of the only true God are called of God to warn His people of pending danger—whether it is from their sin from within or from their enemy without.

> *Son of man, I have made you a watchman for the house of Israel; so hear the word I speak and give them warning from me. When I say to a wicked man, "You will surely die," and you do not warn him or speak out to dissuade him from his evil ways in order to save his life, that wicked man will die for his sin, and I will hold you accountable for his blood. But if you do warn the wicked man and he does not turn from his wickedness or from his evil ways, he will die for his sin; but you will have saved yourself.*
>
> *Again, when a righteous man turns from his righteousness and does evil, and I put a stumbling block before him, he will die. Since you did not warn him, he will die for his sin. The righteous things he did will not be remembered, and I will hold you accountable for his blood. But if you do warn the righteous man not to sin and he does not sin, he will surely live because*

he took warning, and you will have saved yourself. (Ezekiel 3:17-21)

God has given clear instructions. The people of Jehovah God—the pastors and rabbis in particular—are to call sin, *sin*, no matter in whose camp it resides. As the imams of Islam rail from their mosques and rooftops about the "evils" of Christianity and Judaism, the Judeo-Christian community of watchmen remains silent. They are afraid to call the wickedness within Islam sin and an abomination to God Almighty. They are hesitant to call the sinner out of the darkness and bondage of Muhammadism into the light of Jesus Christ. God loves all people and He loves the Muslim too and wants them to experience the light of His salvation. As the Apostle Paul expressed to the Christians who were under oppression in Rome:

How, then, can they call on the one they have not believed in? And how can they believe in the one of whom they have not heard? And how can they hear without someone preaching to them? And how can they preach unless they are sent? As it is written, "How beautiful are the feet of those who bring good news!" (Romans 10:14-15)

The watchmen of God have a great and grave responsibility. He is called to warn God's people of impending doom or attack. If he knows the attack is coming but fails to warn the people, their blood will be on his hands. In like fashion, if the watchman sees a man in sin but does not warn him to repent and turn from his sin, then his eternal damnation shall be the responsibility of the watchman.

Son of man, speak to your countrymen and say to them: "When I bring the sword against a land, and the people of the land choose one of their men and make him their watchman, and he sees the sword coming against the land and blows the trumpet to warn the people, then if anyone hears the trumpet but does not take warning and the sword comes and takes his life, his blood will be on his own head. Since he heard the sound of the trumpet but did not take warning, his blood will be on his own head. If he had taken warning, he would have saved himself. But if the watchman sees the sword coming and does not blow the trumpet to warn the people and the sword comes and takes the life of one of them, that man will be taken away because of his sin, but I will hold the watchman accountable for his blood." (Ezekiel 33:2-6)

Once again, the Spirit of the Lord needs to come upon His watchmen like it did for Gideon; to blow the trumpet of warning for His people (Judges 6:34). "Shout it aloud, do not hold back," Isaiah proclaimed. "Raise your voice like a trumpet. Declare to my people their rebellion and to the house of Jacob their sins" (Isaiah 58:1).

As the venerable Apostle Paul said, "if the trumpet does not sound a clear call, who will get ready for battle?" (1 Corinthians 14:8) Where are the blasts of the trumpets and who will sound the alarm?

"To whom can I speak and give warning? Who will listen to me?" exclaimed Jeremiah the prophet. "Their ears are closed so they cannot hear. The word of the LORD is offensive to them; they find no pleasure in it" (Jeremiah 6:10). When the watchmen do speak up, the people better listen or the consequences could be devastating.

I appointed watchmen over you and said, "Listen to the sound of the trumpet!" But you said, "We will not listen." Therefore hear, O nations; observe, O witnesses, what will happen to them. Hear, O earth: I am bringing disaster on this people, the fruit of their schemes, because they have not listened to my words and have rejected my law." (Jeremiah 6:17-19)

Kingdom of Darkness

Muslims, particularly in the West, if confronted with the realities of the Qur'an and their prophet, will vehemently and aggressively defend Allah, the Qur'an and Muhammad. However, the majority do so with very little personal knowledge of either the Qur'an, or the life of Muhammad and his teaching." This is the verdict: Light has come into the world, but men loved darkness instead of light because their deeds were evil" (John 3:19).

Muhammad was a false prophet from a false god and led those without discernment into a life of darkness and bondage. In referring to such a false prophet, the Apostle Peter had this to say: "These men [false prophets] are springs without water and mists driven by a storm. Blackest darkness is reserved for them. For they mouth empty, boastful words and, by appealing to the lustful desires of sinful human nature, they entice people who are just escaping from those who live in error. They promise them freedom, while they themselves are slaves of depravity—for a man is a slave to whatever has mastered him" (2 Peter 2:17-19). Muhammad, by his own admission, was mastered by an evil spirit, a spirit that led him and all who would follow him into a dark and depraved religion that has deceived and persecuted hundreds of millions of people.

"The good man," Jesus said, "brings good things out of the good stored up in him, and the evil man brings evil things out of the evil stored up in him" (Matthew 12:35). Muhammad had nothing good in him because he was an unredeemed man; a sinner through and through. He did not see the need for a savior, only a way to gain mastery over his enemies.

The Apostle John made it clear: "This is the message we have heard from him and declare to you: God is light; in him there is no darkness at all. If we claim to have fellowship with him yet walk in the darkness, we lie and do not live by the truth" (1 John 1:5-6). Jesus preached "light" and lived in the light of God. Muhammad preached darkness and lived in the dark shadows of Satan. Muhammad could not preach a message of light because he, himself, was darkness. Light begets light; darkness begets darkness. Light illuminates the darkness; darkness can not overcome the light. For those who live in darkness, Paul put it this way. "They are darkened in their understanding and separated from the life of God because of the ignorance that is in them due to the hardening of their hearts" (Ephesians 4:18). Most Muslims are indeed hardened to the truth of the Gospel of Christ. Not necessarily because they have darkened souls but because they have been indoctrinated since birth in the darkness of a dark religion that allows for no freedom of inquiry or questioning; no searching for spiritual truth and no freedom of choice to make a personal decision about God.

Before he became a Christian, Paul the Apostle, then known as Saul of Tarsus, was a relentless persecutor of Christians. Saul, even though he referred to himself as a *Pharisee of the Pharisees*, was living in a spiritual kingdom of darkness. He did not know the truth of God's redemption through Christ. Even some of the Apostles were afraid of him. But then Saul saw the light of day when Jesus appeared to him as he was traveling on the road to Damascus. The appearance of Jesus before him was so brilliant that Saul was blinded for three days. Jesus said to him, "Saul, Saul, why do you persecute me?" (Acts 9:4). Saul had no answer other than, "Who are you Lord?" Saul was living in darkness. He had no idea that he was persecuting the Son of the living God—he, a devout Pharisee, a follower of the Law of Moses. But Jesus illuminated his darkness with the truth of God's word and Saul, the persecutor, became Paul, the liberator.

The Apostle Paul shared his conversion testimony many times. On one such occasion, perhaps his last, he was presenting his defense before King Agrippa (of the Herodian family) in Caesarea, the Roman capitol of Palestine. Paul once again shared what Jesus said to him during his Damascus road encounter. "'I will rescue you from your own people and from the Gentiles. I am sending you to them to open their eyes and turn them from darkness to light, and from the power of Satan to God, so that they may receive forgiveness of sins and a place among those who are sanctified by faith in me'" (Acts 26:17-18). Paul's desire as it was implanted in him by Jesus, was to see everyone set free from the kingdom of darkness. He did not want to persecute anyone who did not believe as he believed. He just wanted to lead them to the light of Christ. Despite Paul's standing as an Apostle, all Christians are called to do the same: Lead those in darkness to the light of Christ. "God is light; in him there is no darkness at all" (1 John 1:5).

The good news is that God knows what dwells in darkness. "He reveals deep and hidden things; he knows what lies in darkness, and light dwells with him" (Daniel 2:22). The light that dwells with God is Jesus Christ. "For he has rescued us from the dominion of darkness and brought us into the kingdom of the Son he loves, in whom we have redemption, the forgiveness of sins"(Colossians 1:13-14).

Of evil men, the Psalmist Asaph wrote: "They know nothing, they understand nothing. They walk about in darkness; all the foundations of the earth are shaken" (Psalm 82:5). Unlike Allah, the God of the Jews and Christians does not take pleasure in evil; nor can the wicked dwell with Him (Psalm 5:4). "For evil men will be cut off," David wrote, "but those who hope in the LORD will inherit the land" (Psalm 37:9).

One day, once again the prophecy of Isaiah will come true again for another people. "The people walking in darkness have seen a great light; on those living in the land of the shadow of death a light has dawned" (Isaiah 9:2). For those Muslims who dwell in darkness but seek the light of truth, they too will see the light in the midst of darkness. They will come to understand that, "Evil men do not understand justice, but those who seek the Lord understand it fully" (Proverbs 28:5). They will see that there is hope for their future and that it resides in the light and life of Jesus Christ.

Muslims who choose Christ will then be able to respond to the Apostle Peter's proclamation. "But you are a chosen people, a royal priesthood, a holy nation, a people belonging to God, that you may declare the praises of him who called you out of darkness into his wonderful light" (1 Peter 2:9).

Not Flesh & Blood

It is hard—very hard—to see beyond the theology of hate that one perceives to reside within many Muslims and not see the person whom God loves and desires to be His own. Despite all the vitriol that spews forth from the mosques in America and abroad; all the vehement anti-American, anti-Western press from the Middle East and elsewhere and the relentless diatribes from imams and Muslim scholars, Christians are called to a higher ground of response. That response must go beyond the skin of the individual to the heart and soul of the person. Christians must realize that a Muslim is also under the attack of Satan. The only difference is that his or her faith condones a theology of hate that is compatible with Satan's plan to destroy what Christ has established. "The thief [Satan] comes only to steal and kill and destroy;" Jesus told His followers, "I have come that they may have life, and have it to the full" (John 10:10).

Witnessing to a Muslim is not a war of words; not a condemnation of their belief system or their prophet or their holy book. It is a spiritual battle requiring much prayer and intercession before engagement. "Be self-controlled and alert," Peter proclaimed. "Your enemy the devil prowls around like a roaring lion looking for someone to devour" (1 Peter 5:8). If you are not prepared to do battle in the spiritual realm, the devil will beat you up and discourage you and make you an ineffective witness for Christ.

Remember, this is a war, but not in the conventional sense. "For though we live in the world," Paul warned, "we do not wage war as the world does. The weapons we fight with are not the weapons of the world. On the contrary, they [our weapons] have divine power to demolish strongholds. We demolish arguments and every pretension that sets itself up against the knowledge of God, and we take captive every thought to make it obedient to Christ" (2 Corinthians 10:3-5). Recall also the words of Apostle John. "There is no fear in love. But perfect love drives out fear, because fear has to do with punishment. The one who fears is not made perfect in love" (1 John 4:18).

The Apostle Paul understood what it meant to be both the persecutor and the persecuted. He was imprisoned, beaten, chained, shipwrecked and faced down death numerous times—often at the hands of those who hated him or his God. Still he kept his focus on the true nature of his quest. "For our struggle is not against flesh and blood, but against the rulers, against the authorities, against the powers of this dark world and against the spiritual forces of evil in the heavenly realms" (Ephesians 6:12). Paul understood that evil was evil no matter which human body it took up residence. It all came from the same source—*the spiritual forces of evil.*

"For I am convinced," Paul told the persecuted Roman Christians, "that neither death nor life, neither angels nor demons, neither the present nor the future, nor any powers, neither height nor depth, nor anything else in all creation, will be able to separate us from the love of God that is in Christ Jesus our Lord" (Romans 8:38-39). If you are going to share Christ with a Muslim you must not do it in the flesh but in the power of the Holy Spirit within you. "For God did not give us a spirit of timidity," Paul wrote to his protégé Timothy, "but a spirit of power, of love and of self-discipline" (2 Timothy 1:7).

Call to Action

On the surface it would seem that it should not be difficult to give witness to the love, peace and joy that a personal relationship with Jesus brings to one who chooses Him as Lord and Savior. After all, the religion of Islam is dark, oppressive, combative and hopeless—all the things that Christianity is not. Their God is impersonal, unapproachable, hateful, and vengeful and leads his followers *into* sin, rather than saving them from it. But therein lays the challenge. Islam is so oppressive and captivating that adherents have a tough time breaking away for fear of their lives and the lives of their love ones. So, Muslims have to be 100% sure that Jesus, and not Allah, is the undisputed way to salvation and eternal life. They do not want to hear theology, they want to know the reality of Jesus and what He can do and mean to them as a person who is hopelessly lost and searching for the truth.

Be strong in faith.

The first step in preparation to be a witness to a Muslim (or to anyone for that matter) is to be sure of your own faith and relationship with Christ and the spiritual power within you. If you are not confident in your own faith, then it's time to reassess your commitment to your Lord and Savior and determine where you went off the track. Back in the fall of 2003, U.S. Army Lt. General William G. Boykin, an unabashed Christian, told a group of evangelicals that Islam's god was an idol and that "We are the army of God, in the house of God, kingdom of God have been raised for such a time as this."[2] The general, of course, was castigated by Muslims and the liberal media. But the general had it right all the way. Islam's god *is* an idol and it is a time just like this that God mobilizes His army of faithful torch bearers. Are you one?

Pray.

Muslims are in spiritual bondage—bondage so oppressive that we in the free world and as Christians can not fully understand. Any effort to set the captives free starts with prayer and intercession, not only for God's guidance, but to break the spiritual strongholds that hold the Muslim captive to the darkness. Jesus told His disciples, "… how can anyone enter a strong man's house and carry off his possessions unless he first ties up the strong man? Then he can rob his house" (Matthew 12:29). Jesus was not teaching His disciples how to be thieves. He was instructing them in spiritual warfare against the spirits of darkness. It is through prayer, fasting and intercession that spiritual bondages are broken. "I have given you authority," Jesus reminded those who follow Him, "to trample on snakes and scorpions and to overcome all the power of the enemy; nothing will harm you" (Luke 10:19).

"When a strong man, fully armed, guards his own house, his possessions are safe," Jesus said. "But when someone stronger attacks and overpowers him, he takes away the armor in which the man trusted and divides up the spoils" (Luke 11:21-22). Again, the analogy is that the strong man is Satan, but Jesus' disciples have one even stronger—Almighty God and the power of the Holy Spirit—who disarm Satan and release his spoils (those held captive).

Remember also, that one way Jesus reaches Muslims is through dreams, visions and manifestations of Himself. Challenge your Muslim friend to pray to God to reveal the truth to him or her and then you pray that Jesus will reveal Himself to them in whatever manner necessary to convince them that He is the one and only way to the Father.

Become knowledgeable.

To be an effective witness you must know your Bible, particularly the Gospel of John. You do not have to memorize scripture, just know it well enough that you can locate a key verse when needed. Then you must know enough about Islam, Muhammad and the Qur'an to converse intelligently. If you have read this book you already know more than most Muslims and will be able to share key points without being confrontational or threatening. Share by asking questions rather than making inflammatory statements that might result in defensive reactions or even anger. "Did you know that Muhammad believed ...?" Not, "You know, Muhammad was a demon-possessed ..."

Make friends.

Despite their outward aggression toward non-Muslims or even those that are fellow believers, Muslims generally place a high value on friendships. "A man who has friends must himself be friendly, But there is a friend *who* sticks closer than a brother" (Proverbs 18:24, NKJV). It takes time to make friends with a Muslim. There are, on both ends, significant trust issues which do not melt away over night.

Often, when Jesus healed someone or shared a word of truth with them, He would tell them, "Go home to your friends, and tell them what great things the Lord has done for you, and how He has had compassion on you" (Mark 5:19, NKJV). Muslims are starving for *good news*. There is not much good about their religion and they know it if they are honest with themselves. They just need a friend who cares about them to tell them the truth about God and the saving grace of Jesus Christ.

Share Christ's love.

Muslims need to see and experience love—true love, the love of Christ in you. Do not forget, that for a Muslim to leave Islam for Christianity it comes with great pain, peril and loss. A new convert will need all the love and acceptance you and fellow believers can muster and to be surrounded with support and guidance in their new life with Christ. "It is not hard for the Holy Spirit to convict and convince the Muslims," wrote author Raza Safa ....[3] "The problem is not *their* hardness, but rather the hardness and unbelief of *our own hearts.*"

"There is much fear in Islam," Safa wrote, "because God is not recognized as a loving Father. Once a Muslim has a real taste of the divine love of God the Father, all his fear will vanish, and he will be ready to be introduced to the salvation available for him through Jesus Christ—God the Son."[4]

Share your testimony.

Tell them about Jesus—not Christianity; not your church. "Salvation is found in no one else, for there is no other name under heaven given to men by which we must be saved" (Acts 4:12). When a Muslim is seeking the truth about God or Jesus, he or she does not want to hear about your denominational theology or doctrines. He or she may not even want to hear about Christianity because it comes with so many trappings depending on where they have lived, what they have heard and seen and what they have personally experienced. They want to know about the reality of Jesus. How did you come to know the reality of Jesus? What is your testimony for Christ?

Paul T. Martindale, director of marketing and training for Arab World Ministries told prospective missionary students at Urbana '06 that, "The job of a missionary is to preach the gospel, not to convert. 'Conversion is the job of the Holy Spirit.'"[5]

Fouad Masri, founder of the Crescent Project, a ministry that trains Christians to reach Muslims with the Gospel, told students, "Your job is not to convert Muslims, your job is to love them .... Muslims know Islam does not work—it's like a house with a leaking roof. We need believers to tell them there's a better house, the house of Jesus."[6]

Rays of Hope.

It is not all doom and gloom. In fact, the power of the Holy Spirit is alive and moving throughout the Muslim world in miraculous ways. In his January 23, 2007 column, Jim Rutz, chairman of Megashift Ministries, briefly summarized the impact of Christianity in the Muslim world.[7] Among his collected tidbits:

• When the Christian allegorical movie *Narnia* was shown in Egypt, Muslims packed the movie houses to see it.

• In 2003, when Mel Gibson's *The Passion of the Christ* was shown throughout the Middle East, Muslims also packed the theaters.

• More Muslims converted to faith in Jesus Christ over the past decade than at any other time in human history. A spiritual revolution is under way throughout North Africa, the Middle East and Central Asia.

• Since 2003 over one million Bibles have been shipped into Iraq.

• In 1979 in Iran there were only 500 known Christians. Today there are more than one million.

• More than one million Sudanese have come to Christ since 2000.

In 2005 alone it has been reported that 250,000 Iranians converted to Christ.[8] Sam Yeghnazar, founder of Elam Ministries, is excited by what he sees happening in Iran. "I believe with all my heart that millions of Iranians can be won for Christ in our generation and profoundly impact not only the character of Iran, but also the whole of the Middle East."[9]

John Reinhold, president of the American Evangelistic Association proclaimed that Iranian Christians "are completely convinced that Iran will become a Christian nation and will be the messenger to the Islamic world, that revival will spill out of there and actually change history."[10]

When Muslims seek the truth and ask God (not Allah) for guidance, Jesus often shows up in a dream, vision or visitation. "Reinhold said an Iranian doctor told him he accepted Christ after seeing a vision in which Jesus told him, 'You are Mine; follow Me' . . . Reinhold said what God is doing in Iran is 'mind-boggling' and can't be attributed solely to traditional evangelism methods. 'The Lord seems to be taking a shortcut to reach the Islamic culture and mind.'"[11]

Al-Jazeera, the main Middle East Arab news service, stated not long ago that approximately six million Muslims are leaving Islam for Christianity each year in Africa.[12]

In July, 2007, thousands of Christians packed the 20,000-seat auditorium of Graha Bethany Church in Surabaya, Indonesia, a country of over 230 million and 88% Muslim.[13] Indonesian Muslims have been notorious and brutal in persecuting Indonesia's Christian minority.

It only takes one believer to change a world. A seventy-year old Coptic Egyptian priest, Father Zakareyah, is a good example. He has dedicated his life to exposing the darkness of the Qur'an and Islam. He has helped "thousands of Muslims convert to Christianity by showing them the perverted teachings of Muhammad and by comparing this man's vile life to the pure and blessed life of Jesus."[14] Through satellite television he has been able to reach millions of Muslims throughout the Middle East and Europe.

Conclusion

The time is now. It is time for the Church and those that profess Christ as their Lord and Savior to step forward and enlist in the Army of God; to suit up with the Armor of God and do battle with the enemy of God and Christ. This is not a war that will be won with guns and bombs, but with power and presence of Almighty God's Holy Spirit working through Christian believers the world over. Satan has a plan, but God has a better and more effective plan.

This battle—the war for the souls in bondage to Islam—must be a top priority for every church, or nothing else will matter. Defeat or acquiescence to Satan and his Islamic hordes is not an option for the body of Christ. The New Hampshire state motto, a carry-over from the Revolutionary War, is still appropriate for every American: "Live free or die."

The God Who Was There

I was studying, going to college, and working [in Iran]. I was under pressure ... I prayed to Allah to help me relax and that the pressure would go away.

I tried my best (as a Muslim). I followed the religious orders of Islam. I did my best to get as deep as possible, gaining access (to Allah) as much as possible. But actually, the stress was growing and the mental pressure was beating me up and absorbing all of my energy ....

One night in my room, I talked to Allah, and complained: "How much pressure? This is enough! How much can I stand? I am working and studying. Why aren't you helping me? Why aren't you giving me relief?"

I threatened: "If you are going to help me, tonight you should show yourself to me. If you don't show me a sign tonight, then I will turn to this material life and will be a sinner." So after I finished, I said, "I will be staying up all night and waiting for your sign so I can see and believe that you are here with me." I was talking to the god of Mohammed .... I was expecting to see Allah. I complained for an hour. I got tired, so I put my head on my prayer mat. It was midnight. I saw a light coming into my room and spreading ....

The room was full of light. I thought it was morning, but later I realized it was midnight. I lifted my head and was seeing Jesus Christ. He was wearing white. While I had never seen a picture of the Messiah, I recognized that this could only be the Messiah.

... Immediately, at that time I started to take notes.

I wrote (in Farsi, the language of Iran), "Come to me, all you who labor and are heavy laden, and I will give you rest."

I got a little angry at this: I was looking for Mohammed's god, and Jesus the Messiah comes to me! What's this?

The next night I dreamed and saw the Messiah. He said, "Didn't I tell you to come under My shadow and come with Me and be safe?" So I was telling myself: "This is the Messiah coming to me. Is this the real God? I should be seeing Allah or Mohammed."

Afrooz
The Voice of the Martyrs
October, 2003, p. 3-4

References

1. Safa, Reza F. *Inside Islam: Exposing and Reaching the World of Islam*, 1996. Charisma House, p. 10.

2. *General: Christian U.S. Fighting Islam*. WorldNetDaily.com., October 17, 2003. Http://www.worldnetdaily.com/news/article.asp?ARTICLE_ ID= 35127. Accessed October 17, 2003.

3. Safa, p. 92.

4. Safa, p. 94.

5. Townsend, Tim, *Followers of Jesus Share Christ With Muslims*. St. Louis Post-Dispatch, December 31, 2006.

6. Ibid.

7. Rutz, Jim, *The Incipient Implosion of Islam*. WorldNetDaily.com., January 23, 2007. Http://www.worldnetdaily.com/news/article. asp?ARTICLE_ID= 53884. Accessed January 23, 2007.

8. Keohane, Steve. *Muhammad: Terrorist or Prophet?* BibleProbe.com, 200402007. Http://bibleprobe.com/muhammad.htm. Accessed April 1, 2007.

9. Cox, Rachael, *Iranian Church Growth 'Mind-Boggling.'* Charisma, October, 2007, p. 36.

10. Ibid.

11. Ibid.

12. Keohane.

13. Karwur, Samuel, *Pentecostal Leaders Gather in Indonesia*. Charisma, October, 2007, p. 35.

14. Salamah, Maged, *Father Zakareya: Our Egyptian Winston Churchill*. Democratic Egypt, April 25, 2006. Http://democraticegypt.blogspot. com/2006/04/father-Zakareya-our-egyptian-winston.html. Accessed June 27, 2007.

Will History Repeat?

"Woe to those who call evil good and good evil,
who put darkness for light and light for darkness,
who put bitter for sweet and sweet for bitter."
(Isaiah 5:20)

Although there is apparently no historical proof that "Nero fiddled while Rome burned," the often used axiom may someday, once again, apply to the Western World.

On July 29, 1921, when Adolf Hitler became the leader of the National Socialist Nazi Party in Germany—less than three years after Germany's defeat in World War I—no one outside of Germany took much notice. Nine years later, in September, 1930, when Germans elected Nazis to lead Germany, no one noticed. On January 30, 1933, when Hitler became Chancellor of Germany and less than two months later opened the first concentration camp outside of Berlin, few world leaders were concerned. Ten days later, when Hitler was given dictatorial powers and four months later when the Nazis were declared the *only* political party in Germany, only a few outside Germany raised their eyebrows in apprehension.

A year later, on August 19, 1934, when Hitler became the Fuhrer (sole leader) of Germany and a month later the German Jews were stripped of their human rights, the world remained silent. When, on November 5, 1937, Hitler revealed his war plans, the Western World stood by. When the Nazis conquered Czechoslovakia on March 16, 1939, it seemed that only Britain took notice. After the Nazis invaded Poland on September 1 of the same year, two days later Britain, France,

Australia and New Zealand had seen enough and declared war on Germany while the United States declared its neutrality.

When Poland was forced to surrender to the Nazis three weeks later and the Nazis started their euthanasia campaign against the sick and disabled, the United States and others kept their distance. In the spring of 1940, the Nazis invaded Denmark, Norway, France, Belgium, Luxembourg and the Netherlands, but the U.S. and other Western nations would have none of it. Within weeks of the German invasion, the Netherlands, Belgium, France and Norway surrendered to the Nazis with little reaction from the United States and elsewhere.

As the German *Blitzkrieg* rolled onward through Europe and Britain prepared for the battle of its life, Prime Minister Winston Churchill made the following enduring speech for freedom before the British House of Commons on June 18, 1940.

> **... I expect that the Battle of Britain is about to begin. Upon this battle depends the survival of Christian civilization. Upon it depends our own British life, and the long continuity of our institutions and our Empire. The whole fury and might of the enemy must very soon be turned on us.**
>
> **Hitler knows that he will have to break us in this Island or lose the war. If we can stand up to him, all Europe may be free and the life of the world may move forward into broad, sunlit uplands. But if we fail, then the whole world, including the United States, including all that we have known and cared for, will sink into the abyss of a new Dark Age made more sinister, and perhaps more protracted, by the lights of perverted science.**
>
> **Let us therefore brace ourselves to our duties, and so bear ourselves that if the British Empire and its Commonwealth last for a thousand years, men will still say, "This was their finest hour."**

After Britain declared war on Germany on September 3, 1939, it would take the United States twenty-seven months to get up the nerve to do the same—but only after Germany declared war on the United States on December 11, 1941, just four days after the shocking Japanese attack on Pearl Harbor in Hawaii. What took so long for the

United States and other countries to join in the fight for the survival of freedom? Denial! Complete denial that such an evil could exist and that it had designs on conquering the world.

Is the world in the grips of the beginning of World War III without knowing it? Some religious leaders and world trend watchers believe so. If so, will the free world repeat the heinous crime of pre-World War II and wait until millions are slaughtered and persecuted? The reality is that millions have already been slaughtered, raped or maimed; homes and churches burned; livelihoods destroyed or forced to flee their towns and country by bands of violent Muslims all over the world acting under the cover of true Islam—often as the local police force, military or government stand by and do nothing or even participate. How many miniature or full-scale holocausts or Dafur (Sudan) genocides will the free world permit before it takes action? Time will tell, but unfortunately, time is not on the side of justice and the freedom-loving peoples of the earth.

For the wrath of God is revealed from heaven against all ungodliness and unrighteousness of men, who suppress the truth in unrighteousness, because what may be known of God is manifest in them, for God has shown it to them. For since the creation of the world His invisible attributes are clearly seen, being understood by the things that are made, even His eternal power and Godhead, so that they are without excuse, because, although they knew God, they did not glorify Him as God, nor were thankful, but became futile in their thoughts, and their foolish hearts were darkened. Professing to be wise, they became fools, and changed the glory of the incorruptible God into an image made like corruptible man and birds and four-footed animals and creeping things.

Therefore God also gave them up to uncleanness, in the lusts of their hearts, to dishonor their bodies among themselves, who exchanged the truth of God for the lie, and worshiped and served the creature rather than the Creator, who is blessed forever. Amen.

For this reason God gave them up to vile passions. For even their women exchanged the natural use for what is against nature. Likewise also the men, leaving the natural use of the woman, burned in their lust for one another, men with men committing what is shameful, and receiving in themselves the penalty of their error which was due.

And even as they did not like to retain God in their knowledge, God gave them over to a debased mind, to do those things which are not fitting; being filled with all unrighteousness, sexual immorality, wickedness, covetousness, maliciousness; full of envy, murder, strife, deceit, evil-mindedness; they are whisperers, backbiters, haters of God, violent, proud, boasters, inventors of evil things, disobedient to parents, undiscerning, untrustworthy, unloving, unforgiving, unmerciful; who, knowing the righteous judgment of God, that those who practice such things are deserving of death, not only do the same but also approve of those who practice them. (Romans 1:18-32, NKJV)

Christians in America are extremely vulnerable in the early 21st century. While militant Islamists threaten America and the Western world with annihilation, "Considerably more intellectual energy," commented Rabbi Daniel Lapin, "is being pumped into the propaganda campaign against Christianity than was ever delivered to the anti-smoking or anti-drunk-driving campaigns. Fervent zealots of secularism are flinging themselves into this anti-Christian war with enormous fanaticism."

And what is the British position of leadership this time around? The dear British are withdrawing their teaching on the Holocaust from their schools because it offends the English Muslim population who deny that the Holocaust ever occurred.

And what is the British response this time to invasion of their country? Are they up to once again defending it at all costs? Apparently not. According to nationally syndicated columnist Cal Thomas in his August 28, 2007 column, Britain is rapidly acquiescing to the large influx of immigrants, the majority of which are of Islamic persuasion. "Between June 2005 and June 2006," wrote Thomas, "nearly 200,000 British citizens chose to leave the country for a new life elsewhere. During the same period, at least 574,000 immigrants came to Britain." This, of course, as Thomas pointed out, does not include the thousands of undocumented immigrants that somehow slipped into the island nation under the radar of British authorities. To further complicate matters, while the Brits are aborting 20% of their pregnancies, the birth rate among new immigrants (again, mostly Muslims) is fifteen times that of the native Englanders.

As millions around the world are persecuted and murdered in the name of Islam and Allah, God—the God of the Jews and Christians—must once again be asking: "Who will rise up for me against the wicked? Who will take a stand for me against evildoers?" (Psalm 94:16).

Books

America Alone: The End of the World As We Know It, Mark Steyn, 2006. Regnery Publishing, Inc.

Infidel, Ayaan Hirsi Ali, 2007. Free Press, a Division of Simon & Schuster, Inc.

Inside Islam: Exposing and Reaching the World of Islam, Reza F. Safa, 1996. Charisma House.

Islam and Terrorism, Mark A. Gabriel, 2002. FrontLine, a Strang Company.

Religion of Peace: Why Christianity Is and Islam Isn't, Robert Spencer, 2007. Regnery Publishing, Inc.

The Truth About Muhammad: Founder of the World's Most Intolerant Religion, Robert Spencer, 2006. Regnery Publishing, Inc.

Unveiling Islam, Ergun Mehmet Canerand Emir Fethi Caner, 2002. Kregel Publications, div. of Kregel. Inc.

Film

Obsession: Radical Islam's War Against the West. Trinity Home Entertainment, 2007.

Ministries

American Congress for Truth. Http://www.
americancongressfortruth.org/

Crescent Project. Http://www.crescentproject.org/

Harvesters World Outreach / Reza Safa Ministries. Http://www.
rezasafa.com

Release International. Http://www.releaseinternational.org/

The Golden Report. Http://www.thegoldenreport.com.

The Voice of the Martyrs. Http://www.persecution.com

Web Sites

Islamic

Answering Christianity. Http://www.answering-christianity.com

Council on American-Islamic Relations. Http://www.cair.com/
factsaboutcair.asp.

Islamic History (Chronology). Http://www.barkati.net/English/
chronology

Quransearch. Http://www.islamicity.com

Sacred Texts. Http://www.sacred-texts.com

Non-Islamic

Answering Islam. Http://answering-islam.org.uk/

BibleProbe.com. Http://bibleprobe.com/muhammad.htm.

Center for Religious Freedom. Http://crf.hudson.org

Faith Freedom International. Http://www.faithfreedom.org/

Islam Review. Http://www.islamreview.com

Jihad Watch. Http://www.jihadwatch.org

The Middle East Media Research Institute. Http://memri.org

The World Fact Book. Http://www.cia.gov/cia/publications/factbook

WorldNetDaily.com. Http://www.worldnetdaily.com

Other Books by James F. Gauss

Y2K, Crying Wolf or World Crisis, 1998, Bridge-Logos (out-of-print)

Christians Confronting Crisis, 1999, Bridge-Logos (out-of-print)

A Champion's Heart, with James Sheard 1999, J Countryman, Div. of Thomas Nelson

We the People, Volume I: Laying the Foundation, 2003, 1st Books (Author House)

We the People, Volume II: Birth of a Nation, 2005, Author House